Red Hat RHCE™ 8 (EX294) Cert Guide

Sander van Vugt

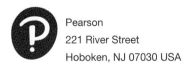

Pearson
221 River Street
Hoboken, NJ 07030 USA

Red Hat RHCE 8 (EX294) Cert Guide

ISBN-13: 978-0-13-687243-6

ISBN-10: 0-13-687243-3

Library of Congress Control Number: 2020941743

2 2020

Trademarks

Warning and Disclaimer

Special Sales

For information about buying this title in bulk quantities, or for special sales opportunities (which may include electronic versions; custom cover designs; and content particular to your business, training goals, marketing focus, or branding interests), please contact our corporate sales department at corpsales@pearsoned.com or (800) 382-3419.

For government sales inquiries, please contact governmentsales@pearsoned.com.

For questions about sales outside the U.S., please contact intlcs@pearson.com.

Editor-in-Chief
Mark Taub

Product Line Manager
Brett Bartow

Executive Editor
Denise Lincoln

Development Editor
Ellie Bru

Managing Editor
Sandra Schroeder

Senior Project Editor
Tonya Simpson

Copy Editor
Chuck Hutchinson

Indexer
Timothy Wright

Proofreader
Donna Mulder

Technical Editors
John McDonough
William "Bo" Rothwell

Publishing Coordinator
Cindy Teeters

Cover Designer
Chuti Prasertsith

Compositor
codeMantra

Contents at a Glance

Table of Contents

Part III: Managing Systems with Ansible

Chapter 12   Managing Software with Ansible   281

About the Author

Sander van Vugt has been teaching Linux classes since 1995 and has written more than 60 books about different Linux-related topics, including the best-selling *RHCSA-RHCE 7 Cert Guide* and the *RHCSA 8 Cert Guide: EX200*. Sander is also the author of more than 25 video courses, including his RHCSA and RHCE Complete Video Courses, *Hands-On Ansible LiveLessons*, and many other titles. He teaches courses for customers around the world and is also a regular speaker at major conferences related to open-source software. Sander is also the founder of the Living Open Source Foundation, a nonprofit organization that teaches open-source courses in African countries.

Dedication

This book is dedicated to my family: Florence, Franck, and Alex. Together we've made great accomplishments over the past year.

Acknowledgments

This book could not have been written without the help of all the people who contributed to it. To start, I want to thank the people at Pearson—Denise Lincoln and Ellie Bru in particular. We've worked a lot together over the past years, and this book is another milestone on our road to success! It has been fantastic how you both have helped me to realize this book in just two months!

Next, I want to thank my technical reviewers. Big thanks to Bo and John! Thanks to your great feedback, I've been able to apply important improvements to the contents of this book. Also, a special thanks to Ettiene Esterhuizen from New Zealand and Santos Venter Chibenga and Robert Charles Muchendu from the African Living Open Source Community, who helped me as volunteer reviewers. And last but not least, thanks to my fellow instructor and colleague Pascal van Dam, who helped me make some important last-minute improvements.

About the Technical Reviewers

John McDonough has more than 30 years of development experience; currently, John is a developer advocate for Cisco DevNet. As a developer advocate, John writes code and creates DevNet Learning Labs about how to write code; writes blogs about writing code; and presents at Cisco Live, SXSW, AnsibleFest, and other industry events. John focuses on the Cisco computing systems products, Cisco UCS, and Cisco Intersight. John's career at Cisco has varied from product engineer to custom application developer, technical marketing engineer, and now a developer advocate.

William "Bo" Rothwell crossed paths with a TRS-80 Micro Computer System (affectionately known as a "Trash 80") at the impressionable age of 14. Soon after, the adults responsible for Bo made the mistake of leaving him alone with the TRS-80. He immediately dismantled it and held his first computer class, showing his friends what made this "computer thing" work.

Since this experience, Bo's passion for understanding how computers work and sharing this knowledge with others has resulted in a rewarding career in IT training. His experience includes Linux, UNIX, and programming languages such as Perl, Python, Tcl, and BASH. He is the founder and president of One Course Source, an IT training organization.

We Want to Hear from You!

As the reader of this book, *you* are our most important critic and commentator. We value your opinion and want to know what we're doing right, what we could do better, what areas you'd like to see us publish in, and any other words of wisdom you're willing to pass our way.

We welcome your comments. You can email to let us know what you did or didn't like about this book—as well as what we can do to make our books better.

Please note that we cannot help you with technical problems related to the topic of this book.

When you write, please be sure to include this book's title and author as well as your name and email address. We will carefully review your comments and share them with the author and editors who worked on the book.

Email: community@informit.com

Reader Services

Register your copy of *Red Hat RHCE 8 (EX294) Cert Guide* at www.pearsonitcertification.com for convenient access to downloads, updates, and corrections as they become available. To start the registration process, go to www.pearsonitcertification.com/register and log in or create an account.* Enter the product ISBN 9780136872436 and click Submit. When the process is complete, you will find any available bonus content under Registered Products.

*Be sure to check the box that you would like to hear from us to receive exclusive discounts on future editions of this product.

Introduction

Welcome to the *Red Hat RHCE 8 (EX294) Cert Guide*! With the release of Red Hat Enterprise Linux 8, Red Hat has decided to take a completely new direction for the RHCE exam. The exam is now completely about managing configurations with Ansible. This is a great choice because in the current IT landscape the days of the system administrator who applies specialized skills to tune individual servers is over. Today the work is all about automation, and Ansible has rapidly become one of the most important solutions to do so.

As a Linux instructor with more than 25 years of experience, I have been certified for both the RHCSA and RHCE exams for every RHEL version since RHEL 4. Taking the exams myself has helped me keep current on the progression of the exam, what is new, and what is different. I am thrilled to be able to share my knowledge with you in this comprehensive Cert Guide so you can get the guidance you need to pass your RHCE RHEL 8 EX294 exam.

As you will see, this Cert Guide covers every objective in the updated RHCE exam, with 16 chapters, more than 40 exercises, 4 practice exams (2 printed in the book and 2 on the companion website), and 1 hour of video training. This *Red Hat RHCE 8 (EX294) Cert Guide* is the best resource you can get to prepare for and pass the exams.

Goals and Methods

To learn the topics described in this book, I recommend that you create your own testing environment, which is explained in Chapter 2, "Installing Ansible." You cannot become an RHCE without practicing a lot. To get familiar with the topics in the chapters, here is what I recommend:

- Read the explanation in the chapters and study the code examples that are provided in the listings. For your convenience, the listings are also provided in the book GitHub repository at https://github.com/sandervanvugt/rhce8-book. Study the examples and try to understand what they do.

- Walk through all of the numbered exercises in the book. The numbered exercises provide step-by-step instructions, and you should follow along with all of them, to walk through configuration tasks and learn how to manage specific features.

- At the end of each chapter, there's an end-of-chapter lab. This lab is much like the lab assignments that you will find on the exam.

Within the exercises included in every chapter of the book, you will find all the examples you need to understand what is on the exam and thoroughly learn the material needed to pass it. The exercises in the chapters provide step-by-step procedure descriptions that you can work through to find working solutions so that you can get real experience before taking the tests. Although you may feel familiar with some topics, it's a good idea to work through all of the exercises in the book. The RHCE exam is hands-on, which can be a lot of pressure on test day. The exercises in each chapter help provide the practice you need to make sure you have the experience you need to not make small errors and mistakes while taking the exam. The exercises are the best way to make sure you work through common errors and learn from your mistakes before you take the test.

Each chapter also includes an end-of-chapter lab. These labs ask questions that are similar to the questions that you might encounter on the exam so you can use them to practice. I have purposely excluded solutions for these labs for a few reasons: (1) you need to train yourself to verify your work before test day because you will be expected to do this on the exam; (2) while taking the test, you will be required to verify for yourself whether your solution is working as expected; and (3) most labs have multiple solutions and I don't want to suggest that my solution is the right one and yours is wrong because it takes a different approach. Your solution is as good as mine, as long as it accomplishes what was asked for in the exercise.

Other Resources

This book contains everything you need to pass the exam, but if you want more guidance and practice, I have a number of video training titles available to help you study, including the following:

- *Red Hat Certified Engineer (RHCE) 3/ed Complete Video Course*
- *Hands-on Ansible LiveLessons*

Apart from these products, you might also appreciate my website: rhatcert.com. Through this website, I provide updates on anything that is useful to exam candidates. I recommend that you register on the website so that I can send you messages about important updates that I've made available. Also, you'll find occasional video updates on my YouTube channel: rhatcert. I hope that all these resources provide you with everything you need to pass the Red Hat exams in an affordable way! Good luck!

Who Should Read This Book?

This book is written as an RHCE exam preparation guide. That means that you should read it if you want to increase your chances of passing the RHCE exam.

I have also written this book to help you become familiar with Ansible. So even if you're not interested in the RHCE EX294 exam at all, this book will teach you everything you need to know to get your Ansible career up and running.

So, why should you consider passing the RHCE exam? That question is simple to answer. Linux has become a very important operating system, and qualified professionals are sought after all over the world. If you want to work as a Linux professional and prove your skills, the RHCE certificate really helps. Having these certificates dramatically increases your chances of becoming hired as a Linux professional. Notice that in order to get RHCE certified, you must hold a current RHCSA certification. You can take the RHCE EX294 exam before you are RHCSA certified, but you can call yourself an RHCE only if you have passed both the RHCSA exam and the RHCE exam.

How This Book Is Organized

This book is organized as a reference guide to help you prepare for the exams. If you're new to the topics, you can just read it cover to cover. You can also read the individual chapters that you need to fine-tune your skills in this book. Every chapter starts with a "Do I Know This Already?" quiz. This quiz asks questions about 10 topics that are covered in each chapter and provides a simple tool to check whether you're already familiar with the topics covered in a chapter. These quizzes do not represent the types of questions you will get on the real exam though.

The best exam preparation is offered in the RHCE practice exams; these are an essential part of readying yourself for the real testing experience. You might be able to provide the right answer to the multiple-choice chapter questions, but that doesn't mean that you can create the configurations when you take the tests. We have included two practice exams in the printed book. The book's companion website then includes two additional practice exams as well as flashcards created from the book's glossary so you can further test your knowledge and skills. You will also find one hour of video from my *Red Hat Certified Engineer (RHCE) 3/ed Complete Video Course*.

The following topics are covered in the chapters:

- **Chapter 1, "Understanding Configuration Management":** In this chapter, you learn about Ansible as a solution. The chapter explains what can be done with Ansible and how Ansible relates to other solutions for configuration management.

- **Chapter 2, "Installing Ansible":** This chapter covers installation of Ansible. You learn what is needed to set up the Ansible control node, as well as the other parts of the Ansible software.

■ **Chapter 3, "Setting Up an Ansible Managed Environment":** In this chapter you learn how to get started with node management. The chapter explains what is needed on the managed nodes as well as the essential Ansible configuration files that are required to reach out to the managed nodes.

■ **Chapter 4, "Using Ad Hoc Commands":** In this chapter you learn about Ansible modules. Modules are the heart of Ansible; they provide solutions for everything that Ansible can do, and the easiest way to use these modules is in ad hoc commands. In this chapter you learn how to work with them.

■ **Chapter 5, "Getting Started with Playbooks":** This chapter provides an introduction to working with playbooks. You learn about YAML, the language used to write playbooks, and how to structure a playbook using plays and tasks.

■ **Chapter 6, "Working with Variables and Facts":** In Ansible, variables can be used to provide dynamic values to specific configuration items. Using variables enables you to separate the static code in a playbook with host-specific information. In this chapter you learn how to work with variables as well as Ansible facts, which are variables that are automatically set for managed nodes.

■ **Chapter 7, "Using Task Control":** To make Ansible smart, you must apply task control. Using task control enables you to run tasks conditionally, and that can be done in many ways. You learn how to use tests, to test for a specific condition, as well as loops that allow you to evaluate a range of items, and handlers, which allow for task execution only if another task was executed successfully.

■ **Chapter 8, "Deploying Files":** Ansible is used for configuration management, and configuration on Linux is stored in files. Hence, managing files is a key skill in Ansible. In this chapter you learn how to use modules to modify files and how to use templates to automatically set up configuration files with specific parameters obtained from facts or variables.

■ **Chapter 9, "Using Ansible Roles":** When you are working with Ansible, it's good if code can be reused. That is what Ansible roles are all about. In this chapter you learn how to work with roles, which are provided through Ansible Galaxy, or as RHEL system roles.

■ **Chapter 10, "Using Ansible in Large Environments":** When working with Ansible in large environments, you should know about a few specific techniques. These techniques are covered in this chapter. You learn how to optimize Ansible by modifying the number of concurrent tasks that can be executed. You also learn how to work with includes and imports, which allow you to set up modular playbooks.

- **Chapter 11, "Troubleshooting Ansible":** In some cases your playbook might not give you the desired result. Then you need to start troubleshooting. This chapter contains not only all you need to know about troubleshooting, including some best practices while developing playbooks, but also information about modules that can be used to make troubleshooting easier.

- **Chapter 12, "Managing Software with Ansible":** This is the first chapter about specific common tasks that you can perform with Ansible. In this chapter you learn how to set up repositories and how to manage software packages with Ansible.

- **Chapter 13, "Managing Users":** To do anything on Linux, you need user accounts. In this chapter you learn all that is needed to create user accounts, including setting encrypted passwords.

- **Chapter 14, "Managing Services and the Boot Process":** Occasionally, you might want to run scheduled jobs. These jobs will be executed at a specific time, using either cron or at. In this chapter you learn how to do that, and you also learn how to manage the systemd default target.

- **Chapter 15, "Managing Storage":** Setting up storage is a key task when working with Linux. In this chapter you learn how to automate storage configuration with Ansible. You also learn how to discover disk devices available on your managed systems and how to set them up, using partitions, logical volumes, filesystems, and mounts.

- **Chapter 16, "Final Preparation":** In this chapter you get some final exam preparation tasks. It contains some test exams and many tips that help you maximize your chances of passing the exam.

How to Use This Book

To help you customize your study time using these books, the core chapters have several features that help you make the best use of your time:

- **"Do I Know This Already?" Quizzes:** Each chapter begins with a quiz that helps you determine the amount of time you need to spend studying that chapter.

- **Foundation Topics:** These are the core sections of each chapter. They explain the protocols, concepts, and configuration for the topics in that chapter.

- **Exam Preparation Tasks:** At the end of the "Foundation Topics" section of each chapter, the "Exam Preparation Tasks" section lists a series of study activities that should be done at the end of the chapter. Each chapter includes the activities that make the most sense for studying the topics in that chapter. The activities include the following:

- **Review Key Topics:** The Key Topic icon is shown next to the most important items in the "Foundation Topics" section of the chapter. The Key Topics Review activity lists the key topics from the chapter and their corresponding page numbers. Although the contents of the entire chapter could be on the exam, you should definitely know the information listed in each key topic.

- **Complete Tables and Lists from Memory:** To help you exercise your memory and memorize some lists of facts, many of the more important lists and tables from the chapter are included in a document on the DVD and companion website. This document lists only partial information, allowing you to complete the table or list.

- **Define Key Terms:** This section lists the most important terms from the chapter, asking you to write a short definition and compare your answer to the glossary at the end of this book.

- **Review Questions:** Questions at the end of each chapter measure insight in the topics that were discussed in the chapter.

- **End-of-Chapter Labs:** These real labs give you the right impression on what an exam assignment looks like. The end-of-chapter labs are your first step in finding out what the exam tasks really look like.

Other Features

In addition to the features in each of the core chapters, this book, as a whole, has additional study resources on the companion website, including the following:

- **Four practice exams:** The companion website contains the four practice exams: two provided in the book and two available on the companion website.

- **Flashcards:** The companion website contains interactive flashcards created from the glossary terms in the book so you can better learn key terms and test your knowledge.

- **More than one hour of video training:** The companion website contains more than one hour of video training from the best-selling *Red Hat Certified Engineer (RHCE) 3/ed Complete Video Course.*

Book Organization, Chapters, and Appendixes

I have also included a table that details where every objective in the RHCE exam is covered in this book so that you can more easily create a successful plan for passing the tests.

Table 1   RHCE Objectives

Objective	Chapter Title	Chapter	Page
Understand core components of Ansible: Inventories	Setting Up an Ansible Managed Environment	3	31
Understand core components of Ansible: Modules	Using Ad Hoc Commands	4	47
Understand core components of Ansible: Variables	Working with Variables and Facts	6	97
Understand core components of Ansible: Facts	Working with Variables and Facts	6	97
Understand core components of Ansible: Plays	Getting Started with Playbooks	5	69
Understand core components of Ansible: Playbooks	Getting Started with Playbooks	5	69
Understand core components of Ansible: Configuration files	Setting Up an Ansible Managed Environment	3	31
Understand core components of Ansible: Use provided documentation	Using Ad Hoc Commands	4	47
Install and configure an Ansible control node: Install required packages	Installing Ansible	2	15
Install and configure an Ansible control node: Create a static host inventory file	Setting Up an Ansible Managed Environment	3	31
Install and configure an Ansible control node: Create a configuration file	Setting Up an Ansible Managed Environment	3	31
Install and configure an Ansible control node: Create and use static inventories	Setting Up an Ansible Managed Environment	3	31
Install and configure an Ansible control node: Manage parallelism	Using Ansible in Large Environments	10	229
Configure Ansible managed nodes: Create and distribute SSH keys to managed nodes	Installing Ansible	2	15
Configure Ansible managed nodes: Configure privilege escalation on managed nodes	Installing Ansible	2	15

Objective	Chapter Title	Chapter	Page
Configure Ansible managed nodes: Validate a working configuration using ad hoc Ansible commands	Using Ad Hoc Commands	4	47
Script administration tasks: Create simple shell scripts	Using Ad Hoc Commands	4	47
Script administration tasks: Create simple shell scripts that run ad hoc Ansible commands	Using Ad Hoc Commands	4	47
Create Ansible plays and playbooks: Know how to work with commonly used Ansible modules	Using Ad Hoc Commands	4	47
Create Ansible plays and playbooks: Use variables to retrieve the results of running a command	Working with Variables and Facts	6	97
Create Ansible plays and playbooks: Use conditionals to control play execution	Using Task Control	7	131
Create Ansible plays and playbooks: Configure error handling	Using Task Control	7	131
Create Ansible plays and playbooks: Create playbooks to configure systems to a specified state	Getting Started with Playbooks	5	69
Use Ansible modules for system administration tasks that work with: Software packages and repositories	Managing Software with Ansible	12	281
Use Ansible modules for system administration tasks that work with: Services	Managing Processes and Tasks	14	333
Use Ansible modules for system administration tasks that work with: Firewall rules	Getting Started with Playbooks	5	69
Use Ansible modules for system administration tasks that work with: File systems	Managing Storage	15	351
Use Ansible modules for system administration tasks that work with: Storage devices	Managing Storage	15	351
Use Ansible modules for system administration tasks that work with: File content	Deploying Files	8	173
Use Ansible modules for system administration tasks that work with: Archiving	Managing Storage	15	351

Objective	Chapter Title	Chapter	Page
Use Ansible modules for system administration tasks that work with: Scheduled tasks	Managing Processes and Tasks	14	333
Use Ansible modules for system administration tasks that work with: Security	Managing Users	13	305
Use Ansible modules for system administration tasks that work with: Users and Groups	Managing Users	13	305
Work with roles: Create roles	Using Ansible Roles	9	205
Work with roles: Download roles from an Ansible Galaxy and use them	Using Ansible Roles	9	205
Use advanced Ansible features: Create and use templates to create customized configuration files	Deploying Files	8	173
Use advanced Ansible features: Use Ansible Vault in playbooks to protect sensitive data	Working with Variables and Facts	6	97

Where Are the Companion Content Files?

Register this print version of *Red Hat RHCE 8 (EX294) Cert Guide* to access the bonus content online.

This print version of this title comes with companion content. You have online access to these files by following these steps:

1. Go to www.pearsonITcertification.com/register and log in or create a new account.

2. Enter the ISBN: **9780136872436**.

3. Answer the challenge question as proof of purchase.

4. Click on the **Access Bonus Content** link in the Registered Products section of your account page to be taken to the page where your downloadable content is available.

Please note that many of our companion content files can be very large, especially image and video files.

If you are unable to locate the files for this title by following the steps, please visit www.pearsonITcertification.com/contact and select the Site Problems/Comments option. Our customer service representatives will assist you.

Credits

Chapter opener images by Charlie Edwards/Photodisc/Getty Images

Chapter 1 quote, "a set of practices intended to reduce the time between committing a change to a system and the change being placed into normal production, while ensuring high quality," © Len Bass, Ingo Weber, and Liming Zhu, *DevOps: A Software Architect's Perspective*, Boston, MA: Addison-Wesley Professional, 2015.

Chapter 4 quote, "Your work will be evaluated by applying the playbooks created during the exam against freshly installed systems and verifying that those systems and services work as specified," © 2020 Red Hat, Inc.

Cover image: Branislav Nenin/Shutterstock

This chapter covers the following subjects:

- Understanding Automation
- Understanding Ansible Essential Components
- Understanding Ansible Use Cases

## CHAPTER 1

Understanding Configuration Management

The following RHCE exam objectives are covered in this chapter:

■ Understand Core Components of Ansible

"Do I Know This Already?" Quiz

The "Do I Know This Already?" quiz allows you to assess whether you should read this entire chapter thoroughly or jump to the "Exam Preparation Tasks" section. If you are in doubt about your answers to these questions or your own assessment of your knowledge of the topics, read the entire chapter. Table 1-1 lists the major headings in this chapter and their corresponding "Do I Know This Already?" quiz questions. You can find the answers in Appendix A, "Answers to the 'Do I Know This Already?' Quizzes and Review Questions."

Table 1-1 "Do I Know This Already?" Section-to-Question Mapping

Foundation Topics Section	Questions
Understanding Automation	1–5
Understanding Ansible Essential Components	6–9
Understanding Ansible Use Cases	10

1. Which of the following are disadvantages of using shell scripts for automation? (Choose two.)

   a. They don't work on any target managed operating system.

   b. They require advanced skills.

   c. It is difficult to guarantee they will always produce the same result if the configuration changes.

   d. Using shell scripts makes sense only when they are used with root privileges.

2. In DevOps, the application life cycle is managed by focusing on different key aspects. Which of the following key aspects comes after releasing?

   a. Testing

   b. Configuring

   c. Monitoring

   d. Packaging

3. Which of the following are advantages of using a CVS to manage the machine-readable configuration files that are used in infrastructure as code?

   a. It is easy to reproduce.

   b. It makes upgrades easy.

   c. It makes rollbacks easy.

   d. All the above are true.

4. Ansible is an automation tool. Other automation solutions exist as well. Which of the following is not one of them?

   a. Puppet

   b. SaltStack

   c. Satellite

   d. Chef

5. When you compare Ansible to competing solutions such as Puppet, SaltStack, and Chef, Ansible offers two significant benefits. Which are these?

   a. Speed

   b. Easy configuration

   c. Agentless operation

   d. Price

6. Ansible provides different solutions to access remote hosts. Which of the following is not one of them?

   a. Agent

   b. API access

   c. winRM

   d. SSH

7. What is the name of the free open-source project that enables you to manage Ansible from a web interface?

   a. Ansible Galaxy

   b. OKD

   c. AWX

   d. Ansible Tower

8. Which of the following is the best description of the declarative approach?

   a. In the declarative approach you run commands to get a specific result.

   b. The declarative approach in Ansible is implemented by using scripts.

   c. The declarative approach enables you to focus on changes that are required to reach the desired state.

   d. The declarative approach uses playbooks.

9. Ansible can be used for provisioning. Which of the following is not a common provisioning scenario that Ansible is used for?

   a. Deploying instances in cloud

   b. Provisioning virtual machines

   c. PXE-booting bare-metal servers

   d. Deploying containers

10. Ansible can be used for different purposes. Which of the following can be considered the core function of Ansible?

   a. Configuration management

   b. Application management

   c. Provisioning

   d. Continuous delivery

Foundation Topics

Understanding Automation

Ansible is often referred to as a configuration management solution. That description doesn't do justice to all that Ansible can do. Ansible is more a solution for automation, allowing system administrators to take care of multiple systems in an efficient way. In this section you learn about all that Ansible can do as an automation tool. We also take a quick look at other automation solutions.

What Is Automation?

In the years of the system administrator, companies used servers. These servers performed a wide range of different tasks, and to ensure that every server was doing what it needed to be doing, a system administrator was needed. System administrators typically had advanced skills in managing different parts of the operating system that ran on their servers.

Even though the years of the system administrator were glorious, and many gurus worked in IT departments, from a company perspective, this scenario was not ideal. First, because system administrator skills are specific to that person, if that person goes away, forgets about brilliant solutions applied earlier, or just has a bad day, things might go wrong.

Another part that was not ideal was that the system administrator typically took care of individual servers, and with the development of IT in recent years, companies have gone from a handful of servers to data centers and cloud environments with hundreds if not thousands of servers. So a more efficient approach was needed.

A first attempt in many sites was the use of shell scripts. Based on the deep knowledge of many system administrators, shell scripts can be used in a flexible way to automate a wide range of tasks on many servers. Using shell scripts, however, does come with some disadvantages:

- Shell scripts cannot be used on a wide range of different devices that need management.

- It is difficult to write shell scripts in a way that will always produce the same result in every situation.

Because of these differences, and also because of changes in the way companies consume IT, a new approach was needed.

Understanding the DevOps Way of Working

Throughout the years the way IT is consumed has changed. In the past, IT was used to provide great services to end users who just had to deal with them. Now the landscape has changed to an environment in which IT is everywhere, and multiple applications can provide a solution to the same IT problem. The years of the system administrator slowly came to an end, and the system administrator's role needed to come closer to that of the developers.

In this new way of working, the developers take care of building applications, and system administrators take care of implementing the code as a working application. Because this change required a deep cooperation between the developer and the system administrator, a new role was created: the role of the DevOps. The term *DevOps* is a contraction of *developer* and *operator*. In this role, tasks performed by the developer and the system administrator come together. A common definition of DevOps is "a set of practices intended to reduce the time between committing a change to a system and the change being placed into normal production, while ensuring high quality" (Len Bass, Ingo Weber, and Liming Zhu, *DevOps: A Software Architect's Perspective*, Boston, MA: Addison-Wesley Professional, 2015).

With this new role, the "DevOps way of working" was introduced. The exact definition is not always the same, but in general, it comes down to managing the entire application life cycle, which consists of the following elements:

- **Coding:** Developing and reviewing application source code

- **Building:** Using continuous integration to include changes in the source code and convert to a working application

- **Testing:** Using a toolchain that takes care of testing the application and making sure that feedback is provided on business risks, if there are any

- **Packaging:** Delivering the code to its end users by bundling it into packages and offering these packages in a repository

- **Releasing:** Approving, managing, and automating new software releases

- **Configuring:** Managing the infrastructure to support the new code

- **Monitoring:** Keeping an eye on application performance and the way it is experienced by the end users

To manage these different elements in the application life cycle, new tools were introduced. Ansible is one of these tools, with a strong focus on managing the configuration of the managed environment according to the infrastructure as code approach.

Some categories in the DevOps approach are more important than others. The most important elements are continuous integration, with solutions such as Jenkins and GitLab, but also OpenShift and even Ansible. The other main component is infrastructure as code, where Ansible, Puppet, and Terraform are important solutions.

Understanding Infrastructure as Code

The essence in infrastructure as code is that machine-readable code (the automation language) is used to describe the state the managed IT infrastructure needs to be in. This is referred to as the *desired state*. This code is next applied to the infrastructure to ensure that it actually is in that state.

In this approach, the machine-readable code files, which basically are simple text files, should be managed like software code, using a version control system, or Concurrent Version System (CVS). That means the tools that are common to the developer are implemented to manage the infrastructure as code. Commonly, Git repositories are used for this purpose.

Putting these files in a CVS makes managing it easy. This approach provides some benefits, such as easy management of change history, upgrades, and rollback. Infrastructure as code is the place where the developer meets the operator in DevOps. Developers can easily review changes, and operators can ensure that the systems are in the state that developers expect.

Other Automation Solutions

To provide automation of configuration management, Ansible is one of the most common solutions. Even if it seems to be currently the most-used configuration management solution, it's not the only one. Other common solutions include Puppet, Chef, and SaltStack.

Like Ansible, Puppet is one of the most important automation solutions. There are a few reasons why Ansible is taking over market share from Puppet though. One of the reasons is YAML. Ansible configurations are written in YAML, which is an easy-to-use and easy-to-understand language. Puppet uses its own language, which is just not as easy. Another major difference is that Ansible uses a push approach, where configurations are sent from the controller node to the managed nodes. Puppet uses a pull approach as its main strategy, where managed nodes use an agent to connect to the Puppet control node to fetch their desired state.

Chef is built as a client/server solution, where the server parts run on the control node machine and the client parts are implemented as an agent on the managed machines. Chef provides its configuration in Ruby DSL, whereas Ansible uses playbooks written in YAML. As a result, Ansible is easier to learn because YAML is a much more accessible data format.

SaltStack is another important alternative to Ansible. The main difference between Ansible and SaltStack is the performance. SaltStack uses the ZeroMQ message queue to realize communication between the SaltStack minions and the control node, and that seems to be faster. Saltstack can work with different languages for configuration files. It uses an agent, which makes implementing SaltStack more complex.

Understanding Ansible Essential Components

Now that you know a bit about Ansible and how it works, let's look at the different components used in Ansible. In this section you learn about the role of Python, the Ansible architecture, the Ansible Tower management platform, and how to manage systems the Ansible way.

Ansible Is Python

There are many programming and scripting languages in use in IT. In open source, the last few decades have seen the rise of the Python scripting language. Python has become the foundation of different solutions, such as Ansible and OpenStack. The reason is that Python is relatively easy to learn. The focus in Python is on readability of code, while at the same time Python makes it possible to do things in an easy way.

Ansible is written in Python, and most components that are used in Ansible are written in Python as well. The default Ansible version that is installed on Red Hat Enterprise Linux 7 is based on Python 2.7; the Ansible release that is used in RHEL 8 is based on Python 3.6. There is no direct relation between an Ansible version and a Python version. Recent versions of Ansible can call either Python 2.x or Python 3.x scripts, but Python 3.x is the better option nowadays because Python 2 is past its end of support life.

The fact that Ansible is written in Python makes it easier to integrate Ansible with custom scripts because Python is a very common and widely known scripting language. This doesn't mean you have to know Python to work with Ansible though. It's true that if you understand the workings of Python it's easier to explain specific behavior in Ansible, but it's perfectly possible to be an expert in Ansible without even knowing how to write a Hello World script in Python.

Ansible Architecture

There are two main node roles in Ansible. The controller node is the node that runs the Ansible software and from which the operator issues Ansible commands. The controller node can be a server running Linux, an operator laptop, or a system running Ansible Tower. The only requirement is that the controller node needs to be Linux.

From the controller node, the managed nodes are addressed. On the controller node, an inventory is maintained to know which managed nodes are available. Ansible doesn't require the use of any agents. That means it can reach out to managed nodes without a need to install anything. To do so, Ansible uses native remote access solutions that are provided by the managed node. On Linux, remote access is realized by using SSH; on Windows, it is realized by using Windows Remote Management (WinRM); and on network devices, it can be provided by using SSH or API access.

To configure the managed nodes, Ansible uses playbooks. A playbook is written in YAML and contains one or more plays. Each play consists of one or more tasks that are executed on the managed nodes.

To implement the tasks, Ansible uses modules. Modules are the pieces of code that do the actual work on the managed nodes, and many modules are available—more than 3000 already, and the number is increasing. Ansible also provides plug-ins. Ansible plug-ins are used to extend Ansible functionality with additional features.

Ansible playbooks should be developed to be idempotent. That means a playbook will always produce the same results, even if it is started multiple times on the same node. As a part of the idempotency, playbooks should also be self-containing and not depend on any other playbooks to be successful.

Understanding Ansible Tower

Ansible can be used in two different ways: Ansible Engine or Ansible Tower. Ansible Engine is the command-line version of Ansible, where modules and plug-ins are used to offer Ansible functionality. Ansible Engine is the solution of choice for people who like to work from the command line in a medium- to mid-sized environment.

Apart from Ansible Engine, there is Ansible Tower, which is based on the AWX open-source solution. It provides a web-based interface to manage Ansible. Ansible Tower adds different features to Ansible Engine, such as

- Web management interface
- Role-based access control
- Job scheduling
- Enhanced security
- Centralized logging

Because the RHCE EX294 exam is about Ansible Engine, you won't find much information about Ansible Tower in this book.

Understanding the Ansible Way

While working with Ansible, you need to make choices on how to approach specific tasks. In many cases, many solutions are available. If, however, you choose to work the Ansible way, making the right solution becomes a lot easier. The Ansible way is focused around the following rules:

- **Keep it simple:** At its launch, Ansible was positioned as a solution that is simpler than the others. That goes for the playbooks and other solutions you'll develop as well. Keep it simple, and it will be easier for others to understand what you had in mind.

- **Make it readable:** As with anything in IT, you can make it very complex and use compact structures to ensure that nobody understands what you were trying to do. That approach doesn't make sense. You should keep it readable, and that starts with your development of Ansible playbooks.

- **Use a declarative approach:** In Ansible, it's all about the desired state. The purpose of Ansible is to bring managed assets into the desired state, regardless of the current state, and make only the modifications that are necessary. The desired state is implemented in playbooks, and using playbooks to make the current state match the desired state is what is known as the declarative approach.

- **Use specific solutions:** On many occasions, you'll find that multiple solutions are available to reach a specific desired state. For instance, you can use the command module to run arbitrary commands, making it possible to accomplish almost anything. You shouldn't, though. To make sure that you get the desired result, use the most specific solution. So if, for instance, a user module allows you to create users, use that module and don't use the Linux **useradd** command with the command module.

Understanding Ansible Use Cases

The core of Ansible is configuration management. The Ansible modules and plug-ins cover a wide range of functions, which means that Ansible can be used for configuration management and beyond. Here are some common use cases.

Using Ansible for Configuration Management

Many people know Ansible only as a configuration management solution, and there's a reason for that. Ansible started as a solution for configuration management, and that is what it still is used for in most cases. In configuration management, Ansible is used to manage configuration files, install software, create users, and perform similar tasks to guarantee that the managed systems all are in the desired state.

Using Ansible for Provisioning

Another common Ansible usage scenario is to deploy and install systems (provisioning). Provisioning is particularly common in virtual and cloud environments, where in the end a new machine is just a configuration file that needs to be pushed to the managed machine and started from there. Ansible does not offer the functionality to PXE-boot and kickstart a bare-metal server but is used in combination with solutions that can take care of that as well. While exploring the different modules that are available, you'll notice that a wide range of modules is provided to work with Ansible in different cloud environments.

Using Ansible for Continuous Delivery

Continuous integration/continuous delivery (CI/CD) makes sure that source code can easily be developed and updated, and the results are easily provisioned as a new version of an application. Ansible cannot take care of the entire CI/CD procedure itself, but Ansible playbooks can play an important role in the CD part of the CI/CD pipeline.

Summary

In this chapter you learned about configuration management in general and the role of Ansible in configuration management solutions. You also read what makes Ansible unique and in which typical use cases Ansible is used. In the next chapter you'll learn how to build your own management infrastructure based on Ansible.

Exam Preparation Tasks

As mentioned in the section "How to Use This Book" in the Introduction, you have a couple of choices for exam preparation: the exercises here, Chapter 16, "Final Preparation," and the exam simulation questions on the companion website.

Review All Key Topics

Review the most important topics in this chapter, noted with the Key Topic icon in the outer margin of the page. Table 1-2 lists a reference of these key topics and the page numbers on which each is found.

Table 1-2 Key Topics for Chapter 1

Key Topic Element	Description	Page Number
List	Application life cycle	7
List	Features Ansible Tower adds to Ansible Engine	10
List	Rules of the Ansible way	11

Define Key Terms

Define the following key terms from this chapter, and check your answers in the glossary:

automation language, CI/CD, current state, CVS, declarative approach, desired state, DevOps, Git repository, idempotent, infrastructure as code, pipelines, provisioning, Python, version control system

This chapter covers the following subjects:

- Understanding an Ansible Environment
- Understanding Controller Host Requirements
- Understanding Installation Methods
- Configuring Managed Hosts
- Configuring the Ansible User

## CHAPTER 2

Installing Ansible

The following RHCE exam objectives are covered in this chapter:

- Install and configure an Ansible control node
  - Install required packages
- Configure Ansible managed nodes
  - Create and distribute SSH keys to managed nodes
  - Configure privilege escalation on managed nodes

"Do I Know This Already?" Quiz

The "Do I Know This Already?" quiz allows you to assess whether you should read this entire chapter thoroughly or jump to the "Exam Preparation Tasks" section. If you are in doubt about your answers to these questions or your own assessment of your knowledge of the topics, read the entire chapter. Table 2-1 lists the major headings in this chapter and their corresponding "Do I Know This Already?" quiz questions. You can find the answers in Appendix A, "Answers to the 'Do I Know This Already?' Quizzes and Review Questions."

Table 2-1 "Do I Know This Already?" Section-to-Question Mapping

Foundation Topics Section	Questions
Understanding an Ansible Environment	1, 2
Understanding Controller Host Requirements	3, 5, 7
Understanding Installation Methods	6
Configuring Managed Hosts	4, 8, 9
Configuring the Ansible User	10

1. Which of the following are required on Ansible managed nodes? (Choose all that apply.)

   a. An Ansible agent

   b. Python

   c. Root access

   d. SSH access

2. Which statements about Python in an Ansible environment are true? (Choose two.)

   a. Python needs to be installed only on the control node.

   b. Python needs to be installed on the managed nodes.

   c. Python 3 is the default version in RHEL 8.

   d. While installing Ansible on CentOS 8, you can select which Python version you want to use.

3. While you are setting up an Ansible managed environment, there are a few requirements. Which of the following is not a mandatory requirement?

   a. Set up a dedicated user account.

   b. Configure SSH key-based login.

   c. Install Python on managed hosts.

   d. Install Python on the Ansible control node.

4. Which statement about sudo is not true?

   a. On managed hosts, the Ansible user must be able to escalate permissions.

   b. Setting up sudo on the control node is not required.

   c. Setting up sudo is not required on all types of managed nodes.

   d. Privilege escalation should be set up to run tasks as root.

5. To set up Ansible to learn for EX294, there are different requirements. Which of the following is not one of them?

   a. RHEL or CentOS 8.x

   b. 1 GB of RAM or more

   c. 20 GB or more disk space

   d. 1 CPU

6. Ansible can be installed in different ways. Which of the following is not one of them?

   a. Use RHEL subscription manager to install from the RHEL Ansible repository.

   b. Use EPEL on either RHEL or CentOS 8.

   c. Use the python-pip installer.

   d. Use the Java installer.

7. Executing tasks as a remote user can be secured in different ways. Which of the following is not one of them?

   a. Protect the SSH private key with a passphrase.

   b. Use password-based SSH login.

   c. Disallow root execution through sudo.

   d. Make password use mandatory while using sudo.

8. Which of the following is not a required setup task while installing Ansible on CentOS 8?

   a. Add the EPEL repository.

   b. Install Python 3.

   c. Configure sudo.

   d. Enable SSH access.

9. Which firewall ports need to be open on Ansible-managed hosts? (Choose all that apply.)

   a. 22

   b. 80

   c. 443

   d. 2022

10. After you use ssh-keygen to create the SSH public/private key pair, what is the next step?

   a. Configure sudo access.

   b. Use ssh-copy-id to copy the private key to the managed machines.

   c. Copy the public key to the remote hosts.

   d. Install Python 3 on the managed hosts.

Foundation Topics

In this chapter you learn how to set up Ansible. This process involves setting up not just the controller host, from which Ansible tasks will be executed on the managed hosts and devices, but also the managed hosts. Because this book was written with the RHCE EX294 in mind, we focus on setting up an environment to manage RHEL/CentOS 8 Linux hosts.

Understanding an Ansible Environment

Ansible is about managing a wide range of different device types. To do so, you need a host that plays the role of the manager. In this book, we call that the controller node. The controller node runs the Ansible software; the managed nodes run nothing in particular. The only requirement on managed nodes is that Ansible should be able to contact them. On Linux and many network devices, that means you need to run Secure Shell (SSH). On Windows that means you need to configure Remote Management or Secure Shell for Windows. To work with Ansible, you don't need to run or configure any agent on managed devices.

To set up this book's test environment, you need a minimum of three nodes. The requirements of these nodes are listed in Table 2-2. One of these nodes is used as the controller node; the other nodes are used as managed nodes. Notice that in this book I've chosen not to manage the controller node with Ansible also. The controller node is an isolated environment to reduce the risk of things going wrong and the controller node accidentally getting changed so that it no longer works.

Notice that the specific operating system version is not very important, which is why Table 2-2 mentions RHEL or CentOS 8.x. While writing this book, I installed on 8.1. By the time you read this, a newer version of the operating system will be available. Even if you are installing Ansible on RHEL or CentOS 8.8, it should not matter. The underlying operating system doesn't change how Ansible approaches things. What matters is the Ansible version that is used, and for RHCE EX294, that is Ansible 2.x—version 2.8 or later, to be even more specific.

Also note that for the node setup in this book, I used a virtual machine installation from the CentOS and Red Hat Enterprise Linux ISO files. It is also possible to use different environments for creating the setup described in this chapter, such as cloud instances for either RHEL or CentOS. While you work with Cloud instances, the operating system will be configured slightly differently, according to the cloud platform that is used. I do not try to cover all these differences in this chapter because there are just too many platforms to consider. Everything in this book is based on virtual machines because that is what you'll work with in the exam. For that reason I recommend you set up your test environment in a virtual machine and not in cloud.

TIP In a production environment, you probably want to manage the controller node with Ansible as well. You would just set up a set of playbooks that allows you to easily configure, update, and manage the controller node.

Table 2-2 Test Environment Node Requirements

Item	Requirement
Operating system	RHEL 8.x or CentOS 8.x
RAM	1 GB or more
Disk space	20 GB or more
Installation profile	Minimal installation

Exercise 2-1   Setting Up the Test Network

1. Set up a test network, consisting of three virtual machines, using the specifications mentioned in Table 2-2. Ensure that the following names are used:

    ▪ control.example.com: the Ansible control machine

    ▪ ansible1.example.com: the first managed node

    ▪ ansible2.example.com: the second managed node

2. Provide fixed IP addresses in each of the virtual machines. Use IP addresses that match your current network environment. The IP addresses should allow your machines to connect to the Internet.

3. While installing, create a user account with the name ansible.

4. Edit the /etc/hosts file on each of the three virtual machines such that you can ping each of the other virtual machines. See Listing 2-1 for an example of the /etc/hosts contents.

Listing 2-1 Sample /etc/hosts Contents

```
127.0.0.1 localhost localhost.localdomain localhost4 \
localhost4.localdomain4
::1  localhost localhost.localdomain localhost6 \
localhost6.localdomain6
192.168.4.200 control.example.com control
192.168.4.201 ansible1.example.com ansible1
192.168.4.202 ansible2.example.com ansible2
```

Understanding Controller Host Requirements

To install Ansible on the controller node, you need a few items:

- Python 3.x

- An SSH client

- Access to an Ansible Repository

- A dedicated user account that is configured with SSH and sudo permissions on managed hosts

Ansible is written in Python, and as a result Python has to be installed on the Ansible controller node as well as the Ansible managed nodes. On older versions of RHEL, this was something you needed to do separately. In RHEL 8, a default Python stack is installed automatically, so you don't have to do anything about that anymore. Notice that on some public cloud instances, a Python stack is not installed by default, and you might still have to manually install it.

Python is needed because, for managing managed hosts, Ansible generates Python scripts. These Python scripts are next executed, using **ssh** on the remote host. Managed network devices are an exception though, as network devices don't typically run a Python stack. But managing network devices with Ansible is outside the scope of the RHCE EX294 exam anyway.

Currently, there are two major versions of Python. Python 3.x slowly has become the standard in recent years, but Python 2.x is still used on many sites. Transitioning from Python 2.x to Python 3.x is not always easy because the scripts are not compatible. On RHEL 8, Ansible uses Python 3 as the default stack though. And even if it is technically possible to use Python 2.x on RHEL 8, this is not something you have to master for the RHCE 8 exam. You shouldn't want to do this anyway. Python 2.x is old and becoming obsolete; Python 3.x is what matters.

Understanding Installation Methods

Ansible is open-source software, and as a result, Ansible can be installed on many platforms, each of which comes with its own installation method. In this book we cover installation of Ansible on either Red Hat Enterprise Linux 8 or CentOS 8. On both platforms you can install Ansible from the distribution repositories or using Python pip. In the following sections you read how to do this.

> **NOTE**   Use the instructions that correspond to the operating system and installation method that you want to use. So do not perform Exercises 2-2, 2-3, and 2-4 but pick the one that applies to your operating system platform.

Installing Ansible on RHEL 8

Obviously, to take the RHCE 8 exam, you run all assignments on Red Hat Enterprise Linux. Using Ansible on Red Hat Enterprise Linux does require you to have a valid license though. Free developer licenses can be requested from https://developers.redhat.com, and using such a license allows you to install RHEL 8 as well as Ansible for free. After you set up the base RHEL 8 environment, the rest of the setup procedure is easy; you just have to add a repository and can then install Ansible. Exercise 2-2 outlines the steps that need to be performed on a pre-installed RHEL 8 machine.

Exercise 2-2   Installing Ansible on RHEL 8

1. On the RHEL 8 control node, open a root shell and type **subscription-manager repos --list**. This shows you a list of currently configured repositories. You should see the standard RHEL 8 repositories.

2. Type **subscription-manager repos --enable=ansible-2-for-rhel-8-x86_64-rpms** to add the Ansible 2.x repository.

3. Use **yum install ansible** to install the Ansible software.

4. Use **ansible --version** to verify that the Ansible software has been installed.

5. Type **rpm -qa | grep python** to verify that Python 3 is also installed.

Installing Ansible on CentOS 8

If you are using CentOS 8, the Ansible software can be installed from the EPEL repository. The EPEL repository contains Extra Packages for Enterprise Linux. Ansible is among the EPEL packages. After enabling access to the EPEL repository, you can install Ansible using a simple **yum install -y ansible**. Exercise 2-3 guides you through this procedure.

Exercise 2-3   Installing Ansible on CentOS 8

1. On the CentOS 8 control node, open a root shell.

2. Type **yum install -y epel-release** to add the EPEL repository.

3. Type **yum install -y ansible** to install the Ansible software.

4. Type **ansible --version** to verify that the Ansible software has been installed.

Using python-pip to Install Ansible

Ansible is completely written in the scripting language Python, and Python includes its own package manager: python-pip. As a result, for software that is written in

Python, you can use either the package manager of your Linux repository or the python-pip software manager. Because Ansible is written in Python, this applies to Ansible as well.

The advantage of using python-pip is that it is an advanced method of managing software, often giving you access to the most recent version of the software before it is available in the repositories of your distribution. The disadvantage is that the software isn't controlled from your distribution, which makes it harder to manage software updates from a generic interface. In Exercise 2-4 you learn how to install Ansible from the python-pip installer.

Exercise 2-4   Using python-pip to Install Ansible

1. From a root shell on your CentOS or RHEL 8 control node, type **yum install -y python3-pip** to install the Python 3 pip installer.

2. Type **alternatives --set python /usr/bin/python3**. This creates a symbolic link with the name python that allows you to start the python3 binary.

3. Exit the root shell, and open a shell as your Ansible user. From the ansible user shell, type **pip3 install ansible --user**.

4. Once the installation completes, type **ansible --version** to verify that Ansible has been installed.

Configuring Managed Hosts

Managed hosts in an Ansible environment don't need a lot. Opposed to what is needed in some other configuration management solutions, no agents need to be installed on the managed hosts. You only have to enable SSH access and ensure that Python is available on the managed hosts.

If you want to manage non-Linux nodes, notice that additional steps might be required. To manage Windows with Ansible, for instance, you must enable a Windows-native remote access mechanism, like Windows Remote Management (WinRM) or the Windows SSH daemon, and if you want to manage network devices, you might have to use device specific requirements. This is not relevant for RHCE EX294 though, where you only have to manage Linux machines with Ansible. Exercise 2-5 guides you through the procedure of setting up Linux-based managed nodes.

Exercise 2-5   Setting Up a RHEL 8 Managed Node

1. On your RHEL 8 managed nodes, open a root shell.

2. Type **systemctl status sshd** to verify whether the SSH process is running and available to receive incoming connections. SSH is automatically installed and started on a RHEL/CentOS 8 installation, so no further action should be required here.

3. Type **rpm -qa | grep python**. You should now see a list of packages. Often, you do not need to manually install Python on RHEL or CentOS 8 because it's a part of the default configuration in most installation types.

4. Finally, type **firewall-cmd --list-all**. In the list of services, you should see that ssh is listed. This means that the remote host is accessible through ssh as well.

5. From the control machine, as user ansible, type **ssh ansible1**. This opens an SSH session to the ansible1 machine, which verifies that everything required is up and running.

In the procedure described in Exercise 2-5, you have manually set up a managed node. This approach is not practical if you're configuring a big Ansible managed environment, and it's not needed for setting up a large Ansible managed environment. To use a more automated approach, you can use the raw module. In Chapter 12, "Managing Software with Ansible," you'll learn how to use this module to configure a managed node.

Configuring the Ansible User

While managing an environment with Ansible, you need a dedicated user account. In this book I use a user with the name "ansible" in all examples. Obviously, in a production environment you can pick any username you would like. Because the examples in this book all use the username "ansible," I advise you to create a user with that name as well.

The ansible user is used to run the ansible scripts on the managed hosts. To do so, Ansible issues an **ssh** command under the hood to push a Python script that performs all configuration tasks on the managed machines. For this procedure to work easily, two steps are required for setting up the ansible user:

1. The user must be able to SSH into the managed machines.

2. The user must be enabled to run tasks as root on the managed machines.

Setting Up SSH for the Ansible User

Setting up SSH to allow the ansible user to log in to a managed host is not difficult. Just ensure the user account exists on all machines and use the **ssh** command. You should consider how to configure SSH access though.

If nothing is configured, the user needs to enter a password each time the remote connection is established. Although secure, this is not convenient, especially not in an environment where Ansible is used to manage remote machines.

The most convenient way to connect to managed machines is by using SSH public/private keys, and that is exactly what we're going to do in our sample configuration. SSH public/private keys can be used as authentication credentials, and because a private key cannot be guessed, it is considered a more secure way to log in to managed hosts.

While working with public/private keys, the public/private key pair is generated on the workstation that the user typically is connecting from. In our case, that is the Ansible control machine. After generating the public/private key pair, the public key needs to be copied over to the managed hosts. While authenticating, the user generates an authentication token using its private key, and this authentication is sent to the managed machine, where it is matched against the public key that is stored on the managed machine. If the matching succeeds, the user is authenticated.

To work with public/private keys, a passphrase may be used to further secure private key access. Normally, the private key should be accessible by the user who owns the key only, which is accomplished by putting the key in a secured place in the user home directory. If, however, someone would be able to copy the user private key, the user identity would be stolen and freely accessible. For that reason, it makes sense to secure the private key with a passphrase.

A passphrase is like a password; it needs to be entered each time the private key is used. Using passphrases makes using public/private key pairs a lot more secure, but it makes working with Ansible a little less convenient as well. For that reason, on the RHCE exam, you don't have to secure SSH setup with passphrases, and you can work with password-less private keys. In Exercise 2-6 you learn how to set up SSH keys that allow the ansible user to connect to the managed machines.

Exercise 2-6   Setting Up SSH Key-Based User Authentication

1. On control.example.com, open a shell as the user ansible.

2. Type **ssh-keygen**. Press Enter to accept the default file name for storing the private key.

3. When prompted for a passphrase, press Enter. This configures a passphrase-less private key. Press Enter again to confirm.

4. After generating the public/private key pair, type **ssh-copy-id ansible1**. This prompts for the user ansible password on server ansible1, after which the public key can be copied to the appropriate location. Repeat this step for ansible2, using **ssh-copy-id ansible2**.

5. Verify that the passphrase-less private key has been correctly configured by using **ssh ansible1**. You should get access to a prompt on ansible1 without having to enter a password or anything.

If you want to secure your environment a bit more than what is required on the exam, you can easily passphrase-protect your user accounts by applying the following procedure:

1. While using **ssh-keygen** to generate the SSH public/private key pair, enter a passphrase to protect the private key.

2. At the start of each Ansible session, type **ssh-agent /bin/bash**.

3. Next, type **ssh-add**. This prompts for the SSH private key passphrase, and after it is entered once, the passphrase can be obtained from the secured SSH passphrase cache for the remainder of the duration of your session.

TIP In a production environment, you might want to consider working with different types of Ansible projects. You might consider setting up a high-security user account with passphrase-protected private keys for the more sensitive jobs and using a low-security user account that can run specific tasks without entering any passphrase.

Configuring sudo for the Ansible User

While working with Ansible, the ansible user account is used not only to gather information from managed hosts but also to install software, change configurations, and perform other tasks that require root privileges. To ensure that Ansible can complete these tasks, you must configure privilege escalation. The default solution to do so on Linux is to use sudo.

To set up sudo, you have two options. You can use the Linux **visudo** command to write the desired configuration to the /etc/sudoers file. Alternatively, you can use drop-in files. These independent files are created in the /etc/sudoers.d/ directory. Using these drop-in files is the preferred way because it allows for easy management of settings for different users, without changing the main /etc/sudoers configuration file.

While setting up a sudo configuration, like when setting up SSH login, you have the choice to do it securely or conveniently. If sudo is used occasionally, it is common to require the user to enter a password before being allowed to escalate permissions. In Ansible playbooks, where tasks often are executed on many hosts, it is very inconvenient if the sudo password needs to be entered every time and on each host. This is why it is common to configure sudo such that no password has to be entered to acquire root privileges. In Exercise 2-7 you are guided through the procedure to do so.

Exercise 2-7   Setting Up Privilege Escalation

1. Ensure that the user ansible exists on all managed nodes and has been configured for SSH key-based access as described in Exercise 2-6.

2. On all managed nodes as well as on the control node, from a root shell, use the command **echo "ansible ALL=(ALL) NOPASSWD: ALL" > /etc/sudoers.d/ansible**.

3. On all managed nodes, as the ansible user, type **sudo ls -l /root/**. This command should show you the contents of the /root/ directory (which is accessible by the root user only) without prompting for a password.

TIP If using password-less privilege escalation is unacceptable in your environment, you might want to consider using Ansible Tower. Ansible Tower is a web-based platform, based on the AWX open-source project, which was developed to meet some inconveniences that are met when using Ansible from the command line. One of its features is to securely store the password that is required to run commands using sudo. Read Appendix B, "Getting Started with Ansible Tower," for a quick impression of what Ansible Tower can do.

Summary

In this chapter you learned how to set up an environment that is ready to be used as the lab environment throughout this book. You installed the required virtual machines, created and configured the user ansible, and ensured that the user ansible is allowed to run tasks with sudo root privileges on the managed nodes. In the next chapter, you'll read how to further set up your Ansible-managed environment.

Exam Preparation Tasks

As mentioned in the section "How to Use This Book" in the Introduction, you have a couple of choices for exam preparation: the exercises here, Chapter 16, "Final Preparation," and the exam simulation questions on the companion website.

Review All Key Topics

Review the most important topics in this chapter, noted with the Key Topic icon in the outer margin of the page. Table 2-3 lists a reference of these key topics and the page numbers on which each is found.

Table 2-3 Key Topics for Chapter 2

Key Topic Element	Description	Page Number
List	Requirements for installing Ansible on the controller node	20
Paragraph	Managed hosts in Ansible	22
List	Setting up Ansible user	23

Memory Tables

Print a copy of Appendix D, "Memory Tables" (found on the companion website), or at least the section for this chapter, and complete the tables and lists from memory. Appendix E, "Memory Tables Answer Key," also on the companion website, includes completed tables and lists to check your work.

Define Key Terms

Define the following key terms from this chapter, and check your answers in the glossary:

Ansible Tower, AWX, controller node, EPEL repository, managed node, pip, WinRM

Review Questions

1. Which installation method should you use when installing Ansible on RHEL 8?

2. What are the requirements on CentOS 8 hosts you want to manage with Ansible?

3. What is the name of the program that can be used to install Ansible from Python?

4. Which agent needs to be running on a RHEL 8 machine to manage it with Ansible?

5. What is the name of the open-source project behind Ansible Tower?

6. If a user wants to configure Ansible to use public/private keys but doesn't want to use passphrase-less private keys, which option can be used?

7. Which directory can be used to create a drop-in file that adds sudo configuration for a specific user?

8. Which solution can be used to make setting up managed nodes in Ansible easier?

9. Is Python always required on managed nodes?

10. A user wants to use SSH passwords and not keys to connect to Ansible-managed machines but doesn't want to enter the password at every new connection that is opened. What solution would you suggest?

End-of-Chapter Lab

In this chapter, you learned how to configure your control node as well as your ansible nodes for Ansible. You can now practice these skills in the end-of-chapter lab. Notice that if you have already worked through the exercises in this chapter, you do not need to perform this lab as well because your environment has already been set up correctly in that case.

Lab 2-1

Set up an Ansible environment according to the directions in this chapter. Make sure this environment meets the following requirements:

- Three hosts are used: control.example.com, ansible1.example.com, and ansible2.example.com.

- A user named ansible is created on all hosts.

- On ansible1 as well as ansible2, the ansible user is allowed to run root commands using sudo, without being required to enter a password.

- User ansible can log in to ansible1 and ansible2 using ssh, based on passphrase-less private keys.

- The ansible software is installed on control.

This chapter covers the following subjects:

- Understanding Projects
- Configuring Static Inventory
- Working with Dynamic Inventory
- Managing Settings in ansible.cfg

## CHAPTER 3

Setting Up an Ansible Managed Environment

The following RHCE exam objectives are covered in this chapter:

- Understand core components of Ansible

  - Inventories

  - Configuration files

- Install and configure an Ansible control node

  - Create a static host inventory file

  - Create a configuration file

  - Create and use static inventories to define groups of hosts

"Do I Know This Already?" Quiz

The "Do I Know This Already?" quiz allows you to assess whether you should read this entire chapter thoroughly or jump to the "Exam Preparation Tasks" section. If you are in doubt about your answers to these questions or your own assessment of your knowledge of the topics, read the entire chapter. Table 3-1 lists the major headings in this chapter and their corresponding "Do I Know This Already?" quiz questions. You can find the answers in Appendix A, "Answers to the 'Do I Know This Already?' Quizzes and Review Questions."

Table 3-1 "Do I Know This Already?" Section-to-Question Mapping

Foundation Topics Section	Questions
Understanding Projects	8
Configuring Static Inventory	1, 2, 3, 6
Working with Dynamic Inventory	4, 5
Managing Settings in ansible.cfg	7, 9, 10

1. Which of the following is not a valid method of using inventory?

   a. If nothing is specified, Ansible looks for a file with the name inventory in the current directory.

   b. Specify the name of the inventory file in ansible.cfg.

   c. Specify the name of the inventory file as a command-line argument using the **-i** option.

   d. Use the default inventory in /etc/ansible/hosts.

2. Which of the following symptoms do you see if no inventory file was specified?

   a. Ansible generates an error message.

   b. Ansible tells you that no inventory hosts could be found.

   c. Ansible tries to run commands against localhost.

   d. The Ansible command doesn't complain but just doesn't give anything as a result.

3. What is the name of the default Ansible inventory?

   a. /etc/hosts

   b. /etc/inventory

   c. /etc/ansible/inventory

   d. /etc/ansible/hosts

4. Which of the following is not a requirement that must be met by a dynamic inventory script?

   a. It must be executable.

   b. It must be written in Python.

   c. It must respect the arguments **--list** and **--host**.

   d. It must produce its output in JSON format.

5. Which statement about using multiple inventory files is true?

   a. Ansible doesn't support using multiple inventory files.

   b. Multiple dynamic inventory files are supported; using multiple static inventory files is not.

   c. When the name of a directory is specified as the inventory that has to be used, all files in that directory are used as inventory.

   d. When multiple inventory files are used, each file has to be specified separately as a command-line option using the **-i** option.

6. Which of the following should not be used in inventory files?

    a. Variables that apply to specific hosts

    b. Host groups

    c. IP addresses

    d. Nested host groups

7. Which of the following should be avoided?

    a. Define privilege escalation in ansible.cfg.

    b. Define privilege escalation in individual playbooks.

    c. Set privilege escalation on the command line.

    d. Define privilege escalation in the inventory file.

8. Where should the inventory file be stored in a big corporation where Ansible is used to manage hundreds of servers and appliances?

    a. In /etc/ansible/hosts

    b. In DNS

    c. In the project directory

    d. In Ansible Tower

9. Which statement about the remote_user setting is not true?

    a. The remote_user typically is defined in the [defaults] section in ansible.cfg.

    b. The remote_user setting refers to the user account that is used to run all tasks on managed hosts after privilege escalation.

    c. The remote_user setting can also be applied on the command line or in a playbook.

    d. Without a remote_user setting, Ansible won't work correctly.

10. Which parameter can be used to disable the requirement to check validity of SSH host keys?

    a. host_key_checking

    b. ssh_host_keys

    c. verify_host_keys

    d. verify_ssh_keys

Foundation Topics

In the preceding chapter you read about the Linux requirements of an Ansible managed environment. At this point your hosts should all meet these requirements, so now it's time to focus on the Ansible part of the configuration. In this chapter you learn about two essential components: the inventory and the ansible.cfg configuration file. But first, we need to spend some time talking about Ansible projects.

Understanding Projects

In some cases, a small IT team may use Ansible to manage just a few servers. In other cases, Ansible is used to manage multiple IT projects in a worldwide organization. These different use cases ask for a different approach in the way Ansible is used. If it is used at a small scale, there's nothing wrong with having just one Ansible configuration take care of all needs in IT. If, however, Ansible is used to manage large-scale environments, it's a good idea to work with different project directories.

A project directory is a self-contained environment that includes everything needed to work in a specific project. The playbooks are found within the project directory. These are the Ansible scripts, written in YAML, that enforce the desired configuration on managed hosts. Apart from these playbooks, other components may also be found in the project directory, such as variable files, additional files used to include tasks, and the inventory and the ansible.cfg configuration files.

Having all of these within the same project directory makes it easy to delegate tasks in an Ansible managed environment. If you're working on just a few servers, this approach might not make too much sense, but once your Ansible environment is taking care of many managed assets, you will recognize the convenience of working with project directories.

Using project directories is good to keep together items that belong together. While using the project directory, you may put the ansible.cfg file and the inventory file in the specific project directory. This approach makes sense if each project has its own specific configuration files. Alternatively, the configuration files may be in the ansible user home directory. This approach makes sense if different user accounts exist for managing Ansible, where each user has his own configuration. You can also choose to manage all Ansible configuration at a system level, where inventory and ansible.cfg are the same for your entire system. Table 3-2 summarizes the different options.

Table 3-2 Options for Storing Configuration Files

Location	Use
Project directory	Useful if specific projects need their own configuration files. Project directories may be changed between users or may be private to a specific user account.
Home directory	Useful to allow one user to work with its specific settings.
/etc/ansible	Useful in small environments where configuration is the same for every Ansible user and every project.

Configuring Static Inventory

The purpose of the Ansible inventory is to identify hosts that Ansible has to manage. Inventory also can be used for other purposes:

- List hosts

- Group hosts

- Specify host variables (deprecated)

Listing Hosts

In its simplest form, the inventory file is just a list of hosts that Ansible uses to identify the hosts that matter in this project. If you prefer a project-oriented approach, you can have different inventories in different projects because in one project you may be addressing different hosts than in other projects. In the project approach, each project directory should have its own inventory file.

In smaller Ansible managed environments, the file /etc/ansible/hosts can be used as the inventory file. If this file exists, it's not necessary to have project inventory files as well.

EXAM TIP If you have doubts about the format of lines in the inventory file on the exam, look at /etc/ansible/hosts. It contains nice examples of how hosts can be specified in the inventory file.

An Ansible inventory can be just a list of host names or IP addresses. You don't need to specify name-resolving information as well because DNS or the /etc/hosts file should be taking care of name resolving. Apart from just listing the names or IP addresses of hosts, the inventory file also can work with ranges. For instance, the line server[1:6].example.com would address all servers between server1 and server6.

Inventory Host Groups

When you're working with many hosts, using host groups is convenient. Host groups can be defined in inventory, and a host may be a member of multiple host groups. You can also work with nested groups, where a group is a member of another group. The example in Listing 3-1 shows what host group definitions should look like.

Listing 3-1   Inventory File with Host Groups

```
ansible1
ansible2
192.168.4.1
192.168.4.2

[web]
web1
web2
[db]
db1
db2

[servers:children]
web
db
```

In Listing 3-1, you first see the hosts ansible1 and ansible2, which are not members of any specific group. Also, you see two IP addresses. You are allowed (though it is not recommended) to include IP addresses as well. Next, a group web and a group db are defined. In the example you also see the group servers that address all hosts in the group [web] as well as the [db] group.

In general, there are three different approaches for using groups. Functional groups are used to be able to address specific groups of hosts, like web servers and file servers. Regional host groups are convenient when working with a region-oriented infrastructure, and staging host groups can be defined to address different hosts according to the staging phase your current environment is in. Table 3-3 gives a summary of a host groups approach.

Table 3-3 Host Group Usage Overview

Group Type	Sample Names	Use
Functional	web, db, lamp	Group hosts according to use.
Regional	africa, europe	Group hosts according to region.
Staging	test, development, prod	Group hosts according to implementation phase.

Apart from the defined host groups, there are also implicit host groups, as shown in Table 3-4. These group names don't have to be defined because they are implicitly there. These are the groups all and ungrouped. Apart from that, there is the implicit host localhost, which doesn't have to be addressed in inventory.

Table 3-4 Implicit Hosts and Host Groups

Name	Use
localhost	Refers to the current host. This may also be the Ansible control host or any other unmanaged host.
all	All hosts that are defined in inventory.
ungrouped	All hosts that are not a member of any group.

Using Inventory in Commands

The inventory file is an essential component of your Ansible configuration because it identifies hosts and allows you to put hosts together in groups. To view the current inventory, you can use the **ansible -i inventory <pattern> --list-hosts** command. Notice the use of the **-i inventory** option, which is mandatory to indicate that a specific inventory must be used.

Another command to show inventory information is **ansible-inventory**:

- Use **ansible-inventory -i inventory --list** to list inventory hosts in JSON output format.

- Use **ansible-inventory -i inventory --graph** to display a graphical overview of hosts in the inventory.

If you're using Ansible commands and don't want to use the default inventory in /etc/ansible/hosts, you must use the **-i** option to point to the inventory file you want to use. This may be an absolute pathname or a relative pathname, so in the example **ansible -i inventory --list-hosts**, a file with the name **inventory** in the local directory is addressed. As an alternative, you may also set the default inventory to use in the ansible.cfg file, which is discussed later.

In Exercise 3-1 you learn how to work with host groups.

Exercise 3-1   Working with Host Groups

1. On the control host, log in as the ansible user and use the command **mkdir base** to create a project directory with the name base. Use **cd base** to get into this directory.

2. In this directory, create a file with the name inventory and give it the following contents:

```
ansible1
ansible2

[web]
web1
web2

[db]
db1
db2

[servers:children]
db
web
```

3. Type **ansible all --list-hosts**. You get a failure message because the **ansible** command does not find any inventory containing hosts.

4. Type **ansible -i inventory all --list-hosts**. Now you see a list of all hosts in inventory.

5. Type **ansible -i inventory ungrouped --list-hosts**. This command shows all hosts that are not a member of any group.

6. Use **ansible-inventory -i inventory --graph**. This command shows a hierarchical overview of inventory, including information about which host is a member of which group.

7. Use **ansible-inventory -i inventory --list**. This command shows the contents of the inventory represented in JSON format.

Specifying Host Variables

In older versions of Ansible, the inventory file was also used to define variables for specific hosts. This behavior is deprecated and should not be used anymore. You might, however, see inventory files that still contain variable definitions, and for that reason, this section describes how it works.

Listing 3-2 shows an inventory file that contains host variables.

Listing 3-2   Sample Inventory with Variables

```
[lamp]
ansible1.example.com

[file]
ansible2.example.com

[win]
windows.example.com

[win:vars]
ansible_user=ansible
ansible_password=@nsible123
ansible_connection=winrm
ansible_winrm_server_cert_validation=ignore
```

As you can see, the variables are set at a group level, using **[groupname:vars]**. You shouldn't use this approach anymore, though. Variables in current versions of Ansible should be set using the host_vars and group_vars directories, as explained in Chapter 6, "Working with Variables and Facts."

Working with Dynamic Inventory

In small environments it is common to manually define the Ansible inventory. If you're using Ansible in big and dynamic environments, like public cloud environments, you should use dynamic inventory instead. In dynamic inventory a script is used to discover inventory hosts in a specific environment. Community-provided inventory scripts are available on GitHub (Google for the exact link of the environment for which you want to find a dynamic inventory script); alternatively, it's not difficult to write your own dynamic inventory scripts.

Working with Community-Provided Dynamic Inventory Scripts

As mentioned, many community-provided inventory scripts are available. The scripts often come with an .ini file that is used to provide specific information on how to connect to the specific resource. To use the community-provided inventory scripts, you have to make sure that they are made executable, using the Linux **chmod +x** command. After making the scripts executable, you must provide required parameters, either by putting them in the .ini file that comes with the inventory script or by providing them as command-line parameters to the **ansible** command. You can obtain good inventory script-specific information on how to do this from the Ansible documentation at https://docs.ansible.com.

Writing Your Own Inventory Scripts

Writing your own inventory script is not too difficult, particularly if you have programming experience. Inventory scripts have a few requirements: they must contain a **--list** option as well as a **--host** option. Also, the output must be produced in JSON format.

In Listing 3-3 you can see an example of the dynamic inventory script pascal.py written in Python. This script generates an inventory that is based on the local Linux host resolving mechanisms in use. This means that it uses the contents of /etc/hosts as the inventory.

Listing 3-3   Dynamic Inventory Script Example

```
#!/usr/bin/python
""" Dynamic Inventory Script Example """

from subprocess import Popen, PIPE
import sys

try:
    import json
except ImportError:
    import simplejson as json

RESULT = {}
RESULT['all'] = {}

PIPE = Popen(['getent', 'hosts'], stdout=PIPE,
universal_newlines=True)

RESULT['all']['hosts'] = []

for line in PIPE.stdout.readlines():
    s = line.split()
    RESULT['all']['hosts'] = RESULT['all']['hosts']+s
```

```
RESULT['all']['vars'] = {}

if len(sys.argv) == 2 and sys.argv[1] == '--list':
    print(json.dumps(RESULT))

elif len(sys.argv) == 3 and sys.argv[1] == '--host':
    print(json.dumps({}))

else:
    print("Requires an argument, please use --list or --host <host>")
```

NOTE   You can download the script in Listing 3-3 from the GitHub repository; it is named listing33.py. Use **git clone https://github.com/sandervanvugt/rhce8-book** to get access to this sample file and many others.

To use the sample inventory script in Listing 3-3, you can run it directly by using the command **./listing33.py --list**. Alternatively, you can use it as an argument to the **ansible** command. You learn how to do this in Exercise 3-2.

Exercise 3-2   Using a Dynamic Inventory Script

1. Type **cd ~** to get back to the current user home directory, and type **sudo yum install -y git** to install the git software.

2. Type **git clone https://github.com/sandervanvugt/rhce8-book** to clone this book's GitHub repository.

3. Type **cd rhce8-book** to go into the rhce8-book directory.

4. Type **sudo alternatives --set python /usr/bin/python3**. This command creates a symbolic link with the name python that points to the python3 binary and thus guarantees that all scripts that are configured to use /usr/bin/python are also working.

5. Type **./listing33.py --list** to show the result of the Python script when it is started by itself. You then see the unformatted command output.

6. Install **json_pp** by typing **sudo yum install perl-JSON-PP**.

7. Type **./listing33.py --list | json_pp** to show output that is formatted in a readable way.

8. Type **ansible -i listing33.py all --list-hosts** to use the script to show all hosts.

Using Multiple Inventory Files

In large environments, it may be useful to access multiple inventory files. You can easily do that by putting all inventory files in a directory and specifying the name of the directory as the inventory file to be used. If it's a static inventory file, you just have to copy it to the inventory directory. If it's a dynamic inventory file, you also need to do that, and in addition you have to make sure that the execute permission is set on the inventory file.

Managing Settings in ansible.cfg

When you're working with Ansible, multiple settings are required to reach out to manage hosts. Table 3-5 lists the most important of these settings. To provide the settings in a persistent way, the ansible.cfg configuration file is used. Specific ansible.cfg files can be created in the current project directory; a generic ansible.cfg file is available as /etc/ansible/ansible.cfg. Listing 3-4 shows an example of an ansible.cfg file.

EXAM TIP   The /etc/ansible/ansible.cfg file is well annotated, and that makes it an excellent resource on the RHCE exam. If you have any doubt about specific parameters to be used, check the /etc/ansible/ansible.cfg file for examples!

Listing 3-4   Sample ansible.cfg File

```
[defaults]
remote_user = ansible
host_key_checking = false
inventory = inventory


[privilege_escalation]
become = True
become_method = sudo
become_user = root
become_ask_pass = False
```

As seen in Listing 3-4, the ansible.cfg file is laid out in .ini file format, with different sections. The section header is between square brackets, and parameters are specified in a key = value format. The common sections in ansible.cfg are [defaults] and [privilege_escalation]. In the default section, generic information is provided. The privilege_escalation section defines how the ansible user should require administrative privileges to connect to the managed hosts.

Table 3-5 ansible.cfg Common Settings

Setting	Use
remote_user	Indicates the name of the user account used to connect to the managed machines
inventory	Indicates the relative or absolute filename that indicates which inventory file to use
become	Is a Boolean value that specifies whether escalation is required
become_method	Indicates which local mechanism should be used for privilege escalation
become_user	Specifies the name of the user account used by become_method to run escalated commands
become_ask_pass	Indicates whether a password should be prompted for when running tasks with escalated privileges
host_key_checking	Specifies whether SSH host keys should be checked

Notice that all of the settings specified in the ansible.cfg file can also be specified in Ansible playbooks. If there are conflicting settings, the most specific setting always wins. So settings defined in a playbook override the settings in the ansible.cfg file. In Exercise 3-3 you practice creating an ansible.cfg file as well as an inventory file in the current user home directory.

Exercise 3-3   Creating an ansible.cfg File

1. Type **cd ~** to ensure that you are in the current user home directory.

2. Type **vim ansible.cfg** to open a new ansible.cfg file that is to be created.

3. Create the defaults section by including the following lines:

```
[defaults]
remote_user = ansible
host_key_checking = false
inventory = inventory
```

4. Configure the privilege escalation section by including the following lines:

```
[privilege_escalation]
become = True
become_method = sudo
become_user = root
become_ask_pass = False
```

5. Copy the inventory file that you created earlier by using **cp base/inventory .**

6. Type **ansible-inventory --list**. This shows you all hosts currently in inventory, without the need to use the **-i inventory** option to specify the name of the inventory file.

Summary

In this chapter you learned about two essential components in every Ansible project: the inventory file and the ansible.cfg file. You read how to create static as well as dynamic inventory files and how to define default settings that Ansible should be working with in the ansible.cfg file. In the next chapter you'll learn how to use all of these settings when working with Ansible ad hoc commands and modules.

Exam Preparation Tasks

As mentioned in the section "How to Use This Book" in the Introduction, you have a couple of choices for exam preparation: the exercises here, Chapter 16, "Final Preparation," and the exam simulation questions on the companion website.

Review All Key Topics

Review the most important topics in this chapter, noted with the Key Topic icon in the outer margin of the page. Table 3-6 lists a reference to these key topics and the page numbers on which each is found.

Table 3-6   Key Topics for Chapter 3

Key Topic Element	Description	Page Number
List	Inventory purposes	35
Table 3-4	Implicit Hosts and Host Groups	37
Tip	ansible.cfg exam tip	42
Table 3-5	ansible.cfg Common Settings	43

Memory Tables

Print a copy of Appendix D, "Memory Tables" (found on the companion website), or at least the section for this chapter, and complete the tables and lists from memory. Appendix E, "Memory Tables Answer Key," also on the companion website, includes completed tables and lists to check your work.

Define Key Terms

Define the following key terms from this chapter, and check your answers in the glossary:

ansible.cfg, inventory, playbook, project, YAML

Review Questions

1. What syntax do you use to define a group named all in inventory?

2. Which name should you use for an inventory file that is created in your local project directory?

3. What is the name of the default inventory file?

4. How do you define a group with the name linux that has as members the groups web and file?

5. Which two command-line options should be respected by any dynamic inventory script?

6. How do you refer to hosts web001 up to web010 from one line in inventory?

7. What is the default name of the group of which hosts are automatically a member if they don't belong to any specific group?

8. Which command should you use to display a graphical overview of inventory hosts, including the groups they are a member of?

9. What is wrong with the following command?

   ansible -i inventory --list-hosts

10. Which parameter in ansible.cfg should you use to specify the mechanism to escalate permissions?

End-of-Chapter Lab

In the preceding chapter you set up the basic Linux environment to work with Ansible. Now it's time to create a project directory.

Lab 3-1

Configure a project directory that meets the following requirements:

- All hosts are entered in a static inventory file.

- An Ansible configuration file is created to take care of the following:

    - The project inventory file is used as the default inventory.

    - Privilege escalation is configured such that the ansible user is used, and sudo is used to run tasks that require privilege escalation.

- After setting up this environment, use the appropriate command to list all hosts in inventory.

This chapter covers the following subjects:

- ■ Understanding Ad Hoc Commands
- ■ Working with Modules
- ■ Consulting Module Documentation
- ■ Running Ad Hoc Commands from Shell Scripts

## CHAPTER 4

Using Ad Hoc Commands

The following RHCE exam objectives are covered in this chapter:

- Understand core components of Ansible

  - Modules

  - Use provided documentation to look up specific information about Ansible modules and commands

- Configure Ansible managed nodes

  - Validate a working configuration using ad hoc Ansible commands

- Script administration tasks

  - Create simple shell scripts

  - Create simple shell scripts that run ad hoc Ansible commands

- Create Ansible plays and playbooks

  - Know how to work with commonly used Ansible modules

"Do I Know This Already?" Quiz

The "Do I Know This Already?" quiz allows you to assess whether you should read this entire chapter thoroughly or jump to the "Exam Preparation Tasks" section. If you are in doubt about your answers to these questions or your own assessment of your knowledge of the topics, read the entire chapter. Table 4-1 lists the major headings in this chapter and their corresponding "Do I Know This Already?" quiz questions. You can find the answers in Appendix A, "Answers to the 'Do I Know This Already?' Quizzes and Review Questions."

Table 4-1 "Do I Know This Already?" Section-to-Question Mapping

Foundation Topics Section	Questions
Understanding Ad Hoc Commands	1–3
Working with Modules	4–7
Consulting Module Documentation	8, 9
Running Ad Hoc Commands from Shell Scripts	10

1. Using ad hoc commands is useful in multiple situations. Which of the following is not one of them?

    a. Making it easy to repeat tasks in a consistent way

    b. Using setup tasks to quickly bring a managed node to a desired state

    c. Performing a quick test to verify that a playbook has executed successfully

    d. Running a discovery task to verify that a node meets certain criteria

2. What is wrong in the following sample ad hoc command?

    ansible all -a "rpm -qa | grep http"

    a. Nothing.

    b. There is no option **-m** to specify which module should be used.

    c. It uses the command module but uses a pipe in the argument.

    d. It misses the key=value format in the specification of the arguments.

3. A user runs the ad hoc command **ansible all -m user -a "name=lisa"** on a host where user lisa already exists. What happens?

    a. A second user with the name lisa_0 is created.

    b. The current user lisa is removed, and a new user lisa is created.

    c. The command gives an error message, and nothing is changed.

    d. The command shows the SUCCESS result, and nothing is changed.

4. Which of the following modules must be used if you want to run a shell command that redirects the output of the command to the file output.txt?

    a. command

    b. shell

    c. raw

    d. bash

5. You want to run a command on an Ansible-managed Cisco router. Which module should you use?

    a. command

    b. shell

    c. raw

    d. bash

6. You want to install software in a network that has multiple Linux distributions. Which module would you use to do this on the Ubuntu nodes?

   a. apt

   b. package

   c. software

   d. install

7. Which of the following is the most accurate statement about the ping module?

   a. It tests connectivity to an Ansible-managed machine.

   b. It tests whether a host is currently running.

   c. It tests the contents of the inventory.

   d. It tests whether the host is in a manageable state.

8. Which command should you use to get a list of all modules installed on your control node?

   a. **ansible-modules**

   b. **ansible -l**

   c. **ansible-doc -l**

   d. **ansible-modules --list**

9. Which command shows you just a list of arguments that can be used with a module in a format that is ready to be used in a playbook?

   a. **ansible-doc**

   b. **ansible-doc -l**

   c. **ansible-doc -s**

   d. **ansible-doc -e**

10. What is the best approach to get a list of modules that can be used for system management?

    a. Grep on the output of **ansible-doc -l**.

    b. Use **ansible-doc system**.

    c. Look up the module index in docs.ansible.com and navigate to the system modules section.

    d. Use **ansible-doc --system**.

Foundation Topics

At this point you should have a base Ansible infrastructure available, so let's start using it! In Ansible, you typically work with playbooks. Playbooks are scripts that are written in YAML and provide all the instructions for getting managed nodes in their desired state. Configuring playbooks will be covered in Chapter 5, "Getting Started with Playbooks." In this chapter we work on some of the preliminary knowledge that is required before you start working with playbooks. You learn about ad hoc commands and modules, which allow you to perform quick tasks on Ansible without having to create any playbooks.

Understanding Ad Hoc Commands

An ad hoc command is an Ansible task that you can run against managed hosts without the need to use any playbook files or other script-like solutions. Ad hoc commands are easy to use and they are fast, and for that reason, they are commonly used.

Ad hoc commands are used in particular on the following:

- Setup tasks that bring nodes to a desired state

- Quick tests to verify that a playbook was indeed successful

- Quick discovery tasks to verify that a node meets certain criteria

Let's look at a sample command, and based on that sample, try to understand what is needed in an ad hoc command:

```
ansible all -m user -a "name=lisa"
```

This command contains a few ingredients. To start with, there is the **ansible** command, which is the command for running ad hoc commands. Next, you need to specify on which hosts you want to run the ad hoc commands, which is accomplished by the **all** part of the command. The third element refers to the module that you want to run. A module is a script that is executed by Ansible to perform a specific task. In the sample command shown, the **-m** option is used to call the module, and the specific module in this example is **user**. Finally, you need to provide arguments to the module by using the **-a** option. In an ad hoc command, all arguments are provided between double quotes. In this case there is just one argument, but if there are many arguments, all of them need to be included between double quotes. Table 4-2 summarizes all these components of the ad hoc command.

Table 4-2 Ad Hoc Command Components

Command	Use
ansible	The command to run ad hoc commands
all	Managed nodes where the command should be issued
-m user	The module to be used
-a "name=lisa"	Arguments to be passed to the module

When running an ad hoc command, you must be using your Ansible user account (not root), and you must be in a project directory where the inventory file and the ansible.cfg file can be found. Next, you run the command **ansible all -m user -a "name=lisa"**, which reaches out to all hosts in inventory to ensure that user lisa exists.

While doing so, Ansible compares the desired state (which is what you just specified in the ad hoc command) with the current state of the managed machine, and if so required, it applies changes to the managed machine. In Listing 4-1 you can see what the output of the command looks like. Notice the listing executed the command on ungrouped, which refers to all hosts that are not a part of any specific group.

Listing 4-1 Ad Hoc Command Output

```
[ansible@control ~]$ ansible ungrouped -m user -a "name=lisa"
ansible2 | SUCCESS => {
    "ansible_facts": {
        "discovered_interpreter_python": "/usr/libexec/
platform-python"
    },
    "append": false,
    "changed": false,
    "comment": "",
    "group": 1002,
    "home": "/home/lisa",
   "move_home": false,
    "name": "lisa",
    "shell": "/bin/bash",
```

```
        "state": "present",
        "uid": 1002
}
ansible1 | CHANGED => {
    "ansible_facts": {
        "discovered_interpreter_python": "/usr/libexec/
platform-python"
    },
    "changed": true,
    "comment": "",
    "create_home": true,
    "group": 1001,
    "home": "/home/lisa",
    "name": "lisa",
    "shell": "/bin/bash",
    "state": "present",
    "system": false,
    "uid": 1001
}
```

Listing 4-1 shows the output of the ad hoc command. You can see that the first line shows ansible2 | SUCCESS. This line indicates that host ansible2 already meets the desired state, and as a result, no changes had to be applied. For host ansible1, you can see ansible1 | CHANGED, which indicates that host ansible1 did not meet the desired state yet, and changes had to be applied.

This is how each Ansible command works. Ansible commands are idempotent, which means that regardless of the current condition, Ansible brings the managed host to the desired state. No matter how often you run the command, it always results in the same desired state. This is what is referred to as the idempotent behavior of Ansible commands: even if you run a command multiple times, the result is always the same. In Exercise 4-1 you can try running an ad hoc command for yourself.

NOTE In this and the following exercises, you need to execute tasks as a non-root user account. To do so, according to the setup instructions in Chapter 2, "Installing Ansible," you have created a user with the name ansible. If you have created a user with a different name, make sure that the name of that specific user is used instead of user ansible.

Exercise 4-1   Running an Ad Hoc Command

1. Open a shell as user ansible on the control host. Make sure that you are in a directory that contains the ansible.cfg configuration file that you created in Exercise 3-3.

2. Create an inventory file with the name inventory and make sure it has the following contents:

   ```
   ansible1
   ansible2
   ```

3. Type **ansible all -m user -a "name=lisa"** to instruct the user module to create a user with the name lisa. This creates user lisa on all managed hosts.

4. Observe the command output, and make sure that all hosts return either the SUCCESS state or the CHANGED state.

5. Run the command again. All hosts now return the SUCCESS state because nothing needed to be changed this time: the current state of the hosts already met the desired state.

6. Type the command **ansible all -m command -a "id lisa"**. In this command you run the **command** module, a module that enables you to run arbitrary commands on managed machines, with the argument **id lisa**, which actually is the command executed on the managed nodes.

7. Observe the output of the command, which should show that user lisa exists and show the groups the user is a member of.

8. Clean up the managed machines using **ansible all -m user -a "name=lisa state=absent"**. This command reaches out to the managed machines and removes user lisa again.

Working with Modules

Ansible functionality is provided by modules. More than 3000 modules are available to take care of a wide range of tasks, allowing administrators to manage Linux servers, Windows servers, cloud infrastructure, cloud instances, containers, network devices, and much more. Knowing Ansible equals knowing modules. Finding the right module for the right task is a key skill, and the more modules you know, the easier working with Ansible will be.

The modules can best be seen as plug-in programs that are used in Ansible playbooks or when using ad hoc commands. The modules themselves are written as Python scripts. That doesn't mean that you have to know Python though. Python knowledge is required only if you are a developer who wants to develop your own modules.

Exploring Essential Modules

Because working with modules is key, let's explore some key modules. Table 4-3 provides an overview.

Table 4-3   Ansible Key Modules

Name	Use
command	Runs arbitrary commands but not using a shell
shell	Runs arbitrary commands using a shell
raw	Runs commands directly on top of SSH without using Python
copy	Copies files or lines of text to files
yum	Manages packages on RHEL family-managed hosts
service	Manages the current state of systemd and system-V services
ping	Checks whether managed hosts are in a manageable state

Let's take a closer look at these core modules.

command

The command module allows users to run arbitrary commands using Ansible. Commands that are run by the command module are not interpreted by a shell. This means that common shell features, such as pipes and redirects, don't work while using the command module. For instance, the command **ansible all -m command -a "rpm -qa | grep nmap"** does not work.

The command module is the default module. This means that if the option **-m command** is omitted, Ansible interprets the argument that is provided by default as an argument to the command module. If another default module is needed, the option **module_name =** *module* can be set in ansible.cfg.

> **EXAM TIP**   You need to perform quite a few tasks on the RHCE exam. For sure, the most elegant way to do so is to use the appropriate module. However, using the command module or the shell module is not wrong; it's just not elegant. So if, on the exam, you cannot accomplish a task using the module that was designed to perform that task, just use the command module instead. All that counts is the result, and on the exam it doesn't really matter how you got there.

shell

The shell module is similar to the command module and allows you to run arbitrary commands, with one important difference: the shell module does run the commands through a shell. That means the usual shell features, such as pipes and redirects, do work while using this module. Compare, for instance, the result of the command **ansible all -m shell -a "rpm -qa | grep nmap"** to the command used before. This time it will work.

raw

The third module that enables you to run arbitrary commands on managed nodes is the raw module. The shell and the command modules, when used, generate a Python script, which is sent over SSH to be executed on the managed host. The raw module, however, doesn't need Python on the managed host; it sends the command straight over the SSH connection. This makes the raw module an excellent choice while setting up a machine or to work on a managed machine that doesn't have a Python stack, such as a network device.

Using the appropriate options, you can use the raw module to perform initial setup tasks on managed hosts. An example is the command **ansible -u root -i inventory ansible3 --ask-pass -m raw -a "yum install python3"**, which can be used to install Python 3 on host ansible3, which may be a node that hasn't received any Ansible configuration yet. Notice that the raw module could be used as an alternative to the command or shell module, but this approach is not recommended. As a generic rule of thumb, you should always try to use the module that is the most specific for the task that you want to accomplish.

> **NOTE**   The command, shell, and raw modules are all used to run arbitrary commands on a managed node. In most cases, it is recommended to avoid using them. Most other modules are idempotent and make it easy to track changes. The command, shell, and raw modules just run an arbitrary command, and it's hard to track what exactly has been changed using these modules, and for that reason it is difficult to guarantee idempotency when they are used.

copy

As its name suggests, the copy module is used to copy things. You can use it to copy files, but you can also use it to copy simple lines of text into a managed file. An example is **ansible all -m copy -a 'content="hello world" dest=/etc/motd'**, which copies the text "hello world" into the /etc/motd file.

yum

The yum module can be used to manage software on the Red Hat Enterprise Linux and related distributions. Use, for example, **ansible all -m yum -a "name=nmap state=latest"** to install the latest version of the nmap package on all managed nodes. Notice that yum is not the only module available for managing software. A more generic module is package, which has the advantage that it works on any Linux distribution. Between the two of them, use the yum module if you need to work with specific yum command features, and use the package module if the highest priority is to manage software on different managed distributions.

service

The service module is used to manage the state of services through either the legacy system V (init) process, or systemd. While using it, make sure that you don't just start the service using the argument state=started, but also enable the service using enabled=yes. If you just use state=started, the managed service is started now but won't be started automatically again after a restart. It's like using **systemctl start myservice** without using **systemctl enable myservice**.

Use, for instance, **ansible all -m service -a "name=httpd state=started enabled=yes"** to enable and start the httpd service. (Obviously, you have to use the yum module to install the httpd service before you can do that.)

ping

The ping module is a simple module that can be used to check whether hosts have been set up correctly to be managed with Ansible. So it doesn't just test connectivity; it tests manageability. It doesn't need any arguments. Just use **ansible all -m ping** to check connectivity for all hosts in inventory. Listing 4-2 shows what the answer looks like for hosts that are available but also shows what you see if a host is not available. To get the same result, just add the hostname ansible3 to the inventory file. In Exercise 4-2 you can practice working with this module as well as the other modules discussed here.

Listing 4-2   Analyzing **ping** Module Output

```
[ansible@control ~]$ ansible all -m ping
ansible3 | UNREACHABLE! => {
    "changed": false,
    "msg": "Failed to connect to the host via ssh: ssh: Could not
resolve hostname ansible3: Name or service not known",
    "unreachable": true
}
```

```
ansible2 | SUCCESS => {
    "ansible_facts": {
        "discovered_interpreter_python": "/usr/libexec/
platform-python"
    },
    "changed": false,
    "ping": "pong"
}
ansible1 | SUCCESS => {
    "ansible_facts": {
        "discovered_interpreter_python": "/usr/libexec/
platform-python"
    },
    "changed": false,
    "ping": "pong"
}
```

Exercise 4-2   Using Modules in Ad Hoc Commands

1. Use **ansible all -m ping** to verify that all hosts in inventory are in a manageable state.

2. Type **ansible ansible1 -m yum -a "name=httpd state=installed"** to install the httpd software package on host ansible1.

3. Verify that the package is installed using **ansible all -m command -a "rpm -qa | grep httpd"**. Analyzing the output, you can see that the **rpm -qa** command runs successfully on the managed hosts, but the pipe is ignored.

4. Use **ansible all -m shell -a "rpm -qa | grep httpd"**. In the output you can see that node ansible2 gives a "non-zero return code" message, meaning that the command did not complete successfully. You can also see a list of matching packages on ansible1. Last, you can see a warning message stating that you should use the yum module instead. Notice that the shell as well as the command modules reported a changed status as the result, even if nothing has really changed.

5. Use **ansible all -m yum -a "list=httpd"** and compare the output to the output of the command used in step 4.

6. Use **ansible all -m command -a "systemctl status httpd"** to verify the current status of the httpd service. It should show the service is not found on ansible2 and the service is inactive and disabled on ansible1.

7. Use **ansible ansible1 -m service -a "name=httpd enabled=yes state=started"** to start and enable the httpd service on ansible1.

8. Run the command **ansible all -m command -a "systemctl status httpd"** again to verify the modification has been applied.

Browsing Available Modules

As mentioned before, to be successful with Ansible, you need to know modules. There are many modules, of course, and to figure out which modules are available, you can use **ansible-doc -l**. This command lists all modules that are installed on your system. When you use it on a CentOS 8.1 installation with a default Ansible installation, you see that no fewer than 3387 modules are installed!

The fact is that many modules are available for Ansible—so many that you'll never use all of them, and also so many that in some cases you'll have a choice between different modules to accomplish the same task. When you're new to Ansible, finding the appropriate module can be hard. By working your way through this Cert Guide, you'll learn about some of the most useful modules, but you're always advised to search whether a better module might be available. You can do that by using **ansible-doc -l** and filtering the output using the Linux grep utility. Use, for instance, the command **ansible-doc -l | grep vmware** to see all the modules available in Ansible to manage VMware environments.

Consulting Module Documentation

Ansible modules are well documented. You can find documentation for all the installed modules using the **ansible-doc** command. Apart from the **ansible-doc** command, which is always available on your Ansible installation, you can visit the Ansible documentation website, which is available at https://docs.ansible.com.

EXAM TIP   Documentation is available on your exam, so learn how to use it. You have access to the **ansible-doc** command but also to a local copy of all documentation at https://docs.ansible.com for the Ansible version used on the exam. As you study for the exam, make sure you practice using these valuable resources!

Using ansible-doc

The **ansible-doc** command provides information about all Ansible modules. This documentation is presented in a structured way. Listing 4-3 shows the result of the command **ansible-doc ping**.

Listing 4-3   Analyzing **ansible-doc** Command Output

```
> PING      (/usr/lib/python3.6/site-packages/ansible/modules/system/
ping.py)


        A trivial test module, this module always returns 'pong' on
        successful contact. It does not make sense in playbooks, but
        it is useful from '/usr/bin/ansible' to verify the ability to
        login and that a usable Python is configured. This is NOT ICMP
        ping, this is just a trivial test module that requires Python
        on the remote-node. For Windows targets, use the [win_ping]
        module instead. For Network targets, use the [net_ping] module
        instead.


  * This module is maintained by The Ansible Core Team
OPTIONS (= is mandatory):

- data
        Data to return for the 'ping' return value.
        If this parameter is set to 'crash', the module will cause an
        exception.
        [Default: pong]
        type: str



SEE ALSO:
        * Module net_ping
            The official documentation on the net_ping module.
            https://docs.ansible.com/ansible/2.9/modules/net_ping
        _module.html
        * Module win_ping
            The official documentation on the win_ping module.
            https://docs.ansible.com/ansible/2.9/modules/win_ping
        _module.html



AUTHOR: Ansible Core Team, Michael DeHaan
        METADATA:
          status:
          - stableinterface
          supported_by: core
```

```
EXAMPLES:

# Test we can logon to 'webservers' and execute python with json lib.
# ansible webservers -m ping
# Example from an Ansible Playbook
- ping:

# Induce an exception to see what happens
- ping:
    data: crash


RETURN VALUES:

ping:
    description: value provided with the data parameter
    returned: success
    type: str
    sample: pong
```

Because all the **ansible-doc** resulting pages show the same structure, it makes sense to understand the different elements. Table 4-4 shows default elements in the **ansible-doc** command output.

Table 4-4   ansible-doc Output Elements

Field	Use
Module name	The name of the module, including the Python script that implements this module
Maintainer information	Information about the person/team responsible for this module
Options	A list of all options (arguments) that can be used with this module
See also	A list of related modules
Author	The person who wrote this module
Examples	Sample code that can be used in playbooks
Return values	The type of result that can be expected

The first interesting element in the result of **ansible-doc** is the name of the module, which is followed by the name of the Python script that is used by this module. Ansible modules are written in Python, and the Python scripts are installed on your control system. So if you want to see what is happening, you can open the Python script, analyze it, and—if you want—even optimize it.

Following the name of the underlying script is a short module description. It's a good idea to read the module description, particularly if you're using a module for the first time. The examples that you may have copied from your Google search often don't provide information about the gotchas in a particular module, so read it!

Next, you see who is responsible for maintaining a module. This is important information that can help you in selecting the best module for your specific purpose. In general, it's a good idea to look for modules that are maintained by the Ansible Core Team, but if you're working on a specific network appliance, using the modules provided by the appliance vendor may be a better idea.

The following element is a list of all the options. Most modules have options, and many modules have at least one option that is mandatory. If your module has mandatory options, you'll find the option indicated as =option (instead of -option). The SEE ALSO section that is next gives information about related and/or similar modules. It's a good idea to have a look at this section because you might find yourself in a specific module where there's also another module that is just a little bit better to accomplish your task.

At the end of the **ansible-doc** output, you'll find the name of the author, and most important, usage examples. In most cases, the examples show sample playbook code. This information is most useful because you'll find examples of the most common use cases and the playbook code you need to use to implement the module in a playbook. All the way at the end of the output you'll find the return values. This section provides information about the type of output that is to be expected from this module.

By default, the **ansible-doc** command provides full documentation about a module. When working on playbooks, you are typically most interested in how to use required parameters in a playbook. To get that information, you can use **ansible-doc -s** *modulename*. The result of this command shows a sample playbook structure, with a list of the arguments that can be used and a short description for each argument. Because the result of **ansible-doc -s** is not as overwhelming as the complete output, many people like using this approach. Listing 4-4 shows partial sample output of this command.

Listing 4-4   Showing Usage Information with **ansible-doc -s service**

```
- name: Manage services
  service:
      arguments:        # Additional arguments provided on the
                        command line.
      enabled:          # Whether the service should start on boot.
                        *At least one of state and
                        enabled are required.*
      name:             # (required) Name of the service.
      pattern:          # If the service does not respond to the
                        status command, name a substring to
                        look for as would be
                        found in the output of
                        the 'ps' command as a
                        stand-in for a status
                        result. If the string
                        is found, the service
                        will be assumed to be
                        started.
      runlevel:         # For OpenRC init scripts (e.g. Gentoo) only.
                        The runlevel that this
                        service belongs to.
      sleep:            # If the service is being 'restarted' then
                        many seconds between
                        the stop and start
                        command. This helps to
                        work around badly-
                        behaving init scripts
                        that exit immediately
                        after signaling a
                        process to stop. Not
                        all service managers
                        support sleep, i.e when
                        using systemd this
                        setting will be
                        ignored.
```

Using https://docs.ansible.com

Apart from the on-system documentation provided by **ansible-doc**, on the exam you'll also have access to the docs.ansible.com website (see Figure 4-1). On this website you can find all you need to know about Ansible, but in some cases it's not obvious where to find that information. For that reason, you must practice using the documentation before taking the exam. In particular, you use the search bar in the upper-left part of the screen. Where appropriate, you'll also find guidelines in this book on where to find specific types of information. You can practice working with the documentation in Exercise 4-3.

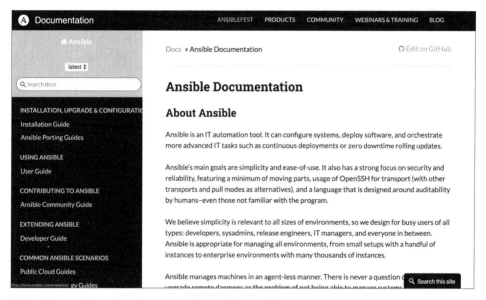

FIGURE 4-1   Browsing documentation at docs.ansible.com

Exercise 4-3   Working with the Documentation

1. Type **ansible-doc -l | grep user**. You see a long list of all modules that have the string "user" either in the module name or in the description of the module.

2. Type **ansible-doc user** and look up mandatory arguments. You should find that the **name** argument is mandatory. Also, look at the SEE ALSO section, where you can find information about related modules.

3. Scroll forward to the EXAMPLES section and look at the examples there.

4. Type **ansible-doc -s user** to see the output of this command. Notice that the output looks like a combination of the list of arguments and the examples in the **ansible-doc** command.

5. Open the Ansible documentation at https://docs.ansible.com from your browser and click **Documentation** in the upper-left corner.

6. In the search bar in the upper-left corner, type **user module system**.

7. In the results list, open the link to **System Modules**. This takes you to a list with all modules that relate to system management tasks. From this list, select the **User** module and look at the web page. Notice that the resulting web page contains the exact same information as what you find in the result of **ansible-doc user**.

Running Ad Hoc Commands from Shell Scripts

To understand why in a book about Ansible there is a section about shell scripting, you need to look at the Exam Format section on the "What you need to know" page in Red Hat's description of the Ansible exam (https://www.redhat.com/en/services/training/ex294-red-hat-certified-engineer-rhce-exam-red-hat-enterprise-linux-8). In this section you find the following text:

> Your work will be evaluated by applying the playbooks created during the exam against freshly installed systems and verifying that those systems and services work as specified.

This means that during the exam, you will be creating Ansible playbooks, and during the exam you can test these playbooks on the managed machines that are provided. Once the exam is over, your playbook will be graded. In the grading process, a new set of managed machines will be provided, and your playbooks will be executed against this new set of managed machines.

In the exam, it is most likely that you will have to work with ad hoc commands as well, and "Create simple shell scripts that run ad hoc Ansible commands" is one of the exam objectives. You'll have to do that in a script because that is the only way the exam evaluation engine will be able to verify your work. As a result, you need to have at least minimal knowledge about using shell scripts. In this section you get a minimal introduction to working with Bash shell scripts. The purpose is not to teach everything there is to know about shell scripts but just to show you the shell scripting essentials required on the exam.

On Red Hat Enterprise Linux, the Bash shell is used as the default command interpreter. Users can type commands at the shell prompt, and the command will provide its output. For complex tasks, it may be useful to create a script that executes all the commands that are needed to run a task. Doing this is not complicated: just enter all commands you want to use as a list in the script. Also, to avoid any interpretation issues, it's a good idea to include a "shebang" (#!) on the first line of the shell script. The shebang indicates which shell should be used while executing the commands in the script.

Listing 4-5 shows a sample script that is created to run two ad hoc commands.

Listing 4-5   Running Ad Hoc Commands from a Script

```
#!/bin/bash


ansible all -m yum -a "name=httpd state=latest"
ansible all -m service -a "name=httpd state=started enabled=yes"
```

If you put the sample lines in Listing 4-5 into a file, you can then run that file as a shell script.

To create a shell script, the file has a few requirements. The contents must be plain ASCII text that is not formatted. The filename itself has no requirements, but many people like using the .sh file extension. This extension is not needed (the Linux operating system doesn't work with extensions), but the extension may make it easier to recognize a script as a script file. If you agree with that statement, call your script file myscript.sh instead of myscript.

After creating the script code, you need to run it. To run a script, it needs to have the execute permission. The easiest way to apply that permission is to use **chmod +x myscript.sh**. This applies the execute permission to all users who currently have read permission to the file. Next, you can run the script.

To run a script from the current directory, you would normally use the command **./myscript.sh**. In this command, the dot refers to the current directory. Using this dot is required if the current directory is not in the $PATH variable. If you want to run the script without having to enter the ./ first, you need to make sure it is in a directory that is in the $PATH variable. You can do that by copying the script to the /usr/local/bin directory, which is in the $PATH variable for normal users. In Exercise 4-4 you can practice writing a shell script that runs Ansible ad hoc commands.

Exercise 4-4   Running Ad Hoc Commands from a Script

1. From the directory that contains the inventory and ansible.cfg files, type **vim setup.sh** to create a setup script.

2. Make sure the script contains the following lines and save the file:

   ```
   #!/bin/bash

   ansible all -m yum -a "name=vsftpd state=installed"
   ansible all -m service -a "name=vsftpd state=started enabled=yes"
   ```

3. Type **chmod +x setup.sh** to make the script file executable.

4. Type the command **./setup.sh** to run the script and perform the selected tasks on the managed hosts.

Summary

In this chapter you learned how to work with ad hoc commands to set up managed hosts and to run quick checks on managed hosts. You also learned about Ansible modules and how to get information about Ansible modules using the appropriate tools. In the next chapter you'll learn how to use playbooks, which allow you to work with Ansible in a consistent way.

Exam Preparation Tasks

As mentioned in the section "How to Use This Book" in the Introduction, you have a couple of choices for exam preparation: the exercises here, Chapter 16, "Final Preparation," and the exam simulation questions on the companion website.

Review All Key Topics

Review the most important topics in this chapter, noted with the Key Topics icon in the outer margin of the page. Table 4-5 lists a reference of these key topics and the page numbers on which each is found.

Table 4-5   Key Topics for Chapter 4

Key Topic Element	Description	Page Number
List	Ad hoc command uses	50

Memory Tables

Print a copy of Appendix D, "Memory Tables" (found on the companion website), or at least the section for this chapter, and complete the tables and lists from memory. Appendix E, "Memory Tables Answer Key," also on the companion website, includes completed tables and lists to check your work.

Define Key Terms

Define the following key terms from this chapter, and check your answers in the glossary:

ad hoc command, bash script, current state, desired state, idempotent, module

Review Questions

1. In what situations would you use ad hoc commands?

2. Which module should you use to install Python on a managed host?

3. Which module should you use to run the **rpm -qa | grep httpd** command?

4. On the RHCE exam, you cannot find the specific module to install software, so you decide to install software using the command module. Is that acceptable?

5. Which arguments should you use to start and enable the httpd service with the service module?

6. You use **ansible-doc** on the user module and find out that this module cannot create users on Windows. Which part of the documentation would you look at to find the command that needs to be used on Windows?

7. You are a Python programmer and want to optimize a module for use in your environment. Where do you get the module source code?

8. While executing a script that runs ad hoc commands, you get a "permission denied" error message. What is the most likely explanation?

9. How would you change the default module used in ad hoc commands?

10. What is the best way to get some examples of playbook code that can be used for a specific module?

End-of-Chapter Lab

In the end-of-chapter lab, this time you create a script that runs some ad hoc commands on managed hosts.

Lab 4-1

Create a bash shell script with the name install.sh that makes sure managed hosts meet the following requirements. It doesn't matter if the hosts already meet the requirements; your script should be created such that it sets up a managed host according to these requirements if it has not yet been configured.

- Install the httpd web server.

- Start and enable the httpd web server.

- Create a user with the name anna.

- Copy the /etc/hosts file from the control machine to the /tmp/ directory on the managed host.

This chapter covers the following subjects:

- Exploring Your First Playbook
- Working with YAML
- Managing Multiplay Playbooks

## CHAPTER 5

Getting Started with Playbooks

The following RHCE exam objectives are covered in this chapter:

- Understand core components of Ansible
  - Plays
  - Playbooks
- Create Ansible plays and playbooks
  - Create playbooks to configure systems to a specified state

"Do I Know This Already?" Quiz

The "Do I Know This Already?" quiz allows you to assess whether you should read this entire chapter thoroughly or jump to the "Exam Preparation Tasks" section. If you are in doubt about your answers to these questions or your own assessment of your knowledge of the topics, read the entire chapter. Table 5-1 lists the major headings in this chapter and their corresponding "Do I Know This Already?" quiz questions. You can find the answers in Appendix A, "Answers to the 'Do I Know This Already?' Quizzes and Review Questions."

Table 5-1 "Do I Know This Already?" Section-to-Question Mapping

Foundation Topics Section	Questions
Exploring Your First Playbook	1, 2
Working with YAML	3, 6, 7
Managing Multiplay Playbooks	4, 5, 8–10

1. Which of the following do you normally find on the first line of a playbook?

    a. The name of the first play

    b. The name of the hosts that are addressed

    c. ---

    d. ...

2. Each play should have at least three parameters in its header. Which of the following is not one of them?

    a. **hosts**

    b. **tasks**

    c. **name**

    d. **become**

3. Which statements about indentation are true?

    a. Indentation is used to identify the relationship between parent and child objects.

    b. Spaces may not be used.

    c. Tabs may not be used.

    d. Plays without indentation are hard to read but do work.

4. How do you undo modifications that are applied from a playbook?

    a. Use **ansible-playbook -u**.

    b. Use **ansible-playbook -u --force**.

    c. You cannot undo changes made by a playbook.

    d. You can create a playbook that accomplishes the opposite of the original playbook.

5. What status would you expect the **ansible-playbook** command to generate while while running a task that has modified the managed system?

    a. ok

    b. changed

    c. modified

    d. applied

6. Which statement about using YAML lists in playbooks is true?

   a. Any module can use a YAML list to specify the names of items that need to be processed.

   b. YAML lists can be used at a play level, not at a tasks level.

   c. The service module does not support YAML lists to manage multiple servers.

   d. A YAML list can be used to run multiple modules.

7. Which option can you use to feed multiple lines of text to a text file, while keeping the newline characters to guarantee proper formatting?

   a. |

   b. >

   c. :

   d. \

8. Which of the following can you use to verify which tasks in a playbook would trigger a change?

   a. **--syntax-check**

   b. **--dry-run**

   c. **-vvv**

   d. **-C**

9. Which of the following indicates the best use case for a multiplay playbook?

   a. A web server must be installed on server1; a database server must be installed on server2.

   b. An FTP server must be installed on server1, after which localhost is used to test connectivity to that server.

   c. A task must run using a different user account.

   d. A play must run with different privilege escalation parameters.

10. Which of the following is not a benefit of using a multiplay playbook?

    a. Different hosts may be addressed.

    b. Plays may run with different user accounts.

    c. Plays can be scheduled separately.

    d. Some plays may be configured to run without privilege escalation.

Foundation Topics

Exploring Your First Playbook

Ansible is all about running playbooks. In this section you learn how to move forward from entering tasks as ad hoc commands on the command line to writing Ansible playbooks.

From Ad Hoc Commands to Playbook

Before we get into the details about playbooks and explore the possibilities of using them, let's run a playbook. In Chapter 4, "Using Ad Hoc Commands," you learned how to work with ad hoc commands, and in Listing 4-5, you created a Bash script to run some of these commands against managed nodes. Listing 5-1 shows you the the commands that were used.

Listing 5-1   Running Ad Hoc Commands from a Script

```
#!/bin/bash

ansible all -m yum -a "name=httpd state=installed"
ansible all -m service -a "name=httpd state=started enabled=yes"
```

All that you do in this script can be done in a playbook as well. Just take a look at the playbook example in Listing 5-2 to see what such a playbook would look like. If you look close enough, you can see that all elements that were specified in the ad hoc commands also occur in the playbook.

Listing 5-2   Configuring Hosts from a Playbook

```
---
- name: install start and enable httpd
  hosts: all
  tasks:
  - name: install package
    yum:
      name: httpd
      state: installed
  - name: start and enable service
    service:
      name: httpd
      state: started
      enabled: yes
```

Playbook Elements

A playbook is a collection of plays. Each play targets specific hosts, and in each play a list of tasks is specified. In the sample playbook in Listing 5-2, one play with the name "install start and enable httpd" is defined.

Playbooks are written in the YAML format and are normally saved with either the .yml or the .yaml extension. YAML format essentially specifies objects as key-value pairs. Dashes can be used to specify lists of embedded objects. For more details about YAML, see the section "Working with YAML" later in this chapter.

At the start of each playbook, you find three dashes. Optionally, you may also find three dots at the end of the playbook. Using these characters makes it easy to embed the playbook code into something else and easily isolate the playbook code when it is included.

While you're working with playbooks, the target hosts are specified in the play, not in the command that runs the playbook (which happens in ad hoc commands). After you indicate the target hosts, you specify a list of tasks. Each item in the list is identified with a hyphen.

For each task, you specify the Ansible module that the task is running and a name. Notice that using names for tasks is not mandatory but is highly recommended, because using names makes it a little easier to identify which tasks have been able to run successfully. Next, you should identify the arguments that the task should be running.

To identify hierarchical relations in playbooks, you use indentation. The basic rules for indentation are easy:

- Data elements at the same level in the hierarchy must have the same indentation.

- Items that are children (properties) and another element are indented more than the parents.

You create indentation using spaces. There is no requirement for how many spaces to use, but using two spaces is common. Using tabs for indentation is not permitted.

Within the playbook, one or more plays are defined. Plays are the highest level in the playbook, and each play starts with a hyphen. The reason is that the playbook defines a list of plays, and it is valid if the list contains just one play. All properties of the play (name, hosts, and the word tasks) are indented at the same level, and next there is a list of tasks. The list of tasks is a property of the play, and these tasks are indented one level deeper than the parent items to show the hierarchical relation between play and tasks. The next level of indentation happens at the task argument level, where each argument that is passed to a task is indented one more level deeper.

> **TIP** To make working with indentation easier, you may configure the vi editor. If the following line is included in the file ~/.vimrc, indentation automatically happens correctly if vi detects that a YAML file is created. Notice this requires you to either use the .yml or the .yaml extension to the files.
>
> ```
> autocmd FileType yaml setlocal ai ts=2 sw=2 et
> ```

In playbooks, you may find one or more plays. Each play has some required elements, which are listed in Table 5-2.

Table 5-2 Playbook Play Required Keys

Key	Use
hosts	Hosts on which this play has to be executed
name	The name of the play
tasks	One or more tasks that should be executed in this play

Running the Playbook

To run the playbook, you use the command **ansible-playbook listing52.yaml**. The result is shown in Listing 5-3. Notice that depending on the state of the managed machine, you might see a slightly different result, showing "changed" instead of "ok."

Listing 5-3 Running a Playbook Output

```
[ansible@control ~]$ ansible-playbook listing52.yaml

PLAY [install start and enable httpd] *******************************

TASK [Gathering Facts] **********************************************
ok: [ansible2]
ok. [ansible1]

TASK [install package] **********************************************
ok: [ansible1]
ok: [ansible2]

TASK [start and enable service] *************************************
ok: [ansible2]
ok: [ansible1]
```

```
PLAY RECAP ***********************************************************
ansible1                      : ok=3      changed=0     unreachable=0
failed=0       skipped=0      rescued=0   ignored=0
ansible2                      : ok=3      changed=0     unreachable=0
failed=0       skipped=0      rescued=0   ignored=0
```

In the output of the **ansible-playbook** command, you always see the same elements. The output starts with the name of the play. This is the name that you defined yourself in the **name** part of each play. Next, you get an overview of the tasks that you defined in the playbook. Each task is identified by the name that you used for the task in the playbook code, and for each task, the **ansible-playbook** command indicates on which managed host it was executed and whether that was successful.

Before the list of tasks that you defined, the **ansible-playbook** command gathers facts. Fact gathering is an important part of Ansible, where Ansible learns about current configuration and settings on managed nodes; you'll learn more about this topic in Chapter 6, "Working with Variables and Facts."

The last element is the Play Recap. In this element you get an overview of the status of each task. If you see "ok" in the task result status, the task has executed successfully and no changes were required. If a task gives the result status "changed," a task has successfully applied modifications to apply the desired state as defined in the playbook. We discuss the other output status options later.

Undoing Playbook Modifications

Undoing playbook modifications is easy to understand. Ansible does not offer any undo functionality, so if you created a playbook and later regret the modifications the playbook has made, you must write a new playbook to define a new desired state that reverts the changes you applied earlier. In Exercise 5-1 you practice all the skills discussed so far and run your first playbook.

Exercise 5-1   Running Your First Playbook

1. Type **vim exercise51.yaml** to open a new file that will contain the desired playbook code. Make sure the file is created in your home directory, where an ansible.cfg and inventory file already exist.

2. Type three dashes to start the playbook code:

    ```
    ---
    ```

3. Start the play definition on a new line. This play definition starts with a dash, which is followed by a space and **name:**, which is followed by the name of the play:

```
---
- name: install and start the vsftpd service
```

4. You need to add a line that defines the hosts that the play should manage. Notice that this line is indented at the same level as the word "name" because this line is a part of the same play definition:

```
---
- name: install and start the vsftpd service
  hosts: all
```

5. In the next part of the play, you define the tasks that will be executed by this play. Under the word **hosts**, indented at the same level, type **tasks:**. There is nothing after the colon because the value of the key **tasks** is a list of tasks, which is provided on the next couple of lines:

```
---
- name: install and start the vsftpd service
  hosts: all
  tasks:
```

6. At this point, you can start defining the tasks. The first task ensures that the yum module is used to define the vsftpd package. Notice the indentation, which identifies that the task is a child element of the play:

```
---
- name: install and start the vsftpd service
  hosts: all
  tasks:
  - name: install vsftpd
    yum:
```

7. At this point, you may specify the arguments to the yum module. Because these arguments are child elements in relation to the yum module, you need another level of indentation:

```
---
- name: install and start the vsftpd service
  hosts: all
  tasks:
  - name: install vsftpd
    yum:
      name: vsftpd
      state: latest
```

8. The first task is now defined, and you can specify the next task that calls the service module to start and enable the vsftpd service. Notice that this task is indented at the same level as the yum task:

```
---
- name: install and start the vsftpd service
  hosts: all
  tasks:
  - name: install vsftpd
    yum:
      name: vsftpd
      state: latest
  - name: start and enable vsftpd service
    service:
      name: vsftpd
      state: started
      enabled: yes
```

9. The playbook is now completed, so write your changes to the file and quit the editor. Next, use **ansible-playbook exercise51.yaml** to run the playbook.

10. Observe the output of the playbook and verify that everything has executed all right.

Working with YAML

YAML (an acronym for YAML Ain't Markup Language according to some, and Yet Another Markup Language according to others) is an easy-to-read data-serialization language. YAML is a common language used for configuration files, not only in Ansible but also in other environments, like Kubernetes and in configuration of some Linux services. YAML isn't difficult to use, but you should know a few things when working with YAML.

Indentation

To start with, YAML uses indentation. As discussed earlier, indentation identifies relations between parts of the configuration so that you can easily see what is a parent object and what is a child object. The most important rule in indentation is that you must use spaces and not tabs.

Using Key-Value Pairs

YAML is all about defining key-value pairs, also known as dictionaries. An example of such a key-value pair is **name: vsftpd**. Key-value pairs can be defined in two ways: **key: value** or **key=value**. Of these two, the first method is preferred, but the second way works also.

If an object in YAML needs multiple key-value pairs to define its properties, it is common to define one key-value pair on a line. If the **key=value** format is used, it's possible to define all the multiple key-value pairs on one line. The sample playbook in Listing 5-4 shows such an example.

Listing 5-4   Multiple Ways to Define Key-Value Pairs

```
---
- name: deploy vsftpd
  hosts: ansible2
  tasks:
  - name: install vsftpd
    yum: name=vsftpd
  - name: enable vsftpd
    service: name=vsftpd enabled=true
  - name: create readme file
    copy:
      content: "welcome to the FTP server\n"
      dest: /var/ftp/pub/README
      force: no
      mode: 0444
...
```

In the sample playbook in Listing 5-4, three tasks are defined. In the first two tasks, all key-value pairs are defined in the **key=value** format on the same line as the name of the module that is used. The third task defines all key-value pairs in the **key: value** format on separate lines. To keep your playbooks readable, you should use only the latter approach.

NOTE   In Ansible, on multiple occasions it's possible to use a different syntax. This section is provided as an introduction to working with YAML, not as a complete overview to working with the language. If you need a more complete overview of YAML syntax variations, look for "YAML Syntax" in the Ansible documentation.

Notice that in the third task the copy module is used to copy a line of text into a destination file. This is an easy way to create a configuration file that contains some standard text. There are other modules to manage text that needs to be copied into a file; you'll learn more about them in Chapter 8, "Deploying Files."

Understanding YAML Lists

While you're working with YAML in Ansible playbooks, keys can have one value, and some keys can have multiple values. No standard rule defines what is the case in which situation. Whether a key can contain multiple values depends on the Ansible module. When you use the yum module, for instance, you can specify a list of packages to the name key. When you use the service module, for instance, it's not possible to specify a list as the argument to the name key. The module documentation normally indicates whether it's possible to specify a list as a value to a specific key. Listing 5-5 shows an example of a playbook that uses a list to define the values of a key.

Listing 5-5 Installing Multiple Packages Using Lists

```
---
- name: using lists
  hosts: all
  tasks:
  - name: install packages
    yum:
      name:
       - nmap
       - httpd
       - vsftpd
      state: latest
```

TIP The yum module can work with different package states. For example, you can use **state: installed** to make sure that a package is installed and use **state: latest** to ensure that the latest version of a package is installed, which triggers a package update if needed.

Using YAML Strings

In YAML files, you include strings on multiple occasions. Using strings is not difficult because the string doesn't have to be escaped by using quotation marks.

However, you are allowed to use quotation marks anyway. This means that all the following notations are valid:

Line of text

"Line of text"

'Line of text'

There are two ways to deal with multiline strings. You can use the | sign in a multiline string to take over all newline characters. If all text in a multiline string just needs to be treated as a line of text, without any further formatting, you can use the > sign. Use the | sign if you want to maintain formatting. Use the > sign if you want to split text over multiple lines in the playbook for better readability, but the lines don't have to be written as multiple lines in the target file.

Verifying Syntax

Because you can easily make a typo or indent items at the wrong level, it might be wise to verify syntax. The **ansible-playbook** command provides the **--syntax-check** option for this task. Listing 5-6 shows what the result of this command might look like.

Listing 5-6   Checking Syntax with **ansible-playbook --syntax-check**

```
[ansible@control ~]$ ansible-playbook --syntax-check listing57.yaml
ERROR! Syntax Error while loading YAML.
  mapping values are not allowed in this context

The error appears to be in '/home/ansible/listing54.yaml': line 8,
column 12, but may
be elsewhere in the file depending on the exact syntax problem.

The offending line appears to be:

    name: httpd
      state: latest
          ^ here
```

As you can see, the **ansible-playbook** command tries to make a reasonable guess about where the syntax problem occurs. Based on the exact error, this guess may be accurate or totally inaccurate. In this case it is quite accurate, as you can see in Listing 5-7, which shows the code that is used to produce the error in Listing 5-6 (as the error occurs just one line earlier).

> **TIP** Where relevant, the playbook code that is used in the listings in this book is available in the book github repository. If you haven't done so yet, you can get the files by using the command **git clone https://github.com/sandervanvugt/rhce8-book**.

Listing 5-7 Sample YAML File with Errors

```
---
- name: install start and enable httpd
  hosts: all
  tasks:
  - name: install package
    yum:
    name: httpd
      state: latest
  - service:
    name: httpd
      state: started
      enabled: yes
```

As seen in the output of the **ansible-playbook --syntax-check** command in Listing 5-6, the output is quite accurate while indicating the exact location of the problem. In Listing 5-7, you might also notice a second problem that was not found in the code; the line **name: httpd** should be indented as a child element to the service: module. The reason is that the **ansible-playbook --syntax-check** stops after finding the first error. You have to fix this error and run the command again to see the second error as well.

One last word about **--syntax-check**. It may be a useful option, but you should realize that the **ansible-playbook** command checks syntax by default. So if you had just run **ansible-playbook listing56.yaml**, you would have seen the exact same message.

Performing a Playbook Dry Run

Before you actually run a playbook and make all modifications to the managed hosts, it may make sense to perform a dry run. You can do this by using the **ansible-playbook -C myplaybook.yaml** command. While you perform a dry run, the **ansible-playbook** command shows you which hosts would be changed by running the playbook without actually applying the changes. See Listing 5-8 for an example. After that, you can work on Exercise 5-2 to practice your YAML skills.

Listing 5-8   Performing a Playbook Dry Run

```
[ansible@control ~]$ ansible-playbook -C listing57.yaml

PLAY [using lists] *********************************************

TASK [Gathering Facts] *****************************************
ok: [ansible2]
ok: [ansible1]

TASK [install packages] ***************************************
changed: [ansible2]
changed: [ansible1]

PLAY RECAP ****************************************************
ansible1                    : ok=2      changed=1    unreachable=0
failed=0     skipped=0      rescued=0    ignored=0
ansible2                    : ok=2      changed=1    unreachable=0
failed=0     skipped=0      rescued=0    ignored=0
```

Exercise 5-2   Practicing YAML Skills

1. Open an editor to create the file exercise52.yaml. Define the playbook header by including the following lines:

```
---
- name: copy multiline text
  hosts: ansible1
  tasks:
```

2. Add the first task. In this task you use the copy module, using **content** and the l sign to copy two lines of text to a file that does not yet exist:

```
---
- name: copy multiline text
  hosts: ansible1
  tasks:
  - name: copy text
    copy:
      content: |
        line 1
        line 2
      dest: /tmp/multiline1.txt
```

3. Add a second task that also uses the copy module but this time uses the **>** sign:

```
---
- name: copy multiline text
  hosts: ansible1
  tasks:
  - name: copy text
    copy:
      content: |
        line 1
        line 2
      dest: /tmp/multiline1.txt
  - name: copy more text
    copy:
      content: >
        line 1
        line 2
      dest: /tmp/multiline2.txt
```

4. Use **ansible-playbook exercise52.yaml** to run the playbook and verify that in the output you see two tasks reporting a changed status.

5. Verify the files that have been created. First, use **ansible ansible1 -a "cat /tmp/ multiline1.txt"** to verify the contents of the first file. Notice that it contains multiple lines.

6. Next, use **ansible ansible1 -a "cat /tmp/multiline2.txt"** to verify that the file contains all the separate lines on one single line.

Managing Multiplay Playbooks

Up to now, you've worked with a playbook that has just one play. Many playbooks that you find out in the wild work with multiple plays though. Using multiple plays in a playbook makes it easy to perform the complete setup of a managed environment, where you can set up one group of servers with one specific configuration and another group of servers with another configuration. When you work with multiplay playbooks, each play has its own list of hosts to address.

Multiplay Playbook Considerations

The main benefit of running a multiplay playbook is that you can configure multiple plays that should all be run in the same procedure. In each play, different connectivity options can be used. To start with, you can define different hosts or host groups, but it's also possible to use different connection parameters that may even overwrite default parameters that have been set in the ansible.cfg file. Think of parameters like **become: no**, which indicates that no privilege escalation is needed, or **remote_ user: bob**, which instructs the playbook to run the remote tasks as user bob instead of using the default user account.

When you are writing playbooks, there are many options. It might seem tempting to write huge playbooks, including many tasks and multiple plays. Doing so is not recommended as a best practice though. To summarize the most important guideline from the best practices: keep it simple. If there is no need to put everything in one playbook, then simply don't. The bigger the playbook, the more difficult it will be to troubleshoot.

In many cases it's a much better solution to write multiple smaller playbooks and use includes to include functionality from other playbooks. One advantage is that this approach makes troubleshooting a lot easier. Another advantage is that this approach makes it easy to develop a toolkit with many small playbooks that can be used in a flexible way to perform a wide range of management tasks. You'll read more about this approach in Chapter 10, "Using Ansible in Large Environments."

Multiplay Playbook Example

Listing 5-9 shows an example of a multiplay playbook. The first play sets up the httpd service on a managed host. In the second play, the uri module is used to test web server accessibility. If no further configuration is used, this module tries to connect to a target web server and expects the HTTP return code 200, indicating that the target web page was accessed successfully.

In this multiplay playbook, the first play is executed on the host group all. This host group includes all hosts that are defined in inventory, but it does not include localhost. The host localhost is not defined in inventory; it's an implicit host that is always usable and that refers to the Ansible control machine. Using localhost can be an efficient way to verify the accessibility of services on managed hosts.

Listing 5-9 Multiplay Playbook Example

```
---
- name: install start and enable httpd
  hosts: all
  tasks:
  - name: install package
    yum:
      name: httpd
      state: latest
```

```
  - name: start and enable service
      service:
        name: httpd
        state: started
        enabled: yes

- name: test httpd accessibility
  hosts: localhost
  tasks:
  - name: test httpd access
    uri:
        url: http://ansible1
```

In Listing 5-10 you can see what happens when you run the playbook. The uri module indicates that the status code is –1, which indicates the httpd service could not be accessed on the managed host. The exit code 200 was expected, and because this is not the case, the uri module returns an error. Do you have any idea why? You don't need to fix this problem yet; you'll do this in the end-of-chapter lab with this chapter.

Listing 5-10   Playbook Result

```
[ansible@control ~]$ ansible-playbook listing59.yaml

PLAY [install start and enable httpd] *******************************

TASK [Gathering Facts] **********************************************
ok: [ansible2]
ok: [ansible1]

TASK [install package] **********************************************
ok: [ansible2]
ok: [ansible1]

TASK [start and enable service] *************************************
ok: [ansible2]
ok: [ansible1]

PLAY [test httpd accessibility] *************************************
```

```
TASK [Gathering Facts] *************************************************
ok: [localhost]


TASK [test httpd access] **********************************************
fatal: [localhost]: FAILED! => {"changed": false, "content": "",
"elapsed": 0, "msg": "Status code was -1 and not [200]: Request
failed: <urlopen error [Errno 113] No route to host>", "redirected":
false, "status": -1, "url": "http://ansible1"}


PLAY RECAP ************************************************************
ansible1                    : ok=3      changed=0     unreachable=0
failed=0     skipped=0     rescued=0    ignored=0
ansible2                    : ok=3      changed=0     unreachable=0
failed=0     skipped=0     rescued=0    ignored=0
localhost                   : ok=1      changed=0     unreachable=0
failed=1     skipped=0     rescued=0    ignored=0
```

Increasing Output Verbosity

While you are analyzing playbook errors, it might be helpful to increase playbook output verbosity. To do so, you can use the **-v** command-line option one time or multiple times. Table 5-3 gives an overview.

Table 5-3 Output Verbosity Options Overview

Option	Use
-v	Shows task results
-vv	Shows task results as well as task configuration
-vvv	Shows task results, task configuration, and information about connections to managed hosts
-vvvv	Same as **-vvv** but also includes verbosity options about connection plug-ins, user accounts, and scripts that have been executed

Increasing output verbosity can be useful and provide you with additional information. Output verbosity must be used with moderation, though. While **-vv** can be useful in many cases, the **-vvvv** option just overloads you with irrelevant information in most cases. Listing 5-11 shows partial output of the command **ansible-playbook -vv listing59.yaml**, and Listing 5-12 shows partial output of the command **ansible-playbook -vvvv listing59.yaml**.

Listing 5-11   ansible-playbook -vv Partial Output

```
[ansible@control ~]$ ansible-playbook -vv listing59.yaml
ansible-playbook 2.9.5
  config file = /home/ansible/ansible.cfg
  configured module search path = ['/home/ansible/.ansible/plugins/
modules', '/usr/share/ansible/plugins/modules']
  ansible python module location = /usr/lib/python3.6/site-packages/
ansible
  executable location = /usr/bin/ansible-playbook
  python version = 3.6.8 (default, Nov 21 2019, 19:31:34) [GCC 8.3.1
20190507 (Red Hat 8.3.1-4)]
Using /home/ansible/ansible.cfg as config file


PLAYBOOK: listing59.yaml **********************************************
2 plays in listing59.yaml


PLAY [install start and enable httpd] ********************************

TASK [Gathering Facts] **********************************************
task path: /home/ansible/listing59.yaml:2
ok: [ansible2]
ok: [ansible1]
META: ran handlers


TASK [install package] **********************************************
task path: /home/ansible/listing59.yaml:5
ok: [ansible2] => {"changed": false, "msg": "Nothing to do", "rc": 0,
"results": []}
ok: [ansible1] => {"changed": false, "msg": "Nothing to do", "rc": 0,
"results": []}
```

Listing 5-12   ansible-playbook -vvvv Partial Output

```
[ansible@control ~]$ ansible-playbook -vvvv listing59.yaml
ansible-playbook 2.9.5
  config file = /home/ansible/ansible.cfg
  configured module search path = ['/home/ansible/.ansible/plugins/
modules', '/usr/share/ansible/plugins/modules']
ansible python module location = /usr/lib/python3.6/site-packages/
ansible
  executable location = /usr/bin/ansible-playbook
```

```
   python version = 3.6.8 (default, Nov 21 2019, 19:31:34) [GCC 8.3.1
20190507 (Red Hat 8.3.1-4)]
Using /home/ansible/ansible.cfg as config file
setting up inventory plugins
host_list declined parsing /home/ansible/inventory as it did not pass
its verify_file() method
script declined parsing /home/ansible/inventory as it did not pass its
verify_file() method
auto declined parsing /home/ansible/inventory as it did not pass its
verify_file() method
Parsed /home/ansible/inventory inventory source with ini plugin
Loading callback plugin default of type stdout, v2.0 from /usr/lib/
python3.6/site-packages/ansible/plugins/callback/default.py


PLAYBOOK: listing59.yaml ***********************************************
Positional arguments: listing59.yaml
verbosity: 4
remote_user: ansible
connection: smart
timeout: 10
become: True
become_method: sudo
tags: ('all',)
inventory: ('/home/ansible/inventory',)
forks: 5
2 plays in listing57.yaml


PLAY [install start and enable httpd] *********************************

TASK [Gathering Facts] ***********************************************
task path: /home/ansible/listing59.yaml:2
<ansible2> ESTABLISH SSH CONNECTION FOR USER: ansible
<ansible2> SSH: EXEC ssh -vvv -C -o ControlMaster=auto
-o ControlPersist=60s -o StrictHostKeyChecking=no -o
KbdInteractiveAuthentication=no -o PreferredAuthentications=gssapi-
with-mic,gssapi-keyex,hostbased,publickey -o PasswordAuthentication=no
-o 'User="ansible"' -o ConnectTimeout=10 -o ControlPath=/home/
ansible/.ansible/cp/b95d9eb347 ansible2 '/bin/sh -c '"'"'echo ~ansible
&& sleep 0'"'"''
<ansible1> ESTABLISH SSH CONNECTION FOR USER: ansible
<ansible1> SSH: EXEC ssh -vvv -C -o ControlMaster=auto
-o ControlPersist=60s -o StrictHostKeyChecking=no -o
KbdInteractiveAuthentication=no -o PreferredAuthentications=gssapi-
with-mic,gssapi-keyex,hostbased,publickey -o PasswordAuthentication=no
-o 'User="ansible"' -o ConnectTimeout=10 -o ControlPath=/home/
```

```
ansible/.ansible/cp/88f8e128b5 ansible1 '/bin/sh -c '"'"'echo ~ansible
&& sleep 0'"'"''

<ansible2> (0, b'/home/ansible\n', b"OpenSSH_8.0p1, OpenSSL 1.1.1c
FIPS  28 May 2019\r\ndebug1: Reading configuration data /etc/ssh/
ssh_config\r\ndebug3: /etc/ssh/ssh_config line 51: Including file /
etc/ssh/ssh_config.d/05-redhat.conf depth 0\r\ndebug1: Reading
configuration data /etc/ssh/ssh_config.d/05-redhat.conf\r\ndebug2:
checking match for 'final all' host ansible2 originally ansible2\r\
ndebug3: /etc/ssh/ssh_config.d/05-redhat.conf line 3: not matched
'final'\r\ndebug2: match not found\r\ndebug3: /etc/ssh/ssh_
config.d/05-redhat.conf line 5: Including file /etc/crypto-policies/
back-ends/openssh.config depth 1 (parse only)\r\ndebug1: Reading
configuration data /etc/crypto-policies/back-ends/openssh.config\r\
ndebug3: gss kex names ok: [gss-gex-sha1-,gss-group14-sha1-]\r\
ndebug3: kex names ok: [curve25519-sha256,curve25519-sha256@libssh.
org,ecdh-sha2-nistp256,ecdh-sha2-nistp384,ecdh-sha2-nistp521,diffie-
hellman-group-exchange-sha256,diffie-hellman-group14-sha256,diffie-
hellman-group16-sha512,diffie-hellman-group18-sha512,diffie-
hellman-group-exchange-sha1,diffie-hellman-group14-sha1]\r\
ndebug1: configuration requests final Match pass\r\ndebug1:
re-parsing configuration\r\ndebug1: Reading configuration data /
etc/ssh/ssh_config\r\ndebug3: /etc/ssh/ssh_config line 51:
Including file /etc/ssh/ssh_config.d/05-redhat.conf depth 0\r\
ndebug1: Reading configuration data /etc/ssh/ssh_config.d/05-
redhat.conf\r\ndebug2: checking match for 'final all' host ansible2
originally ansible2\r\ndebug3: /etc/ssh/ssh_config.d/05-redhat.
conf line 3: matched 'final'\r\ndebug2: match found\r\ndebug3: /
etc/ssh/ssh_config.d/05-redhat.conf line 5: Including file /etc/
crypto-policies/back-ends/openssh.config depth 1\r\ndebug1: Reading
configuration data /etc/crypto-policies/back-ends/openssh.config\r\
ndebug3: gss kex names ok: [gss-gex-sha1-,gss-group14-sha1-]\r\
ndebug3: kex names ok: [curve25519-sha256,curve25519-sha256@libssh.
org,ecdh-sha2-nistp256,ecdh-sha2-nistp384,ecdh-sha2-nistp521,diffie-
hellman-group-exchange-sha256,diffie-hellman-group14-sha256,diffie-
hellman-group16-sha512,diffie-hellman-group18-sha512,diffie-hellman-
group-exchange-sha1,diffie-hellman-group14-sha1]\r\ndebug1: auto-mux:
Trying existing master\r\ndebug2: fd 4 setting O_NONBLOCK\r\ndebug2:
mux_client_hello_exchange: master version 4\r\ndebug3: mux_client_
forwards: request forwardings: 0 local, 0 remote\r\ndebug3: mux_
client_request_session: entering\r\ndebug3: mux_client_request_alive:
entering\r\ndebug3: mux_client_request_alive: done pid = 2384\r\
ndebug3: mux_client_request_session: session request sent\r\ndebug3:
mux_client_read_packet: read header failed: Broken pipe\r\ndebug2:
Received exit status from master 0\r\n")

<ansible2> ESTABLISH SSH CONNECTION FOR USER: ansible

<ansible2> SSH: EXEC ssh -vvv -C -o ControlMaster=auto
-o ControlPersist=60s -o StrictHostKeyChecking=no -o
KbdInteractiveAuthentication=no -o PreferredAuthentications=gssapi-
with-mic,gssapi-keyex,hostbased,publickey -o PasswordAuthentication=no
-o 'User="ansible"' -o ConnectTimeout=10 -o ControlPath=/home/
ansible/.ansible/cp/b95d9eb347 ansible2 '/bin/sh -c '"'"'(
umask 77 && mkdir -p "' echo /home/ansible/.ansible/tmp/
```

```
ansible-tmp-1585565643.3326187-58978915363330 '" && echo ansible-
tmp-1585565643.3326187-58978915363330="' echo /home/ansible/.ansible/
tmp/ansible-tmp-1585565643.3326187-58978915363330 '" ) && sleep
0'"'"''

<ansible1> (0, b'/home/ansible\n', b"OpenSSH_8.0p1, OpenSSL 1.1.1c
FIPS  28 May 2019\r\ndebug1: Reading configuration data /etc/ssh/
ssh_config\r\ndebug3: /etc/ssh/ssh_config line 51: Including file /
etc/ssh/ssh_config.d/05-redhat.conf depth 0\r\ndebug1: Reading
configuration data /etc/ssh/ssh_config.d/05-redhat.conf\r\ndebug2:
checking match for 'final all' host ansible1 originally ansible1\r\
ndebug3: /etc/ssh/ssh_config.d/05-redhat.conf line 3: not matched
'final'\r\ndebug2: match not found\r\ndebug3: /etc/ssh/ssh_
config.d/05-redhat.conf
```

If you think Listing 5-12 is too much, that's exactly the idea I want to transmit. The **-vvvv** output shows all there is to show, and it's not uncommon to see it producing thousands of lines of output code. There are very few situations in which that information may be useful, however.

EXAM TIP   Of the troubleshooting options you've seen so far, the output verbosity options are not the most useful. Using common sense is. Most errors in playbooks are the result of logic errors, where the flow of tasks in a playbook has not been well thought through. It is relatively easy to avoid those types of errors: don't include too many tasks in a play, and don't include too many plays in a playbook. That way, you make it easy to avoid losing oversight.

In Exercise 5-3 you work on a multiplay playbook.

Exercise 5-3   Creating a Multiplay Playbook

1. Use an editor to create the file **exercise53.yaml** and create the first play:

```
---

- name: enable web server
  hosts: ansible1
  tasks:
  - name: install stuff
    yum:
    - httpd
    - firewalld
  - name: create a welcome page
    copy:
```

```
      content: "welcome to the webserver\n"
      dest: /var/www/html/index.html
- name: enable webserver
  service:
    name: httpd
    state: started
    enabled: true
- name: enable firewall
  service:
    name: firewalld
    state: started
    enabled: true
- name: open service in firewall
  firewalld:
    service: http
    permanent: true
    state: enabled
    immediate: yes
```

2. Continue by adding the second play to complete the playbook. Notice the use of the **return_content** in the uri module, which ensures that the result of the command is shown while running the playbook:

```
---
- name: enable web server
  hosts: ansible1
  tasks:
  - name: install stuff
    yum:
      name:
      - httpd
      - firewalld
  - name: create a welcome page
    copy:
      content: "welcome to the webserver\n"
      dest: /var/www/html/index.html
  - name: enable webserver
    service:
      name: httpd
      state: started
      enabled: true
  - name: enable firewall
    service:
```

```
        name: firewalld
        state: started
        enabled: true
     - name: open service in firewall
       firewalld:
          service: http
          permanent: true
          state: enabled
          immediate: yes


   - name: test webserver access
     hosts: localhost
     become: no
     tasks:
     - name: test webserver access
       uri:
          url: http://ansible1
          return_content: yes
          status_code: 200
```

3. Verify playbook syntax by using **ansible-playbook --syntax-check exercise53.yaml**.

4. Run the playbook by using **ansible-playbook -vv exercise53.yaml**.

Summary

In this chapter you read how to work with playbooks. To start with, you ran a sample playbook and verified its results. Next, you learned about the YAML file format used in playbooks and some of its most important features. In the last section you read how to work with multiplay playbooks and learned when using them makes sense.

Exam Preparation Tasks

As mentioned in the section "How to Use This Book" in the Introduction, you have a couple of choices for exam preparation: the exercises here, Chapter 16, "Final Preparation," and the exam simulation questions on the companion website.

Review All Key Topics

Review the most important topics in this chapter, noted with the Key Topics icon in the outer margin of the page. Table 5-4 lists a reference of these key topics and the page numbers on which each is found.

Table 5-4   Key Topics for Chapter 5

Key Topic Element	Description	Page Number
Table 5-2	Playbook Play Required Keys	74

Memory Tables

Print a copy of Appendix D, "Memory Tables" (found on the companion website), or at least the section for this chapter, and complete the tables and lists from memory. Appendix E, "Memory Tables Answer Key," also on the companion website, includes completed tables and lists to check your work.

Define Key Terms

Define the following key terms from this chapter, and check your answers in the glossary:

dictionary, key-value, list, play, playbook, task, YAML

Review Questions

1. Which option do you use to show the most verbose output to the **ansible-playbook** command?

2. What characters must be used for indentation in YAML files?

3. How can you verify syntax of an Ansible playbook?

4. Which module can you use to verify connectivity to a web server?

5. Which module can you use to add a few lines of text to a file?

6. What is the use case for using a > sign before specifying a string of text in a playbook?

7. When should multiple playbooks be used instead of multiplay playbooks?

8. What does a task show that has successfully been executed but does not trigger any changes?

9. If a playbook has run three tasks, and none of these tasks trigger any changes on the managed hosts, how many times would you see "ok" in the playbook output?

10. Which exit code does the uri module look for to check whether web content is accessible?

End-of-Chapter Lab

In the end-of-chapter lab with this chapter, you analyze what is wrong with a play-book and fix it.

Lab 5-1

Run the playbook listing57.yaml. As you've seen before, it generates an error. Fix the error by using the following directions:

- What specific information do you obtain when increasing verbosity?

- Does it help to perform a syntax check?

- Does it help to perform a dry run?

- Which module is required to fix this playbook?

This chapter covers the following subjects:

- Understanding the Use of Variables in Ansible Playbooks
- Working with Ansible Facts
- Working with Variables
- Using Vault to Manage Sensitive Values
- Capturing Command Output Using **register**

## CHAPTER 6

Working with Variables and Facts

The following RHCE exam objectives are covered in this chapter:

- Understand core components of Ansible
    - Variables
    - Facts
- Create Ansible plays and playbook
    - Use variables to retrieve the results of running a command
- Use advanced Ansible features
    - Use Ansible Vault in playbooks to protect sensitive data

"Do I Know This Already?" Quiz

The "Do I Know This Already?" quiz allows you to assess whether you should read this entire chapter thoroughly or jump to the "Exam Preparation Tasks" section. If you are in doubt about your answers to these questions or your own assessment of your knowledge of the topics, read the entire chapter. Table 6-1 lists the major headings in this chapter and their corresponding "Do I Know This Already?" quiz questions. You can find the answers in Appendix A, "Answers to the 'Do I Know This Already?' Quizzes and Review Questions."

Table 6-1 "Do I Know This Already?" Section-to-Question Mapping

Foundation Topics Section	Questions
Understanding the Use of Variables in Ansible Playbooks	1
Working with Ansible Facts	2–4
Working with Variables	5–7
Using Vault to Manage Sensitive Values	8, 9
Capturing Command Output Using **register**	10

1. A user wants to print the message "lisa is created," where lisa refers to the value of a variable. How should this variable be written in the playbook YAML code?

   a. "{{ ansible_user }}"

   b. {{ ansible_user }}

   c. '{{ user }}'

   d. "{{ user }}"

2. Which module is used to gather facts using an ad hoc command?

   a. facter

   b. setup

   c. gather

   d. collect

3. There are different valid methods to address the value of a fact. Which of the following should be considered the preferred way?

   a. ansible_facts['default_ipv4']['address']

   b. ansible_facts.default_ipv4.address

   c. ansible_default_ipv4.address

   d. ansible_default_ipv4['address']

4. Custom facts have different requirements. Which of the following is not one of them?

   a. Custom facts must be stored on the managed host in the directory /etc/ansible/facts.d.

   b. Custom fact files must be executable.

   c. Custom facts are written in INI or JSON format.

   d. Custom fact files must use the .fact extension.

5. Which of the following variable names is correct?

   a. my.file1

   b. 1file

   c. my_file1

   d. my-file

6. Which of the following is not a valid way to define variables in a playbook?

   a. Use vars_files: in the playbook header.

   b. Create a file with the name group_vars/groupname that contains variables that apply to a host group.

   c. Create a file with the name host_vars/hostname that contains variables that apply to a specific host.

   d. Define the variables: key in the play header and give it a list value.

7. Which of the following is used as a magic variable and cannot be overwritten for that reason?

   a. hostvars

   b. host_groups

   c. inventory

   d. config_file

8. Which command can you use to change the password on an Ansible Vault-encrypted file?

   a. **ansible-vault change**

   b. **ansible-vault rekey**

   c. **ansible-vault create**

   d. **ansible-vault password**

9. Which option can you use with the **ansible-vault** command to decrypt multiple Ansible Vault-encrypted files with different passwords from one playbook?

   a. **--ask-vault-pass**

   b. **--vault-id @prompt**

   c. **--vault-password-file=password-file**

   d. Use **--ask-vault-pass** multiple times.

10. How can the result of a command be used as a variable in Ansible?

   a. Get it from Ansible facts.

   b. Use the command_facts module.

   c. Use the **register** parameter.

   d. Redirect the standard output to a file and analyze that.

Foundation Topics

Understanding the Use of Variables in Ansible Playbooks

Up to now you've learned how to work with playbooks. Although convenient, a playbook that just works with static data is not very impressive. That's why using variables is important in Ansible. Variables are labels that refer to data that can be dynamically changed, and that makes Ansible really flexible, particularly when variables are used in combination with conditionals, as discussed in Chapter 7, "Using Task Control." Before learning about variables and facts in detail, let's look at the example in Listing 6-1 showing how variables are used.

Listing 6-1   Using Variables Example

```
---
- name: create a user using a variable
  hosts: ansible1
  vars:
    users: lisa
  tasks:
    - name: create a user {{ users }} on host {{ ansible_hostname }}
      user:
        name: "{{ users }}"
```

As you can see, the sample playbook in Listing 6-1 has a vars section. In this section, one variable is defined, using the common *key: value* syntax. Next, in the task definition the user module is used to work with this variable. To refer to the variable, you just place the name definition between double curly brackets. However, in the **name** argument to the user module, the variable is between double quotes and double curly braces. The reason is that the value in this case starts with the variable. If a value starts with a variable, the variable must be placed between double quotes. If more than just the variable name in the line specifies the value, the entire line that starts with the variable must be between double quotes.

Next you see the variable ansible_hostname, which is not defined anywhere. That is because this variable is an Ansible fact. Ansible facts are also used as variables, but they are variables that are automatically set, based on properties of the managed system. Fact discovery is used by default to discover all that Ansible possibly might want to know about a machine to use in conditionals. You don't have to define facts; facts are a part of the system properties.

Listing 6-2 shows the command output when running the playbook in Listing 6-1.

Listing 6-2   Running the Listing 6-1 Sample Playbook

```
[ansible@control ~]$ ansible-playbook listing61.yaml


PLAY [create a user using a variable] *******************************
**************************************

TASK [Gathering Facts] **********************************************
***********************
ok: [ansible1]


TASK [create a user lisa on host ansible1] **************************
**************************************
changed: [ansible1]


PLAY RECAP **********************************************************
************
ansible1                      : ok=2      changed=1    unreachable=0
failed=0      skipped=0     rescued=0    ignored=0
```

As shown in Listing 6-2, the **ansible-playbook** command shows the task description "create a user lisa on host ansible1," in which the variable defined in the playbook is used along with the Ansible fact ansible_hostname, which is the discovered variable that reveals system properties.

Working with Ansible Facts

In Ansible, there are three types of variables. Table 6-2 provides an overview.

Table 6-2   Ansible Variable Types Overview

Type	Use
Fact	Discovered variable that contains values describing specific system properties
Variable	Variable that is defined at the discretion of the user
Magic variable	System variable that is automatically set

Ansible facts are system properties that are collected when Ansible executes on a remote system. After facts are gathered, the facts can be used as variables. Apart from the system facts, which just exist as a system property, there can be custom facts. These facts are defined by an administrator and stored as a file on the managed hosts. In the following sections, you learn how to work with facts on Ansible-managed systems. Magic variables are specific system variables, which will be discussed later in this chapter.

Gathering Facts

When any Ansible playbook is used, it first gathers facts for all the managed hosts. This is done by an implicit fact-gathering task in every playbook. The result of this process is stored in the ansible_facts variable. Let's run the simple playbook in Listing 6-3 to analyze fact gathering.

Listing 6-3   Simple Playbook to Show Fact Gathering

```
---
- name: show fact gathering
  hosts: all
  tasks:
  - name: show all facts
    debug:
      var: ansible_facts
```

The playbook in Listing 6-3 collects all known facts about the managed hosts and stores them in the variable ansible_facts. To show how this process works, Listing 6-3 uses the debug module. This module can be used for debugging purposes, and it is used to either show a message or print the contents of a variable. In this case, the debug module prints all the contents of the multivalued variable ansible_facts; see Listing 6-4 for a partial result. Notice that when variables are referred to using the var argument to the debug module, the name of the variables doesn't have to be between curly brackets and quotes. This is one of many exceptions that you may find while working with variables.

Listing 6-4   Fact Gathering Partial Result

```
TASK [show all facts] *********************************************
*************************************
ok: [ansible1] => {
    "ansible_facts": {
        "_facts_gathered": true,
        "all_ipv4_addresses": [
            "192.168.122.1",
            "192.168.4.201"
        ],
```

```
        "all_ipv6_addresses": [
            "fe80::e564:5033:5dec:aead"
        ],
        "ansible_local": {},
        "apparmor": {
            "status": "disabled"
        },
        "architecture": "x86_64",
        "bios_date": "07/29/2019",
        "bios_version": "6.00",
        "cmdline": {
            "BOOT_IMAGE": "(hd0,msdos1)/vmlinuz-4.18.0-147.el8.x86_64",
            "crashkernel": "auto",
            "quiet": true,
            "rd.lvm.lv": "cl/swap",
            "resume": "/dev/mapper/cl-swap",
            "rhgb": true,
            "ro": true,
            "root": "/dev/mapper/cl-root"
        },
        "date_time": {
            "date": "2020-03-30",
            "day": "30",
            "epoch": "1585579970",
            "hour": "10",
            "iso8601": "2020-03-30T14:52:50Z",
            "iso8601_basic": "20200330T105250355357",
            "iso8601_basic_short": "20200330T105250",
            "iso8601_micro": "2020-03-30T14:52:50.355419Z",
            "minute": "52",
            "month": "03",
            "second": "50",
            "time": "10:52:50",
            "tz": "EDT",
            "tz_offset": "-0400",
            "weekday": "Monday",
            "weekday_number": "1",
            "weeknumber": "13",
            "year": "2020"
        },
        "default_ipv4": {
            "address": "192.168.4.201"
```

The result of fact gathering is stored in a multivalued variable with the name ansible_facts, which is organized as a dictionary (see the "Using Multivalued Variables" section). To address specific values in this dictionary, you can use two formats:

- Notation with square brackets: **ansible_facts['default_ipv4']['address']**

- Dotted notation: **ansible_facts.default_ipv4.address**

Of these two notations, the notation with the square brackets is preferred.

As you can see when browsing through the result of Ansible fact gathering, a wide range of facts is collected. Table 6-3 provides an overview of some of the most commonly used facts.

Table 6-3   Commonly Used Ansible Facts

Variable	Use
ansible_facts['hostname']	Short hostname
ansible_facts['distribution']	Linux distribution
ansible_facts['default_ipv4']['address']	The main IPv4 address
ansible_facts['interfaces']	A list of network interfaces
ansible_facts['devices']	A list of attached storage devices
ansible_facts['devices']['sda']['partitions']['sda1']['size']	The size of partition /dev/sda1
ansible_facts['distribution_version']	The version of the current distribution

Note that Ansible gathers a lot of facts by default. Some information is not included, though, and if that type of information is needed, it may be collected using additional modules. For an overview of all available modules for gathering specific types of facts, type **ansible-doc -l | grep fact**. This command shows that a wide range of fact-gathering modules is available. One of these modules is package_facts, which collects information about software packages installed on managed hosts.

Understanding How Facts Are Displayed

While working with facts, you may encounter two different ways in which facts are displayed. In the current way, all facts are stored in a dictionary with the name ansible_facts, and items in this dictionary are addressed using the notation with square brackets, which can be seen in Table 6-3. In the old way, Ansible facts were injected as individual variables, which were prefixed with the string ansible_ (like ansible_hostname), allowing the variables to be addressed individually. This approach is known as injected variables.

The confusing thing is that the old approach and the new approach both still occur. Compare, for instance, the output of the **ansible ansible1 -m setup** command shown in Listing 6-5 with the output of the playbook that displays contents of the ansible_fact variable, which you saw in Listing 6-4. As you can see, in Listing 6-5 Ansible facts are injected as variables.

Listing 6-5   ansible -m setup Shows Facts Injected as Variables

```
ansible1 | SUCCESS => {
    "ansible_facts": {
        "ansible_all_ipv4_addresses": [
            "192.168.122.1",
            "192.168.4.201"
        ],
        "ansible_all_ipv6_addresses": [
            "fe80::e564:5033:5dec:aead"
        ],
        "ansible_apparmor": {
            "status": "disabled"
        },
        "ansible_architecture": "x86_64",
        "ansible_bios_date": "07/29/2019",
        "ansible_bios_version": "6.00",
        "ansible_cmdline": {
            "BOOT_IMAGE": "(hd0,msdos1)/vmlinuz-4.18.0-147.el8.
x86_64",
            "crashkernel": "auto",
            "quiet": true,
            "rd.lvm.lv": "cl/swap",
            "resume": "/dev/mapper/cl-swap",
            "rhgb": true,
            "ro": true,
            "root": "/dev/mapper/cl-root"
        },
        "ansible_date_time": {
            "date": "2020-03-31",
            "day": "31",
            "epoch": "1585645366",
            "hour": "05",
            "iso8601": "2020-03-31T09:02:46Z",
            "iso8601_basic": "20200331T050246844129",
```

```
            "iso8601_basic_short": "20200331T050246",
            "iso8601_micro": "2020-03-31T09:02:46.844200Z",
            "minute": "02",
            "month": "03",
            "second": "46",
            "time": "05:02:46",
            "tz": "EDT",
            "tz_offset": "-0400",
            "weekday": "Tuesday",
            "weekday_number": "2",
            "weeknumber": "13",
            "year": "2020"
        },
        "ansible_default_ipv4": {
            "address": "192.168.4.201",
            "alias": "ens33",
            "broadcast": "192.168.4.255",
            "gateway": "192.168.4.2",
            "interface": "ens33",
            "macaddress": "00:0c:29:1f:c1:23",
            "mtu": 1500,
            "netmask": "255.255.255.0",
            "network": "192.168.4.0",
            "type": "ether"
        },
```

When you are working with facts, the recommended way is to use the ansible_facts variable, not injected facts, because at some point, injected variables won't be supported anymore. Table 6-4 shows how injected variables compare to the new ansible_facts style to address variables.

Table 6-4 Comparing ansible_facts Versus Injected Facts as Variables

ansible_facts	Injected Variable
ansible_facts['hostname']	ansible_hostname
ansible_facts['distribution']	ansible_distribution
ansible_facts['default_ipv4']['address']	ansible_default_ipv4['address']
ansible_facts['interfaces']	ansible_interfaces
ansible_facts['devices']	ansible_devices

ansible_facts	Injected Variable
ansible_facts['devices']['sda']\ 'partitions']['sda1']['size']	ansible_devices['sda']['partitions']['sda1'] ['size']
ansible_facts['distribution_version']	ansible_distribution_version

Listing 6-6 and Listing 6-7 show two playbooks. Listing 6-6 addresses facts in the old way, and Listing 6-7 addresses the facts using the new way, using the ansible_facts variable. To make sure you understand that different notations can be used in either method, the listings address the facts in dotted notation, not in the notation with square brackets.

Listing 6-6 Addressing Facts with Injected Variables

```
---
- hosts: all
  tasks:
  - name: show IP address
    debug:
      msg: >
         This host uses IP address {{ ansible_default_ipv4.address }}
```

Listing 6-7 Addressing Facts Using the ansible_facts Variable

```
---
- hosts: all
  tasks:
  - name: show IP address
    debug:
      msg: >
         This host uses IP address {{ ansible_facts.default_ipv4.
address }}
```

TIP If, for some reason, you want the method where facts are injected into variables to be the default method, you can use **inject_facts_as_vars=true** in the **[default]** section of the ansible.cfg file.

Because there are many different ways to refer to facts, they may be quite confusing. Let's finish this section with an overview of all options:

- In Ansible versions since 2.5, all facts are stored in one variable: ansible_facts. This method is used while gathering facts from a playbook.

- Before Ansible version 2.5, facts were injected into variables such as ansible_hostname. This method is still used by the setup module. (Note that this may change in future versions of Ansible.)

- Facts can be addressed in dotted notation: **{{ ansible_facts.default_ipv4.address }}**.

- Alternatively, facts can be addressed in square brackets notation: **{{ ansible_facts['default_ipv4']['address'] }}**. This notation is preferred.

Managing Fact Gathering

By default, upon execution of each playbook, facts are gathered. This does slow down playbooks, and for that reason, it is possible to disable fact gathering completely. To do so, you can use the **gather_facts: no** parameter in the play header. If later in the same playbook it is necessary to gather facts, you can do this by running the setup module in a task.

Even if it is possible to disable fact gathering for all of your Ansible configurations, this practice is not recommended. Too many playbooks use conditionals that are based on the current value of facts, and all of these conditionals would stop working if fact gathering were disabled altogether.

As an alternative to make working with facts more efficient, you can disable a fact cache. To do so, you need to install an external plug-in. Currently, two plug-ins are available for this purpose: jsonfile and redis. To configure fact caching using the redis plug-in, you need to install it first. Next, you can enable fact caching through ansible.cfg. The following procedure describes how to do this (note that you don't have to know this for the RHCE exam):

1. Use **yum install redis**.

2. Use **service redis start**.

3. Use **pip install redis**.

4. Edit /etc/ansible/ansible.cfg and ensure it contains the following parameters:

```
[defaults]
gathering = smart
fact_caching = redis
fact_caching_timeout = 86400
```

NOTE   Fact caching can be convenient but should be used with caution. If, for instance, a playbook installs a certain package only if a sufficient amount of disk space is available, it should not do this based on information that may be up to 24 hours old. For that reason, using a fact cache is not recommended in many situations.

Working with Custom Facts

Apart from the facts that can be gathered in all cases, Ansible also offers an option to work with custom facts. A custom fact is used to provide a host with arbitrary values that Ansible can use to change the behavior of plays. Custom facts can be provided as static files. These files must be in either INI or JSON format, have the extension .fact, and on the managed hosts must be stored in the /etc/ansible/facts.d directory.

Alternatively, custom facts can be generated by a script, and in that case the only requirement is that the script must generate its output in JSON format. Dynamic custom facts are useful because they allow the facts to be determined at the moment that a script is running. Listing 6-8 provides an example of a static custom fact file.

Listing 6-8 Custom Facts Sample File

```
[packages]
web_package = httpd
ftp_package = vsftpd


[services]
web_service = httpd
ftp_service = vsftpd
```

To get the custom facts files on the managed hosts, you can use a playbook. Listing 6-9 provides an example of a playbook that copies a local custom fact file (existing in the current Ansible project directory) to the appropriate location on the managed hosts. Notice that this playbook uses variables, which are explained in more detail in the section titled "Working with Variables."

Listing 6-9 Sample Playbook to Copy Custom Facts

```
---
- name: Install custom facts
  hosts: all
  vars:
    remote_dir: /etc/ansible/facts.d
    facts_file: listing68.fact
  tasks:
  - name: create remote directory
    file:
```

```
        state: directory
        recurse: yes
        path: "{{ remote_dir }}"
    - name: install new facts
      copy:
        src: "{{ facts_file }}"
        dest: "{{ remote_dir }}"
```

Custom facts are stored in the variable ansible_facts.ansible_local. In this variable, you use the filename of the custom fact file and the label in the custom fact file. For instance, after you run the playbook in Listing 6-9, the web_package fact that was defined in listing68.fact is accessible as

```
{{ ansible_facts['ansible_local']['listing68']['packages']
['web_package'] }}
```

To verify, you can use the setup module with the filter argument. Notice that because the setup module produces injected variables as a result, the ad hoc command to use is **ansible all -m setup -a "filter=ansible_local"**. The command **ansible all -m setup -a "filter=ansible_facts['ansible_local']"** does not work. In Exercise 6-1 you practice working with facts.

Exercise 6-1   Working with Ansible Facts

1. Create a custom fact file with the name custom.fact and the following contents:
    ```
    [software]
    package = httpd
    service = httpd
    state = started
    enabled = true
    ```

2. Write a playbook with the name copy_facts.yaml and the following contents:
    ```
    ---
      name: copy custom facts
      hosts: ansible1
      tasks:
      - name: create the custom facts directory
        file:
          state: directory
          recurse: yes
          path: /etc/ansible/facts.d
      - name: copy the custom facts
        copy:
    ```

```
        src: custom.fact
        dest: /etc/ansible/facts.d
```

3. Apply the playbook using **ansible-playbook copy_facts.yaml**.

4. Check the availability of the custom facts by using **ansible all -m setup -a "filter=ansible_local"**.

5. Use an ad hoc command to ensure that the httpd service is not installed on any of the managed servers: **ansible all -m yum -a "name=httpd state=absent"**.

6. Create a playbook with the name setup_with_facts.yaml that installs and enables the httpd service, using the custom facts. (Notice that all fact names referred to in the variables in this playbook should be in one line—also see the example in the book GitHub repository.)

```
---
- name: install and start the web service
  hosts: ansible1
  tasks:
  - name: install the package
    yum:
      name: "{{ ansible_facts['ansible_local']['custom']
['software']['package'] }}"
      state: latest
  - name: start the service
    service:
      name: "{{ ansible_facts['ansible_local']['custom']
['software']['service'] }}"
      state: "{{ ansible_facts['ansible_local']['custom']
['software']['state'] }}"
      enabled: "{{ ansible_facts['ansible_local']['custom']
['software']['enabled'] }}"
```

7. Run the playbook to install and set up the service by using **ansible-playbook setup_with_facts.yaml**.

8. Use an ad hoc command to verify the service is running: **ansible ansible1 -a "systemctl status httpd"**.

Working with Variables

In the previous section you learned how you can use Ansible facts to work with dynamic values that are based on something that exists on a managed host. In this section you learn about variables. Variables in general are used to separate static data from dynamic data. By putting the dynamic data in variables, you make it easier to manage the dynamic data, in particular if the variables are excluded from external files.

Variables can be used to refer to a wide range of dynamic data, such as names of files, services, packages, users, URLs to specific servers, and much more.

Defining Variables

To define a variable, you can just use the key: value structure in a vars section in the play header. Other ways to define and include variables are discussed later in this section. A variable definition may look like the sample in Listing 6-10.

Listing 6-10   Defining Variables in a Playbook Header

```
---
- name: using variables
  hosts: ansible1
  vars:
    ftp_package: vsftpd
  tasks:
  - name: install package
    yum:
      name: "{{ ftp_package }}"
      state: latest
```

In the example in Listing 6-10, a vars section is included in the play header to define the variable ftp_package. This variable is next referred to in the yum task. As the variable is the first item in the value, its name must be placed between double curly brackets as well as double quotes.

When you define variables, there are a few requirements:

- Variable names must start with a letter.

- Variable names are case sensitive.

- Variable names can contain only letters, numbers, and underscores.

Using Include Files

When you are defining variables, you can define them all in the header of the play. For small playbooks this approach can work fine, but as a playbook grows bigger and gets more complex, you can easily lose oversight. For that reason, it is common to define variables in include files. Specific host and host group variables can be used as include files (see the section "Managing Host and Group Variables" later in this chapter), but it's also possible to include an arbitrary file as a variable file, using the **vars_files:** statement. Notice that the **vars_files:** parameter can have a single value or a list providing multiple values. If a list is used, each item needs to start with a dash; see the "Using Multivalued Variables" section for more information about using lists.

When you include variables from files, it's a good idea to work with a separate directory that contains all variables because that makes it easier to manage as your projects grow bigger.

Listing 6-11 shows a sample playbook, where the line **vars_files: vars/common** is used to include variables defined in the file vars/common, for which contents are displayed in Listing 6-12.

Listing 6-11   Using a Variable Include File

```
---
- name: using a variable include file
  hosts: ansible1
  vars_files: vars/common
  tasks:
  - name: install package
    yum:
      name: "{{ my_package }}"
      state: latest
```

Listing 6-12   Variable Include File Contents

```
my_package: nmap
my_ftp_service: vsftpd
my_file_service: smb
```

Among the most important benefits of using variable include files is the option to manage variables from one central location. If variables are defined in individual playbooks, they are spread all over, and it may be difficult to get an overview of all variables that are used on a site. When you put variables in variable files, it's much easier to manage them in a consistent way and to guarantee that the same variables are used throughout a site.

Managing Host and Group Variables

In some cases you might want to set variables for specific hosts or specific host groups. You can do this by using host_vars and group_vars inclusions. In older versions of Ansible, it was common to set host variables and group variables in inventory, but this practice is now deprecated.

If you want to use host variables, you must create a subdirectory with the name host_vars within the Ansible project directory. In this directory, create a file that matches the inventory name of the host to which the variables should be applied. So the variables for host ansible1 are defined in host_vars/ansible1. To use host group variables, you use a similar approach. To start, you create a directory with the name group_vars. In this directory, a file with the name of the host group is created, and in this file all variables are defined. So if you want to define variables for the host group web servers, you need to create a file with the name group_vars/webservers. In Exercise 6-2 you practice working with host and host group variables.

Exercise 6-2   Using Host and Host Group Variables

1. Create a project directory in your home directory. Type **mkdir ~/chapter6** to create the chapter6 project directory, and use **cd ~/chapter6** to go into this directory.

2. Type **cp ../ansible.cfg .** to copy the ansible.cfg file that you used before. No further modifications to this file are required.

3. Type **vim inventory** to create a file with the name inventory, and ensure it has the following contents:

```
[webservers]
ansible1

[dbservers]
ansible2
```

4. Create the file webservers.yaml, containing the following contents. Notice that nothing is really changed by running this playbook. It just uses the debug module to show the current value of the variables.

```
---
- name: configure web services
  hosts: webservers
  tasks:
  - name: this is the {{ web_package }} package
    debug:
       msg: "Installing {{ web_package }}"
  - name: this is the {{ web_service }} service
    debug:
       msg: "Starting the {{ web_service }}"
```

5. Create the file group_vars/webservers with the following contents:

```
web_package: httpd
web_service: httpd
```

6. Run the playbook with some verbosity to verify it is working by using **ansible-playbook -vv webservers.yaml**.

As you saw in Exercise 6-2, the host group variables are automatically picked up, even if there is not any specific reference to the file that should be included anywhere in the playbook.

> **NOTE**   Using host and host group variables this way is efficient, but at the same time it's confusing. In Ansible it's possible to get variables and other contents from multiple locations, and because the group_vars and host_vars locations are not specified in the playbook, it's easy to overlook where they are coming from. Therefore, it's a good idea to analyze the entire project directory to understand what is happening in a playbook. And using these includes is also one reason why it makes sense to work with project directories and to ensure that these project directories don't become too big.

Using Multivalued Variables

When you work with variables in Ansible, it is common to work with multivalued variables. Two types of multivalued variables can be used: the array (also known as a list) and the dictionary (also known as a hash). Each of these has its own specific use cases.

In variable definition, a list (also known as an array) is a key that can have multiple items as its value. Each item in a list starts with a dash (-). Individual items in a list can be addressed using the index number (starting at zero), as in {{ users[1] }} (which would print the key-value pairs that are set for user lisa). Listing 6-13 shows an example of a variable that is defined as an array.

Listing 6-13   Array Example

```
users:
  - linda:
    username: linda
    homedir: /home/linda
    shell: /bin/bash
  - lisa:
    username: lisa
    homedir: /home/lisa
    shell: /bin/bash
  - anna:
    username: anna
    homedir: /home/anna
    shell: /bin/bash
```

In Python, a dictionary (also known as a hash) is an unordered collection of items, a collection of key-value pairs. In Python, a dictionary is defined as my_dict = { key1: 'car', key2:'bike' }. Because it is based on Python, Ansible lets users use dictionaries as an alternative notation to arrays, though dictionaries are not as common in use as arrays. Items in values in a dictionary are not started with a dash. Using dictionaries is one way; the alternative is to use a list. Listing 6-14 shows an example of a variable that is defined as a dictionary.

Listing 6-14   Dictionary Example

```
users:
  linda:
    username: linda
    homedir: /home/linda
    shell: /bin/bash
  lisa:
    username: lisa
    homedir: /home/lisa
    shell: /bin/bash
  anna:
    username: anna
    homedir: /home/anna
    shell: /bin/bash
```

Using multivalued variables is particularly useful in combination with task control structures such as loops because this allows you to iterate through the multiple values of the variable. Read Chapter 7 for more examples about this. Listing 6-15 shows a sample playbook that uses the debug module to show how to address different keys in a dictionary multivalued variable.

Listing 6-15   Addressing Specific Keys in a Dictionary Multivalued Variable

```
---
- name: show dictionary also known as hash
  hosts: ansible1
  vars_files:
  - vars/users-dictionary
  tasks:
  - name: print dictionary values
    debug:
      msg: "User {{ users.linda.username }} has homedirectory {{
users.linda.homedir }} and shell {{ users.linda.shell }}"
```

As you saw in "Working with Ansible Facts," multivalued variables can be addressed in two ways. In Listing 6-15 the dotted notation is used. In Listing 6-16 you can see how to use the square brackets notation as an alternative. Of these two notations, the recommendation is to use the notation with square brackets.

Listing 6-16 Using the Square Brackets Notation to Address Multivalued Variables

```
---
- name: show dictionary also known as hash
  hosts: ansible1
  vars_files:
    - vars/users-dictionary
  tasks:
    - name: print dictionary values
      debug:
        msg: "User {{ users['linda']['username'] }} has homedirectory
{{ users['linda']['homedir'] }} and shell {{ users['linda']['shell']
}}"
```

Working with Magic Variables

Apart from the variables that can be set by the Ansible user or administrator and the variables that are discovered as Ansible facts, there are also the so-called magic variables. Magic variables are variables that are set automatically by Ansible to reflect an Ansible internal state. There are about 30 magic variables; Table 6-5 shows an overview of some of the most important magic variables.

Table 6-5 Magic Variables Overview

Variable	Use
hostvars	Contains all hosts in inventory and their assigned variables
groups	Contains all groups in inventory
group_names	Lists groups this host is currently a member of
inventory_hostname	Specifies the inventory host name for the current host
inventory_file	Specifies the name of the current inventory file that is used

The most important thing that you should remember about magic variables is that you cannot use their name for anything else. If you try to set a magic variable to another value anyway, it always resets to the default internal value. So don't try to set your own variable groups to store usergroups; the variable groups is already used as a magic variable! In Listing 6-17 you can see how the debug module is used to show the current values assigned to the hostvars magic variable. As you can see, this variable shows many settings that you can change by modifying the ansible.cfg configuration file. If local facts are defined on the host, you will see them also.

Listing 6-17   Using the debug Module to Show Hostvars Variables

```
[ansible@control ~]$ ansible localhost -m debug -a
'var=hostvars["ansible1"]'
localhost | SUCCESS => {
    "hostvars[\"ansible1\"]": {
        "ansible_check_mode": false,
        "ansible_diff_mode": false,
        "ansible_facts": {},
        "ansible_forks": 5,
        "ansible_inventory_sources": [
            "/home/ansible/inventory"
        ],
        "ansible_playbook_python": "/usr/bin/python3.6",
        "ansible_verbosity": 0,
        "ansible_version": {
            "full": "2.9.5",
            "major": 2,
            "minor": 9,
            "revision": 5,
            "string": "2.9.5"
        },
        "group_names": [
            "ungrouped"
        ],
        "groups": {
            "all": [
                "ansible1",
                "ansible2"
            ],
            "ungrouped": [
                "ansible1",
                "ansible2"
            ]
        },
        "inventory_dir": "/home/ansible",
        "inventory_file": "/home/ansible/inventory",
        "inventory_hostname": "ansible1",
        "inventory_hostname_short": "ansible1",
        "omit": "__omit_place_holder__38849508966537e44da5c665d4a784c
3bc0060de",
        "playbook_dir": "/home/ansible"
    }
}
```

Understanding Variable Precedence

With all the different locations where variables can be set, it's important to know what happens if variables are set at multiple levels. Understanding variable precedence is not always easy because they can be set at so many different levels. The most important advice is to just keep it simple and avoid using variables with the same names that are defined at different levels. That way, you avoid having to think about variable precedence.

If a variable with the same name is defined at different levels anyway, the most specific variable always wins. Variables that are defined while running the **playbook** command using the **-e key=value** command-line argument have the highest precedence. After variables that are passed as command-line options, playbook variables are considered. Next are variables that are defined for inventory hosts or host groups. Consult the Ansible documentation item "Variable precedence" for more details and an overview of the 22 different levels where variables can be set and how precedence works for them.

The following list shows precendence for some of the most commonly used variable types:

1. Variables passed on the command line
2. Variables defined in or included from a playbook
3. Inventory variables

Using Vault to Manage Sensitive Values

Sometimes, you must deal with sensitive data when working with Ansible—think about webkeys, passwords, and other types of sensitive data that you really shouldn't store as plain text in a playbook. Ansible Vault is the solution to that problem. You can use Ansible Vault to encrypt and decrypt sensitive data to make it unreadable, and only while accessing data does it ask for a password so that it is decrypted.

Understanding Vault

Ansible may need to access environments where passwords, webkeys, or other authentication tokens are needed. Storing these elements as plain text in a playbook would be a huge risk, so Ansible Vault is the solution. Ansible Vault can be used to encrypt and decrypt any data file in Ansible.

The following approach is used while working with Ansible Vault:

1. Sensitive data is stored as values in variables in a separate variable file.
2. The variable file is encrypted, using the **ansible-vault** command.
3. While accessing the variable file from a playbook, you enter a password to decrypt.

Managing Encrypted Files

The foundation of working with Ansible Vault is the creation of encrypted files. When the command **ansible-vault create secret.yaml** is used, Ansible Vault prompts for a password and then opens the file using the default editor. Alternatively, the password can be provided in a password file. In that case, the password file must be really well protected (for example, by putting it in the user root home directory). If a password file is used, the encrypted variable file can be created using **ansible-vault create --vault-password-file=passfile secret.yaml**.

Apart from using **ansible-vault create** to create a new encrypted file, you can use the command **ansible-vault encrypt** to encrypt one or more existing files. The encrypted file can next be used from a playbook, where a password needs to be entered to decrypt. Alternatively, the **ansible-vault decrypt** command can be used to decrypt the file. Table 6-6 gives an overview of the most commonly used **ansible-vault** commands.

Table 6-6   ansible-vault Command Options

Command	Use
create	Creates a new encrypted file
encrypt	Encrypts an existing file
encrypt_string	Encrypts a string
decrypt	Decrypts an existing file
rekey	Changes the password on an encrypted file
view	Shows contents of an encrypted file
edit	Edits an existing encrypted file

Using Vault in Playbooks

When a Vault-encrypted file is accessed from a playbook, a password must be entered. To have the **ansible-playbook** command prompt for a password, you need to provide the appropriate option. The option **--vault-id @prompt** provides the most elegant option, where the **ansible-playbook** command prompts for a password for each of the Vault-encrypted files that may be used.

Using **--vault-id @prompt** enables a playbook to work with multiple Vault-encrypted files where these files are allowed to have different passwords set. If all Vault-encrypted files a playbook refers to have the same password set, you can use the command **ansible-playbook --ask-vault-pass**.

Alternatively, you can use the command **ansible-playbook --vault-password-file=secret** to obtain the Vault password from a password file. The password file should contain a string that is stored as a single line in the file. Make sure the vault password file is protected through file permissions, such that it is not accessible by unauthorized users!

Managing Files with Sensitive Variables

When you work with Vault-encrypted variable files, it's good practice to separate files containing unencrypted variables from files that contain encrypted variables. A good approach to do so is to use group_vars and host_vars variable inclusion. You read earlier that in the group_vars directory, a file with the name of a host group can be used. Likewise, in the host_vars directory, a file with the name of a host can be created.

While separating encrypted variables from unencrypted files, you may create a directory (instead of a file) with the name of the host or host group. Next, within that directory you can create a file with the name vars, which contains unencrypted variables, and a file with the name vault, which contains Vault-encrypted variables. Alternatively, Vault-encrypted variables can be included from a file using the **vars_files** parameter. In Exercise 6-3 you practice your skills working with Ansible Vault.

Exercise 6-3   Working with Ansible Vault

1. Create a secret file containing encrypted values for a variable user and a variable password by using **ansible-vault create secrets.yaml**. Set the password to **password** and enter the following lines:

```
username: bob
pwhash: password
```

> **NOTE**   When creating users, you cannot provide the password in plain text; it needs to be provided as a hashed value. Because this exercise focuses on the use of Vault, the password is not provided as a hashed value, and as a result, a warning is displayed while using it. You may ignore this warning. In Chapter 13, "Managing Users," you'll learn how to create users with a password provided as a properly hashed value.

2. Create the file create-users.yaml and provide the following contents:

```
---

- name: create a user with vaulted variables
  hosts: ansible1
  vars_files:
```

```
              - secrets.yaml
          tasks:
          - name: creating user
            user:
              name: "{{ username }}"
              password: "{{ pwhash }}"
```

3. Run the playbook by using **ansible-playbook --ask-vault-pass create-users. yaml**. Provide the password when asked for it.

4. Change the current password on **secrets.yaml** by using **ansible-vault rekey secrets.yaml** and set the new password to **secretpassword**.

5. To automate the process of entering the password, use **echo secretpassword > vault-pass**.

6. Use **chmod 400 vault-pass** to ensure the file is readable for the ansible user only; this is about as much as you can do to secure the file.

7. Verify that it's working by using **ansible-playbook --vault-password-file=vault-pass create-users.yaml**.

Capturing Command Output Using register

Variables can be set by the user or the Ansible administrator. Alternatively, the result of commands can be used as a variable, using the **register** parameter in a task. Let's look at the example in Listing 6-18 to understand how it works.

Listing 6-18   Sample Playbook That Uses **register**

```
---
- name: test register
  hosts: ansible1
  tasks:
  - shell: cat /etc/passwd
    register: passwd_contents
  - debug:
      var: "passwd_contents"
```

In the sample playbook in Listing 6-18, the **cat /etc/passwd** command is executed by the shell module. Notice that in this playbook no names are used for tasks. Using names for tasks is not mandatory; it's just recommended in more complex playbooks because this convention makes identification of the tasks easier. The entire contents of the command are next stored in the variable passwd_contents. This variable contains the output of the command, stored in different keys. Table 6-7 provides an overview of the most useful keys, and Listing 6-19 shows the partial result of the **ansible-playbook listing618.yaml** command.

Table 6-7   Keys Used with **register**

Key	Use
cmd	The command that was used
rc	The return code of the command; should be 0 for a successful command
stderr	If applicable, error messages generated by the command
stderr_lines	Error messages shown line by line
stdout	The command output
stdout_lines	The command output shown line by line

Listing 6-19   Partial Result of Running **ansible-playbook listing618.yaml**

```
[ansible@control ~]$ ansible-playbook listing618.yaml

PLAY [test register] **********************************************
******************

TASK [Gathering Facts] *******************************************
******************
ok: [ansible2]
ok: [ansible1]

TASK [shell] *****************************************************
******************
changed: [ansible2]
changed: [ansible1]

TASK [debug] *****************************************************
******************
ok: [ansible1] => {
    "passwd_contents": {
        "changed": true,
        "cmd": "cat /etc/passwd",
        "delta": "0:00:00.004149",
        "end": "2020-04-02 02:28:10.692306",
        "failed": false,
```

```
        "rc": 0,
        "start": "2020-04-02 02:28:10.688157",
        "stderr": "",
        "stderr_lines": [],
        "stdout": "root:x:0:0:root:/root:/bin/bash\nbin:x:1:1:bin:/
bin:/sbin/nologin\ndaemon:x:2:2:daemon:/sbin:/sbin/nologin\nadm:x:
3:4:adm:/var/adm:/sbin/nologin\nlp:x:4:7:lp:/var/spool/lpd:/sbin/
nologin\nsync:x:5:0:sync:/sbin:/bin/sync\nshutdown:x:6:0:shutdown:/
sbin:/sbin/shutdown\nhalt:x:7:0:halt:/sbin:/sbin/halt\nansible:x:
1000:1000:ansible:/home/ansible:/bin/bash\napache:x:48:48:Apache:/usr/
share/httpd:/sbin/nologin\nlinda:x:1002:1002::/home/linda:/bin/bash\
nlisa:x:1003:1003::/home/lisa:/bin/bash",
        "stdout_lines": [
            "root:x:0:0:root:/root:/bin/bash",
            "bin:x:1:1:bin:/bin:/sbin/nologin",
            "daemon:x:2:2:daemon:/sbin:/sbin/nologin",
            "adm:x:3:4:adm:/var/adm:/sbin/nologin",
            "lp:x:4:7:lp:/var/spool/lpd:/sbin/nologin",
            "sync:x:5:0:sync:/sbin:/bin/sync",
            "shutdown:x:6:0:shutdown:/sbin:/sbin/shutdown",
            "halt:x:7:0:halt:/sbin:/sbin/halt",
            "ansible:x:1000:1000:ansible:/home/ansible:/bin/bash",
            "apache:x:48:48:Apache:/usr/share/httpd:/sbin/nologin",
            "linda:x:1002:1002::/home/linda:/bin/bash",
            "lisa:x:1003:1003::/home/lisa:/bin/bash"
        ]
    }
}
```

Using **register** is particularly useful in combination with conditionals, as discussed in Chapter 7. While doing so, you can ensure that a task runs only if a command produces a specific result.

Notice that **register** shows the values that are returned by specific tasks. Tasks have common return values, but modules may have specific return values. That means you cannot assume, based on the result of an example using a specific module, that the return values you see are available for all modules. Consult the module documentation for more information about specific return values.

Summary

In this chapter you learned how to work with variables in many different ways. First you read about Ansible facts, the variables that are automatically set to contain many different system parameters. You also read how to use Ansible facts to set local variables on a host, using custom facts. Next, you explored working with variables and saw how single-valued as well as multivalued variables can be used. After that you read how to secure variables using Ansible Vault, and in the last part of this chapter, you saw how the **register** parameter can be used to store the result of a command that is used in a playbook.

Exam Preparation Tasks

As mentioned in the section "How to Use This Book" in the Introduction, you have a couple of choices for exam preparation: the exercises here, Chapter 16, "Final Preparation," and the exam simulation questions on the companion website.

Review All Key Topics

Review the most important topics in this chapter, noted with the Key Topics icon in the outer margin of the page. Table 6-8 lists a reference of these key topics and the page numbers on which each is found.

Table 6-8 Key Topics for Chapter 6

Key Topic Element	Description	Page Number
List	Facts notations	104
Table 6-3	Commonly Used Ansible Facts	104
Paragraph	Using facts	104
List	Referring to facts	107
List	Defining variables	112
List	Variable precedence overview	119
List	Ansible Vault approach	119

Memory Tables

Print a copy of Appendix D, "Memory Tables" (found on the companion website), or at least the section for this chapter, and complete the tables and lists from memory.

Appendix E, "Memory Tables Answer Key," also on the companion website, includes completed tables and lists to check your work.

Define Key Terms

Define the following key terms from this chapter, and check your answers in the glossary:

array, dictionary, fact, hash, list, local fact, magic variable, register, Vault

Review Questions

1. What are the two requirements for working with custom facts?

2. Which module is used to enable fact gathering or to run fact gathering manually?

3. What needs to be done to use a fact cache?

4. How can you include a variables file in a playbook?

5. How do you set variables that apply to a group of hosts as defined in the inventory?

6. Which type of multivalued variable should you use if you want to use a loop to parse through the different values?

7. Which magic variable can be used to request current settings for variables on a specific host?

8. How do you change the password on a file that has been encrypted with **ansible-vault**?

9. How can a Vault-encrypted file that contains variables be assigned to hosts in a specific inventory host group?

10. You have used **register** in a playbook to register the result of a command in a variable **cmd_result**. How would you show the exit code of the command in a playbook?

End-of-Chapter Labs

Now that we're at the end of this chapter, it's time to do a more complex end-of-chapter lab. This lab consists of two parts: in the first part, you work with custom facts, and in the second part, you use the custom facts in a second playbook.

Lab 6-1

Configure a playbook that works with custom facts and meets the following requirements:

- Use the project directory chapter6.

- Create an inventory file where ansible1 is member of the host group named file and ansible2 is member of the host group named lamp.

- Create a custom facts file that contains a section named packages and set the following variables:

```
smb_package = samba
ftp_package = vsftpd
db_package = mariadb
web_package = httpd
firewall_package = firewalld
```

- Create another custom facts file that contains a section named services and set the following variables:

```
smb_service = smbd
ftp_service = vsftpd
db_service = mariadb
web_service = httpd
firewall_service = firewalld
```

- Create a playbook with the name copy_facts.yaml that copies these facts to all managed hosts. In this playbook define a variable remote_dir to specify the directory the fact files should be copied to. Use the variable fact_file to copy the fact files to the appropriate directories.

- Run the playbook and verify whether it works.

Lab 6-2

After copying over the facts files, create a playbook that uses the facts to set up the rest of the environment. Make sure it meets the following requirements:

- Use a variable inclusion file with the name allvars.yaml and set the following variables:

```
web_root = /var/www/html
ftp_root = /var/ftp
```

- Create a playbook that sets up the file services and the web services. Also ensure the playbook opens the firewalld firewall to provide access to these servers.

- Make sure the webservice provides access to a file index.html, which contains the text "Welcome to the Ansible Web Server."

- Run the playbook and use ad hoc commands to verify that the services have been started.

This chapter covers the following subjects:

- Using Loops and Items
- Using **when** to Run Tasks Conditionally
- Using Handlers
- Dealing with Failures

## CHAPTER 7

Using Task Control

The following RHCE exam objectives are covered in this chapter:

- Create Ansible plays and playbooks
  - Use conditionals to control play execution
  - Configure error handling
  - Create playbooks to configure systems to a specified state

"Do I Know This Already?" Quiz

The "Do I Know This Already?" quiz allows you to assess whether you should read this entire chapter thoroughly or jump to the "Exam Preparation Tasks" section. If you are in doubt about your answers to these questions or your own assessment of your knowledge of the topics, read the entire chapter. Table 7-1 lists the major headings in this chapter and their corresponding "Do I Know This Already?" quiz questions. You can find the answers in Appendix A, "Answers to the 'Do I Know This Already?' Quizzes and Review Questions."

Table 7-1 "Do I Know This Already?" Section-to-Question Mapping

Foundation Topics Section	Questions
Using Loops and Items	1, 2
Using **when** to Run Tasks Conditionally	3–6
Using Handlers	7–9
Dealing with Failures	10

1. Which of the following should you use to iterate through a variable that contains a list of items as its value?
   a. **with_items**
   b. **with_value**
   c. **item**
   d. **loop**

2. Which statement about using variables in **when** conditional statements is true?

    a. Loops cannot be used in **when** statements.

    b. When used in a **when** statement, the variable name is written without curly brackets.

    c. When using variables in a **when** statement, you always need to write them between curly brackets as well as double quotes.

    d. When using variables in a **when** statement, you need to address them using a %% sign.

3. Which of the following shows the proper test to verify whether a Boolean variable is true?

    a. **variable is defined**

    b. **variable**

    c. **variable = "true"**

    d. **variable == 1**

4. Which of the following shows correct syntax for a string test used to check whether **variable** has a specific value?

    a. **variable = value**

    b. **variable == value**

    c. **variable = "value"**

    d. **variable == "value"**

5. Which of the following shows correct syntax for a test that checks whether a variable has a specific numeric value?

    a. **key == "n"**

    b. **key = "n"**

    c. **key == n**

    d. **key = n**

6. What can you use in a playbook to show a prompt while a user executes the playbook, asking the user to provide a specific value for a variable?

    a. **prompt**

    b. **ask_vars**

    c. **vars_prompt**

    d. **prompt_vars**

7. Which of the following can be used in a playbook to activate a handler upon successful execution of a task?

   a. **notify**

   b. **alert**

   c. **handler**

   d. **call**

8. While working with handlers, different requirements apply. Which of the following is not one of them?

   a. If one task in the play fails, no handlers will run.

   b. Handlers will run only after all tasks in the play have been processed.

   c. Handlers will run only if the task results in an ok or a changed status.

   d. Handlers will run in the order specified in the handlers section.

9. Which of the following can be used to ensure that handlers will also run if any task finishes with an error?

   a. **force_handlers**

   b. **ignore_errors**

   c. **run_always**

   d. **ignore_all**

10. Which module should be used to generate a specific error message if a specific failure occurs?

   a. failed_when

   b. failed

   c. fail

   d. failure

Foundation Topics

Using Loops and Items

Some modules allow you to provide a list that needs to be processed. Many modules don't, and in these cases, it makes sense to use a loop mechanism to iterate over a list of items. Take, for instance, the yum module. While specifying the names of packages, you can use a list of packages. If, however, you want to do something similar for the service module, you find out that this is not possible. That is where loops come in. In this section you learn how to work with loops.

Working with Loops

To help you understand working with loops, Listing 7-1 shows a simple playbook that installs software packages using the yum module and then ensures that services installed from these packages are started using the service module.

Listing 7-1   Using **loop**

```
---
- name: install and start services
  hosts: ansible1
  tasks:
  - name: install packages
    yum:
      name:
      - vsftpd
      - httpd
      - samba
      state: latest
  - name: start the services
    service:
      name: "{{ item }}"
      state: started
      enabled: yes
    loop:
    - vsftpd
    - httpd
    - smb
```

In Listing 7-1, you can see that a loop is defined at the same level as the service module. The loop has a list of services in the list (array) statement that you have seen before. Items in the loop can be accessed by using the system internal variable item. At no place in the playbook is there a definition of the variable item; the loop takes care of defining it.

In Listing 7-1 you can also see that a different approach is used for the yum module. The name in the yum module does support a list by default, so in this case there is no further need to use **loop** and **item**.

When considering whether to use a loop, you should first investigate whether a module offers support for providing lists as values to the keys that are used. If this is the case, just provide a list, as all items in the list can be considered in one run of the module. If not, define the list using **loop** and provide "{{ item }}" as the value to the key. Notice that when using **loop**, the module is activated again on each iteration.

Using Loops on Variables

Although it's possible to define a loop within a task, it's not the most elegant way. To create a flexible environment where static code is separated from dynamic site-specific parameters, it's a much better idea to define loops outside the static code, in variables. When you define loops within a variable, all the normal rules for working with variables apply: The variables can be defined in the play header, using an include file, or as host/hostgroup variables. In Listing 7-2 you can see how the example from Listing 7-1 has been rewritten to include the loop from a variable.

Listing 7-2   Providing the Loop by a Variable

```
---
- name: install and start services
  hosts: ansible1
  vars:
    services:
    - vsftpd
    - httpd
    - smb
  tasks:
  - name: install packages
    yum:
      name:
      - vsftpd
      - httpd
      - samba
    state: latest
  - name: start the services
```

```
    service:
      name: "{{ item }}"
      state: started
      enabled: yes
    loop: "{{ services }}"
```

Using Loops on Multivalued Variables

An item can be a simple list, but it can also be presented as a multivalued variable, as long as the multivalued variable is presented as a list. Consider the sample playbook in Listing 7-4, which uses variables that are imported from the file vars/users-list shown in Listing 7-3.

Listing 7-3   Variables File

```
users:
  - username: linda
    homedir: /home/linda
    shell: /bin/bash
    groups: wheel
  - username: lisa
    homedir: /home/lisa
    shell: /bin/bash
    groups: users
  - username: anna
    homedir: /home/anna
    shell: /bin/bash
    groups: users
```

Listing 7-4   Using Multivalued Variables

```
---
- name: create users using a loop from a list
  hosts: ansible1
  vars_files: vars/users-list
  tasks:
  - name: create users
    user:
      name: "{{ item.username }}"
      state: present
      groups: "{{ item.groups }}"
      shell: "{{ item.shell }}"
    loop: "{{ users }}"
```

Working with multivalued variables is possible, but the variables in that case must be presented as a list; using dictionaries is not supported. The only way to loop over dictionaries is to use the dict2items filter. Use of filters is not included in the RHCE topics and for that reason is not explained further here. You can look up "Iterating over a dictionary" in the Ansible documentation for more information. Listing 7-5 shows the output of the command **ansible-playbook listing74.yaml**.

Listing 7-5   Working with Multivalued Variables Output

```
[ansible@control ~]$ ansible-playbook listing74.yaml

PLAY [create users using a loop from a list] ************************

TASK [Gathering Facts] *********************************************
ok: [ansible1]

TASK [create users] ***********************************************
changed: [ansible1] => (item={'username': 'linda', 'homedir': '/home/
linda', 'shell': '/bin/bash', 'groups': 'wheel'})
changed: [ansible1] => (item={'username': 'lisa', 'homedir': '/home/
lisa', 'shell': '/bin/bash', 'groups': 'users'})
changed: [ansible1] => (item={'username': 'anna', 'homedir': '/home/
anna', 'shell': '/bin/bash', 'groups': 'users'})

PLAY RECAP ********************************************************
ansible1                    : ok=2    changed=1    unreachable=0
failed=0    skipped=0    rescued=0    ignored=0
```

Understanding with_items

Since Ansible 2.5, using **loop** has been the way to iterate over the values in a list. In earlier versions of Ansible, the **with_*keyword*** statement was used instead. In this approach, the ***keyword*** is replaced with the name of an Ansible lookup plug-in, but the rest of the syntax is very common. Table 7-2 provides an overview of some of the most common options. Notice that the syntax was still supported at the time this book was written but will be deprecated in a future version of Ansible.

Table 7-2   with_*keyword* Options Overview

Keyword	Use
with_items	Used like **loop** to iterate over values in a list
with_file	Used to iterate over a list of filenames on the control node
with_sequence	Used to generate a list of values based on a numeric sequence

In Listing 7-6 you can see how the playbook from Listing 7-2 is rewritten to use **with_items**. Notice that it has only one change: **loop** has been changed to **with_items**.

Listing 7-6   Using **with_items**

```
---
- name: install and start services
  hosts: ansible1
  vars:
    services:
    - vsftpd
    - httpd
    - smb
  tasks:
  - name: install packages
    yum:
      name:
      - vsftpd
      - httpd
      - samba
      state: latest
  - name: start the services
    service:
      name: "{{ item }}"
      state: started
      enabled: yes
    with_items: "{{ services }}"
```

In Exercise 7-1 you practice working with **loop**.

Exercise 7-1   Working with loop

1. Use your editor to define a variables file with the name vars/packages and the following contents:

```
packages:
- name: httpd
  state: absent
- name: vsftpd
  state: installed
- name: mysql-server
  state: latest
```

2. Use your editor to define a playbook with the name exercise71.yaml and create the play header:

```
- name: manage packages using a loop from a list
  hosts: ansible1
  vars_files: vars/packages
  tasks:
```

3. Continue the playbook by adding the yum task that will manage the packages, using the **packages** variable as defined in the vars/packages variable include file:

```
- name: manage packages using a loop from a list
  hosts: ansible1
  vars_files: vars/packages
  tasks:
  - name: install packages
    yum:
      name: "{{ item.name }}"
      state: "{{ item.state }}"
    loop: "{{ packages }}"
```

4. Run the playbook using **ansible-playbook exercise71.yaml**, and observe the results. In the results you should see which packages it is trying to manage and in which state it is trying to get the packages.

Using when to Run Tasks Conditionally

In Ansible, you can use a **when** statement to run tasks conditionally. Multiple tests can be done using **when**; for instance, you can test whether a variable has a specific value, whether a file exists, whether a minimal amount of memory is available, and more.

Working with when

Let's get started with a simple playbook to explore the workings of **when**. In the sample playbook in Listing 7-7, you can see how a **when** statement is used to install the right software package for the Apache web server, based on the Linux distribution that was found in the Ansible facts. Notice that when used in **when** statements, the variable that is evaluated is not placed between double curly braces.

Listing 7-7   Using **when** for Conditional Software Installation

```
---
- name: conditional install
  hosts: all
  tasks:
  - name: install apache on Red Hat and family
    yum:
      name: httpd
      state: latest
    when: ansible_facts['os_family'] == "RedHat"
  - name: install apache on Ubuntu and family
    apt:
      name: apache2
      state: latest
    when: ansible_facts['os_family'] == "Debian"
```

Notice the use of **when**: Because it is not a part of any properties of the modules on which it is used, the **when** statement must be indented at the same level as the module itself. In the example in Listing 7-7, a string test is used to check whether the value of the Ansible fact **ansible_os_family** (which in the playbook is written as the equivalent **ansible_facts['os_family']**) is equal to the string RedHat. Because this is a string test, the string itself must be between double quotes. Without the double quotes, it would be considered an integer test. A string test is just one of the many conditional tests that can be executed. Table 7-3 provides an overview with some other examples of conditional tests.

Listing 7-8 shows the output of the playbook in Listing 7-7. Because no hosts use a Linux distribution from the Debian family, the second task reports a status of **skipped**.

Listing 7-8   Conditional Playbook Result

```
[ansible@control ~]$ ansible-playbook listing77.yaml

PLAY [conditional install] *******************************************

TASK [Gathering Facts] ***********************************************
ok: [ansible2]
ok: [ansible1]

TASK [install apache on Red Hat and family] *************************
ok: [ansible1]
changed: [ansible2]
```

```
TASK [install apache on Ubuntu and family] ***************************
skipping: [ansible1]
skipping: [ansible2]


PLAY RECAP ***********************************************************
ansible1                    : ok=2    changed=0    unreachable=0
failed=0       skipped=1    rescued=0    ignored=0
ansible2                    : ok=2    changed=1    unreachable=0
failed=0       skipped=1    rescued=0    ignored=0
```

Using Conditional Test Statements

When working with **when**, you use conditional test statements. In the example in Listing 7-7 you saw a string test, but many other tests are also available. Table 7-3 gives an overview of some common conditional tests that you can perform with the **when** statement.

Table 7-3   Conditional Tests Overview

Conditional Test	Example
Variable exists	variable is defined
Variable does not exist	variable is not defined
First variable is present in list mentioned as second	ansible_distribution in distributions
Variable is true, 1 or yes	variable
Variable is false, 0 or no	not variable
Equal (string)	key == "value"
Equal (numeric)	key == value
Less than	key < value
Less than or equal to	key <= value
Greater than	key > value
Greater than or equal to	key >= value
Not equal to	key != value

EXAM TIP   Conditional tests are important, but you won't find a nice table like Table 7-3 in the Ansible documentation. Look for "Tests" in the Ansible documentation, and use the item that is found in Templating (Jinja2). This section contains useful examples that might help you during the exam.

When referring to variables in **when** statements, you don't have to use curly brackets because items in a **when** statement are considered to be variables by default. So you can write **when: text == "hello"** instead of **when: "{{ text }}" == "hello"**.

As you can see in Table 7-3, there are roughly four types of **when** conditional tests:

- Checks related to variable existence

- Boolean checks

- String comparisons

- Integer comparisons

The first type of test checks whether a variable exists or is a part of another variable, such as a list. This is a useful test to figure out if, for instance, a specific Ansible fact has been set. An example is shown in Listing 7-9 where the sample playbook checks for the existence of a specific disk device, using **variable is defined** and **variable is not defined**. When you run this playbook, you'll notice that all failing tests result in the message "skipping."

Listing 7-9   Using **when** to Check Whether a Variable Exists

```
---
- name: check for existence of devices
  hosts: all
  tasks:
  - name: check if /dev/sda exists
    debug:
       msg: a disk device /dev/sda exists
    when: ansible_facts['devices']['sda'] is defined
  - name: check if /dev/sdb exists
    debug:
       msg: a disk device /dev/sdb exists
    when: ansible_facts['devices']['sdb'] is defined
  - name: dummy test, intended to fail
    debug:
       msg: failing
    when: dummy is defined
  - name: check if /dev/sdc does not exist
    debug:
       msg: there is no /dev/sdc device
    when: ansible_facts['devices']['sdc'] is not defined
```

Closely related to the **is defined** check is the check that finds whether the first variable value is present in the second variable's list. This scenario is demonstrated in Listing 7-10, which executes the **debug** task if the variable **my_answer** is in **supported_packages**. Notice that in this listing **vars_prompt** is used. This stops the playbook, asks the user for input, and stores the input in a variable with the name my_answer.

Listing 7-10   Checking Whether a Variable Occurs in a List

```
---
- name: test if variable is in another variables list
  hosts: all
  vars_prompt:
  - name: my_answer
    prompt: which package do you want to install
  vars:
    supported_packages:
    - httpd
    - nginx
  tasks:
  - name: something
    debug:
      msg: you are trying to install a supported package
    when: my_answer in supported_packages
```

The next type of check is the Boolean check. This check works on variables that have a Boolean value, but these variables are not very common. The most important thing to know about this type of check is that it should not be defined with the check for existence. Boolean checks are used to check the Boolean value of a variable; **is defined** is used to check whether a variable is defined.

The last types of checks are string comparisons and integer comparisons. You already saw a string test in Listing 7-7. In an integer comparison, you check whether a variable has a specific value. You can, for instance, check if more than 1 GB of disk space is available. When doing checks on available disk space and available memory, carefully look at the expected value. Memory is shown in megabytes, by default, whereas disk space is expressed in bytes. Listing 7-11 shows an example that will install vsftpd if more than 50 MB of memory is available.

Listing 7-11   Using an Integer Check

```
---
- name: conditionals test
  hosts: all
  tasks:
  - name: install vsftpd if sufficient memory available
    package:
      name: vsftpd
      state: latest
    when: ansible_facts['memory_mb']['real']['free'] > 50
```

Testing Multiple Conditions

Apart from doing single evaluations, **when** statements can also be used to evaluate multiple conditions. To do so, you can group the conditions with parentheses and combine them with **and** and **or** keywords. Listing 7-12 shows an example where **and** is used and that runs the task only if both conditions are true. Alternatively, consider using **or** to allow a task to run if one of the conditions is true.

Listing 7-12   Combining Multiple Conditions

```
---
- name: testing multiple conditions
  hosts: all
  tasks:
  - name: showing output
    debug:
      msg: using CentOS 8.1
    when: ansible_facts['distribution_version'] == "8.1" and ansible_
facts['distribution'] == "CentOS"
```

Apart from the simple **and** statement in Listing 7-12, you can make more complex statements by grouping conditions together in parentheses. Listing 7-13 shows an example. Note that in this example the **when** statement starts with a > sign because the statement is wrapped over the next five lines for readability. The > sign makes sure that all the values provided to the **when** statement are interpreted as one line and not as five.

Listing 7-13 Combining Complex Statements

```
---
- name: using multiple conditions
  hosts: all
  tasks:
  - package:
      name: httpd
      state: removed
    when: >
      ( ansible_facts['distribution'] == "RedHat" and
        ansible_facts['memfree_mb'] < 512 )
      or
      ( ansible_facts['distribution'] == "CentOS" and
        ansible_facts['memfree_mb'] < 256 )
```

Combining loop and when

Although you use **when** to execute a task only if a specific condition is true, you can use **loop** to iterate over a list of items. To unleash the full power of Ansible play-books, you can use a combination. The playbook in Listing 7-14 performs a kernel update only if /boot is on a dedicated mount point and at least 200 MB is available in the mount.

Listing 7-14 Combining **loop** and **when**

```
---
- name: conditionals test
  hosts: all
  tasks:
  - name: update the kernel if sufficient space is available in /boot
    package:
      name: kernel
      state: latest
    loop: "{{ ansible_facts['mounts'] }}"
    when: item.mount == "/boot" and item.size_available > 200000000
```

Because the sample playbook from Listing 7-14 loops over all the mounts that were found, it's interesting to observe its output. In Listing 7-15 you can see how the task first skips the / mount and next performs the task on the /boot mount as it meets the conditions. Later in Exercise 7-2 you practice working with **when**.

Listing 7-15   Listing 7-14 Task Result

```
[ansible@control ~]$ ansible-playbook listing714.yaml


PLAY [conditionals test] ***********************************************
*******************

TASK [Gathering Facts] *************************************************
*******************
ok: [ansible2]
ok: [ansible1]


TASK [update kernel if sufficient space in /boot] *********************
*******************
skipping: [ansible1] => (item={'mount': '/', 'device': '/dev/
mapper/cl-root', 'fstype': 'xfs', 'options': 'rw,seclabel,rela
time,attr2,inode64,noquota', 'size_total': 18238930944, 'size_
available': 13722013696, 'block_size': 4096, 'block_total': 4452864,
'block_available': 3350101, 'block_used': 1102763, 'inode_total':
8910848, 'inode_available': 8790863, 'inode_used': 119985, 'uuid':
'ef0bb39c-5a29-4c0a-9152-7dd3fd5254c2'})
skipping: [ansible2] => (item={'mount': '/', 'device': '/dev/
mapper/cl-root', 'fstype': 'xfs', 'options': 'rw,seclabel,rela
time,attr2,inode64,noquota', 'size_total': 18238930944, 'size_
available': 16635084800, 'block_size': 4096, 'block_total': 4452864,
'block_available': 4061300, 'block_used': 391564, 'inode_total':
8910848, 'inode_available': 8877221, 'inode_used': 33627, 'uuid':
'acdeb1af-c439-4030-b9ba-c21d4d4fb0a8'})
changed: [ansible2] => (item={'mount': '/boot', 'device': '/dev/
sda1', 'fstype': 'ext4', 'options': 'rw,seclabel,relatime', 'size_
total': 1023303680, 'size_available': 811139072, 'block_size': 4096,
'block_total': 249830, 'block_available': 198032, 'block_used': 51798,
'inode_total': 65536, 'inode_available': 65227, 'inode_used': 309,
'uuid': 'cc870ab6-1e0e-4d27-9df3-9e5961d9fa62'})
changed: [ansible1] => (item={'mount': '/boot', 'device': '/dev/
sda1', 'fstype': 'ext4', 'options': 'rw,seclabel,relatime', 'size_
total': 1023303680, 'size_available': 803180544, 'block_size': 4096,
'block_total': 249830, 'block_available': 196089, 'block_used': 53741,
'inode_total': 65536, 'inode_available': 65227, 'inode_used': 309,
'uuid': '7acd65d6-115f-499f-a02f-90364a18b9fc'})


PLAY RECAP ************************************************************
*******************
ansible1                   : ok=2    changed=1    unreachable=0
failed=0    skipped=0    rescued=0    ignored=0
ansible2                   : ok=2    changed=1    unreachable=0
failed=0    skipped=0    rescued=0    ignored=0
```

Combining loop and register

In Chapter 6, "Working with Variables and Facts," you learned that the results of a command can be stored in a variable when you use **register**. Using **register**, you store the result of a command in a multivalued variable, and based on this result, another conditional task can run. In the example in Listing 7-16, you can see how this statement is used in a playbook.

Listing 7-16 Combining **register** and **loop**

```
---
- name: test register
  hosts: all
  tasks:
    - shell: cat /etc/passwd
      register: passwd_contents
    - debug:
        msg: passwd contains user lisa
      when: passwd_contents.stdout.find('lisa') != -1
```

You might notice that in this playbook, the **when** statement makes use of some particular items that we haven't seen before. To start with, it refers to **passwd_contents.stdout.find**, but **passwd_contents.stdout** does not contain any item with the name **find**. The construction that is used here is **variable.find**, which enables a task to search a specific string in a variable. To do so, the **find** function in Python is used—after all, Ansible is written in Python. When the Python **find** function does not find a string, it returns a value of –1. If the requested string is found, the **find** function returns an integer that returns the position where the string was found. For instance, if the string lisa is found in /etc/passwd, it returns an unexpected value like 2604, which is the position in the file, expressed as a byte offset from the beginning, where the string is found for the first time.

Because of the behavior of the Python **find** function, **variable.find** needs *not* to be equal to –1 to have the task succeed. So don't write **passwd_contents.stdout. find('lisa') = 0** (because it is not a Boolean), but instead write **passwd_contents. stdout.find('lisa') != -1**. In Exercise 7-2 you practice working with conditionals using **register**.

Note that when using **register**, you might want to define a task that runs a command that will fail, just to capture the return code of that command, after which the playbook should continue. If that is the case, you must ensure that **ignore_errors: yes** is used in the task definition. The default behavior is that if a task fails, execution of the playbook is aborted, and no other tasks run.

Exercise 7-2   Using when

1. Use your editor to create a new file with the name exercise72.yaml. Start writing the play header as follows:

    ```
    ---

    - name: restart sshd service if httpd is running
      hosts: ansible1
      tasks:
    ```

2. Add the first task, which checks whether the httpd service is running, using command output that will be registered. Notice the use of **ignore_errors: yes**. This line makes sure that if the service is *not* running, the play is still executed further.

    ```
    ---

    - name: restart sshd service if httpd is running
      hosts: ansible1
      tasks:
      - name: get httpd service status
        command: systemctl is-active httpd
        ignore_errors: yes
        register: result
    ```

3. Add a debug task that shows the output of the command so that you can analyze what is currently in the registered variable:

    ```
    ---

    - name: restart sshd service if httpd is running
      hosts: ansible1
      tasks:
      - name: get httpd service status
        command: systemctl is-active httpd
        ignore_errors: yes
        register: result
      - name: show result variable contents
        debug:
           msg: printing contents of the registered variable
    {{ result }}
    ```

4. Complete the playbook by including the **service** task, which is started only if the value stored in **result.rc** (which is the return code of the command that was registered) contains a 0. This is the case if the previous command executed successfully.

    ```
    ---

    - name: restart sshd service if httpd is running
      hosts: ansible1
    ```

```
    tasks:
    - name: get httpd service status
      command: systemctl is-active httpd
      ignore_errors: yes
      register: result
    - name: show result variable contents
      debug:
        msg: printing contents of the registered variable
{{ result }}
    - name: restart sshd service
      service:
        name: sshd
        state: restarted
      when: result.rc == 0
```

5. Use an ad hoc command to make sure the httpd service is installed: **ansible ansible1 -m yum -a "name=httpd state=latest"**.

6. Use an ad hoc command to make sure the httpd service is stopped: **ansible ansible1 -m service -a "name=httpd state=stopped"**.

7. Run the playbook using **ansible-playbook exercise72.yaml** and analyze the result. You should see that the playbook skips the **service** task.

8. Type **ansible ansible1 -m service -a "name=httpd state=started"** and run the playbook again, using **ansible-playbook exercise72.yaml**. Playbook execution at this point should be successful.

Using Handlers

Playbooks contain lists of tasks. Tasks are always executed in order, and if one task fails, none of the following tasks are executed. In some cases, you might need to manage execution dependencies in a more specific way. That is when handlers can come in handy. A handler is a conditional task that is triggered and is executed by a successful task.

Working with Handlers

To work with handlers, you should define a **notify** statement at the level where the task is defined. The **notify** statement should list the name of the handler that is to be executed, and the handlers are listed at the end of the play. Make sure the name of the handler matches the name of the item that is called in the **notify** statement, because that is what the handler is looking for.

The playbook in Listing 7-17 shows how to work with handlers. It is a multiplay playbook, where the first play is used to define the file index.html on localhost. Next, this file is used in the second play to set up the web server.

The handler is triggered from the task where the copy module is used to copy the index.html file. If this task is successful, the **notify** statement calls the handler. Notice that handlers can be specified as a list, so one task can call multiple handlers. Also notice that in Listing 7-17 a second task is defined, which is intended to fail.

Listing 7-17 Working with Handlers

```
---
- name: create file on localhost
  hosts: localhost
  tasks:
  - name: create index.html on localhost
    copy:
      content: "welcome to the webserver"
      dest: /tmp/index.html

- name: set up web server
  hosts: all
  tasks:
    - name: install httpd
      yum:
        name: httpd
        state: latest
    - name: copy index.html
      copy:
        src: /tmp/index.html
        dest: /var/www/html/index.html
      notify:
        - restart_web
    - name: copy nothing - intended to fail
      copy:
        src: /tmp/nothing
        dest: /var/www/html/nothing.html
  handlers:
    - name: restart_web
      service:
        name: httpd
        state: restarted
```

Listing 7-18 shows the result of the command **ansible-playbook listing717.yaml**.

Listing 7-18   ansible-playbook listing717.yaml Command Result

```
[ansible@control ~]$ ansible-playbook listing717.yaml

PLAY [create file on localhost] ***************************************

TASK [Gathering Facts] ***********************************************
ok: [localhost]

TASK [create index.html on localhost] *******************************
changed: [localhost]

PLAY [set up web server] *********************************************

TASK [Gathering Facts] ***********************************************
ok: [ansible2]
ok: [ansible1]

TASK [install httpd] ************************************************
changed: [ansible2]
changed: [ansible1]

TASK [copy index.html] *********************************************
changed: [ansible2]
changed: [ansible1]

TASK [copy nothing - intended to fail] ******************************
An exception occurred during task execution. To see the full
traceback, use -vvv. The error was: If you are using a module and
expect the file to exist on the remote, see the remote_src option
fatal: [ansible2]: FAILED! => {"changed": false, "msg": "Could not
find or access '/tmp/nothing' on the Ansible Controller.\nIf you are
using a module and expect the file to exist on the remote, see the
remote_src option"}
An exception occurred during task execution. To see the full
traceback, use -vvv. The error was: If you are using a module and
expect the file to exist on the remote, see the remote_src option
fatal: [ansible1]: FAILED! => {"changed": false, "msg": "Could not
find or access '/tmp/nothing' on the Ansible Controller.\nIf you are
using a module and expect the file to exist on the remote, see the
remote_src option"}
```

```
RUNNING HANDLER [restart_web] ************************************

PLAY RECAP ********************************************************
ansible1                    : ok=3      changed=2     unreachable=0
failed=1      skipped=0     rescued=0    ignored=0
ansible2                    : ok=3      changed=2     unreachable=0
failed=1      skipped=0     rescued=0    ignored=0
localhost                   : ok=2      changed=1     unreachable=0
failed=0      skipped=0     rescued=0    ignored=0
```

As you can see in the command result in Listing 7-18, all tasks up to **copy index.html** run successfully. However, the task **copy nothing** fails, which is why the handler does not run. The solution seems easy: the handler doesn't run because the task that copies the file /tmp/nothing fails as the source file doesn't exist. So the solution seems simple: create the source file using **touch /tmp/nothing** on the control host and run the task again. Listing 7-19 shows the result of this approach.

Listing 7-19   Running **playbook listing717.yaml** Again

```
[ansible@control ~]$ ansible-playbook listing717.yaml

PLAY [create file on localhost] *********************************

TASK [Gathering Facts] **********************************************
ok: [localhost]

TASK [create index.html on localhost] *******************************
ok: [localhost]

PLAY [set up web server] ********************************************

TASK [Gathering Facts] **********************************************
ok: [ansible2]
ok: [ansible1]

TASK [install httpd] ***********************************************
ok: [ansible2]
ok: [ansible1]

TASK [copy index.html] *********************************************
ok: [ansible2]
ok: [ansible1]
```

```
TASK [copy nothing - intended to fail] ******************************
changed: [ansible2]
changed: [ansible1]


PLAY RECAP ***********************************************************
ansible1                    : ok=4    changed=1    unreachable=0
failed=0    skipped=0    rescued=0    ignored=0
ansible2                    : ok=4    changed=1    unreachable=0
failed=0    skipped=0    rescued=0    ignored=0
localhost                   : ok=2    changed=0    unreachable=0
failed=0    skipped=0    rescued=0    ignored=0
```

As you can see, despite what you might have expected, after creating the source file and running the playbook again, the handler still doesn't run. The reason is that handlers run only if the task that triggers them gives a **changed** status, and that doesn't happen in Listing 7-19 because the task that triggers the handler executed successfully while running the playbook in Listing 7-18. To see the handler being triggered successfully, you must run an ad hoc command to remove the /var/www/html/index.html file on the managed hosts and run the playbook again. Listing 7-20 shows the result.

Listing 7-20   Successfully Running Listing 7-17

```
[ansible@control ~]$ ansible ansible2 -m file -a "name=/var/www/html/
index.html state=absent"
ansible2 | CHANGED => {
    "ansible_facts": {
        "discovered_interpreter_python": "/usr/libexec/
platform-python"
    },
    "changed": true,
    "path": "/var/www/html/index.html",
    "state": "absent"
}
[ansible@control ~]$ ansible-playbook listing717.yaml

PLAY [create file on localhost] *************************************

TASK [Gathering Facts] *********************************************
ok: [localhost]

TASK [create index.html on localhost] ******************************
ok: [localhost]

PLAY [set up web server] *******************************************
```

```
TASK [Gathering Facts] ********************************************
ok: [ansible2]
ok: [ansible1]

TASK [install httpd] **********************************************
ok: [ansible2]
ok: [ansible1]

TASK [copy index.html] ********************************************
changed: [ansible2]
ok: [ansible1]

TASK [copy nothing - intended to fail] ***************************
ok: [ansible2]
ok: [ansible1]

RUNNING HANDLER [restart_web] ************************************
changed: [ansible2]

PLAY RECAP *******************************************************
ansible1                   : ok=4      changed=0     unreachable=0
failed=0     skipped=0     rescued=0    ignored=0
ansible2                   : ok=5      changed=2     unreachable=0
failed=0     skipped=0     rescued=0    ignored=0
localhost                  : ok=2      changed=0     unreachable=0
failed=0     skipped=0     rescued=0    ignored=0
```

Understanding Handler Execution and Exceptions

When a task fails, none of the following tasks run. How does that make handlers different? A handler runs only on the success of a task, but the next task in the list also runs only if the previous task was successful. What, then, is so special about handlers?

The difference is in the nature of the handler. Handlers are meant to perform an extra action when a task makes a change to a host. So in the design of the playbook, handlers should be considered an extension to the regular task. They are a conditional task that runs only upon the success of a previous task.

If a handler is triggered and a task that is later in the play fails, the handler will not be executed on the node where the subsequent task has failed. There are two solutions to prevent this. To start with, you can use **force_handlers: true** in the play header to ensure that the handler will run anyway. You also can use the more generic

ignore_errors: true statement in the play header to accomplish the same thing. Because **force_handlers: true** is more specific, using that option is preferred if you just need to make sure that your handlers will run. In Exercise 7-3 you can practice how this works.

When you work with handlers, there are a few specifics to be aware of:

- Handlers are specified in a handlers section at the end of the play.

- Handlers run in the order they occur in the handlers section and not in the order as triggered.

- Handlers run only if the task calling them generates a changed status.

- Handlers by default will not run if any task in the same play fails, unless **force_handlers** or **ignore_errors** is used.

- Handlers run only after *all* tasks in the play where the handler is activated have been processed. You might want to define multiple plays to avoid this behavior.

Exercise 7-3   Working with Handlers

1. Open a playbook with the name exercise73.yaml.

2. Define the play header:

```
---
- name: update the kernel
  hosts: all
  force_handlers: true
  tasks:
```

3. Add a task that updates the current kernel:

```
---
- name: update the kernel
  hosts: all
  force_handlers: true
  tasks:
  - name: update kernel
    yum:
      name: kernel
      state: latest
    notify: reboot_server
```

4. Add a handler that reboots the server in case the kernel was successfully updated:

```
---
- name: update the kernel
  hosts: all
```

```
        force_handlers: true
        tasks:
        - name: update kernel
          yum:
            name: kernel
            state: latest
          notify: reboot_server
        handlers:
        - name: reboot_server
          command: reboot
```

5. Run the playbook using **ansible-playbook exercise73.yaml** and observe its result. You will get a failure on the handlers, as it has rebooted the managed node, and for that reason the command cannot send back its success status. Notice that the handler runs only if the kernel was updated. If the kernel already was at the latest version, nothing has changed and the handler does not run. Also notice that it wasn't really necessary to use **force_handlers** in the play header, but by using it anyway, at least you now know where to use it.

Dealing with Failures

When working with playbooks, you can get unexpected results. To deal with these situations, you need to understand normal playbook operations. Based on your understanding of the expected result, you can handle a situation if something doesn't go as expected.

Understanding Task Execution

Tasks in Ansible playbooks are executed in the order they are specified. If a task in the playbook fails to execute on a host, the task generates an error and the play does not further execute on that specific host. This also goes for handlers: if any task that follows the task that triggers a handler fails, the handlers do not run. In both of these cases, it is important to know that the tasks that have run successfully still generate their result. Because this can give an unexpected result, it is important to always restore the original situation if that happens.

In some cases you might want the entire playbook to stop executing on all hosts when a failing task is encountered. If that is the case, you can use **any_errors_fatal** in the play header or on a block (blocks are explained later in this chapter).

Managing Task Errors

Generically, tasks can generate three different types of results. Table 7-4 gives an overview.

Table 7-4 Tasks Result Overview

Result	Explanation
ok	The task has run successfully but no changes were applied.
changed	The task has run successfully and changes have been applied.
failed	While running the task, a failure condition was encountered.

As you saw before, if a task fails, all execution stops. This outcome can be prevented by using **ignore_errors** and **force_handlers**. If you specify **ignore_errors: yes** in a task, the playbook continues, even after processing the failing task. Likewise, **force_handlers** can be used to ensure that handlers will be executed, even if a failing task was encountered. Listing 7-21 shows an example of a playbook that uses **ignore_errors**.

Listing 7-21   Example with **ignore_errors**

```
---
- name: restart sshd only if crond is running
  hosts: all
  tasks:
    - name: get the crond server status
      command: /usr/bin/systemctl is-active crond
      ignore_errors: yes
      register: result
    - name: restart sshd based on crond status
      service:
        name: sshd
        state: restarted
      when: result.rc == 0
```

The essence of the playbook in Listing 7-21 is that the sshd service needs to be restarted, based on the result of the current status of the crond service. To find the current status of the crond service, you use the command **systemctl is-active crond**, and the result of that command is registered. To allow the playbook to continue, even if the service currently is not running, you include **ignore_errors: yes** in the task definition. This allows the result of the command module to be recorded using **register**. Next, the sshd service is restarted based on the value of the registered command result.

In Listing 7-17 you learned how to work with handlers. Also in this playbook, you saw how the handlers aren't triggered if any task in the play will fail. You can easily fix this issue by including **force_handlers** in the play header. Listing 7-22 shows the modified playbook where this approach is applied.

Listing 7-22   Forcing Handlers to Run

```
---
- name: create file on localhost
  hosts: localhost
  tasks:
  - name: create index.html on localhost
    copy:
      content: "welcome to the webserver"
      dest: /tmp/index.html

- name: set up web server
  hosts: all
  force_handlers: yes
  tasks:
    - name: install httpd
      yum:
        name: httpd
        state: latest
    - name: copy index.html
      copy:
        src: /tmp/index.html
        dest: /var/www/html/index.html
      notify:
        - restart_web
    - name: copy nothing - intended to fail
      copy:
        src: /tmp/nothing
        dest: /var/www/html/nothing.html
  handlers:
    - name: restart_web
      service:
        name: httpd
        state: restarted
```

As you can see, regardless of the fact that the **copy nothing** task fails, the handler is executed anyway because of the use of **force_handlers**.

Specifying Task Failure Conditions

If a task successfully runs a command, according to Ansible it has run successfully, even if the command output itself indicates a failure. In that case it makes sense to set a failure condition anyway. You can do so by using the **failed_when** conditional. Notice that **failed_when** is a true conditional, so it must be used to evaluate some expression. Listing 7-23 shows a sample script where this conditional is demonstrated.

Listing 7-23   Using **failed_when**

```
---
- name: demonstrating failed_when
  hosts: all
  tasks:
  - name: run a script
    command: echo hello world
    ignore_errors: yes
    register: command_result
    failed_when: "'world' in command_result.stdout"
  - name: see if we get here
    debug:
      msg: second task executed
```

In Listing 7-23, the command module is used to run a simple command. As it runs the **echo** command, the command itself would be considered successful. However, **register** is used to capture command output, and **failed_when** is used to define the command as failed when the text "world" occurs in the stdout of the command. That means the command generates a failed status in all cases. At the same time, the **ignore_errors: yes** statement enables the task to fail, after which the playbook still continues. As a result, after showing the failure on the first task, the second task does get executed, as you can see in Listing 7-24.

Listing 7-24   Result of Running **ansible-playbook listing723.yaml**

```
[ansible@control ~]$ ansible-playbook listing723.yaml

PLAY [demonstrating failed_when] ************************************

TASK [Gathering Facts] *********************************************
ok: [ansible1]
ok: [ansible2]

TASK [run a script] ***********************************************
fatal: [ansible2]: FAILED! => {"changed": true, "cmd": ["echo",
"hello", "world"], "delta": "0:00:00.004303", "end": "2020-04-06
03:44:56.748552", "failed_when_result": true, "rc": 0, "start": "2020-
04-06 03:44:56.744249", "stderr": "", "stderr_lines": [], "stdout":
"hello world", "stdout_lines": ["hello world"]}
...ignoring
```

```
fatal: [ansible1]: FAILED! => {"changed": true, "cmd": ["echo",
"hello", "world"], "delta": "0:00:00.004261", "end": "2020-04-06
03:44:56.770166", "failed_when_result": true, "rc": 0, "start": "2020-
04-06 03:44:56.765905", "stderr": "", "stderr_lines": [], "stdout":
"hello world", "stdout_lines": ["hello world"]}
...ignoring

TASK [see if we get here] ********************************************
ok: [ansible1] => {
    "msg": "second task executed"
}
ok: [ansible2] => {
    "msg": "second task executed"
}

PLAY RECAP **********************************************************
ansible1                   : ok=3    changed=1   unreachable=0
failed=0    skipped=0    rescued=0    ignored=1
ansible2                   : ok=3    changed=1   unreachable=0
failed=0    skipped=0    rescued=0    ignored=1
```

Alternatively, you can use the fail module to specify when a task fails. Using this module makes sense only if **when** is used to define the exact condition when a failure should occur. Listing 7-25 shows how the playbook from Listing 7-23 can be rewritten using the fail module.

Listing 7-25   Using the fail Module

```
---
- name: demonstrating the fail module
  hosts: all
  ignore_errors: yes
  tasks:
  - name: run a script
    command: echo hello world
    register: command_result
  - name: report a failure
    fail:
      msg: the command has failed
    when: "'world' in command_result.stdout"
  - name: see if we get here
    debug:
      msg: second task executed
```

Notice that in the rewritten playbook in Listing 7-25, the **ignore_errors** statement has moved from the task definition to the play header. Without this move, the message "second task executed" would never be shown because the fail module always generates a failure message. The main advantage of using the fail module instead of using **failed_when** is that the fail module can easily be used to set a clear failure message, which is not possible when using **failed_when**.

Managing Changed Status

In Ansible, there are commands that change something and commands that don't. Some commands, however, are not very obvious in reporting their status. Run the playbook in Listing 7-26, for example.

Listing 7-26   Sample Playbook Contents

```
---
- name: demonstrate changed status
  hosts: all
  tasks:
  - name: check local time
    command: date
    register: command_result

  - name: print local time
    debug:
        var: command_result.stdout
```

As you can see in Listing 7-27, this playbook reports a changed status, even if nothing really was changed!

Listing 7-27   Result of Running **ansible-playbook listing726.yaml**

```
[ansible@control ~]$ ansible-playbook listing726.yaml

PLAY [demonstrate changed status] *********************************

TASK [Gathering Facts] ********************************************
ok: [ansible2]
ok: [ansible1]

TASK [check local time] *******************************************
changed: [ansible2]
changed: [ansible1]
```

```
TASK [print local time] ************************************************
ok: [ansible1] => {
    "command_result.stdout": "Mon Apr  6 04:11:26 EDT 2020"
}
ok: [ansible2] => {
    "command_result.stdout": "Mon Apr  6 04:11:26 EDT 2020"
}

PLAY RECAP ************************************************************
ansible1                    : ok=3    changed=1    unreachable=0
failed=0      skipped=0    rescued=0    ignored=0
ansible2                    : ok=3    changed=1    unreachable=0
failed=0      skipped=0    rescued=0    ignored=0
```

In some cases, managing the changed status can be useful in avoiding unexpected results while running a playbook. Listing 7-28 shows how the sample playbook from Listing 7-26 can be changed accordingly, using **changed_when**, and Listing 7-29 shows the result of running the playbook in Listing 7-28. If you set **changed_when** to false, the playbook reports only an ok or failed status and never reports a changed status.

Listing 7-28   Using **changed_when**

```
---
- name: demonstrate changed status
  hosts: all
  tasks:
  - name: check local time
    command: date
    register: command_result
    changed_when: false

  - name: print local time
    debug:
      var: command_result.stdout
```

Listing 7-29   Result of Running **ansible-playbook listing728.yaml**

```
[ansible@control ~]$ ansible-playbook listing728.yaml


PLAY [demonstrate changed status] ***********************************


TASK [Gathering Facts] **********************************************
ok: [ansible2]
ok: [ansible1]


TASK [check local time] *********************************************
ok: [ansible2]
ok: [ansible1]


TASK [print local time] *********************************************
ok: [ansible1] => {
    "command_result.stdout": "Mon Apr  6 04:15:26 EDT 2020"
}
ok: [ansible2] => {
    "command_result.stdout": "Mon Apr  6 04:15:26 EDT 2020"
}


PLAY RECAP **********************************************************
ansible1                   : ok=3    changed=0    unreachable=0
failed=0    skipped=0    rescued=0    ignored=0
ansible2                   : ok=3    changed=0    unreachable=0
failed=0    skipped=0    rescued=0    ignored=0
```

Using Blocks

When you are working with conditional statements, blocks can be very useful. A
block is a group of tasks to which a **when** statement can be applied. As a result, if a
single condition is true, multiple tasks can be executed. To do so, between the **tasks:**
statement in the play header and the actual tasks that run the specific modules, you
can insert a **block:** statement. Listing 7-30 shows an example.

Listing 7-30   Using Blocks

```
- name: simple block example
  hosts: all
  tasks:
  - name: setting up http
    block:
    - name: installing http
       yum:
          name: httpd
          state: present
     - name: restart httpd
       service:
          name: httpd
          state: started
    when: ansible_distribution == "CentOS"
```

To understand the sample playbook in Listing 7-30, notice that the **when** statement is applied at the same level as the **block** definition. When you define it this way, the tasks in the block are executed only if the **when** statement is true.

Using Blocks with rescue and always Statements

Listing 7-30 shows how a block is used to group different tasks together. Blocks can be used for simple error handling as well, in such a way that if any task that is defined in the **block** statement fails, the tasks that are defined in the **rescue** section are executed. Besides that, an **always** section can be used to define tasks that should always run, regardless of the success or failure of the tasks in the block. Listing 7-31 shows an example.

EXAM TIP   On the RHCE exam, you definitely need to work out a playbook that handles complex conditional statements. Make sure you fully understand how to use blocks, because they provide an excellent way to do this.

Listing 7-31   Using Blocks, **rescue**, and **always**

```
---
- name: using blocks
  hosts: all
  tasks:
  - name: intended to be successful
    block:
    - name: remove a file
      shell:
        cmd: rm /var/www/html/index.html
    - name: printing status
      debug:
      msg: block task was operated
    rescue:
    - name: create a file
      shell:
        cmd: touch /tmp/rescuefile
    - name: printing rescue status
      debug:
        msg: rescue task was operated
    always:
    - name: always write a message to logs
      shell:
        cmd: logger hello
    - name: always printing this message
      debug:
        msg: this message is always printed
```

In Listing 7-32 you can see the output of the command **ansible-playbook listing731.yaml**.

Listing 7-32   Output of Command **ansible-playbook listing731.yaml**

```
[ansible@control ~]$ ansible-playbook listing731.yaml

PLAY [using blocks] ********************************************************

TASK [Gathering Facts] ****************************************************
ok: [ansible2]
ok: [ansible1]

TASK [remove a file] ******************************************************
*******************
[WARNING]: Consider using the file module with state=absent rather
than running 'rm'. If you need to use command because file is
insufficient you can add 'warn: false' to this command task or set
'command_warnings=False' in ansible.cfg to get rid of this message.
changed: [ansible2]
changed: [ansible1]
TASK [printing status] ****************************************************
ok: [ansible1] => {
    "msg": "block task was operated"
}
ok: [ansible2] => {
    "msg": "block task was operated"
}


TASK [always write a message to logs] *************************************
changed: [ansible2]
changed: [ansible1]


TASK [always printing this message] **************************************
ok: [ansible1] => {
    "msg": "this message is always printed"
}
ok: [ansible2] => {
    "msg": "this message is always printed"
}


PLAY RECAP ****************************************************************
ansible1                    : ok=5     changed=2     unreachable=0
failed=0      skipped=0      rescued=0      ignored=0
ansible2                    : ok=5     changed=2     unreachable=0
failed=0      skipped=0      rescued=0      ignored=0
```

As you can see in the output in Listing 7-32, the tasks in the **block** were successfully executed, and for that reason, the tasks in the **rescue** section were all skipped, and the tasks in the **always** section were also executed successfully. As a result of the code in this specific playbook, the next time that the same playbook is used, it will not be able to run the tasks in the **block** statement (as the file was already removed in the previous run) and, for that reason, run the tasks in the **rescue** statement as well as the tasks in **always**. You can see this in the output in Listing 7-33.

Listing 7-33   Tasks in **rescue** Are Executed If Tasks in **block** Are Failing

```
[ansible@control ~]$ ansible-playbook listing731.yaml


PLAY [using blocks] *******************************************
***

TASK [Gathering Facts] ****************************************
***
ok: [ansible2]
ok: [ansible1]


TASK [remove a file] ******************************************
***
[WARNING]: Consider using the file module with state=absent rather
than running 'rm'. If you need to use command because file is
insufficient you can add 'warn: false' to this command task or set
'command_warnings=False' in ansible.cfg to get rid of this message.
fatal: [ansible2]: FAILED! => {"changed": true, "cmd": "rm /var/
www/html/index.html", "delta": "0:00:00.003018", "end": "2020-04-06
05:16:29.810703", "msg": "non-zero return code", "rc": 1, "start":
"2020-04-06 05:16:29.807685", "stderr": "rm: cannot remove '/var/www/
html/index.html': No such file or directory", "stderr_lines": ["rm:
cannot remove '/var/www/html/index.html': No such file or directory"],
"stdout": "", "stdout_lines": []}
fatal: [ansible1]: FAILED! => {"changed": true, "cmd": "rm /var/
www/html/index.html", "delta": "0:00:00.012466", "end": "2020-04-06
05:16:29.836735", "msg": "non-zero return code", "rc": 1, "start":
"2020-04-06 05:16:29.824269", "stderr": "rm: cannot remove '/var/www/
html/index.html': No such file or directory", "stderr_lines": ["rm:
cannot remove '/var/www/html/index.html': No such file or directory"],
"stdout": "", "stdout_lines": []}


TASK [create a file] ******************************************
***
[WARNING]: Consider using the file module with state=touch rather
than running 'touch'. If you need to use command because file is
insufficient you can add 'warn: false' to this command task or set
'command_warnings=False' in ansible.cfg to get rid of this message.
changed: [ansible2]
changed: [ansible1]
```

```
TASK [printing rescue status] *****************************************
***
ok: [ansible1] => {
    "msg": "rescue task was operated"
}
ok: [ansible2] => {
    "msg": "rescue task was operated"
}


TASK [always write a message to logs] ********************************
changed: [ansible2]
changed: [ansible1]
TASK [always printing this message] **********************************
ok: [ansible1] => {
    "msg": "this message is always printed"
}
ok: [ansible2] => {
    "msg": "this message is always printed"
}


PLAY RECAP ***********************************************************
ansible1                   : ok=5     changed=2    unreachable=0
failed=0     skipped=0     rescued=1   ignored=0
ansible2                   : ok=5     changed=2    unreachable=0
failed=0     skipped=0     rescued=1   ignored=0
```

As you can see in Listing 7-33, the tasks in the **block** statement have failed, which is why the tasks in the **rescue** statement are executed instead.

In the output of Listing 7-32 as well as Listing 7-33, a warning is shown because the command module is used to run a command that can also be issued using the file module. This is just a warning in which Ansible informs you that a better solution is available. This relates to one of the basic principles while working with Ansible: Don't use the command module if a specific module is available to do the same thing. As indicated, you can set **command_warnings=False** in ansible.cfg to avoid seeing this message. Or you can rewrite the task that uses the shell module to remove a file (which is not a very Ansible way of doing things). Better use the file module and set its argument state to absent to remove the file.

NOTE   Blocks are useful, but one thing is inconvenient: you cannot use a block on a loop. If you need to iterate over a list of values, think of using a different solution.

Summary

In this lesson you learned about using conditionals in Ansible. In the first part you explored how to work with **loop**, allowing iteration over a list of items. Next, you learned how to define conditional tasks using **when**. After that, we explored the workings of handlers, which allow for conditional task execution. In the last part of this chapter, you read how to manage error handling in Ansible playbook, in which using blocks plays an important role.

Exam Preparation Tasks

As mentioned in the section "How to Use This Book" in the Introduction, you have a couple of choices for exam preparation: the exercises here, Chapter 16, "Final Preparation," and the exam simulation questions on the companion website.

Review All Key Topics

Review the most important topics in this chapter, noted with the Key Topic icon in the outer margin of the page. Table 7-5 lists a reference of these key topics and the page numbers on which each is found.

Table 7-5   Key Topics for Chapter 7

Key Topic Element	Description	Page Number
Table 7-3	Conditional Tests Overview	141
Paragraph	Conditional statement types	142
Paragraph	Using **register** on failed tasks	147
List	Tips for working with handlers	155

Memory Tables

Print a copy of Appendix D, "Memory Tables" (found on the companion website), or at least the section for this chapter, and complete the tables and lists from memory. Appendix E, "Memory Tables Answer Key," also on the companion website, includes completed tables and lists to check your work.

Define Key Terms

Define the following key terms from this chapter, and check your answers in the glossary:

block, failure condition, handler, item, lookup plug-in, **when**

Review Questions

1. If a loop is used on the contents of the variable **"{{ services }}"**, what is the name of the specific variable that should be used while iterating over the different values?

2. What should you do to loop over the values in a dictionary?

3. Which statement should you use to run a task only if a specific condition is true?

4. What do you need to include in your playbook to have it execute a task only if the variable **myvar** exists?

5. How do you write a **when** statement that tests whether the variable **myvar** has the string value "myvalue"?

6. Which conditional test should you use to verify that mypackage is a value in the list mypackages?

7. How would you write a test that checks whether var1 has the value value1 and var2 has the value value2, or var3 has the value value3 and var4 has the value value4?

8. What can you do to check whether the output of a command, as registered in the variable **cmd_out using register**, contains the text "error"?

9. How can you make sure that a play continues, even if a specific task has resulted in an error?

10. How can you stop execution of a complete playbook if any task generates an error?

End-of-Chapter Lab

Now that we're at the end of this chapter, let's do a lab. In this lab, you install and set up an Apache web server.

Lab 7-1

Write a playbook that meets the following requirements. Use multiple plays in a way that makes sense.

- Write a first play that installs the httpd and mod_ssl packages on host ansible2.

- Use variable inclusion to define the package names in a separate file.

- Use a conditional to loop over the list of packages to be installed.

- Install the packages only if the current operating system is CentOS or Red Hat (but not Fedora) version 8.0 or later. If that is not the case, the playbook should fail with the error message "Host *hostname* does not meet minimal requirements," where *hostname* is replaced with the current host name.

- On the Ansible control host, create a file /tmp/index.html. This file must have the contents "welcome to my webserver".

- If the file /tmp/index.html is successfully copied to /var/www/html, the web server process must be restarted. If copying the package fails, the playbook should show an error message.

- The firewall must be opened for the http as well as the https services.

This chapter covers the following subjects:

- Using Modules to Manipulate Files
- Managing SELinux Properties
- Using Jinja2 Templates

## CHAPTER 8

Deploying Files

The following RHCE exam objectives are covered in this chapter:

- Use Ansible modules for system administration tasks that work with:
  - File contents
- Use advanced Ansible features
  - Create and use templates to create customized configuration files

"Do I Know This Already?" Quiz

The "Do I Know This Already?" quiz allows you to assess whether you should read this entire chapter thoroughly or jump to the "Exam Preparation Tasks" section. If you are in doubt about your answers to these questions or your own assessment of your knowledge of the topics, read the entire chapter. Table 8-1 lists the major headings in this chapter and their corresponding "Do I Know This Already?" quiz questions. You can find the answers in Appendix A, "Answers to the 'Do I Know This Already?' Quizzes and Review Questions."

Table 8-1 "Do I Know This Already?" Section-to-Question Mapping

Foundation Topics Section	Questions
Using Modules to Manipulate Files	1–6
Managing SELinux Properties	7, 8
Using Jinja2 Templates	9, 10

1. Which module should you use to check the current permission mode on a file?
   - a. stat
   - b. file
   - c. permissions
   - d. acl

2. Which module should you use to replace a line of text in a configuration file with another line of text?

   a. copy

   b. regex

   c. lineinfile

   d. blockinfile

3. Which of the following shows correct syntax for a **when** statement that runs a task only if the permission mode as discovered by the stat module and registered to the st variable is not set to 0640?

   a. st.mode != '0640'

   b. st.stat.mode != 0640

   c. st.stat.mode != '0640'

   d. st.mode != 0640

4. Which of the following lines shows correct use of the lineinfile module to find a line that begins with PermitRootLogin based on a regular expression?

   a. line: "PermitRootLogin"

   b. line: "^PermitRootLogin"

   c. regexp: "PermitRootLogin"

   d. regexp: "^PermitRootLogin"

5. Which of the following is not a common task that the file module can do?

   a. Remove files

   b. Copy a line of text into a file

   c. Create links

   d. Set permissions

6. Which module can you use to copy a file from a managed node to the control node?

   a. copy

   b. file

   c. sync

   d. fetch

7. Different modules can be used when working with SELinux. Which of the following modules should you avoid?

   a. file

   b. sefcontext

   c. command

   d. selinux

8. After you set an SELinux context, the Linux **restorecon** command must be executed. How would you do this?

   a. Use the command module to run the **restorecon** command.

   b. Use the restorecon module.

   c. Use the selinux module.

   d. No further action is needed; this is done automatically when using the appropriate SELinux module.

9. What do you need to transform the contents of a variable to the JSON format?

   a. The lineinfile module

   b. A Jinja2 template

   c. A filter

   d. The copy module

10. What should you use to process host-specific facts from a template?

    a. The hostvars macro

    b. The hostvars magic variable

    c. The hostvars module

    d. The hostvars filter

Foundation Topics

Using Modules to Manipulate Files

Managing files is an important task for Linux administrators. Different types of manipulations are performed on files on a frequent basis. They include managing files, managing file contents, and moving files around. In this section you learn how to use Ansible modules to apply these different tasks.

File Module Manipulation Overview

Many modules are available to manage different aspects of files. Table 8-2 provides an overview of some of the most commonly used file modules.

Table 8-2 File Manipulation Module Overview

Module	Use
copy	Copies files to remote locations
fetch	Fetches files from remote locations
file	Manages files and file properties
acl	Works with file system ACLs
find	Finds files based on any property
lineinfile	Manages lines in text files
blockinfile	Manages blocks in text files
replace	Replaces strings in text files based on regex
synchronize	Performs rsync-based synchronization tasks
stat	Retrieves file or file system status

Most of these modules are discussed in the following sections. When using file-related modules, you might need a module that is not discussed here. If that is the case, the best approach is to use the **ansible-doc** command. When you use this command on any module, you always see related modules mentioned in the SEE ALSO section of the documentation.

Managing File Attributes

If you need to work with file attributes, the stat module and the file module come in handy. The stat module enables you to retrieve file status information. Because this module gets status information and is not used to change anything, you mainly use it to check specific file properties and perform an action if the properties are not set as expected. In Listing 8-1 you can see a playbook that uses the stat and debug modules to explore what exactly the stat module is doing. Listing 8-2 shows the output shown while running **ansible-playbook listing81.yaml**.

Listing 8-1   Exploring the stat Module

```
---
- name: stat module tests
  hosts: ansible1
  tasks:
  - stat:
      path: /etc/hosts
    register: st
  - name: show current values
    debug:
      msg: current value of the st variable is {{ st }}
```

Listing 8-2   Running **ansible-playbook listing81.yaml**

```
[ansible@control ~]$ ansible-playbook listing81.yaml

PLAY [stat module tests] *********************************************

TASK [Gathering Facts] **********************************************
ok: [ansible1]

TASK [stat] *********************************************************
ok: [ansible1]

TASK [show current values] ******************************************
ok: [ansible1] => {
    "msg": "current value of the st variable is {'changed':
False, 'stat': {'exists': True, 'path': '/etc/hosts', 'mode':
'0644', 'isdir': False, 'ischr': False, 'isblk': False, 'isreg':
True, 'isfifo': False, 'islnk': False, 'issock': False, 'uid': 0,
'gid': 0, 'size': 158, 'inode': 16801440, 'dev': 64768, 'nlink':
1, 'atime': 1586230060.147566, 'mtime': 1536580263.0, 'ctime':
1584958718.8117938, 'wusr': True, 'rusr': True, 'xusr': False, 'wgrp':
False, 'rgrp': True, 'xgrp': False, 'woth': False, 'roth': True,
'xoth': False, 'isuid': False, 'isgid': False, 'blocks': 8, 'block_
size': 4096, 'device_type': 0, 'readable': True, 'writeable': True,
'executable': False, 'pw_name': 'root', 'gr_name': 'root', 'checksum':
'7335999eb54c15c67566186bdfc46f64e0d5a1aa', 'mimetype': 'text/plain',
'charset': 'us-ascii', 'version': '408552077', 'attributes': [],
'attr_flags': ''}, 'failed': False}"
}
```

```
PLAY RECAP ***********************************************************
ansible1                   : ok=3      changed=0      unreachable=0
failed=0      skipped=0      rescued=0      ignored=0
```

As you can see from Listing 8-2, the stat module returns many file properties. It tests which permission mode is set, whether it is a link, which checksum is set on the file, and much more. For a complete list of output data, you can consult the documentation as provided while running **ansible-doc stat**.

Based on the output that is provided, a conditional test can be performed. The sample playbook in Listing 8-3 shows how this can be done and how the playbook can write a message if the expected permissions mode is not set.

Listing 8-3   Performing File State Tests with the stat Module

```
---
- name: stat module tests
  hosts: ansible1
  tasks:
  - command: touch /tmp/statfile
  - stat:
      path: /tmp/statfile
    register: st
  - name: show current values
    debug:
      msg: current value of the st variable is {{ st }}
  - fail:
      msg: "unexpected file mode, should be set to 0640"
    when: st.stat.mode != '0640'
```

As you can see in the playbook output in Listing 8-4, the playbook fails with the unexpected file mode message. Also notice the warning in the Listing 8-4 output: it tells you that there is a better solution to do what you wanted to do here. This happens on multiple occasions when you might have selected a module that is not the best solution for the task you want to perform. Remember: Using the command module will work in almost all cases, but often a better solution is available.

Listing 8-4   Running **ansible-playbook listing83.yaml** Result

```
[ansible@control ~]$ ansible-playbook listing83.yaml

PLAY [stat module tests] ***********************************************
```

```
TASK [Gathering Facts] ***********************************************
ok: [ansible1]
TASK [command] *******************************************************
[WARNING]: Consider using the file module with state=touch rather
than running 'touch'. If you need to use command because file is
insufficient you can add 'warn: false' to this command task or set
'command_warnings=False' in ansible.cfg to get rid of this message.
changed: [ansible1]

TASK [stat] **********************************************************
ok: [ansible1]

TASK [show current values] *******************************************
ok: [ansible1] => {
    "msg": "current value of the st variable is {'changed':
False, 'stat': {'exists': True, 'path': '/tmp/statfile', 'mode':
'0644', 'isdir': False, 'ischr': False, 'isblk': False, 'isreg':
True, 'isfifo': False, 'islnk': False, 'issock': False, 'uid': 0,
'gid': 0, 'size': 0, 'inode': 51440456, 'dev': 64768, 'nlink': 1,
'atime': 1586253087.057596, 'mtime': 1586253087.057596, 'ctime':
1586253087.057596, 'wusr': True, 'rusr': True, 'xusr': False, 'wgrp':
False, 'rgrp': True, 'xgrp': False, 'woth': False, 'roth': True,
'xoth': False, 'isuid': False, 'isgid': False, 'blocks': 0, 'block_
size': 4096, 'device_type': 0, 'readable': True, 'writeable': True,
'executable': False, 'pw_name': 'root', 'gr_name': 'root', 'checksum':
'da39a3ee5e6b4b0d3255bfef95601890afd80709', 'mimetype': 'inode/x-
empty', 'charset': 'binary', 'version': '158303785', 'attributes': [],
'attr_flags': ''}, 'failed': False}"
}

TASK [fail] **********************************************************
fatal: [ansible1]: FAILED! => {"changed": false, "msg": "unexpected
file mode, should be set to 0640"}

PLAY RECAP ***********************************************************
ansible1                  : ok=4      changed=1      unreachable=0
failed=1     skipped=0     rescued=0     ignored=0
```

In the earlier examples in this section, you saw how you can use the stat module to show different types of file properties. Based on the output of the stat module, you may use the file module to set specific file properties. In Listing 8-5 you can see how the playbook from Listing 8-3 is rewritten to automatically set the desired permissions state.

Listing 8-5   Using the file Module to Correct File Properties Discovered with stat

```
---
- name: stat module tests
  hosts: ansible1
  tasks:
  - command: touch /tmp/statfile
  - stat:
      path: /tmp/statfile
    register: st
  - name: show current values
    debug:
      msg: current value of the st variable is {{ st }}
  - name: changing file permissions if that's needed
    file:
      path: /tmp/statfile
      mode: 0640
    when: st.stat.mode != '0640'
```

EXAM TIP   In the examples in this chapter, some tasks don't have a name assigned. Using a name for each task is not required; however, it does make troubleshooting a lot easier if each task does have a name. For that reason, on the exam it's a good idea to use names anyway. Doing so makes it easier to identify which tasks lead to which specific result.

Managing File Contents

If you need to manage file contents, multiple modules can be useful. The find module enables you to find files, just like the Linux **find** command. The lineinfile module enables you to manipulate lines in files, and blockinfile enables you to manipulate complete blocks of text. Also don't forget the copy module. We look at it in the next section, but you can also use it to copy a specified text to a file. For managing text operations on files, however, it is recommended that you use lineinfile or blockinfile instead because these give more options to specify where exactly the text should be written to.

Listing 8-6 shows an example where lineinfile is used to change a string, based on a regular expression.

Listing 8-6 Changing File Contents Using lineinfile

```
---
- name: configuring SSH
  hosts: all
  tasks:
  - name: disable root SSH login
    lineinfile:
        dest: /etc/ssh/sshd_config
        regexp: "^PermitRootLogin"
        line: "PermitRootLogin no"
      notify: restart sshd

  handlers:
  - name: restart sshd
    service:
      name: sshd
      state: restarted
```

As you can see in Listing 8-6, lineinfile uses the **dest** key to specify the filename. Next, a regular expression is used to search for lines that have text starting with **PermitRootLogin**. If this regular expression is found, it is changed into the line **PermitRootLogin no**.

You can use the lineinfile module to manipulate a single line in a file. In some cases you have to manage multiple lines in a file. In that case, you can use the blockinfile module. Listing 8-7 provides an example.

Listing 8-7 Using blockinfile to Manipulate Multiple Lines of Text

```
---
- name: modifying file
  hosts: all
  tasks:
  - name: ensure /tmp/hosts exists
    file:
        path: /tmp/hosts
        state: touch
  - name: add some lines to /tmp/hosts
    blockinfile:
        path: /tmp/hosts
        block: |
          192.168.4.110 host1.example.com
          192.168.4.120 host2.example.com
        state: present
```

Based on what you've learned so far, the use of blockinfile should be easy to understand. Just remember the use of the | after **block:**. This character is used to specify that the next couple of lines should be treated as lines, adding the newline character to the end of the line. Alternatively, you could use **block: >**, but that would add one long line to the destination file.

Notice that when blockinfile is used, the text specified in the block is copied with a start and end indicator. See Listing 8-8 for an example:

Listing 8-8   Resulting File Modification by blockinfile

```
127.0.0.1    localhost localhost.localdomain localhost4 localhost4.
localdomain4
::1           localhost localhost.localdomain localhost6 localhost6.
localdomain6
192.168.4.200.   control.example.com.        control
192.168.4.201    ansible1.example.com        ansible1
192.168.4.202    ansible2.example.com        ansible2


# BEGIN ANSIBLE MANAGED BLOCK
192.168.4.110 host1.example.com
192.168.4.120 host2.example.com
# END ANSIBLE MANAGED BLOCK
```

Creating and Removing Files

In an earlier example in this chapter you saw how the command module was used to create a new file by using the Linux **touch** command. While running this playbook, you saw a warning that you shouldn't do it this way, but you should use the file module instead, and that is totally right.

You can use the file module to perform some pretty common tasks:

- Create new files or directories
- Create links
- Remove files
- Set permissions and ownership

Listing 8-9 shows a sample playbook where the file module is used to create a new directory and in that directory create an empty file, after which the same file module is used again to remove the directory recursively. This approach is not very useful, but at least it shows you some of the most common uses of the file module.

Listing 8-9   Creating and Removing Files with the file Module

```
---
- name: using the file module
  hosts: ansible1
  tasks:
  - name: create directory
    file:
      path: /newdir
      owner: ansible
      group: ansible
      mode: 770
      state: directory
  - name: create file in that directory
    file:
      path: /newdir/newfile
      state: touch
  - name: show the new file
    stat:
      path: /newdir/newfile
    register: result
  - debug:
      msg: |
          This shows that newfile was created
          "{{ result }}"
  - name: removing everything again
    file:
      path: /newdir
      state: absent
```

In Listing 8-9, you can see that the last task is configured to remove a directory. Just specifying the path to the directory and **state: absent** recursively removes the directory. You don't need to specify any other options here, and the **recurse** key also is not required.

Moving Files Around

Three modules are particularly useful for moving files around. The copy module copies a file from the Ansible control host to a managed machine. The fetch module enables you to do the opposite, and the synchronize module performs Linux rsync-like tasks, ensuring that a file from the control host is synchronized to a file with that name on the managed host. The main difference between copy and synchronize is that the copy module always creates a new file, whereas the synchronize module updates a current existing file. In Listing 8-10 you can see how these modules are used.

Listing 8-10   Moving a File Around with Ansible

```
---
- name: file copy modules
  hosts: all
  tasks:
  - name: copy file demo
    copy:
      src: /etc/hosts
      dest: /tmp/
  - name: add some lines to /tmp/hosts
    blockinfile:
      path: /tmp/hosts
      block: |
        192.168.4.110 host1.example.com
        192.168.4.120 host2.example.com
      state: present
  - name: verify file checksum
    stat:
      path: /tmp/hosts
      checksum_algorithm: md5
    register: result
  - debug:
      msg: "The checksum of /tmp/hosts is {{ result.stat.checksum }}"
  - name: fetch a file
    fetch:
      src: /tmp/hosts
      dest: /tmp/
```

After running the playbook in Listing 8-10, you might expect to find the file /tmp/hosts on the Ansible control machine. This, however, is not the case, and the reason is easy to understand. Ansible playbooks typically are used on multiple hosts, so if a file is fetched from a managed host, it must be stored in a unique location. To guarantee the uniqueness, Ansible creates a subdirectory for each managed host in the dest directory and puts the file that fetch has copied from the remote host in that subdirectory. So the result of the playbook in Listing 8-10 is stored as /tmp/ansible1/hosts and /tmp/ansible2/hosts. You practice working with files in Exercise 8-1.

Exercise 8-1   Managing Files with Ansible

1. Create a file with the name exercise81.yaml and give it the following play header:

```
---

- name: testing file manipulation skills
  hosts: ansible1
  tasks:
```

2. Add a task that creates a new empty file:

```
---

- name: testing file manipulation skills
  hosts: ansible1
  tasks:
  - name: create a new file
    file:
      name: /tmp/newfile
      state: touch
```

3. Use the stat module to check on the status of the new file:

```
---

- name: testing file manipulation skills
  hosts: ansible1
  tasks:
  - name: create a new file
    file:
      name: /tmp/newfile
      state: touch
  - name: check status of the new file
    stat:
      path: /tmp/newfile
    register: newfile
```

4. To see what the status module is doing, add a line that uses the debug module:

```
- name: testing file manipulation skills
  hosts: ansible1
  tasks:
  - name: create a new file
    file:
      name: /tmp/newfile
      state: touch
  - name: check status of the new file
    stat:
      path: /tmp/newfile
```

```
      register: newfile
    - name: for debugging only
      debug:
        msg: the current values for newfile are {{ newfile }}
```

5. Now that you understand which values are stored in newfile, you can add a
   conditional playbook that changes the current owner if not set correctly:

```
---
- name: testing file manipulation skills
  hosts: ansible1
  tasks:
  - name: create a new file
    file:
      name: /tmp/newfile
      state: touch
  - name: check status of the new file
    stat:
      path: /tmp/newfile
    register: newfile
  - name: for debugging only
    debug:
      msg: the current values for newfile are {{ newfile }}
  - name: change file owner if needed
    file:
      path: /tmp/newfile
      owner: ansible
    when: newfile.stat.pw_name != 'ansible'
```

6. Add a second play to the playbook that fetches a remote file:

```
- name: fetching a remote file
  hosts: ansible1
  tasks:
  - name: fetch file from remote machine
    fetch:
      src: /etc/motd
      dest: /tmp
```

7. Now that you have fetched the file so that it is on the Ansible control machine,
   use blockinfile to edit it:

```
- name: adding text to the file that is now on localhost
  hosts: localhost
  tasks:
  - name: add a message
    blockinfile:
```

```
                path: /tmp/ansible1/etc/motd
                block: |
                  welcome to this server
                  for authorized users only
                state: present
```

8. In the final step, copy the modified file to ansible2 by including the following play:

```
- name: copy the modified file to ansible2
  hosts: ansible2
  tasks:
  - name: copy motd file
    copy:
      src: /tmp/ansible1/etc/motd
      dest: /tmp
```

9. At this point you're ready to run the playbook. Type **ansible-playbook exercise81.yaml** to run it and observe the results.

10. Type **ansible ansible2 -a "cat /tmp/motd"** to verify that the modified motd file was successfully copied to ansible2.

Managing SELinux Properties

In the security of any Linux system, SELinux is an important component. SELinux can be used on files to manage file context; apart from that, context can be set on ports; and SELinux properties can be managed using Booleans. Ansible has a few modules that allow for making changes to the SELinux configuration, which are listed in Table 8-3.

TIP To work with SELinux in Ansible, you need to have knowledge about SELinux. This is a part of the RHCSA-level knowledge that is required for anyone who wants to take EX294. This section does not explain SELinux itself. For more information about SELinux, consult the Red Hat RHCSA 8 Cert Guide.

Table 8-3 Modules for Managing Changes on SELinux

Module	Use
file	Manages context on files but not in the SELinux policy
sefcontext	Manages file context in the SELinux policy
command	Is required to run the **restorecon** command after using sefcontext
selinux	Manages current SELinux state
seboolean	Manages SELinux Booleans

Managing SELinux File Context

The essential thing to understand when working with SELinux to secure files is that the context type that is set on the file defines which processes can work with the files. The file context type can be set on a file directly, or it can be set on the SELinux policy.

When you're working with SELinux, all of its properties should be set in the SELinux policy. To do this, you use the Ansible sefcontext module. Setting a context type in the policy doesn't automatically apply it to files though. You still need to run the Linux **restorecon** command to do this. Ansible does not offer a module to run this command; it needs to be invoked using the command module.

As an alternative, you can use the file module to set SELinux context. The disadvantage of this approach is that the context is set directly on the file, not in the SELinux policy. As a result, if at any time default context is applied from the policy to the file system, all context that has been set with the Ansible file module risks being overwritten. For that reason, the recommended way to manage SELinux context in Ansible is to use the sefcontext module.

To be able to work with the Ansible sefcontext module and the Linux **restorecon** command, you also need to make sure that the appropriate software is installed on Linux. This software comes from the policycoreutils-python-utils RPM package, which is not installed by default in all installation patterns.

Listing 8-11 shows a sample playbook that uses this module to manage SELinux context type.

Listing 8-11   Managing SELinux Context with sefcontext

```
---
- name: show selinux
  hosts: all
  tasks:
  - name: install required packages
    yum:
      name: policycoreutils-python-utils
      state: present
  - name: create testfile
    file:
      name: /tmp/selinux
      state: touch
  - name: set selinux context
    sefcontext:
```

```
      target: /tmp/selinux
      setype: httpd_sys_content_t
      state: present
   notify:
      - run restorecon
 handlers:
 - name: run restorecon
   command: restorecon -v /tmp/selinux
```

In the sample playbook in Listing 8-11, the required software package is installed first. Next, a test file is created using the file module; then in the next task the **sefcontext** command is used to write the new context to the policy. If executed successfully, this task will trigger a handler to run the Linux **restorecon** command by using the command module.

Don't forget: A handler will run only if the task that triggers it generates a changed status. If the current state already matches the desired state, no changes are applied and the handler won't run!

EXAM TIP   The exam assignment might not be as specific as to ask you to change a context using SELinux. You might just have to configure a service with a nondefault documentroot, which means that SELinux will deny access to the service. So also on the EX294 exam, with all tasks, you should ask yourself if this task requires any changes at an SELinux level.

Applying Generic SELinux Management Tasks

Some additional SELinux related modules are available as well. The selinux module enables you to set the current state of SELinux to either permissive, enforcing, or disabled. The seboolean module enables you to easily enable or disable functionality in SELinux using Booleans. Listing 8-12 shows an example of a playbook that uses both of these modules.

Listing 8-12   Changing SELinux State and Booleans

```
---
- name: enabling SELinux and a boolean
  hosts: ansible1
  vars:
    myboolean: httpd_read_user_content
  tasks:
  - name: enabling SELinux
    selinux:
```

```
      policy: targeted
      state: enforcing
 - name: checking current {{ myboolean }} Boolean status
   shell: getsebool -a | grep {{ myboolean }}
   register: bool_stat
 - name: showing boolean status
   debug:
     msg: the current {{ myboolean }} status is {{ bool_stat.stdout }}
 - name: enabling boolean
   seboolean:
     name: "{{ myboolean }}"
     state: yes
     persistent: yes
```

In the sample playbook in Listing 8-12, to start with, the selinux module is used to ensure that SELinux is in the enforcing state. When using this module, you also have to specify the name of the policy, which in most cases is the targeted policy.

Next, the seboolean module is used to enable a Boolean. As you can see, this Boolean is defined as the variable **myboolean**. Before the Boolean is enabled, the shell and debug modules are used to show its current status. In Exercise 8-2 you practice working with SELinux.

Exercise 8-2   Changing SELinux Context

In this exercise you configure a more complicated playbook, running different tasks. To guide you through this process, which will prepare you for the exam in a somewhat better way, I show you a different approach this time. To start with, this is the assignment you're going to work on.

Install, start, and configure a web server that has the DocumentRoot set to the /web directory. In this directory, create a file named index.html that shows the message "welcome to the Exercise 8-2 webserver." Ensure that SELinux is enabled and allows access to the web server document root. Also ensure that SELinux allows users to publish web pages from their home directory.

1. Because this is a complex task, you should start this time by creating a playbook outline. A good approach for doing this is to create the playbook play header

and list all tasks that need to be accomplished by providing a name as well as the name of the task that you want to run. Create this structure as follows:

```
---

- name: Managing web server SELinux properties
  hosts: ansible1
  tasks:
  - name: ensure SELinux is enabled and enforcing
  - name: install the webserver
  - name: start and enable the webserver
  - name: open the firewall service
  - name: create the /web directory
  - name: create the index.html file in /web
  - name: use lineinfile to change webserver configuration
  - name: use sefcontext to set context on new documentroot
  - name: run the restorecon command
  - name: allow the web server to run user content
```

2. Now that the base structure has been defined, you can define the rest of the task properties. To start with, enable SELinux and set to the enforcing state:

```
---

- name: Managing web server SELinux properties
  hosts: ansible1
  tasks:
  - name: ensure SELinux is enabled and enforcing
    selinux:
      policy: targeted
      state: enforcing
```

3. You can install the web server, start and enable it, create the /web directory, and create the index.html file in the /web directory. You should be familiar with these tasks, so you can do them all in one run:

```
  - name: install the webserver
    yum:
      name: httpd
      state: latest
  - name: start and enable the webserver
    service:
      name: httpd
      state: started
      enabled: yes
  - name: open the firewall service
    firewalld:
```

```
        service: http
        state: enabled
        immediate: yes

    - name: create the /web directory
      file:
        name: /web
        state: directory
    - name: create the index.html file in /web
      copy:
        content: 'welcome to the exercise82 web server'
        dest: /web/index.html
    - name: use lineinfile to change webserver configuration
    - name: use sefcontext to set context on new documentroot
    - name: run the restorecon command
    - name: allow the web server to run user content
```

4. You must use the lineinfile module to change the httpd.conf contents. Two different lines need to be changed, which you accomplish by making the following modifications:

```
    - name: use lineinfile to change webserver configuration
      lineinfile:
        path: /etc/httpd/conf/httpd.conf
        regexp: '^DocumentRoot "/var/www/html"'
        line: DocumentRoot "/web"
    - name: use lineinfile to change webserver security
      lineinfile:
        path: /etc/httpd/conf/httpd.conf
        regexp: '^<Directory "/var/www">'
        line: '<Directory "/web">'
    - name: use sefcontext to set context on new documentroot
    - name: run the restorecon command
    - name: allow the web server to run user content
```

5. In the final steps, you take care of configuring the SELinux-specific settings:

```
    - name: use sefcontext to set context on new documentroot
      sefcontext:
        target: '/web(/.*)?'
        setype: httpd_sys_content_t
        state: present
    - name: run the restorecon command
      command: restorecon -Rv /web
```

```
     - name: allow the web server to run user content
       seboolean:
         name: httpd_read_user_content
         state: yes
         persistent: yes
```

6. At this point, the complete playbook should look as follows:

```
---
- name: Managing web server SELinux properties
  hosts: ansible1
  tasks:
  - name: ensure SELinux is enabled and enforcing
    selinux:
        policy: targeted
        state: enforcing
  - name: install the webserver
    yum:
        name: httpd
        state: latest
  - name: start and enable the webserver
    service:
        name: httpd
        state: started
        enabled: yes
  - name: open the firewall service
    firewalld:
        service: http
        state: enabled
        immediate: yes
  - name: create the /web directory
    file:
        name: /web
        state: directory
  - name: create the index.html file in /web
    copy:
        content: 'welcome to the exercise82 web server'
        dest: /web/index.html
  - name: use lineinfile to change webserver configuration
    lineinfile:
        path: /etc/httpd/conf/httpd.conf
        regexp: '^DocumentRoot "/var/www/html"'
        line: DocumentRoot "/web"
```

```
     - name: use lineinfile to change webserver security
       lineinfile:
           path: /etc/httpd/conf/httpd.conf
           regexp: '^<Directory "/var/www">'
           line: '<Directory "/web">'
     - name: use sefcontext to set context on new documentroot
       sefcontext:
           target: '/web(/.*)?'
           setype: httpd_sys_content_t
           state: present
     - name: run the restorecon command
       command: restorecon -Rv /web
     - name: allow the web server to run user content
       seboolean:
           name: httpd_read_user_content
           state: yes
           persistent: yes
```

7. Run the playbook by using **ansible-playbook exercise82.yaml** and verify its output.

8. Verify that the web service is accessible by using **curl http://ansible1**. In this case, it should not show the expected welcome text. Try to analyze why. You can find the answer at the end of this chapter before the end-of-chapter. So what should you learn from this? A playbook may run without any errors, but that doesn't mean that it has produced the desired results. You should always verify!

Using Jinja2 Templates

A template is a configuration file that contains variables and, based on the variables, is generated on the managed hosts according to host-specific requirements. Using templates allows for a structural way to generate configuration files, which is much more powerful than changing specific lines from specific files. Ansible uses Jinja2 to generate templates.

Working with Simple Templates

Jinja2 is a generic templating language for Python developers. It is used in Ansible templates, but Jinja2-based approaches are also found in other parts of Ansible. For instance, the way variables are referred to is based on Jinja2.

In a Jinja2 template, three elements can be used. Table 8-4 provides an overview.

Table 8-4 Jinja2 Template Elements

Element	Example
data	**sample text**
comment	**{# sample text #}**
variable	**{{ ansible_facts['default_ipv4']['address'] }}**
expression	**{% for myhost in groups['web'] %}**
	{{ myhost }}
	{% endfor %}

To work with a template, you must create a template file, written in Jinja2. Next, this template file must be included in an Ansible playbook that uses the template module. Listing 8-13 shows what a template file might look like, and Listing 8-14 shows an example of a playbook that calls the template.

Listing 8-13 Sample Template

```
# {{ ansible_managed }}

<VirtualHost *:80>
        ServerAdmin webmaster@{{ ansible_facts['fqdn'] }}
        ServerName {{ ansible_facts['fqdn'] }}
        ErrorLog logs/{{ ansible_facts['hostname'] }}-error.log
        CustomLog        logs/{{ ansible_facts['hostname'] }}-common.
log common
        DocumentRoot /var/www/vhosts/{{ ansible_facts['hostname'] }}/

        <Directory /var/www/vhosts/{{ ansible_facts['hostname'] }}>
                Options +Indexes +FollowSymlinks +Includes
                Order allow,deny
                Allow from all
        </Directory>
</VirtualHost>
```

The sample template in Listing 8-13 starts with **# {{ ansible_managed }}**. This string is commonly used to identify that a file is managed by Ansible so that administrators are not going to change file contents by accident. While processing the template, this string is replaced with the value of the **ansible_managed** variable.

This variable can be set in ansible.cfg. For instance, you can use **ansible_managed = This file is managed by Ansible** to substitute the variable with its value while generating the template.

As for the remainder, the template file is just a text file that uses variables to substitute specific variables to their values. In this case that is just the **ansible_fqdn** and **ansible_hostname** variables that are set as Ansible facts. To generate the template, you need a playbook that uses the template module to call the template. Listing 8-14 shows an example.

Listing 8-14 Sample Playbook

```
---
- name: installing a template file
  hosts: ansible1
  tasks:
  - name: install http
    yum:
      name: httpd
      state: latest
  - name: start and enable httpd
    service:
      name: httpd
      state: started
      enabled: true
  - name: install vhost config file
    template:
      src: listing813.j2
      dest: /etc/httpd/conf.d/vhost.conf
      owner: root
      group: root
      mode: 0644
  - name: restart httpd
    service:
      name: httpd
      state: restarted
```

In the sample playbook in Listing 8-14, the template module is used to work on the source file specified as **src**, to generate the destination file, specified as **dest**. The result is that on the managed host the template is generated, with all the variables substituted to their values.

Applying Control Structures in Jinja2 Using for

In templates, control structures can be used to dynamically generate contents. A **for** statement can be used to iterate over all elements that exist as the value of a variable. Let's look at some examples.

To start with, Listing 8-15 shows a template where a **for** statement is shown.

Listing 8-15   Exploring Jinja2 **for** Statements

```
{% for node in groups['all'] %}
host_port={{ node }}:8080
{% endfor %}
```

In this Jinja2 file, a variable with the name **host_ports** is defined on the second line (which is the line that will be written to the target file). To produce its value, the host group **all** is processed in the **for** statement on the first line. While processing the host group, a temporary variable with the name **node** is defined. This value of the **node** variable is replaced with the name of the host while it is processed, and after the host name, the string **:8080** is copied, which will result in a separate line for each host that was found. As the last element, **{% endfor %}** is used to close the **for** loop. In Listing 8-16 you can see an example of a playbook that runs this template.

Listing 8-16   Generating a Template with a Conditional Statement

```
---
- name: generate host list
  hosts: ansible2
  tasks:
  - name: template loop
    template:
      src: listing815.j2
      dest: /tmp/hostports.txt
```

As you can see, the sample playbook in Listing 8-16 uses the template as the source file and, based on the template, produces the file /tmp/hostports.txt on the managed host. To verify, you can use the ad hoc command **ansible ansible2 -a "cat /tmp/hostports.txt"**.

Using Conditional Statements with if

The **for** statement can be used in templates to iterate over a series of values. The **if** statement can be used to include text only if a variable contains a specific value or evaluates to a Boolean true. Listing 8-17 shows a sample template file that reacts on a variable that is set in the sample playbook in Listing 8-18.

Listing 8-17   Template Example with **if**

```
{% if apache_package == 'apache2' %}
  Welcome to Apache2
{% else %}
  Welcome to httpd
{% endif %}
```

Listing 8-18   Using the Template with **if**

```
---
- name: work with template file
  vars:
      apache_package: 'httpd'
  hosts: ansible2
  tasks:
  - template:
      src: listing817.j2
      dest: /tmp/httpd.conf
```

Using Filters

In Jinja2 templates, you can use filters. Filters are a way to perform an operation on the value of a template expression, such as a variable. The filter is included in the variable definition itself, and the result of the variable and its filter is used in the file that is generated. Table 8-5 gives an overview of some common filters. In Exercise 8-3 you practice your skills and work with templates that use a conditional statement.

Table 8-5   Common Filters Overview

Filter Example	Use
{{ myvar | to_json}}	Writes the contents of **myvar** in JSON format
{{ myvar || to_yaml }}	Writes the contents of **myvar** in YAML format
{{ myvar | ipaddr }}	Tests whether **myvar** contains an IP address

EXAM TIP   The Ansible documentation at https://docs.ansible.com contains a section with the title "Frequently Asked Questions." In this section you can find the question "How do I loop over a list of hosts in a group, inside a template?" Read it now, and study it. The response here provides a very nice example of using conditional statements in templates, and that information might be useful on the exam.

Exercise 8-3   Working with Conditional Statements in Templates

1. Use your editor to create the file exercise83.j2. Include the following line to open the Jinja2 conditional statement:

   ```
   {% for host in groups['all'] %}
   ```

2. This statement defines a variable with the name **host**. This variable iterates over the magic variable **groups**, which holds all Ansible host groups as defined in inventory. Of these groups, the **all** group (which holds all inventory host names) is processed.

3. Add the following line (write it as one line; it will wrap over two lines, but do not press Enter to insert a newline character):

   ```
   {{ hostvars[host]['ansible_default_ipv4']['address'] }} {{
   hostvars[host]['ansible_fqdn']  }} {{ hostvars[host]['ansible_
   hostname'] }}
   ```

   This line writes a single line for each inventory host, containing three items. To do so, you use the magic variable **hostvars**, which can be used to identify Ansible facts that were discovered on the inventory host. The **[host]** part is replaced with the name of the current host, and after that, the specific facts are referred to. As a result, for each host a line is produced that holds the IP address, the FQDN, and next the host name.

4. Add the following line to close the **for** loop:

   ```
   {% endfor %}
   ```

5. Verify that the complete file contents look like the following and write and quit the file:

   ```
   {% for host in groups['all'] %}
   {{ hostvars[host]['ansible_default_ipv4']['address'] }} {{
   hostvars[host]['ansible_fqdn']  }} {{
   hostvars[host]['ansible_hostname'] }}
   {% endfor %}
   ```

6. Use your editor to create the file exercise83.yaml. It should contain the following lines:

   ```
   ---
   - name: generate /etc/hosts file
   ```

```
        hosts: all
        tasks:
        - name:
          template:
            src: exercise83.j2
            dest: /tmp/hosts
```

7. Run the playbook by using **ansible-playbook exercise83.yaml**.

8. Verify the /tmp/hosts file was generated by using **ansible all -a "cat /tmp/hosts"**.

Summary

In this chapter you learned how to manipulate text files with Ansible. In the first section you learned about the most important Ansible modules that can be used. Next, you learned how to manage SELinux with Ansible. In the last part of this chapter, you read about generating configuration files using Jinja2 templates.

Exam Preparation Tasks

As mentioned in the section "How to Use This Book" in the Introduction, you have a couple of choices for exam preparation: the exercises here, Chapter 16, "Final Preparation," and the exam simulation questions on the companion website.

Review All Key Topics

Review the most important topics in this chapter, noted with the Key Topics icon in the outer margin of the page. Table 8-6 lists a reference of these key topics and the page numbers on which each is found.

Table 8-6 Key Topics for Chapter 8

Key Topic Element	Description	Page Number
List	File module tasks	182
Table 8-4	Jinja2 Template Elements	195

Memory Tables

Print a copy of Appendix D, "Memory Tables" (found on the companion website), or at least the section for this chapter, and complete the tables and lists from memory. Appendix E, "Memory Tables Answer Key," also on the companion website, includes completed tables and lists to check your work.

Define Key Terms

Define the following key terms from this chapter, and check your answers in the glossary:

Jinja2, template

Review Questions

1. Which module should you use to work with file system ACLs?

2. Which modules can you use to replace strings in text files based on regex? (List two.)

3. Which module should you use to retrieve file status?

4. List three tasks that are commonly executed using the file module.

5. Which module should you use to synchronize the contents of a file with the contents of a file on the control host?

6. What is wrong with using the file module to manipulate SELinux file context?

7. Which module can you use to change SELinux Booleans?

8. A playbook runs successfully, but the handler in that playbook is not triggered. What is the most common explanation?

9. How do you include a comment line in a Jinja2 template?

10. What is the **if** statement used for in Ansible templates?

Exercise Answers

After you perform all the steps in Exercise 8-2, the web server still doesn't work. Further analysis shows that the changes in httpd.conf have been made successfully and also that the SELinux context is set correctly. However, after you apply the changes with lineinfile, the web server needs to be started. You can do this either by using a handler or by moving the service task to be performed after the lineinfile task.

End-of-Chapter Labs

Lab 8-1: Generate an /etc/hosts File

Write a playbook that generates an /etc/hosts file on all managed hosts. Apply the following requirements:

- All hosts that are defined in inventory should be added to the /etc/hosts file.

Lab 8-2: Manage a vsftpd Service

Write a playbook that uses at least two plays to install a vsftpd service, configure the vsftpd service using templates, and configure permissions as well as SELinux. Apply the following requirements:

- Install, start, and enable the vsftpd service. Also open a port in the firewall to make it accessible.

- Use the /etc/vsftpd/vsftpd.conf file to generate a template. In this template, you should use the following variables to configure specific settings. Replace these settings with the variables and leave all else unmodified:

  - anonymous_enable: yes

  - local_enable: yes

  - write_enable: yes

  - anon_upload_enable: yes

- Set permissions on the /var/ftp/pub directory to mode 0777.

- Configure the **ftpd_anon_write** Boolean to allow anonymous user writes.

- Set the **public_content_rw_t** SELinux context type to the /var/ftp/pub directory.

- If any additional tasks are required to get this done, take care of them.

This chapter covers the following subjects:

- Using Ansible Roles
- Using Ansible Galaxy Roles
- Using RHEL System Roles

## CHAPTER 9

Using Ansible Roles

The following RHCE exam objectives are covered in this chapter:

■ Work with roles

■ Create roles

■ Download roles from Ansible Galaxy and use them

"Do I Know This Already?" Quiz

The "Do I Know This Already?" quiz allows you to assess whether you should read this entire chapter thoroughly or jump to the "Exam Preparation Tasks" section. If you are in doubt about your answers to these questions or your own assessment of your knowledge of the topics, read the entire chapter. Table 9-1 lists the major headings in this chapter and their corresponding "Do I Know This Already?" quiz questions. You can find the answers in Appendix A, "Answers to the 'Do I Know This Already?' Quizzes and Review Questions."

Table 9-1 "Do I Know This Already?" Section-to-Question Mapping

Foundation Topics Section	Questions
Using Ansible Roles	1–5
Using Ansible Galaxy Roles	6–8
Using RHEL System Roles	9, 10

1. In which role directory should you define role variables that are not supposed to be overwritten from a playbook?

   a. vars

   b. meta

   c. files

   d. defaults

2. Roles can be found in many locations. Which of the following locations should not be used for storing custom-made roles?

   a. ./roles

   b. ~/.ansible/roles

   c. /etc/ansible/roles

   d. /usr/share/ansible/roles

3. Where do you find Ansible community-provided roles?

   a. In the Ansible registry

   b. In the Ansible Git repository

   c. In Ansible Galaxy

   d. On the Ansible website

4. You want to define a task that is executed after the handlers in a playbook. How can you do that?

   a. You can't; handlers are always executed last.

   b. You include these tasks in a role.

   c. You make sure these tasks are defined after the tasks that call the handlers.

   d. You include them in a post_tasks section.

5. Which file is used to define role dependencies?

   a. README.md in the role directory

   b. meta/main.yml in the role

   c. meta/main.yml in the project directory

   d. The Ansible playbook

6. Which of the following commands allows you to set up a directory structure for a custom role easily?

   a. **mkdir**

   b. **ansible init**

   c. **ansible-galaxy init**

   d. **ansible-galaxy setup**

7. When working with Ansible Galaxy, you can specify a requirements file. Which of the following specifies the correct way to indicate the requirements file that should be used?

    a. Include **requirements_file: filename** in the playbook that calls the roles.

    b. Use **ansible-galaxy install -r filename**.

    c. Include a dependencies section in the playbook, and in this section specify the name of the requirements file.

    d. Use the **ansible galaxy -r filename** command.

8. Which command-line switch must be used with the **ansible-galaxy search** command to find roles that work on RHEL and CentOS?

    a. **--platforms EL**

    b. **--platforms RHEL-family**

    c. **--platforms RHEL**

    d. **--platforms CentOS**

9. Which variable is used in the RHEL Timesync System Role to identify that fast synchronization should be used?

    a. **iburst**

    b. **fast_sync**

    c. **hostname**

    d. **timesync_ntp_servers**

10. Which variables should be used in the RHEL SELinux System Role to manage file context? (Choose two.)

    a. **selinux_context**

    b. **selinux_fcontext**

    c. **selinux_dirs**

    d. **selinux_restore_dirs**

Foundation Topics

Using Ansible Roles

In Ansible, playbooks are used to perform common tasks. Tasks in an Ansible environment are rarely unique, however. If you write a playbook to install, enable, and expose the latest version of Nginx, it is very likely that someone else has done that before. That is exactly what roles are all about. Ansible roles are ready-to-use, playbook-based Ansible solutions that you can easily include in your own playbooks. Community roles are provided through Ansible Galaxy, but it's also possible to create your own roles. And apart from that, Red Hat provides RHEL System Roles. In this chapter you learn all about roles.

Working with Ansible roles has many benefits. The most important benefit is that roles make it possible to provide Ansible code in a reusable way. You can easily define a specific task in a role, and after defining it in a role, you can easily redistribute that and ensure that tasks are handled the same way, no matter where they are executed. Roles can be custom-made for specific environments, or default roles provided from Ansible Galaxy can be used.

Understanding Ansible Roles

The essence of using Ansible roles is that they work with include files. All the different components that you may use in a playbook are used in roles and stored in separate directories. While defining the role, you don't need to tell the role that it should look in some of these specific directories; it does that automatically. The only thing you need to do is tell your Ansible playbook that it should include a role. While you are doing that, the different components of the role are stored in different subdirectories. Listing 9-1 shows an example of the default role directory structure.

Table 9-2 provides an overview of the use of these subdirectories and where you'll find which type of file.

Listing 9-1 Roles Sample Directory Structure

```
[ansible@control roles]$ tree testrole/
testrole/
|-- defaults
|    '-- main.yml
|-- files
|-- handlers
|    '-- main.yml
|-- meta
```

```
|       '-- main.yml
|-- README.md
|-- tasks
|       '-- main.yml
|-- templates
|-- tests
|       |-- inventory
|       '-- test.yml
'-- vars
        '-- main.yml
```

Table 9-2 Role Directory Structure

Directory	Contents
defaults	Default variables that may be overwritten by other variables
files	Static files that are needed by role tasks
handlers	Handlers for use in this role
meta	Metadata, such as dependencies, plus license and maintainer information
tasks	Role task definitions
templates	Jinja2 templates
tests	Optional inventory and a test.yml file to test the role
vars	Variables that are not meant to be overwritten

Most of the role directories have a main.yml file. This is the entry-point YAML file that is used to define components in the role.

Understanding Role Location

Before creating your own custom role, you need to decide where to store it. Roles can be stored in different locations:

- ./roles is used to store roles in the current project directory. This location has the highest precedence.

- ~/.ansible/roles exists in the current user home directory and makes the role available to the current user only. This location has second-highest precedence.

- /etc/ansible/roles is the location where roles are stored to make them accessible to any user.

■ /usr/share/ansible/roles is the location where roles are stored after they are installed from RPM files. This location has lowest precedence and should not be used for storing custom-made roles.

To create a custom role, you just have to create the default role directory structure with a main.yml file at the location where it is expected. To easily create the custom directory structure, you can use the **ansible-galaxy init** command. This command creates all directories including sample files for you, after which you just have to provide the specific contents.

Using Roles from Playbooks

After making the roles you want to use available, you need to use them from a playbook. Using roles from a playbook is not difficult: you call them in a way that is similar to calling tasks from a playbook, and roles are included as a list. Listing 9-2 shows what this process may look like.

Listing 9-2   Calling Roles from a Playbook

```
---
- name: include some roles
  roles:
  - role1
  - role2
```

When roles are included in a playbook, that does change the order of execution in the playbook. Normally, all tasks in the playbook are executed, after which the handlers that are triggered are executed. When roles are included, the roles are executed before the tasks. In specific cases you might have to execute tasks before the roles. To do so, you can specify these tasks in a pre_tasks section. Also, it's possible to use the post_tasks section to include tasks that will be executed after the roles, but also after tasks specified in the playbook as well as the handlers they call.

Creating Custom Roles

Creating roles is not difficult; you just have to provide the required components in specific locations. Listing 9-3 shows an example of the motd role that you'll create yourself in Exercise 9-1. Look at how it is composed before starting the exercise.

Listing 9-3   Sample motd Role Structure

```
motd
|-- defaults
|    '-- main.yml
|          ---
|          # defaults file for motd
|          system_manager: anna@example.com
|-- meta
|    '-- main.yml
|          galaxy_info:
|          author: Sander van V
|          description: your description
|          company: your company (optional)
|          license: license (GPLv2, CC-BY, etc)
|          min_ansible_version: 2.5
|-- README.md
|-- tasks
|    '-- main.yml
|          ---
|          # tasks file for motd
|          - name: copy motd file
|            template:
|              src: templates/motd.j2
|              dest: /etc/motd
|              owner: root
|              group: root
|              mode: 0444
'-- templates
    '-- motd.j2
          Welcome to {{ ansible_hostname }}

          This file was created on {{ ansible_date_time.date }}
          Disconnect if you have no business being here

          Contact {{ system_manager }} if anything is wrong
```

The best way to learn how to create a custom role is to do it. So let's look at Exercise 9-1, which guides you through the procedure to create roles.

Exercise 9-1   Creating a Custom Role

1. Use **mkdir roles** to create a roles subdirectory in the current directory, and use **cd roles** to get into that subdirectory.

2. Use **ansible-galaxy init motd** to create the motd role structure.

3. Open the file motd/tasks/main.yml with an editor and ensure it has the following contents:

```
---
- name: copy motd file
  template:
    src: templates/motd.j2
    dest: /etc/motd
    owner: root
    group: root
    mode: 0444
```

4. Create the file motd/templates/motd.j2 and give it the following contents:

```
Welcome to {{ ansible_hostname }}

This file was created on {{ ansible_date_time.date }}
Disconnect if you have no business being here

Contact {{ system_manager }} if anything is wrong
```

5. Add the following contents to the file motd/defaults/main.yml:

```
---
system_manager: anna@example.com
```

6. Open the file motd/meta/main.yml and give it the following contents:

```
galaxy_info:
  author: student
  description: sample motd role
  company: mycompany
  license: license GPLv2
  min ansible_version: 2.5
```

7. This is all that you need to include in the role. Now create the playbook exercise91.yaml with the following contents:

```
---
- name: use the motd role playbook
  hosts: ansible2
  roles:
```

```
        - role: motd
          system_manager: bob@example.com
```

8. Run the playbook by using **ansible-playbook exercise91.yaml**.

9. Verify that modifications have been applied correctly by using the ad hoc command **ansible ansible2 -a "cat /etc/motd"**.

Managing Role Dependencies

Roles may have dependencies, meaning that one role might need another role to do what is needed. Using role dependencies makes sense if, for instance, you develop a custom role that installs an e-commerce solution that is based on a generic Apache web server and a generic Mariadb database server. In that case the custom role should trigger the dependencies, which can be done in the role meta/main.yml file.

When you're working with dependencies, dependent roles are always executed before the roles that depend on them. Also they are executed once. That means when two roles that are used in a playbook call the same dependency, the dependent role is executed once only. When calling dependent roles, it is possible to pass variables to the dependent role. Also you can define a **when** statement to ensure that the dependent role is executed only in specific situations. Listing 9-4 shows an example.

Listing 9-4   Defining Role Dependencies in meta/main.yml

```
dependencies:
- role: apache
  port: 8080
- role: mariabd
  when: environment == 'production'
```

Understanding File Organization Best Practices

Working with roles splits the contents of the role off the tasks that are run through the playbook. Splitting files to store them in a location that makes sense is common in Ansible, and this approach is documented in the Ansible Best Practices, which you can find at the Ansible documentation website. In this section you find a summary of some of the most important best practices from this document. Notice that in this book the best practice of using project directories is not applied.

- When you're working with Ansible, it's a good idea to work with project directories in bigger environments. Working with project directories makes it easier to delegate tasks and have the right people responsible for the right things.

- Each project directory may have its own ansible.cfg file, inventory file, and playbooks.

- If the project grows bigger, variable files and other include files may be used, and they are normally stored in subdirectories.

- At the top-level directory, create the main playbook from which other playbooks are included. The suggested name for the main playbook is site.yml.

- Use group_vars/ and host_vars/ to set host-related variables and do not define them in inventory.

- Consider using different inventory files to differentiate between production and staging phases.

- Use roles to standardize common tasks.

When you are working with roles, some additional recommendations apply:

- Use a version control repository to maintain roles in a consistent way. Git is commonly used for this purpose.

- Sensitive information should never be included in roles. Use Ansible Vault to store sensitive information in an encrypted way.

- Use **ansible-galaxy init** to create the role base structure. Remove files and directories you don't use.

- Don't forget to provide additional information in the role's README.md and meta/main.yml files.

- Keep roles focused on a specific function. It is better to use multiple roles to perform multiple tasks.

- Try to develop roles in a generic way, such that they can be used for multiple purposes.

Using Ansible Galaxy Roles

As an Ansible user or administrator, you can develop your own roles. The fact is, however, many tasks are common and need to be executed in different environments, so you might not have to develop roles yourself. For all of these standard tasks, there is Ansible Galaxy. Ansible Galaxy is a public library of Ansible content and contains thousands of roles that have been provided by community members.

Working with Galaxy

The easiest way to work with Ansible Galaxy is to use the website at https://galaxy.ansible.com, which is shown in Figure 9-1.

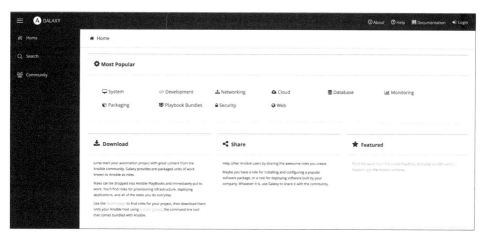

FIGURE 9-1   Ansible Galaxy Website Main Page

On the main page of the Galaxy website, you can see different categories of content that are provided. If you're looking for something specific, you can use the Search option. This option enables you to type what you're looking for, and you see a list of matching results next (see Figure 9-2).

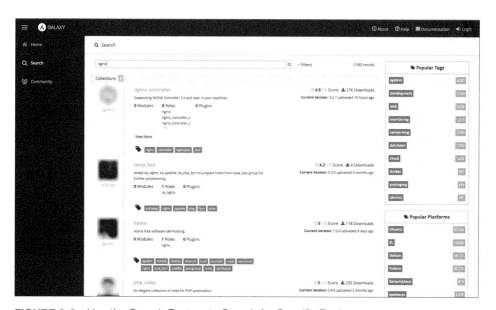

FIGURE 9-2   Use the Search Feature to Search for Specific Packages

In the result of any Search action, you see a list of collections as well as a list of roles. An Ansible Galaxy collection is a distribution format for Ansible content. It can contain roles as well as playbooks, modules, and plug-ins. In most cases you just need the roles, not the collection: roles contain all that you include in the playbooks you're working with.

When you select a role, Ansible Galaxy shows information about it. Some important indicators are the number of times the role has been downloaded and the score of the role. This information enables you to easily distinguish between commonly used roles and roles that are not used that often. Also you can use tags to make identifying Galaxy roles easier. These tags provide more information about a role and make it possible to search for roles in a more efficient way. Figure 9-3 shows an example of these role properties.

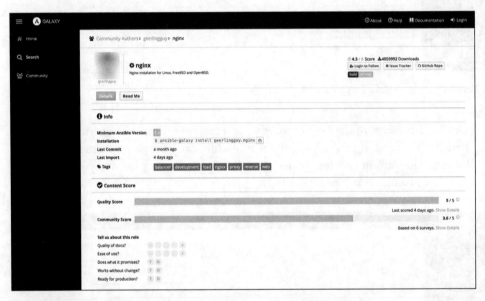

FIGURE 9-3   Ansible Galaxy Shows Appreciation Information for Roles

You can download roles directly from the Ansible Galaxy website; alternatively, you can use the **ansible-galaxy** command.

Using the ansible-galaxy Command

As an alternative to using the website, you can use the **ansible-galaxy** command to find roles based on many different keywords and manage them as well. When you use **ansible-galaxy search**, you need to provide a string as an argument. Ansible searches for this string in the name and description of the roles. Because you may get a lot of results, it makes sense to filter down the result of the search action a bit. Some useful command-line arguments are listed in Table 9-3.

Table 9-3 **ansible-galaxy** Useful Command-Line Options

Option	Use
--platforms	Operating system platform to search for
--author	GitHub username of the author
--galaxy-tags	Additional tags to filter by

After finding a role, you may use **ansible-galaxy info** to get more information about a role. Listing 9-5 shows what the information provided about the geerlingguy. docker role looks like.

Listing 9-5 Requesting Additional Information with **ansible-galaxy info**

```
[ansible@control ~]$ ansible-galaxy info geerlingguy.docker

Role: geerlingguy.docker
        description: Docker for Linux.
        active: True
        commit: c94e327a74a16a85f23d73be386c161a9cfe81d4
        commit_message: Allow rc 1 on centos7 when waiting for
systemctl.
        commit_url: https://api.github.com/repos/geerlingguy/
ansible-role-docker/gi>
        company: Midwestern Mac, LLC
        created: 2017-02-24T04:13:02.804883Z
        download_count: 5311691
        forks_count: 404
        github_branch: master
        github_repo: ansible-role-docker
        github_server: https://github.com
        github_user: geerlingguy
        id: 15836
        imported: 2020-04-12T10:53:22.695455-04:00
        is_valid: True
        issue_tracker_url: https://github.com/geerlingguy/
ansible-role-docker/issues
        license: license (BSD, MIT)
        min_ansible_version: 2.4
```

```
          modified: 2020-04-12T14:53:22.705998Z
          open_issues_count: 18
          path: ('/home/ansible/.ansible/roles', '/usr/share/ansible/
roles', '/etc/an>
          role_type: ANS
          stargazers_count: 596
          travis_status_url: https://travis-ci.org/geerlingguy/ansible-
role-docker.sv
```

Managing Ansible Galaxy Roles

Once the role you need has been identified, you can install it using **ansible-galaxy install**. This command normally installs the role into the ~/.ansible/roles directory because this role is specified in the **role_path** setting in ansible.cfg. If you want roles to be installed in another directory, consider changing this parameter. Alternatively, use **ansible-galaxy install** with the **-p** option to install the role to a different role path directory.

When working with Ansible roles, you can use a requirements file. The requirements file is a YAML file that you can include when using the **ansible-roles** command. The content of the file itself is quite simple and may look like the code in Listing 9-6. It's also possible to add roles from sources other than Ansible Galaxy, such as a Git repository or a tarball. In that case, you must specify the exact URL to the role using the **src** option. When you are installing roles from a Git repository, the **scm** keyword is also required and must be set to **git**.

Listing 9-6   Ansible Role Requirements File Example

```
- src: geerlingguy.nginx
  version: "2.7.0"
```

To install a role using the requirements file, you can use the **-r** option with the **ansible-galaxy install** command like this: **ansible-galaxy install -r roles/requirements.yml**.

To get an overview of currently installed roles, you can use the **ansible-galaxy list** command. Based on the role name that is found, you can use the **ansible-galaxy remove** command to remove roles from your system. You can practice working with **ansible-galaxy** in Exercise 9-2.

Exercise 9-2   Using ansible-galaxy to Manage Roles

1. Type **ansible-galaxy search --author geerlingguy --platforms EL** to see a list of roles that geerlingguy has created.

2. Make the command more specific and type **ansible-galaxy search nginx --author geerlingguy --platforms EL** to find the geerlingguy.nginx role.

3. Request more information about this role by using **ansible-galaxy info geerlingguy.nginx**.

4. Create a requirements file with the name listing96.yaml and give this file the following contents:

   ```
   - src: geerlingguy.nginx
     version: "2.7.0"
   ```

5. Add the line **roles_path = /home/ansible/roles** to the ansible.cfg file.

6. Use the command **ansible-galaxy install -r listing96.yaml** to install the role from the requirements file. It is possible that by the time you run this exercise, the specified version 2.7.0 is no longer available. If that is the case, use **ansible-galaxy info** again to find a version that still is available, and change the requirements file accordingly.

7. Type **ansible-galaxy list** to verify that the new role was successfully installed on your system.

8. Write a playbook with the name exercise92.yaml that uses the role and has the following contents:

   ```
   ---
   - name: install nginx using Galaxy role
     hosts: ansible2
     roles:
     - geerlingguy.nginx
   ```

9. Run the playbook using **ansible-playbook exercise92.yaml** and observe that the new role is installed from the custom roles path.

Using RHEL System Roles

Some parts of the RHEL operating system have changed significantly between RHEL versions. Examples are networking, which has changed from the init-based network script to the current solution that is based on NetworkManager. Another example is time synchronization, which has evolved from an NTP-based solution to a Chrony-based solution.

To allow for a uniform approach while managing multiple RHEL versions, Red Hat provides RHEL System Roles. RHEL System Roles make managing different parts of the operating system easy. Table 9-4 provides an overview.

Table 9-4   RHEL System Roles Overview

Role	Use
rhel-system-roles.kdump	Configures the kdump crash recovery service
rhel-system-roles.network	Configures network interfaces
rhel-system-roles.postfix	Configures hosts as a Mail Transfer Agent using Postfix
rhel-system-roles.selinux	Manages SELinux settings
rhel-system-roles.storage	Configures storage
rhel-system-roles.timesync	Configures time synchronization

Understanding RHEL System Roles

RHEL System Roles are based on the community Linux System Roles and provide a uniform interface to make configuration tasks easier where significant differences may exist between versions of the managed operating system. RHEL System Roles can be used to manage Red Hat Enterprise Linux 6.10 and later, as well as RHEL 7.4 and later, and all versions of RHEL 8. The RHEL System Roles listed in Table 9-4 are based on the generic Linux System Roles. Although they may be used for the specific task you want to accomplish, the Linux System Roles are not supported by RHEL technical support.

Installing RHEL System Roles

To use RHEL System Roles, you need to install the rhel-system-roles package on the control node by using **sudo yum install rhel-system-roles**. This package can be found in the RHEL 8 AppStream repository. After installation, the roles are copied to the /usr/share/ansible/roles directory, a directory that is a default part of the Ansible **roles_path** setting. If a modification to the **roles_path** setting has been made in ansible.cfg, the roles are applied to the first directory listed in the **roles_ path**. With the roles, some very useful documentation is installed also; you can find it in the /usr/share/doc/rhel-system-roles directory.

To pass configuration to the RHEL System Roles, variables are important. In the documentation directory, you can find information about variables that are required and used by the role. Some roles also contain a sample playbook that can be used as a blueprint when defining your own role. It's a good idea to use these as the basis for your own RHEL System Roles–based configuration. The next two sections describe the SELinux and the TimeSync System Roles, which provide nice and easy-to-implement examples of how you can use the RHEL System Roles.

Using the RHEL SELinux System Role

You learned earlier how to manage SELinux settings using task definitions in your own playbooks. Using the RHEL SELinux System Role provides an easy-to-use alternative. To use this role, start by looking at the documentation, which is in the /usr/share/doc/rhel-system-roles/selinux directory. A good file to start with is the README.md file, which provides lists of all the ingredients that can be used.

The SELinux System Role also comes with a sample playbook file. The most important part of this file is the **vars:** section, which defines the variables that should be applied by SELinux. Listing 9-7 shows an example of the section that contains the variable definitions.

Listing 9-7 Variable Definition in the SELinux System Role

```
---
- hosts: all
  become: true
  become_method: sudo
  become_user: root
  vars:
    selinux_policy: targeted
    selinux_state: enforcing
    selinux_booleans:
      - { name: 'samba_enable_home_dirs', state: 'on' }
      - { name: 'ssh_sysadm_login', state: 'on', persistent: 'yes' }
    selinux_fcontexts:
      - { target: '/tmp/test_dir(/.*)?', setype: 'user_home_dir_t',
ftype: 'd' }
    selinux_restore_dirs:
      - /tmp/test_dir
    selinux_ports:
      - { ports: '22100', proto: 'tcp', setype: 'ssh_port_t', state:
'present' }
    selinux_logins:
      - { login: 'sar-user', seuser: 'staff_u', serange: 's0-s0:c0.
c1023', state: 'present' }
```

As you can see in Listing 9-7, the variables are used to define the most important parts of what needs to be configured with SELinux. Using the RHEL SELinux System Role is just as easy as copying over the sample playbook in the documentation directory, edit the variables to represent the configuration that you want to create, and run the playbook. Table 9-5 provides an overview of the variables and the way they should be used.

Table 9-5   SELinux Variables Overview

Variable	Use
selinux_policy	The name of the policy to use; normally set to targeted
selinux_state	The state SELinux should be in, as managed with **setenforce**
selinux_booleans	A list of Booleans that need to be set
selinux_fcontext	A list of file contexts that need to be set, including the target file or directory to which they should be applied
selinux_restore_dirs	A list of directories at which the Linux **restorecon** command needs to be executed to apply a new context
selinux_ports	A list of ports and SELinux port types
selinux_logins	A list of SELinux users and roles that can be created

Most of the time while configuring SELinux, you need to apply the correct state as well as file context. To set the appropriate file context, you first need to define the **selinux_fcontext** variable. Next, you have to define **selinux_restore_dirs** also to ensure that the desired context is applied correctly. In Listing 9-8 you can see what a playbook looks like; this one sets the httpd_sys_content_t context type to the /web directory. Notice that this playbook is completely based on the sample playbook in /usr/share/doc. The most significant change is that unnecessary lines are removed and the values of two variables have been set.

Listing 9-8   Sample Playbook That Uses the SELinux RHEL System Role

```
---
- hosts: ansible2
  vars:
    selinux_policy: targeted
    selinux_state: enforcing
    selinux_fcontexts:
      - { target: '/web(/.*)?', setype: 'httpd_sys_content_t', ftype:
'd' }
    selinux_restore_dirs:
      - /web

  # prepare prerequisites which are used in this playbook
  tasks:
    - name: Creates directory
      file:
```

```
        path: /web
        state: directory
    - name: execute the role and catch errors
      block:
        - include_role:
            name: rhel-system-roles.selinux
```

When you use the RHEL SELinux System Role, some changes require the managed host to be rebooted. To take care of this, a block structure is used, where the System Role runs in the block. When a change that requires a reboot is applied, the SELinux System Role sets the variable **selinux_reboot_required** and fails. As a result, the rescue section in the playbook is executed. This rescue section first makes sure that the playbook fails because of the **selinux_reboot_required** variable being set to true. If that is the case, the reboot module is called to reboot the managed host. While rebooting, playbook execution waits for the rebooted host to reappear, and when that happens, the RHEL SELinux System Role is called again to complete its work. Listing 9-9 shows the part of the sample playbook that takes care of this task.

Listing 9-9 Rebooting Managed Hosts If Required

```
- name: execute the role and catch errors
      block:
        - include_role:
            name: rhel-system-roles.selinux
      rescue:
        # Fail if failed for a different reason than
selinux_reboot_required.
        - name: handle errors
          fail:
            msg: "role failed"
          when: not selinux_reboot_required

        - name: restart managed host
          shell: sleep 2 && shutdown -r now "Ansible updates
triggered"
          async: 1
          poll: 0
          ignore_errors: true
```

```
   - name: wait for managed host to come back
     wait_for_connection:
       delay: 10
       timeout: 300

   - name: reapply the role
     include_role:
       name: rhel-system-roles.selinux
```

Using the RHEL TimeSync System Role

Another example of a RHEL System Role is the TimeSync role. Using this role is convenient and relatively easy, and using it comes down to setting the appropriate variables in the playbook that calls the role. The most important setting that needs to be changed is the **timesync_ntp_servers** variable. This variable specifies attributes to indicate which time servers should be used. The **hostname** attribute identifies the name of IP address of the time server. The **iburst** option is used to enable or disable fast initial time synchronization using the **timesync_ntp_servers** variable.

All the other benefits of using this RHEL System Role happen under the hood. The System Role finds out which version of RHEL is used, and according to the currently used version, it either configures NTP or Chronyd. Because this is automatically detected, no further action is required. In Exercise 9-3 you practice how to use the RHEL TimeSync System Role.

Exercise 9-3   Using a RHEL System Role to Manage Time Synchronization

1. Use **cp /usr/share/doc/rhel-system-roles/timesync/example-timesync-playbook.yml exercise93.yaml** to copy the sample timesync playbook to the current directory.

2. Edit the file exercise93.yaml to look like the following:

```
---
- hosts: ansible
  vars:
    timesync_ntp_servers:
    - hostname: pool.ntp.org
      iburst: yes
  roles:
  - rhel-system-roles.timesync
```

3. Add the timezone module and the **timezone** variable to the playbook to set the timezone as well. The complete playbook should look like the following:

```
---
- hosts: ansible2
  vars:
    timesync_ntp_servers:
    - hostname: pool.ntp.org
      iburst: yes
    timezone: UTC
  roles:
  - rhel-system-roles.timesync
  tasks:
  - name: set timezone
    timezone:
      name: "{{ timezone }}"
```

4. Use **ansible-playbook exercise93.yaml** to run the playbook. Observe its output. Notice that some messages in red are shown, but these can safely be ignored.

5. Use **ansible ansible2 -a "timedatectl show"** and notice that the **timezone** variable is set to UTC.

Summary

Ansible roles make working with Ansible easier because they provide standard chunks of code that can easily be included in a playbook. Ansible roles can be provided to playbooks in multiple ways: you can write them yourself, you can obtain them from Ansible Galaxy, and you can also use them as provided by the rhel-system-roles RPM package. In this chapter you learned how to work with all these approaches.

Exam Preparation Tasks

As mentioned in the section "How to Use This Book" in the Introduction, you have a couple of choices for exam preparation: the exercises here, Chapter 16, "Final Preparation," and the exam simulation questions on the companion website.

Review All Key Topics

Review the most important topics in this chapter, noted with the Key Topics icon in the outer margin of the page. Table 9-6 lists a reference of these key topics and the page numbers on which each is found.

Table 9-6   Key Topics for Chapter 9

Key Topic Element	Description	Page Number
Paragraph	Ansible Galaxy Roles	218

Memory Tables

Print a copy of Appendix D, "Memory Tables" (found on the companion website), or at least the section for this chapter, and complete the tables and lists from memory. Appendix E, "Memory Tables Answer Key," also on the companion website, includes completed tables and lists to check your work.

Define Key Terms

Define the following key terms from this chapter, and check your answers in the glossary:

role, Galaxy, requirements file, RHEL System Role

Review Questions

1. How do you specify that roles should be stored in a nonstandard directory?

2. Where in a role should you define default variables that may be overwritten?

3. Which file in the role specification should contain dependency specifications?

4. If no changes have been made to the default directory where roles should be stored, in which directory will you find newly installed roles?

5. What can you do to make sure that tasks in a playbook are executed before the roles?

6. What can you do to set tasks to be executed after all roles, but also after all other tasks and their handlers in a playbook?

7. Which command should you use to define the default role directory and file structure?

8. How can you install multiple roles from Ansible Galaxy all at once?

9. What is the best way to start writing a playbook that is based on a RHEL System Role?

10. While investigating what to modify while working with RHEL System Roles, what should you look at first?

End-of-Chapter Labs

This chapter includes two labs. The first lab allows you to practice working with Ansible roles, and in the second lab, you apply a RHEL System Role.

Lab 9-1

Create a playbook that starts the Nginx web server on ansible1, according to the following requirements:

- A requirements file must be used to install the Nginx web server. Do NOT use the latest version of the Galaxy role, but instead use the version before that.

- The same requirements file must also be used to install the latest version of postgresql.

- The playbook needs to ensure that neither httpd nor mysql is currently installed.

Lab 9-2

Use the RHEL SELinux System Role to manage SELinux properties according to the following requirements:

- A Boolean is set to allow SELinux relabeling to be automated using cron.

- The directory /var/ftp/uploads is created, permissions are set to 777, and the context label is set to public_content_rw_t.

- SELinux should allow web servers to use port 82 instead of port 80.

- SELinux is in enforcing state.

This chapter covers the following subjects:

- Advanced Inventory Usage
- Optimizing Ansible Processing
- Including and Importing Files

## CHAPTER 10

Using Ansible in Large Environments

The following RHCE exam objectives are covered in this chapter:

- Install and configure an Ansible control node
  - Create a static host inventory file
  - Manage parallelism

"Do I Know This Already?" Quiz

The "Do I Know This Already?" quiz allows you to assess whether you should read this entire chapter thoroughly or jump to the "Exam Preparation Tasks" section. If you are in doubt about your answers to these questions or your own assessment of your knowledge of the topics, read the entire chapter. Table 10-1 lists the major headings in this chapter and their corresponding "Do I Know This Already?" quiz questions. You can find the answers in Appendix A, "Answers to the 'Do I Know This Already?' Quizzes and Review Questions."

Table 10-1 "Do I Know This Already?" Section-to-Question Mapping

Foundation Topics Section	Questions
Advanced Inventory Usage	1–4
Optimizing Ansible Processing	5, 6
Including and Importing Files	7–10

1. Which of the following host name patterns is invalid?
   a. **webservers***
   b. **192.168.4.200,web1**
   c. **all,!web1**
   d. **web&,file**

2. Dynamic inventory scripts can be used in many environments. Which of the following environments is not supported?

   a. Red Hat Satellite

   b. Active Directory

   c. OpenStack

   d. None of the above

3. The **ansible-inventory** command can be used with different options. Which of the following is not one of them?

   a. **--list**

   b. **--graph**

   c. **--host**

   d. **--all**

4. Dynamic inventory scripts have some requirements. Which of the following is not one of them?

   a. Is written in Python

   b. Produces output in JSON format

   c. Implements a **--list** option

   d. Implements a **--host <hostname>** option

5. How would you make sure that all tasks in one specific playbook are fully executed on a group of three hosts before moving over to the next group of three hosts?

   a. Use **forks: 3** in ansible.cfg.

   b. Start the play using the **--forks 3** parameter.

   c. Use **serial: 3** in ansible.cfg.

   d. Use **serial: 3** in the play header.

6. How would you improve performance and make sure that tasks can be executed on 50 hosts simultaneously?

   a. Use **forks: 50** in ansible.cfg.

   b. Start the play using the **--forks 50** parameter.

   c. Use **serial: 50** in ansible.cfg.

   d. Use **serial: 50** in the play header.

7. Which solution should you use if contents from an external file need to be processed in a playbook if a specific condition is true?

   a. Role

   b. Include

   c. Import

   d. Expansion

8. Which of the following do you need if you want tasks to be included in the playbook before the work on any task in the playbook is started?

   a. **import_playbook**

   b. **import_tasks**

   c. **include_playbook**

   d. **include_tasks**

9. When you use **include_tasks**, several limitations apply. Which of the following is not one of them?

   a. When you use **ansible-playbook --list-tasks**, tasks that are included tasks are not displayed.

   b. You cannot use **ansible-playbook --start-at-task** to start a playbook at a task from an included task file.

   c. You cannot use notify to trigger a handler that is in the included tasks file.

   d. You cannot use a conditional statement on included task files.

10. When you use **import_tasks**, several limitations apply. Which of the following is not one of them?

    a. Loops cannot be used.

    b. If a variable is used to specify the name of the file to import, it cannot be a host or group inventory variable.

    c. The ansible-playbook **--start-at-task** command cannot be used.

    d. When using a **when** statement on an entire **import_tasks** file, the conditional statements are applied to each of the tasks in this file.

Foundation Topics

Advanced Inventory Usage

You have already learned how to create an inventory file. Up to now, you have worked with a small inventory file that contains just a couple of hosts, which can be put into inventory groups. When an environment is getting bigger, you'll probably want some more flexibility regarding inventory files. This section is about advanced inventory usage. You learn how to make inventory flexible by working with host name patterns, dynamic inventory, and multiple inventory files.

Working with Host Name Patterns

To work with hosts, you need to list them in inventory. This can be done by including host names, as well as IP addresses. If you want to use an IP address in a playbook, the IP address must be specified as such in the inventory. You cannot use IP addresses that are based only on DNS name resolving. So specifying an IP address in the playbook but not in the inventory file—assuming DNS name resolution is going to take care of the IP address resolving—doesn't work.

The easiest way to refer to multiple hosts is to use host groups. Groups can be specified in inventory, and apart from the specified groups, there are the implicit host groups all and ungrouped. Apart from that, host name wildcards may be used. For instance, you can use **ansible -m ping 'ansible*'** to match all hosts that have a name starting with ansible. When you use wildcards in host name patterns, it is important to always put the pattern between quotes: the command **ansible -m ping ansible*** will fail with a no matching hosts error. Wildcards can be used at any place in the host name. So you also can use **ansible -m ping '*ble1'**, as long as the pattern is placed between quotes.

Notice that when you use wildcards to match host names, Ansible doesn't distinguish between IP addresses, host names, or hosts; it just matches anything. So the pattern 'web*' matches all servers that are members of the group 'webservers', but also hosts 'web1' and 'web2'.

To address multiple hosts, you can also specify a comma-separated list of targets, as in **ansible -m ping ansible1,192.168.4.202**. The comma-separated list can be a mix of anything and can include host names, IP addresses, and host group names.

Some more advanced patterns are possible as well. You can specify a logical AND condition by including an ampersand (&), and a logical NOT by using an exclamation point (!). So the pattern **web,&file** applies to hosts only if they are members of the web and file groups, and the pattern **web,!webserver1** applies to all hosts in the web group, except host webserver1. When you use the logical AND operator, the position of the ampersand doesn't really matter. So you can rewrite **web,&file** as **&web,file** also. Notice that you can use a colon (:) instead of a comma (,), but using a comma is better to avoid confusion when using IPv6 addresses, which contain colons by default.

Configuring Dynamic Inventory

Static inventories work well for a small environment. However, if the environment is getting bigger and more dynamic, static inventories are not that efficient anymore, so dynamic inventories may be considered. A dynamic inventory is a script that can be used to detect whether new hosts have been added to the managed environment.

 Dynamic inventory scripts are provided by the community and exist for many different environments. Alternatively, it is fairly easy to write your own dynamic inventory script. The main requirement is that the dynamic inventory script works with a **--list** and a **--host <hostname>** option and produces its output in JSON format. Also, the script must have the Linux execute permission set. Many dynamic inventory scripts are written in Python, but this is not a requirement. Any script that supports the **--list** and **--host** options and generates JSON output will do.

Writing dynamic inventory scripts is not an exam requirement, but Listing 10-1 shows what a sample dynamic inventory script looks like.

Listing 10-1   Sample Dynamic Inventory Script

```
#!/usr/bin/python

from subprocess import Popen,PIPE
import sys

try:
     import json
except ImportError:
     import simplejson as json

result = {}
result['all'] = {}

pipe = Popen(['getent', 'hosts'], stdout=PIPE,
universal_newlines=True)
```

```
result['all']['hosts'] = []

for line in pipe.stdout.readlines():
    s = line.split()
    result['all']['hosts']=result['all']['hosts']+s

result['all']['vars'] = {}

if len(sys.argv) == 2 and sys.argv[1] == '--list':
    print(json.dumps(result))

elif len(sys.argv) == 3 and sys.argv[1] == '--host':
    print(json.dumps({}))

else:
    print("Requires an argument, please use --list or --host <host>")
```

As you can see in Listing 10-1, the script core is the line **pipe = Popen(['getent',
'hosts'], stdout=PIPE, universal_newline=True)**, which gets a list of hosts using
the **getent** function. This queries all hosts in /etc/hosts and other mechanisms
where host name resolving is enabled. To show the resulting host list, you can use
the **--list** command, and to show details for a specific host, you can use the option
--host hostname. Listing 10-2 shows an example of the output in JSON format.

Listing 10-2   JSON Output of the listing101.py Script

```
[ansible@control rhce8-book]$ ./listing101.py --list
{"all": {"hosts": ["127.0.0.1", "localhost", "localhost.localdomain",
"localhost4", "localhost4.localdomain4", "127.0.0.1", "localhost",
"localhost.localdomain", "localhost6", "localhost6.localdomain6",
"192.168.4.200", "control.example.com", "control", "192.168.4.201",
"ansible1.example.com", "ansible1", "192.168.4.202", "ansible2.
example.com", "ansible2"], "vars": {}}}
```

Even if simple, the script in Listing 10-1 is beneficial because it automatically
detects when new hosts have been added to DNS or the /etc/hosts file. Dynamic
inventory scripts are activated in the same way as regular inventory scripts: you
use the **-i** option to either the **ansible** or the **ansible-playbook** command to pass
the name of the inventory script as an argument. You just need to make sure that
the dynamic inventory script has the Linux execute permission set. Use **chmod +x
scriptname** if this is not the case.

You can see the real value of dynamic inventory scripts when they are used in large environments. That can be an environment where an external directory service is used, one that keeps track of all hosts in the environment. Such a directory service can be based on a wide range of solutions, including FreeIPA, Active Directory, or Red Hat Satellite. Dynamic inventory scripts also are available for virtual machine-based infrastructures such as VMware of Red Hat Enterprise Virtualization, where virtual machines can be discovered dynamically. Another main area where dynamic inventory scripts can be found is in cloud environments, where scripts are available for many solutions, including AWS, GCE, Azure, and OpenStack.

When you are working with dynamic inventory, additional parameters are normally required. For instance, to get an inventory from an EC2 cloud environment, you need to enter your web keys. To pass these parameters, many inventory scripts come with an additional configuration file that is formatted in .ini style. The community-provided ec2.py script, for instance, comes with an ec2.ini parameter file.

Another feature that is seen in many inventory scripts is cache management. To make working with inventory scripts more efficient, you can use a cache to store names and parameters of recently discovered hosts. If a cache is provided, options exist to manage the cache, allowing you, for instance, to make sure that the inventory information really is recently discovered.

Using the ansible-inventory Command

As shown in Listing 10-2, the default output of a dynamic inventory script is unformatted. To show formatted JSON output of the scripts, you can use the **ansible-inventory** command. Apart from the **--list** and **--host** options, this command also uses the **--graph** option to show a list of hosts, including the host groups they are a member of. In Listing 10-3, you can see the output of the **ansible-inventory -i listing101.py --graph** command. Remember this will work only if the Linux execute permission is set on the dynamic inventory file.

Listing 10-3 Showing Output of the **ansible-inventory** Command

```
[ansible@control rhce8-book]$ ansible-inventory -i listing101.py
--graph
[WARNING]: A duplicate localhost-like entry was found (localhost).
First found
localhost was 127.0.0.1
@all:
  |--@ungrouped:
  |   |--127.0.0.1
  |   |--192.168.4.200
```

```
|    |--192.168.4.201
|    |--192.168.4.202
|    |--ansible1
|    |--ansible1.example.com
|    |--ansible2
|    |--ansible2.example.com
|    |--control
|    |--control.example.com
|    |--localhost
|    |--localhost.localdomain
|    |--localhost4
|    |--localhost4.localdomain4
|    |--localhost6
|    |--localhost6.localdomain6
```

Working with Multiple Inventory Files

Ansible supports working with multiple inventory files. One way of using multiple inventory files is to enter multiple **-i** parameters with the **ansible** or **ansible-playbook** commands to specify the name of the files to be used. So **ansible-inventory -i inventory -i listing101.py --list** would produce an output list based on the static inventory in the inventory file, as well as the dynamic inventory that is generated by the listing101.py Python script. Alternatively, you can specify the name of a directory using the **-i** command-line option. This approach uses all files in the directory as inventory files. Notice that when using an inventory directory, dynamic inventory files still must be executable for this approach to work. In Exercise 10-1, you practice working with multiple inventories.

Exercise 10-1   Using Multiple Inventories

1. Open a shell as the ansible user and create a directory with the name inventories.

2. Copy the file listing101.py to the directory inventories.

3. Also copy the inventory file to the directory inventories.

4. To make sure both inventories have some unique contents, add the following lines to the file inventories/inventory:

   ```
   webserver1
   webserver2
   ```

5. Add the following lines to the Linux /etc/hosts file:

```
192.168.4.203     ansible3.example.com     ansible3
192.168.4.204     ansible4.example.com     ansible4
```

6. Use the command **ansible-inventory -i inventories --list**. In the result you should see the web servers that you added to the static inventory file, as well as the hosts that you added to /etc/hosts, which is the input file for the dynamic inventory. This result proves that the new inventory directory works.

Optimizing Ansible Processing

To optimize the working of Ansible, you can manage parallel as well as serial task execution. Parallel task execution manages the number of hosts on which tasks are executed simultaneously. Serial task execution can be used to make sure that all tasks are executed on a host or group of hosts before proceeding to the next host or group of hosts.

Managing Parallel Task Execution

While processing a playbook, Ansible can apply the tasks to multiple hosts simultaneously. Theoretically, Ansible can run tasks on all hosts at the same time, and in many cases that would not be a problem because processing is executed on the managed host anyway. If, however, network devices or other nodes that do not have their own Python stack are involved, processing needs to be done on the control host. To prevent the control host from being overloaded in that case, the maximum number of simultaneous connections by default is set to 5. You can manage this setting by using the **forks** parameter in ansible.cfg. Alternatively, you can use the **-f** option with the **ansible** and **ansible-playbook** commands.

Processing a maximum of five managed nodes simultaneously is good if processing needs to be done on the control host. Because processing in most environments is done on the managed hosts, the maximum setting of five forks just slows down the working of Ansible, and it is a good idea to increase this maximum to something significantly higher. If only Linux hosts are managed, there is no reason to keep the maximum number of simultaneous tasks much lower than 100.

While executing tasks, Ansible processes tasks in a playbook one by one. This means that, by default, the first task is executed on all managed hosts. Once that is done, the next task is processed, until all tasks have been executed. Notice that there is no specific order in the execution of tasks, so you may see that in one run ansible1 is processed before ansible2, while on another run they might be processed in the opposite order.

Managing Serial Task Execution

By default, Ansible runs task by task. This means that it runs the first task on all hosts, and once that is done, it proceeds to run the next task on all hosts. In some cases, this is undesired behavior. If, for instance, a playbook is used to update a cluster of hosts this way, this would create a situation where the old software has been updated, but the new version has not been started yet and the entire cluster would be down. To prevent this situation from happening, you can configure serial task execution. To do so, you use the **serial** keyword in the play header.

When, for instance, the **serial: 3** keyword is used in the header of a play, all tasks are executed on three hosts, and after completely running all tasks on three hosts, the next group of three hosts is handled. In Exercise 10-2, you practice using the **serial** and **forks** parameters.

Exercise 10-2   Managing Parallelism

1. Apply the instructions in Chapter 2, "Installing Ansible," to add two more managed nodes with the names ansible3.example.com and ansible4.example.com. Specific steps are shown in Exercises 2-1, 2-5, 2-6, and 2-7.

2. Open the inventory file with an editor and add the following lines:
   ```
   ansible3
   ansible4
   ```

3. Open the ansible.cfg file and add the line **forks = 4** to the [defaults] section.

4. Write a playbook with the name exercise102-install that installs and enables the Apache web server and another playbook with the name exercise102-remove that disables and removes the Apache web server. Because this is a fairly basic task, no specific instructions are provided. Consult the files **exercise102-install.yaml** and **exercise102-remove.yaml** in the GitHub repository at https://github.com/sandervanvugt/rhce8-book if you need additional help with these tasks.

5. Run **ansible-playbook exercise102-remove.yaml** to remove and disable the Apache web server on all hosts. This is just to make sure you start with a clean configuration.

6. Run the playbook to install and run the web server, using **time ansible-playbook exercise102-install.yaml**, and notice the time it takes to run the playbook.

7. Run **ansible-playbook exercise102-remove.yaml** again to get back to a clean state.

8. Edit **ansible.cfg** and change the **forks** parameter to **forks = 2**. Run the **time ansible-playbook exercise102-install.yaml** command again to see how much time it takes now; it should take considerably longer. Notice that apart from the time that it takes, you see no output in the playbook execution while it runs.

9. Edit the **exercise102-install.yaml** playbook and include the line **serial: 2** in the play header.

10. Run the **ansible-playbook exercise102-remove.yaml** command again to get back to a clean state.

11. Run the **ansible-playbook exercise102-install.yaml** command again and observe that the entire play is executed on two hosts only before the next group of two hosts is taken care of.

Including and Importing Files

When playbooks get larger, the recommendation is to split them into separate files. This makes managing large playbooks easier and allows you to dedicate specific management tasks to specific administrators. Also, splitting the files makes it possible to reuse playbook contents in different projects.

You have already seen how roles can be used to include generic code from other playbooks. Apart from using roles, you also can include and import files. When content is included, it is dynamically processed at the moment that Ansible reaches that content. If content is imported, Ansible performs the import operation before starting to work on the tasks in the playbook.

Files can be included and imported at different levels:

- **Roles:** Roles are typically used to process a complete set of instructions provided by the role. Roles have a specific structure as well.

- **Playbooks:** Playbooks can be imported as a complete playbook. You cannot do this from within a play. Playbooks can be imported only at the top level of the playbook.

- **Tasks:** A task file is just a list of tasks and can be imported or included in another task.

- **Variables:** As discussed in Chapter 6, "Working with Variables and Facts," variables can be maintained in external files and included in a playbook. This makes managing generic multipurpose variables easier.

Importing Playbooks

Importing playbooks is common in a setup where one master playbook is used, from which different additional playbooks are included. According to the Ansible Best Practices Guide (which is a part of the Ansible documentation), the master playbook could have the name site.yaml, and it can be used to include playbooks for each specific set of servers, for instance. When a playbook is imported, this replaces the entire play. So, you cannot import a playbook at a task level; it needs to happen at a play level. Listing 10-4 gives an example of the playbook imported in Listing 10-5. In Listing 10-6, you can see the result of running the **ansible-playbook listing105.yaml** command.

Listing 10-4   Sample Playbook to Be Imported

```
- hosts: all
  tasks:
  - debug:
      msg: running the imported play
```

Listing 10-5   Importing a Playbook

```
---
- name: run a task
  hosts: all
  tasks:
  - debug:
      msg: running task1

- name: importing a playbook
  import_playbook: listing104.yaml
```

Listing 10-6   Running **ansible-playbook listing105.yaml** Result

```
[ansible@control rhce8-book]$ ansible-playbook listing105.yaml


PLAY [run a task] ******************************************************
**********


TASK [Gathering Facts] ************************************************
**********
```

```
ok: [ansible2]
ok: [ansible1]
ok: [ansible3]
ok: [ansible4]

TASK [debug] ********************************************************
**********
ok: [ansible1] => {
    "msg": "running task1"
}
ok: [ansible2] => {
    "msg": "running task1"
}
ok: [ansible3] => {
    "msg": "running task1"
}
ok: [ansible4] => {
    "msg": "running task1"
}

PLAY [all] *********************************************************
**********

TASK [Gathering Facts] *********************************************
**********
ok: [ansible2]
ok: [ansible1]
ok: [ansible3]
ok: [ansible4]

TASK [debug] ********************************************************
**********
ok: [ansible1] => {
    "msg": "running the imported play"
}
ok: [ansible2] => {
    "msg": "running the imported play"
}
ok: [ansible3] => {
    "msg": "running the imported play"
}
```

```
ok: [ansible4] => {
    "msg": "running the imported play"
}


PLAY RECAP *************************************************************
**********
ansible1                        : ok=4      changed=0    unreachable=0
failed=0     skipped=0       rescued=0    ignored=0
ansible2                        : ok=4      changed=0    unreachable=0
failed=0     skipped=0       rescued=0    ignored=0
ansible3                        : ok=4      changed=0    unreachable=0
failed=0     skipped=0       rescued=0    ignored=0
ansible4                        : ok=4      changed=0    unreachable=0
failed=0     skipped=0       rescued=0    ignored=0
```

Importing and Including Task Files

Instead of importing complete playbooks, you may include task files. When you use **import_tasks**, the tasks are statically imported while executing the playbook. When you use **include_tasks**, the tasks are dynamically included at the moment they are needed. Dynamically including task files is recommended when the task file is used in a conditional statement. If task files are mainly used to make development easier by working with separate task files, they can be statically imported.

There are a few considerations when working with **import_tasks** to statically import tasks:

- Loops cannot be used with **import_tasks**.

- If a variable is used to specify the name of the file to import, this cannot be a host or group inventory variable.

- When you use a **when** statement on the entire **import_tasks** file, the conditional statements are applied to each task that is involved.

As an alternative, **include_tasks** can be used to dynamically include a task file. This approach also comes with some considerations:

- When you use the **ansible-playbook --list-tasks** command, tasks that are in the included tasks are not displayed.

- You cannot use **ansible-playbook --start-at-task** to start a playbook on a task that comes from an included task file.

- You cannot use a **notify** statement in the main playbook to trigger a handler that is in the included tasks file.

TIP   When you use includes and imports to work with task files, the recommendation is to store the task files in a separate directory. Doing so makes it easier to delegate task management to specific users.

Using Variables When Importing and Including Files

The main goal to work with imported and included files is to make working with reusable code easy. To make sure you reach this goal, the imported and included files should be as generic as possible. That means it's a bad idea to include names of specific items that may change when used in a different context. Think, for instance, of the names of packages, users, services, and more.

To deal with include files in a flexible way, you should define specific items as variables. Within the **include_tasks** file, for instance, you refer to {{ package }}, and in the main playbook from which the include files are called, you can define the variables. Obviously, you can use this approach with a straight variable definition or by using host variable or group variable include files.

EXAM TIP   It's always possible to configure items in a way that is brilliant but quite complex. On the exam it's not a smart idea to go for complex. Just keep your solution as easy as possible. The only requirement on the exam is to get things working, and it doesn't matter exactly how you do that.

In Listings 10-7 through 10-10, you can see how include and import files are used to work on one project. The main playbook, shown in Listing 10-9, defines the variables to be used, as well as the names of the include and import files. Listings 10-7 and 10-8 show the code from the include files, which use the variables that are defined in Listing 10-9. The result of running the playbook in Listing 10-9 can be seen in Listing 10-10.

Listing 10-7   The Include Tasks File tasks/service.yaml Used for Services Definition

```
- name: install {{ package }}
  yum:
    name: "{{ package }}"
    state: latest
- name: start {{ service }}
  service:
    name: "{{ service }}"
    enabled: true
    state: started
```

The sample tasks file in Listing 10-7 is straightforward; it uses the yum module to install a package and the service module to start and enable the package. The variables this file refers to are defined in the main playbook in Listing 10-9.

Listing 10-8   The Import Tasks File tasks/firewall.yaml Used for Firewall Definition

```
- name: install the firewall
  package:
    name: "{{ firewall_package }}"
    state: latest
- name: start the firewall
  service:
    name: "{{ firewall_service }}"
    enabled: true
    state: started
- name: open the port for the service
  firewalld:
    service: "{{ item }}"
    immediate: true
    permanent: true
    state: enabled
  loop: "{{ firewall_rules }}"
```

In the sample firewall file in Listing 10-8, the firewall service is installed, defined, and configured. In the configuration of the firewalld service, a loop is used on the variable firewall_rules. This variable obviously is defined in Listing 10-9, which is the file where site-specific contents such as variables are defined.

Listing 10-9   Main Playbook Example

```
---
- name: setup a service
  hosts: ansible2
  tasks:
  - name: include the services task file
    include_tasks: tasks/service.yaml
    vars:
      package: httpd
      service: httpd
```

```
     when: ansible_facts['os_family'] == 'RedHat'
  - name: import the firewall file
    import_tasks: tasks/firewall.yaml
    vars:
      firewall_package: firewalld
      firewall_service: firewalld
      firewall_rules:
      - http
      - https
```

The main playbook in Listing 10-9 shows the site-specific configuration. It performs two main tasks: it defines variables, and it calls an include file and an import
file. The variables that are defined are used by the include and import files. The
include_tasks statement is executed in a **when** statement. Notice that the **firewall_
rules** variable contains a list as its value, which is used by the loop that is defined in
the import file.

Listing 10-10   Running **ansible-playbook listing109.yaml**

```
[ansible@control rhce8-book]$ ansible-playbook listing109.yaml

PLAY [setup a service] **********************************************

TASK [Gathering Facts] **********************************************
ok: [ansible2]

TASK [include the services task file] ******************************
included: /home/ansible/rhce8-book/tasks/service.yaml for ansible2

TASK [install httpd] ***********************************************
ok: [ansible2]

TASK [start httpd] *************************************************
changed: [ansible2]

TASK [install the firewall] ***************************************
changed: [ansible2]
```

```
TASK [start the firewall] ********************************************
ok: [ansible2]

TASK [open the port for the service] ********************************
changed: [ansible2] => (item=http)
changed: [ansible2] => (item=https)

PLAY RECAP **********************************************************
ansible2                    : ok=7    changed=3    unreachable=0
failed=0    skipped=0    rescued=0    ignored=0
```

The interesting thing in the Listing 10-10 output is that the include file is dynamically included while running the playbook. This is not the case for the statically imported file. In Exercise 10-3 you practice working with include files.

Exercise 10-3   Using Includes and Imports

In this exercise you create a simple master playbook that installs a service. The name of the service is defined in a variable file, and the specific tasks are included through task files.

1. Open the file exercise103-vars.yaml and define three variables as follows:

   ```
   packagename: vsftpd
   servicename: vsftpd
   firewalld_servicename: ftp
   ```

2. Create the exercise103-ftp.yaml file and give it the following contents to install, enable, and start the vsftpd service and also to make it accessible in the firewall:

   ```
   - name: install {{ packagename }}
     yum:
       name: "{{ packagename }}"
       state: latest
   - name: enable and start {{ servicename }}
     service:
       name: "{{ servicename }}"
       state: started
       enabled: true
   - name: open the service in the firewall
     firewalld:
       service: "{{ firewalld_servicename }}"
       permanent: yes
       state: enabled
   ```

3. Create the exercise103-copy.yaml file that manages the /var/ftp/pub/README file and make sure it has the following contents:

```
- name: copy a file
  copy:
    content: "welcome to this server"
    dest: /var/ftp/pub/README
```

4. Create the master playbook exercise103.yaml that includes all of them and give it the following contents:

```
---
- name: install vsftpd on ansible2
  vars_files: exercise103-vars.yaml
  hosts: ansible2
  tasks:
  - name: install and enable vsftpd
    import_tasks: exercise103-ftp.yaml
  - name: copy the README file
    import_tasks: exercise103-copy.yaml
```

5. Run the playbook and verify its output.

6. Run an ad hoc command to verify the /var/ftp/pub/README file has been created: **ansible ansible2 -a "cat /var/ftp/pub/README"**.

Summary

In this chapter you learned how to work with Ansible in a large environment. We focused on three different aspects. First, you learned how to manage large numbers of hosts in an efficient way, using dynamic inventory and host name patterns. Next, you learned how to optimize working with Ansible by modifying the number of hosts in parallel as well as serial task execution. In the last part of this chapter, you learned how to work with includes and imports of plays and tasks.

Exam Preparation Tasks

As mentioned in the section "How to Use This Book" in the Introduction, you have a couple of choices for exam preparation: the exercises here, Chapter 16, "Final Preparation," and the exam simulation questions on the companion website.

Review All Key Topics

Review the most important topics in this chapter, noted with the Key Topics icon in the outer margin of the page. Table 10-2 lists a reference of these key topics and the page numbers on which each is found.

Table 10-2   Key Topics for Chapter 10

Key Topic Element	Description	Page Number
Paragraph	Dynamic inventory script requirements	233
Paragraph	Working with multiple inventory files	236
List	Using includes and imports	239
List	Import tasks considerations	242
List	Include tasks considerations	242

Define Key Terms

Define the following key terms from this chapter, and check your answers in the glossary:

fork, import, include, parallel task execution, serial task execution

Review Questions

1. How would you address only hosts that are a member of the group web as well as a member of the group file?

2. Which two arguments must be implemented in every dynamic inventory script?

3. If a dynamic inventory script needs additional parameters, how do you normally provide them?

4. Which command do you use to show in a tree-like output all currently known hosts, including the groups of which they are members?

5. Which command-line option can you use with the **ansible-playbook** command to ensure that 10 hosts are configured at the same time while running a playbook?

6. How do you write a playbook in such a way that all tasks are first executed on three hosts before the next group of three hosts is dealt with?

7. What should you do if you want to dynamically include tasks?

8. What is the recommended way to work with variables, assuming that you want to separate static code from dynamic parameters?

9. You have split up your project into different task files, but now you cannot use **ansible-playbook --list-tasks** anymore. How can you fix this?

10. What is a good reason to import playbooks instead of tasks?

End-of-Chapter Lab

In the end-of-chapter lab with this chapter, you reorganize a playbook to work with several different files instead of one big file. Do this according to the instructions in Lab 10-1.

Lab 10-1

The lab82.yaml file, which you can find in the GitHub repository that goes with this course, is an optimal candidate for optimization. Optimize this playbook according to the following requirements:

- Use includes and imports to make this a modular playbook where different files are used to distinguish between the different tasks.

- Optimize this playbook such that it will run on no more than two hosts at the same time and completes the entire playbook on these two hosts before continuing with the next host.

This chapter covers the following subjects:

- Managing Ansible Errors and Logs
- Using Modules for Troubleshooting and Testing
- Using Tags
- Troubleshooting Common Scenarios

## CHAPTER 11

Troubleshooting Ansible

The following RHCE exam objectives are covered in this chapter:

- Create Ansible plays and playbooks
  - Configure error handling

"Do I Know this Already?" Quiz

The "Do I Know This Already?" quiz allows you to assess whether you should read this entire chapter thoroughly or jump to the "Exam Preparation Tasks" section. If you are in doubt about your answers to these questions or your own assessment of your knowledge of the topics, read the entire chapter. Table 11-1 lists the major headings in this chapter and their corresponding "Do I Know This Already?" quiz questions. You can find the answers in Appendix A, "Answers to the 'Do I Know This Already?' Quizzes and Review Questions."

Table 11-1 "Do I Know This Already?" Section-to-Question Mapping

Foundation Topics Section	Questions
Managing Ansible Errors and Logs	1–4
Using Modules for Troubleshooting and Testing	5–7
Using Tags	8
Troubleshooting Common Scenarios	9, 10

1. Which of the following is the most important reason why it doesn't really make sense to configure Ansible to write log files containing command output?

   a. The log files would get very big fast.

   b. All relevant output while running a command is written to the STDOUT.

   c. Writing log files requires root privileges.

   d. Ansible doesn't work with rsyslogd.

2. Which command-line option to the **ansible-playbook** command should you use to preview differences that would be made while processing template files without actually writing the modifications?

    a. **--diff**

    b. **--check**

    c. **--check --diff**

    d. **--template**

3. What would you see in the playbook output if a task was not executed because it did not meet a requirement that was set by a conditional statement?

    a. failed

    b. skipped

    c. rescued

    d. ignored

4. You are trying to get an overview of all tasks that are executed by a playbook that has been set up in a modular way by using the **ansible-playbook --list-tasks** command. You notice that you don't see all tasks. Which of the following is the most likely explanation?

    a. Tasks that are added from an included or imported file are not shown.

    b. If a file is dynamically included, you don't see its tasks.

    c. The playbook uses roles and tasks from roles that are not displayed.

    d. The tasks that don't show in the overview work with variables that are undefined.

5. To analyze what a play is doing, you want to include easy-to-understand messages about what is going wrong and what is going well. Which of the following modules should you use?

    a. debug

    b. fail

    c. assert

    d. stat

6. Which module would you use to check values that are returned by an API?

  a. uri

  b. api

  c. url

  d. web

7. You want to check the owner of a file. Which module should you use?

  a. file

  b. user

  c. mode

  d. stat

8. You want to use tags to run a debug task only if it is specifically requested, and you decide to tag this task using the **tags [debug, never]** line. Which commands run all tasks, including the task with this tag?

  a. **ansible-playbook --tags debug**

  b. **ansible-playbook --tags never**

  c. **ansible-playbook --tags all,debug**

  d. **ansible-playbook --tags untagged,debug**

9. You can use the ping module to verify connectivity to the remote host. When it is used without further arguments, which of the following is not tested while using the ping module?

  a. IP connectivity

  b. Accessibility of the SSH service

  c. Availability of a Python stack

  d. None of the above

10. While running an Ansible playbook, a user receives the error message "Missing sudo password." Which of the following is the most likely explanation?

  a. SSH keys have not been copied successfully.

  b. The remote_user has not been set.

  c. Passwordless sudo has not been configured for remote_user.

  d. The become_user has not been set.

Foundation Topics

Managing Ansible Errors and Logs

When a playbook is processed or an ad hoc command is executed, Ansible produces output. This output gives a first indication of what has happened. If the output does not provide enough information, you can use additional solutions. In this section you learn about them.

Using Check Mode

Before actually running a playbook in a way that all changes are implemented, you can start the playbooks in check mode. To do this, you use the **--check** or **-C** command-line argument to the **ansible** or **ansible-playbook** command. The effect of using check mode is that changes that would have been made are shown but not executed. You should realize, though, that check mode is not supported in all cases. You will, for instance, have problems with check mode if it is applied to conditionals, where a specific task can do its work only after a preceding task has made some changes. Also, to successfully use check mode, the modules need to support it, but some don't. Modules that don't support check mode don't show any result while running check mode, but also they don't make any changes.

Apart from the command-line argument, you can use **check_mode: yes** or **check_mode: no** with any task in a playbook. If **check_mode: yes** is used, the task always runs in check mode (and does not implement any changes), regardless of the use of the **--check** option. If a task has **check_mode: no** set, it never runs in check mode and just does its work, even if the **ansible-playbook** command is used with the **--check** option. Using check mode on individual tasks might be a good idea if using check mode on the entire playbook gives unpredicted results: you can enable it on just a couple of tasks to ensure that they run successfully before proceeding to the next set of tasks. Notice that using **check_mode: no** for specific tasks can be dangerous; these tasks will make changes, even if the entire playbook was started with the **--check** option!

NOTE   The **check_mode** argument is a replacement for the **always_run** option that was used in Ansible 2.5 and earlier. In current Ansible versions, you should not use **always_run** anymore.

Another option that is commonly used with the **--check** option is **--diff**. This option reports changes to template files without actually applying them. Listing 11-1 shows a sample playbook, Listing 11-2 shows the template that it is processing, and Listing 11-3 shows the result of running this playbook with the **ansible-playbook listing111.yaml --check --diff** command.

Listing 11-1   Sample Playbook

```
---
- name: simple template example
  hosts: ansible2
  tasks:
  - template:
      src: listing112.j2
      dest: /etc/issue
```

Listing 11-2   Sample Template File

```
{# /etc/issue #}
Welcome to {{ ansible_facts['hostname'] }}
```

Listing 11-3   Running the listing111.yaml Sample Playbook

```
[ansible@control rhce8-book]$ ansible-playbook listing111.yaml --check
--diff

PLAY [simple template example] ****************************************

TASK [Gathering Facts] ***********************************************
ok: [ansible2]

TASK [template] *****************************************************
--- before
+++ after: /home/ansible/.ansible/tmp/ansible-local-4493uxbpju1e/
tmpm5gn7crg/listing112.j2
@@ -0,0 +1,3 @@
+Welcome to ansible2
+
+

changed: [ansible2]

PLAY RECAP **********************************************************
ansible2                    : ok=2    changed=1    unreachable=0
failed=0    skipped=0    rescued=0    ignored=0
```

Understanding Output

When you run the **ansible-playbook** command, output is generated. You've probably had a glimpse of it before, but let's look at the output in a more structured way now. Listing 11-4 shows some typical sample output generated by running the **ansible-playbook** command.

Listing 11-4   ansible-playbook Command Output

```
[ansible@control rhce8-book]$ ansible-playbook listing52.yaml

PLAY [install start and enable httpd] ********************************

TASK [Gathering Facts] **********************************************
ok: [ansible2]
ok: [ansible1]
ok: [ansible3]
ok: [ansible4]

TASK [install package] *********************************************
changed: [ansible2]
changed: [ansible1]
changed: [ansible3]
changed: [ansible4]

TASK [start and enable service] ************************************
changed: [ansible2]
changed: [ansible1]
changed: [ansible3]
changed: [ansible4]

PLAY RECAP *********************************************************
ansible1                   : ok=3      changed=2     unreachable=0
failed=0      skipped=0      rescued=0     ignored=0
ansible2                   : ok=3      changed=2     unreachable=0
failed=0      skipped=0      rescued=0     ignored=0
ansible3                   : ok=3      changed=2     unreachable=0
failed=0      skipped=0      rescued=0     ignored=0
ansible4                   : ok=3      changed=2     unreachable=0
failed=0      skipped=0      rescued=0     ignored=0
```

In the output of any **ansible-playbook** command, you can see different items:

■ An indicator of the play that is started

■ If not disabled, the Gathering Facts task that is executed for each play

- Each individual task, including the task name if that was specified

- The Play Recap, which summarizes the play results

In the Play Recap, different results can be shown. Table 11-2 gives an overview.

Table 11-2 Playbook Recap Overview

Result	Explanation
ok	The current state of the managed node already matches the desired state.
changed	A change was applied to implement the desired state.
unreachable	The target node could not be reached.
failed	The task contains an error and could not be executed.
skipped	Due to a nonmatching conditional, the task was skipped.
rescued	The main task in a block failed, and the rescue action defined in the block was used instead.
ignored	The target host was ignored because of the use of **ignore_errors** in the playbook.

As discussed before, when you use the **ansible-playbook** command, you can increase the output verbosity level using one or more **-v** options. Table 11-3 lists what these options accomplish. For generic troubleshooting, you might want to consider using **-vv**, which shows output as well as input data. In particular cases using the **-vvv** option can be useful because it adds connection information as well.

The **-vvvv** option just brings too much information in many cases but can be useful if you need to analyze which exact scripts are executed or whether any problems were encountered in privilege escalation. Make sure to capture the output of any command that runs with **-vvvv** to a text file, though, so that you can read it in an easy way. Even for a simple playbook, it can easily generate more than 10 screens of output.

Table 11-3 Verbosity Options Overview

Option	Use
-v	Output data is displayed.
-vv	Output and input data is displayed.
-vvv	Output data, input data, and connection information are shown.
-vvvv	Information about scripts that are executed and how they are executed is shown.

In Listing 11-5 you can see the output of a small playbook that runs different tasks on the managed hosts. Listing 11-5 shows details about execution of one task on host ansible4, and as you can see, it goes deep in the amount of detail that is shown. One component is worth looking at, and that is the escalation succeeded that you can see in the output. This means that privilege escalation was successful and tasks were executed because **become_user** was defined in ansible.cfg. Failing privilege escalation is one of the common reasons why playbook execution may go wrong, which is why it's worth keeping an eye on this indicator.

Listing 11-5   Analyzing Partial **-vvvv** Output

```
<ansible4> ESTABLISH SSH CONNECTION FOR USER: ansible
<ansible4> SSH: EXEC ssh -vvv -C -o ControlMaster=auto
-o ControlPersist=60s -o StrictHostKeyChecking=no -o
KbdInteractiveAuthentication=no -o PreferredAuthentications=gssapi-
with-mic,gssapi-keyex,hostbased,publickey -o PasswordAuthentication=no
-o 'User="ansible"' -o ConnectTimeout=10 -o ControlPath=/
home/ansible/.ansible/cp/859d5267e3 ansible4 '/bin/
sh -c '"'"'chmod u+x /home/ansible/.ansible/tmp/ansible-
tmp-1587544652.4716983-118789810824208/ /home/ansible/.ansible/tmp/
ansible-tmp-1587544652.4716983-118789810824208/AnsiballZ_systemd.py &&
sleep 0'"'"''

Escalation succeeded

<ansible4> (0, b'', b"OpenSSH_8.0p1, OpenSSL 1.1.1c FIPS  28 May
2019\r\ndebug1: Reading configuration data /etc/ssh/ssh_config\r\
ndebug3: /etc/ssh/ssh_config line 51: Including file /etc/ssh/
ssh_config.d/05-redhat.conf depth 0\r\ndebug1: Reading configuration
data /etc/ssh/ssh_config.d/05-redhat.conf\r\ndebug2: checking match
for 'final all' host ansible4 originally ansible4\r\ndebug3: /
etc/ssh/ssh_config.d/05-redhat.conf line 3: not matched 'final'\r\
ndebug2: match not found\r\ndebug3: /etc/ssh/ssh_config.d/05-redhat.
conf line 5: Including file /etc/crypto-policies/back-ends/openssh.
config depth 1 (parse only)\r\ndebug1: Reading configuration data /
etc/crypto-policies/back-ends/openssh.config\r\ndebug3: gss kex
names ok: [gss-gex-sha1-,gss-group14-sha1-]\r\ndebug3: kex names
ok: [curve25519-sha256,curve25519-sha256@libssh.org,ecdh-sha2-
nistp256,ecdh-sha2-nistp384,ecdh-sha2-nistp521,diffie-hellman-group-
exchange-sha256,diffie-hellman-group14-sha256,diffie-hellman-group16-
sha512,diffie-hellman-group18-sha512,diffie-hellman-group-exchange-
sha1,diffie-hellman-group14-sha1]\r\ndebug1: configuration requests
final Match pass\r\ndebug1: re-parsing configuration\r\ndebug1:
Reading configuration data /etc/ssh/ssh_config\r\ndebug3: /etc/ssh/
ssh_config line 51: Including file /etc/ssh/ssh_config.d/05-redhat.
conf depth 0\r\ndebug1: Reading configuration data /etc/ssh/ssh_
config.d/05-redhat.conf\r\ndebug2: checking match for 'final all'
host ansible4 originally ansible4\r\ndebug3: /etc/ssh/ssh_config.d/05-
redhat.conf line 3: matched 'final'\r\ndebug2: match found\r\ndebug3:
/etc/ssh/ssh_config.d/05-redhat.conf line 5: Including file /etc/
crypto-policies/back-ends/openssh.config depth 1\r\ndebug1: Reading
configuration data /etc/crypto-policies/back-ends/openssh.config\r\
ndebug3: gss kex names ok: [gss-gex-sha1-,gss-group14-sha1-]\r\
```

```
ndebug3: kex names ok: [curve25519-sha256,curve25519-sha256@libssh.
org,ecdh-sha2-nistp256,ecdh-sha2-nistp384,ecdh-sha2-nistp521,diffie-
hellman-group-exchange-sha256,diffie-hellman-group14-sha256,diffie-
hellman-group16-sha512,diffie-hellman-group18-sha512,diffie-hellman-
group-exchange-sha1,diffie-hellman-group14-sha1]\r\ndebug1: auto-mux:
Trying existing master\r\ndebug2: fd 4 setting O_NONBLOCK\r\ndebug2:
mux_client_hello_exchange: master version 4\r\ndebug3: mux_client_
forwards: request forwardings: 0 local, 0 remote\r\ndebug3: mux_
client_request_session: entering\r\ndebug3: mux_client_request_alive:
entering\r\ndebug3: mux_client_request_alive: done pid = 4764\r\
ndebug3: mux_client_request_session: session request sent\r\ndebug3:
mux_client_read_packet: read header failed: Broken pipe\r\ndebug2:
Received exit status from master 0\r\n")
<ansible4> ESTABLISH SSH CONNECTION FOR USER: ansible
<ansible4> SSH: EXEC ssh -vvv -C -o ControlMaster=auto
-o ControlPersist=60s -o StrictHostKeyChecking=no -o
KbdInteractiveAuthentication=no -o PreferredAuthentications=gssapi-
with-mic,gssapi-keyex,hostbased,publickey -o PasswordAuthentication=no
-o 'User="ansible"' -o ConnectTimeout=10 -o ControlPath=/home/
ansible/.ansible/cp/859d5267e3 -tt ansible4 '/bin/sh -c '"'"'sudo
-H -S -n  -u root /bin/sh -c '"'"'"'"'"'"'"'"'echo BECOME-SUCCESS-
muvtpdvqkslnlegyhoibfcrilvlyjcqp ; /usr/libexec/platform-python /home/
ansible/.ansible/tmp/ansible-tmp-1587544652.4716983-118789810824208/
AnsiballZ_systemd.py'"'"'"'"'"'"'"'"' && sleep 0'"'"''
Escalation succeeded
```

Optimizing Command Output Error Formatting

You might have noticed that the formatting of error messages in Ansible command output can be a bit hard to read. Fortunately, there's an easy way to make it a little more readable by including two options in the ansible.cfg file. These options are **stdout_callback = debug** and **stdout_callback = error**. After including these options, you'll notice it's a lot easier to read error output and distinguish between its different components!

Logging to Files

By default, Ansible does not write anything to log files. The reason is that the Ansible commands have all the options that may be useful to write output to the STDOUT. If so required, it's always possible to use shell redirection to write the command output to a file.

If you do need Ansible to write log files, you can set the **log_path** parameter in ansible.cfg. Alternatively, Ansible can log to the filename that is specified as the argument to the $ANSIBLE_LOG_PATH variable. Notice that Ansible logs can grow big very fast, so if logging to output files is enabled, make sure that Linux log rotation is configured to ensure that files cannot grow beyond a specific maximum size.

Running Task by Task

When you analyze playbook behavior, it's possible to run playbook tasks one by one or to start running a playbook at a specific task. The **ansible-playbook --step** command runs playbooks task by task and prompts for confirmation before running the next task. Alternatively, you can use the **ansible-playbook --start-at-task= "task name"** command to start playbook execution as a specific task. Before using this command, you might want to use **ansible-playbook --list-tasks** for a list of all tasks that have been configured. To use these options in an efficient way, you must configure each task with its own name. In Listing 11-6 you can see what running playbooks this way looks like. This listing first shows how to list tasks in a playbook and next how the **--start-at-task** and **--step** options are used.

Listing 11-6   Running Tasks One by One

```
[ansible@control rhce8-book]$ ansible-playbook --list-tasks
exercise81.yaml

playbook: exercise81.yaml

  play #1 (ansible1): testing file manipulation skills.    TAGS: []
    tasks:
      create a new file              TAGS: []
      check status of the new file   TAGS: []
      for debugging purposes only    TAGS: []
      change file owner if needed    TAGS: []

  play #2 (ansible1): fetching a remote file.    TAGS: []
    tasks:
      fetch file from remote machine.    TAGS: []

  play #3 (localhost): adding text to the file that is now on
localhost TAGS: []
    tasks:
      add a message.    TAGS: []

  play #4 (ansible2): copy the modified file to ansible2.    TAGS: []
    tasks:
      copy motd file.    TAGS: []
[ansible@control rhce8-book]$ ansible-playbook --start-at-task "add a
message"  --step exercise81.yaml
```

```
PLAY [testing file manipulation skills] ******************************

PLAY [fetching a remote file] ****************************************

PLAY [adding text to the file that is now on localhost]
************************
Perform task: TASK: Gathering Facts (N)o/(y)es/(c)ontinue:
```

In Exercise 11-1 you learn how to apply check mode while working with templates.

Exercise 11-1   Using Templates in Check Mode

1. Locate the file httpd.conf; you can find it in the rhce8-book directory, which you can download from the GitHub repository at https://github.com/sandervanvugt/rhce8-book. Use **mv httpd.conf exercise111-httpd.j2** to rename it to a Jinja2 template file.

2. Open the exercise111-httpd.j2 file with an editor, and apply modifications to existing parameters so that they look like the following:
   ```
   ServerRoot "{{ apache_root }}"
   User {{ apache_user }}
   Group {{ apache_group }}
   ```

3. Write a playbook that takes care of the complete Apache web server setup and installation, starts and enables the service, opens a port in the firewall, and uses the template module to create the /etc/httpd/conf/httpd.conf file based on the template that you created in step 2 of this exercise. The complete playbook with the name exercise111.yaml looks like the following (make sure you have the *exact* contents shown below and do *not* correct any typos):
   ```
   ---

   - name: perform basic apache setup
     hosts: ansible2
     vars:
       apache_root: /etc/httpd
       apache_user: httpd
       apache_group: httpd
     tasks:
     - name: install RPM package
       yum:
         name: httpd
         state: latest
   ```

```
    - name: copy template file
      template:
        src: exercise111-httpd.j2
        dest: /etc/http/httpd.conf
    - name: start and enable service
      service:
        name: httpd
        state: started
        enabled: yes
    - name: open port in firewall
      firewalld:
        service: http
        permanent: yes
        state: enabled
        immediate: yes
```

4. Run the command **ansible-playbook --syntax-check exercise111.yaml**. If no errors are found in the playbook syntax, you should just see the name of the playbook.

5. Run the command **ansible-playbook --check --diff exercise111.yaml**. In the output of the command, pay attention to the task copy template file. After the line that starts with **+++ after**, you should see the lines in the template that were configured to use a variable, using the right variables.

6. Run the playbook to perform all its tasks step by step, using the command **ansible-playbook --step exercise111.yaml**. Press **y** to confirm the first step. Next, press **c** to automatically continue. The playbook will fail on the copy template file task because the target directory does not exist. Notice that the **--syntax-check** and the **--check** options do not check for any logical errors in the playbook and for that reason have not detected this problem.

7. Edit the exercise111.yaml file and ensure the **template** task contains the following corrected line: (replace the old line starting with **dest:**):
   ```
   dest: /etc/httpd/conf/httpd.conf
   ```

8. Type **ansible-playbook --list-tasks exercise111.yaml** to list all the tasks in the playbook.

9. To avoid running the entire playbook again, use **ansible-playbook --start-at-task="copy template file" exercise111.yaml** to run the playbook to completion.

Using Modules for Troubleshooting and Testing

While working with playbooks, you may use different modules for troubleshooting. The debug module was used in previous chapters and is particularly useful for analyzing variable behavior. Some other modules may prove useful when troubleshooting Ansible. Table 11-4 gives an overview.

Table 11-4 Troubleshooting Modules Overview

Module	Use
debug	Writes debug information, which is useful for checking variable values
uri	Tests the answer coming from any URL, which is useful for API calls
fail	Uses a **when** conditional to determine when a module should be considered failing
script	Allows for the execution of a shell script on the managed host
stat	Gathers status information about files
assert	Tests whether the expected result is present and otherwise fails

The following sections discuss how these modules can be used.

Using the Debug Module

The debug module is useful to visualize what is happening at a certain point in a playbook. It works with two arguments: the **msg** argument can be used to print a message, and the **var** argument can be used to print the value of a variable. Notice that when you use the **var** argument, the variable does not have to be referred to using the usual **{{ varname }}** structure, just use **varname** instead. If variables are used in the **msg** argument, they must be referred to the normal way, using the **{{ varname }}** syntax.

Because you have already seen the debug module in action in numerous examples in previous chapters of this book, no new examples are included here.

Using the uri Module

The best way to learn how to work with these modules is to look at some examples. Listing 11-7 shows an example where the uri module is used.

Listing 11-7   Using the uri Module

```
---
- name: test webserver access
  hosts: localhost
  become: no
  tasks:
  - name: connect to the web server
    uri:
        url: http://ansible2.example.com
        return_content: yes
    register: this
    failed_when: "'welcome' not in this.content"
  - debug:
      var: this.content
```

The playbook in Listing 11-7 uses the uri module to connect to a web server. The **return_content** argument captures the web server content, which is stored in a variable using **register**. Next, the **failed_when** statement makes this module fail if the text "welcome" is not in the registered variable. For debugging purposes, the debug module is used to show the contents of the variable.

In Listing 11-8 you can see the partial result of running this playbook. Notice that the playbook does not generate a failure because the default web page that is shown by the Apache web server contains the text "welcome."

Listing 11-8   ansible-playbook listing117.yaml Command Result

```
[ansible@control rhce8-book]$ ansible-playbook listing117.yaml

PLAY [test webserver access] *****************************************

TASK [Gathering Facts] **********************************************
ok: [localhost]

TASK [connect to the web server] ************************************
ok: [localhost]

TASK [debug] *******************************************************
ok: [localhost] => {
```

```
    "this.content": "<?xml version=\"1.0\" encoding=\"utf-8\"?>\
n<!DOCTYPE HTML>\n<html lang=\"en\">\n  <head>\n    <title>CentOS
Apache HTTP </title>\n    <meta charset=\"utf-8\"/>\n    <meta
name=\"viewport\" content=\"width=device-width, initial-scale=1,
shrink-to-fit=no\"/>\n    <link rel=\"shortcut icon\" href=\"http://
www.centos.org/favicon.ico\"/>\n    <link rel=\"stylesheet\"
media=\"all\" href=\"noindex/common/css/bootstrap.min.
css\"/>\n    <link rel=\"stylesheet\" media=\"all\" href=\"noindex/
common/css/styles.css\"/>\n  </head>\n  <body>\n    <header
class=\"container\">\n      <section class=\"row\">\n        <div
class=\"header-graphic v3-banner platform-banner centos-banner\"
role=\"banner\">\n        <div class=\"graphic-inner\">\n
<div class=\"graphic-inner2\">\n          <div class=\"banner-...
href=\"https://www.centos.org/legal/\"></a> | <a href=\"https://www.
centos.org/legal/privacy/\"></a></p>\n    </footer>\n  </body>\n</
html>\n"
}


PLAY RECAP *********************************************************
localhost                 : ok=3    changed=0    unreachable=0
failed=0    skipped=0    rescued=0    ignored=0
```

Using the uri module can be useful to perform a simple test to check whether a web server is available, but you can also use it to check accessibility or returned information from an API endpoint.

Using the stat Module

You can use the stat module to check on the status of files. Although this module can be useful for checking on the status of just a few files, it's not a file system integrity checker that was developed to check file status on a large scale. If you need large-scale file system integrity checking, you should use Linux utilities such as aide.

The stat module is useful in combination with **register**. In this use, the stat module is used to register the status of a specific file, and in a **when** statement, a check can be done to see whether the file status is not as expected. In combination with the fail module, you can use this module to generate a failure and error message if the file does not meet the expected status. Listing 11-9 shows an example, and Listing 11-10 shows the resulting output, where you can see that the fail module fails the playbook because the file owner is not root.

Listing 11-9 Using stat to Check Expected File Status

```
---
- name: create a file
  hosts: all
  tasks:
  - file:
      path: /tmp/statfile
      state: touch
      owner: ansible

- name: check file status
  hosts: all
  tasks:
  - stat:
      path: /tmp/statfile
    register: stat_out
  - fail:
      msg: "/tmp/statfile file owner not as expected"
    when: stat_out.stat.pw_name != 'root'
```

Listing 11-10 **ansible-playbook listing119.yaml** Command Result

```
[ansible@control rhce8-book]$ ansible-playbook listing119.yaml

PLAY [create a file] *********************************************

TASK [Gathering Facts] ******************************************
ok: [ansible2]
ok: [ansible1]
ok: [ansible3]
ok: [ansible4]
fatal: [ansible6]: UNREACHABLE! => {"changed": false, "msg": "Failed
to connect to the host via ssh: ansible@ansible6: Permission denied
(publickey,gssapi-keyex,gssapi-with-mic,password).", "unreachable":
true}
fatal: [ansible5]: UNREACHABLE! => {"changed": false, "msg": "Failed
to connect to the host via ssh: ssh: connect to host ansible5 port
22: No route to host", "unreachable": true}

TASK [file] *****************************************************
changed: [ansible2]
```

```
changed: [ansible1]
changed: [ansible3]
changed: [ansible4]


PLAY [check file status] *******************************************


TASK [Gathering Facts] *********************************************
ok: [ansible1]
ok: [ansible2]
ok: [ansible3]
ok: [ansible4]


TASK [stat] ********************************************************
ok: [ansible2]
ok: [ansible1]
ok: [ansible3]
ok: [ansible4]


TASK [fail] ********************************************************
fatal: [ansible2]: FAILED! => {"changed": false, "msg": "/tmp/statfile
file owner not as expected"}
fatal: [ansible1]: FAILED! => {"changed": false, "msg": "/tmp/statfile
file owner not as expected"}
fatal: [ansible3]: FAILED! => {"changed": false, "msg": "/tmp/statfile
file owner not as expected"}
fatal: [ansible4]: FAILED! => {"changed": false, "msg": "/tmp/statfile
file owner not as expected"}


PLAY RECAP *********************************************************
ansible1                   : ok=4    changed=1    unreachable=0
failed=1      skipped=0    rescued=0    ignored=0
ansible2                   : ok=4    changed=1    unreachable=0
failed=1      skipped=0    rescued=0    ignored=0
ansible3                   : ok=4    changed=1    unreachable=0
failed=1      skipped=0    rescued=0    ignored=0
ansible4                   : ok=4    changed=1    unreachable=0
failed=1      skipped=0    rescued=0    ignored=0
ansible5                   : ok=0    changed=0    unreachable=1
failed=0      skipped=0    rescued=0    ignored=0
ansible6                   : ok=0    changed=0    unreachable=1
failed=0      skipped=0    rescued=0    ignored=0
```

Using the assert Module

The assert module is a bit like the fail module. You can use it to perform a specific conditional action. The assert module works with a **that** option that defines a list of conditionals. If any one of these conditionals is false, the task fails, and if all the conditionals are true, the task is successful. Based on the success or failure of a task, the module uses the **success_msg** or **fail_msg** options to print a message. Listing 11-11 shows an example that uses the assert module.

Listing 11-11   Using the assert Module

```
---
- hosts: localhost
  vars_prompt:
  - name: filesize
    prompt: "specify a file size in megabytes"
  tasks:
  - name: check if file size is valid
    assert:
      that:
      - "{{ (filesize | int) <= 100 }}"
      - "{{ (filesize | int) >= 1 }}"
      fail_msg: "file size must be between 0 and 100"
      success_msg: "file size is good, let\'s continue"
  - name: create a file
    command: dd if=/dev/zero of=/bigfile bs=1 count={{ filesize }}
```

The example in Listing 11-11 contains a few new items. As you can see, the play header starts with a **vars_prompt**. This defines a variable named **filesize**, which is based on the input provided by the user. This **filesize** variable is next used by the assert module. The **that** statement contains a list in which two conditions are stated. If specified like this, all conditions stated in the **that** condition must be true. So you are looking for **filesize** to be equal to or bigger than 1 and smaller than or equal to 100.

Before this can be done, one little problem needs to be managed: when **vars_prompt** is used, the variable type is set to be a string by default. This means that a statement like **filesize <= 100** would fail with a type mismatch. That is why a Jinja2 filter is used to convert the variable type from string to integer.

Filters are a powerful feature provided by the Jinja2 templating language and can be used in Ansible to modify variables before processing. For more information about filters, see https://docs.ansible.com/ansible/latest/user_guide/playbooks_filters. html. The int filter can be used to convert the value of a string variable to an integer. To do this, you need to rewrite the entire variable as a Jinja2 operation, which is done using "{{ (filesize | int) <= 100 }}".

In this line, the entire string is written as a variable. The variable is further treated in a Jinja2 context. In this context, the part **(filesize | int)** ensures that the string is converted to an integer, which makes it possible to check if the value is smaller than 100.

When you run the code in Listing 11-11, and enter a value of 200 when prompted, the result shown in Listing 11-12 is produced.

Listing 11-12   ansible-playbook listing1111.yaml Output

```
[ansible@control rhce8-book]$ ansible-playbook listing1111.yaml

PLAY [localhost] ********************************************************

TASK [Gathering Facts] *************************************************
ok: [localhost]

TASK [check if file size is valid] ************************************
fatal: [localhost]: FAILED! => {
    "assertion": "filesize <= 100",
    "changed": false,
    "evaluated_to": false,
    "msg": "file size must be between 0 and 100"
}

PLAY RECAP ************************************************************
localhost                  : ok=1    changed=0    unreachable=0
failed=1    skipped=0    rescued=0    ignored=0
```

As you can see, the task that is defined with the assert module fails because the variable has a value that is not between the minimum and maximum sizes that are defined.

Understanding the need for using the filter to convert the variable type might not be easy. So, let's also look at Listing 11-13, which shows an example of a playbook that will fail. You can see its behavior in Listing 11-14, where the playbook is executed.

Listing 11-13   Failing Version of the Listing 11-11 Playbook

```
---
- hosts: localhost
  vars_prompt:
  - name: filesize
    prompt: "specify a file size in megabytes"
  tasks:
  - name: check if file size is valid
    assert:
      that:
      - filesize <= 100
      - filesize >= 1
      fail_msg: "file size must be between 0 and 100"
      success_msg: "file size is good, let\'s continue"
  - name: create a file
    command: dd if=/dev/zero of=/bigfile bs=1 count={{ filesize }}
```

Listing 11-14   ansible-playbook listing1113.yaml Failing Result

```
[ansible@control rhce8-book]$ ansible-playbook listing1113.yaml
specify a file size in megabytes:

PLAY [localhost] *****************************************************

TASK [Gathering Facts] **********************************************
ok: [localhost]

TASK [check if file size is valid] *********************************
fatal: [localhost]: FAILED! => {"msg": "The conditional check
'filesize <= 100' failed. The error was: Unexpected templating type
error occurred on ({% if filesize <= 100 %} True {% else %} False {%
endif %}): '<=' not supported between instances of 'str' and 'int'"}

PLAY RECAP *********************************************************
localhost                  : ok=1    changed=0    unreachable=0
failed=1    skipped=0    rescued=0    ignored=0
```

As you can see, the code in Listing 11-13 fails because the <= test is not supported between a string and an integer.

In Exercise 11-2 you work with some of the modules discussed in this section.

Exercise 11-2   Using Modules for Troubleshooting

1. Open your editor to create the file exercise112.yaml and define the play header:

```
---
- name: using assert to check if volume group vgdata exists
  hosts: all
  tasks:
```

2. Add a task that uses the command **vgs vgdata** to check whether a volume group with the name vgdata exists. The task should use **register** to register the command result, and it should continue if this is not the case.

```
- name: check if vgdata exists
  command: vgs vgdata
  register: vg_result
  ignore_errors: true
```

3. To make it easier to use **assert** in the next step on the right variable, include a **debug** task to show the value of the variable:

```
- name: show vg_result variable
  debug:
     var: vg_result
```

4. Add a task to print a success or failure message, depending on the result of the **vgs** command from the first task:

```
- name: print a message
  assert:
     that:
     - vg_result.rc == 0
     fail_msg: volume group not found
     success_msg: volume group was found
```

5. Use the command **ansible-playbook exercise112.yaml** to verify its contents. Assuming that the LVM Volume Group vgdata was not found, it should print "volume group not found."

6. Change the playbook to verify that it will print the **success_msg** if the requested volume group was found. You can do so by having it run the command **vgs cl**, which on CentOS 8 should give a positive result.

Using Tags

When you are using larger playbooks, Ansible enables you to use the **tags** attribute. A tag is a label that is applied to a task or another item like a block or a play, and while using the **ansible-playbook --tags** or **ansible-playbook --skip-tags** command, you can specify which tags need to be executed. Listing 11-15 shows a simple playbook example where tags are used, and in Listing 11-16 you can see the output generated while running this playbook.

Listing 11-15   Using **tags** in a Playbook

```
---
- name: using tags example
  hosts: all
  vars:
    services:
    - vsftpd
    - httpd
  tasks:
  - yum:
      name:
      - httpd
      - vsftpd
      state: present
    tags:
    - install
  - service:
      name: "{{ item }}"
      state: started
      enabled: yes
    loop: "{{ services }}"
    tags:
    - services
```

Listing 11-16   **ansible-playbook --tags "install" listing1115.yaml** Output

```
[ansible@control rhce8-book]$ ansible-playbook --tags "install"
listing1115.yaml

PLAY [using tags example] *********************************************

TASK [Gathering Facts] ************************************************
ok: [ansible2]
ok: [ansible1]
ok: [ansible4]
ok: [ansible3]
```

```
TASK [yum] **********************************************************
ok: [ansible2]
ok: [ansible1]
changed: [ansible3]
changed: [ansible4]


PLAY RECAP **********************************************************
ansible1                    : ok=2      changed=0      unreachable=0
failed=0      skipped=0      rescued=0      ignored=0
ansible2                    : ok=2      changed=0      unreachable=0
failed=0      skipped=0      rescued=0      ignored=0
ansible3                    : ok=2      changed=1      unreachable=0
failed=0      skipped=0      rescued=0      ignored=0
ansible4                    : ok=2      changed=1      unreachable=0
failed=0      skipped=0      rescued=0      ignored=0
```

Tags can be applied to many structures, such as imported plays, tasks, and roles, but the easiest way to get familiar with tags is to use them on a task. Note that tags cannot be applied on items that are dynamically included (instead of imported), using **include_roles** or **include_tasks**.

While writing playbooks, you may apply the same tag multiple times. This capability allows you to define groups of tasks, where multiple tasks are configured with the same tag, and as a result, you can easily run a specific part of the requested configuration. When multiple tasks with multiple tags are used, you can get an overview of each using the **ansible-playbook --list-tasks --list-tags** command. In Listing 11-17 you can see an example that is based on the playbook listing1115.yaml.

Listing 11-17   Listing Tasks and Tags

```
[ansible@control rhce8-book]$ ansible-playbook --list-tags --list-
tasks listing1115.yaml


playbook: listing1115.yaml

  play #1 (all): using tags example.    TAGS: []
    tasks:
      yum.        TAGS: [install]
      service.    TAGS: [services]
      TASK TAGS: [install, services]
```

When working with tags, you can use some special tags. Table 11-5 gives an overview.

Table 11-5   Special Tags Overview

Tag	Use
always	Makes sure a task always runs, unless specifically skipped with **--skip-tags always**
never	Never runs a task, unless it is specifically requested
tagged	Runs all tagged tasks
untagged	Runs all untagged tasks
all	Runs all tasks

Apart from these special tags, you might also want to set a **debug** tag to easily identify tasks that should be run only if you specifically want to run debug tasks as well. If combined with the **never** tag, the task that is tagged with the **debug,never** tasks runs only if the **debug** tag is specifically requested. So in case you want to run the entire playbook, including tasks that have been tagged with **debug**, you need to use the **ansible-playbook --tags all,debug** command. In Exercise 11-3 you can see how this can be used to optimize the playbook that was previously used in Exercise 11-2.

Exercise 11-3   Using Tags to Make Debugging Easier

1. Rewrite the exercise112.yaml playbook that you created in the previous exercise, and include the line **tags: [never, debug]** in the **debug** task. The complete playbook looks as follows:

```
---
- name: using assert to check if volume group vgdata exists
  hosts: all
  tasks:
  - name: check if vgdata exists
    command: vgs vgdata
    register: vg_result
    ignore_errors: true
  - name: show vg_result variable
    debug:
       var: vg_result
    tags: [ never, debug ]
  - name: print a message
    assert:
```

```
          that:
          - vg_result.rc == 0
          fail_msg: volume group not found
          success_msg: volume group was found
```

2. Run the playbook using **ansible-playbook --tags all exercise113.yaml**. Notice that it does not run the **debug** task.

3. Run the playbook using **ansible-playbook --tags all,debug exercise113.yaml**. Notice that it now does run the **debug** task as well.

Troubleshooting Common Scenarios

Apart from the problems that may arise in playbooks, another type of error relates to connectivity issues. To connect to managed hosts, SSH must be configured correctly, and also authentication and privilege escalation must work as expected.

Analyzing Connectivity Issues

To be able to connect to a managed host, you need to have an IP network connection. Apart from that, you need to make sure that the host has been set up correctly:

- The SSH service needs to be accessible on the remote host.

- Python must be installed.

- Privilege escalation needs to be set up.

Apart from these, inventory settings may be specified to indicate how to connect to a remote host. Normally, the inventory contains a host name only. If a host resolves to multiple IP addresses, you may want to specify how exactly the remote host must be connected to. The **ansible_host** parameter can be configured to do so. In inventory, for instance, you may include the following line to ensure that your host is connected in the right way:

```
ansible5.example.com ansible_host=192.168.4.55
```

Notice that this setting makes sense only in an environment where a host can be reached on multiple different IP addresses.

To test connectivity to remote hosts, you can use the ping module. It checks for IP connectivity, accessibility of the SSH service, sudo privilege escalation, and the availability of a Python stack. The ping module does not take any arguments. Listing 11-18 shows the result of running the ad hoc command **ansible all -m ping** where hosts that are available send "pong" as a reply, and for hosts that are not available, you see why they are not available.

Listing 11-18   Verifying Connectivity Using the ping Module

```
[ansible@control rhce8-book]$ ansible all -m ping
ansible2 | SUCCESS => {
    "ansible_facts": {
        "discovered_interpreter_python": "/usr/libexec/
platform-python"
    },
    "changed": false,
    "ping": "pong"
}
ansible1 | SUCCESS => {
    "ansible_facts": {
        "discovered_interpreter_python": "/usr/libexec/
platform-python"
    },
    "changed": false,
    "ping": "pong"
}
ansible3 | SUCCESS => {
    "ansible_facts": {
        "discovered_interpreter_python": "/usr/libexec/
platform-python"
    },
    "changed": false,
    "ping": "pong"
}
ansible4 | FAILED! => {
    "msg": "Missing sudo password"
}
```

Analyzing Authentication Issues

A few settings play a role in authentication on the remote host to execute tasks:

- The **remote_user** setting determines which user account to use on the managed nodes.

- SSH keys need to be configured for the remote_user to enable smooth authentication.

- The **become** parameter needs to be set to true.

- The **become_user** needs to be set to the root user account.

- Linux sudo needs to be set up correctly.

In Exercise 11-4 you work on troubleshooting some common scenarios.

Exercise 11-4   Troubleshooting Connectivity Issues

1. Use an editor to create the file exercise114.yaml and give it the following contents:

   ```
   ---
   - name: remove user from wheel group
     hosts: ansible4
     tasks:
     - user:
         name: ansible
         groups: ''
   ```

2. Run the playbook using **ansible-playbook exercise114.yaml** and use **ansible ansible4 -m reboot** to reboot node ansible4.

3. Once the reboot is completed, use **ansible all -m ping** to verify connectivity. Host ansible4 should give a "Missing sudo password" error.

4. Type **ansible ansible4 -m raw -a "usermod -aG wheel ansible" -u root -k** to make user ansible a member of the group wheel again.

5. Repeat the **ansible all -m ping** command. You should now be able to connect normally to the host ansible4 again.

Summary

In this chapter you read about troubleshooting Ansible. We covered four different troubleshooting-related topics. First, you learned how to make sure that sufficient troubleshooting information is printed while running tasks. This section covered working with log files, running in check mode, and increasing the verbosity level. Next you learned how to use different modules that can be useful to make playbook success or failure more insightful. The third topic was about using tags, which may be particularly useful to run only specific tasks. In the last topic you learned about troubleshooting some common scenarios.

Exam Preparation Tasks

As mentioned in the section "How to Use This Book" in the Introduction, you have a couple of choices for exam preparation: the exercises here, Chapter 16, "Final Preparation," and the exam simulation questions on the companion website.

Review All Key Topics

Review the most important topics in this chapter, noted with the Key Topics icon in the outer margin of the page. Table 11-6 lists a reference of these key topics and the page numbers on which each is found.

Table 11-6   Key Topics for Chapter 11

Key Topic Element	Description	Page Number
List	Items seen in the output of any **ansible-playbook** command	256
List	Requirements for successful authentication	276

Memory Tables

Print a copy of Appendix D, "Memory Tables" (found on the companion website), or at least the section for this chapter, and complete the tables and lists from memory. Appendix E, "Memory Tables Answer Key," also on the companion website, includes completed tables and lists to check your work.

Define Key Terms

Define the following key terms from this chapter, and check your answers in the glossary:

check mode, filter, tag

Review Questions

1. What can you do to ensure a task will not run in check mode?

2. What would you expect to see in the playbook output summary if the main task in a block has failed and the rescue action is executed instead?

3. Which parameter can you set in the ansible.cfg file to specify where Ansible command output is logged?

4. Which module would you use to analyze API output?

5. You want to write a playbook in which you define a condition to specify when a task would be considered failing. Which module should you use to do so?

6. Which module would you use to test whether an expected result is present and fail in all other cases?

7. How would you convert a variable data type from a string to an integer?

8. Which tag would you use to make sure that a task never runs unless specifically requested?

9. A task has been configured with the [debug, never] tasks. How can you run the playbook to run all tasks, including this one?

10. Which command should you use to verify connectivity to Ansible-managed machines?

End-of-Chapter Lab

Now that we are at the end of this chapter, let's do a lab! The following lab enables you to practice your troubleshooting skills.

Lab 11-1

The lesson11-lab.yaml playbook contains some errors. Fix them according to the following instructions:

- Use command-line tools and arguments to find the errors. Don't fix them by just reading the YAML file, even if some errors are obvious.

- After fixing an error in one task, start running the playbook with the next task. Try to avoid running the same task over and over again.

- Before applying the template, use a dry-run and a diff to see what the template will change.

- Use the debug module where necessary.

This chapter covers the following subjects:

- Using Modules to Manage Packages
- Using Modules to Manage Repositories and Subscriptions
- Implementing a Playbook to Manage Software

## CHAPTER 12

Managing Software with Ansible

The following RHCE exam objectives are covered in this chapter:

- Using Ansible modules for system administration tasks that work with
  - Software packages and repositories

"Do I Know This Already?" Quiz

The "Do I Know This Already?" quiz allows you to assess whether you should read this entire chapter thoroughly or jump to the "Exam Preparation Tasks" section. If you are in doubt about your answers to these questions or your own assessment of your knowledge of the topics, read the entire chapter. Table 12-1 lists the major headings in this chapter and their corresponding "Do I Know This Already?" quiz questions. You can find the answers in Appendix A, "Answers to the 'Do I Know This Already?' Quizzes and Review Questions."

Table 12-1 "Do I Know This Already?" Section-to-Question Mapping

Foundation Topics Section	Questions
Using Modules to Manage Packages	1–5
Using Modules to Manage Repositories and Subscriptions	6–8
Implementing a Playbook to Manage Software	9, 10

1. Which module should you use to set up access to a yum repository?

   a. yum

   b. dnf

   c. repository

   d. yum_repository

2. How do you get access to facts about packages that are installed on managed machines?

    a. Package facts are collected by the default fact gathering as performed with the setup module.

    b. Package facts need to be gathered separately using the package_facts module.

    c. There is no module for gathering package facts. Use the command module instead.

    d. There is no module for gathering package facts. Use the shell module instead.

3. Which argument should be used with the yum_repository module to specify the name of the repository file that should be created on the RHEL managed machine?

    a. **file**

    b. **name**

    c. **filename**

    d. **repofile**

4. Which of the following lines shows correct syntax for installing an AppStream module?

    a. **name: 'mymodule:1.2/devel'**

    b. **name: mymodule:1.2/devel**

    c. **name: '@mymodule:1.2/devel'**

    d. **name: @mymodule:1.2/devel**

5. How would you perform an update to all packages on your system?

    a. Use the yum_update module.

    b. Use **update: all** as an argument to the yum module.

    c. Use **name: '*'** and **state: latest** as arguments to the yum module.

    d. Use **update: '*'** as an argument to the yum module.

6. While setting up a repository server, which module can you use to generate the repository metadata?

    a. yumrepository

    b. command

    c. yumrepo

    d. createrepo

7. You can use the yum module to download packages using the **download_only** argument. Which of the following statements about using this argument is true?

   a. The **download_only** argument downloads packages to the current directory.

   b. The **download_only** argument downloads packages to the /var/lib/rpm directory.

   c. The **download_only** argument downloads packages to the /tmp directory.

   d. When **download_only** is used, you also must use the **download_dir** argument to specify to which directory the packages are downloaded.

8. Which modules can you use to set up repository access on a RHEL system that is registered with Subscription Manager? (Choose two.)

   a. rhsm_repository

   b. yum_repository

   c. rhel_repository

   d. redhat_subscription

9. You want to configure a new host using a playbook. To do so, you want to set the host name as a variable, such that it can be used in all plays in the playbook. How do you do this?

   a. Set the variable in the playbook header.

   b. Set the variable in the header of the first play.

   c. Use **vars_prompt** to prompt for the variable value.

   d. Use the **-e varname=value** option to provide the variable as a startup option while running the playbook.

10. To use the redhat_subscription module in Ansible, you must set a username and password. How should you provide them? (Choose two.)

   a. Set the username and password arguments to the redhat_subscription module.

   b. Use **vars_prompt** to prompt for the variables when the playbook runs.

   c. Use Ansible Vault to securely store the values of these variables.

   d. Specify the variables using the **-e** command-line option, while running the playbook with the **ansible-playbook** command.

Foundation Topics

Using Modules to Manage Packages

Managing software packages on managed nodes is one of the first requirements when working with Ansible. Different modules are available. Table 12-2 provides an overview.

Table 12-2   Software Management Modules Overview

Module	Use
yum	Manages software packages on RHEL and CentOS
dnf	Manages software packages on Fedora
apt	Manages software packages on Ubuntu
package	Manages software packages on any Linux distribution
yum_repository	Manages repositories
package_facts	Includes package facts in the Ansible facts

Configuring Repository Access

Before you can manage any software packages, you need to set up access to a repository. To do so, the yum_repository module is provided. If you have worked with yum repository files in the /etc/yum.repos.d/ directory, using the yum_repository module is not difficult because it uses the same information.

Listing 12-1 shows an example of a playbook that sets up access to a yum repository. Notice that this is an example only, and it doesn't work yet because the repository has not been set up yet.

Listing 12-1   Configuring Repository Access

```
---
- name: setting up repository access
  hosts: all
  tasks:
  - name: connect to example repo
    yum_repository:
      name: example repo
      description: RHCE8 example repo
      file: examplerepo
      baseurl: ftp://control.example.com/repo/
      gpgcheck: no
```

While setting up repository access, you should use a few arguments. You can see an example of them in Listing 12-1. Table 12-3 provides an overview.

Table 12-3   yum_repository Key Arguments

Argument	Use
name	Identifies the name of the repository
description	Provides more details about the repository
file	Identifies the .repo file created in /etc/yum.repos.d on the managed machine to store the repository information
baseurl	Indicates the URL that identifies how to access the repository
gpgcheck	Indicates whether to check files in the repository using a GPG key

Notice that use of the **gpgcheck** argument is recommended but not mandatory. Most repositories are provided with a GPG key to verify that packages in the repository have not been tampered with. However, if no GPG key is set up for the repository, the **gpgcheck** parameter can be set to no to skip checking the GPG key.

Managing Software with yum

The yum module can be used to manage software packages. You use it to install and remove packages or to update packages. This can be done for individual packages, as well as package groups and modules. Let's look at some examples that go beyond the mere installation or removal of packages, which was covered sufficiently in earlier chapters.

Listing 12-2 shows a playbook that will update all packages on this system.

Listing 12-2   Using yum to Perform a System Update

```
---
- name: updating all packages
  hosts: ansible2
  tasks:
  - name: system update
    yum:
      name: '*'
      state: latest
```

Notice the use of the **name** argument to the yum module. It has `'*'` as its argument. To prevent the wildcard from being interpreted by the shell, you must make sure it is placed between single quotes.

Listing 12-3 shows an example where yum package groups are used to install the Virtualization Host package group.

Listing 12-3   Installing Package Groups

```
---
- name: install or update a package group
  hosts: ansible2
  tasks:
  - name: install or update a package group
    yum:
      name: '@Virtualization Host'
      state: latest
```

When a yum package group instead of an individual package needs to be installed, the name of the package group needs to start with an at sign (@), and the entire package group name needs to be put between single quotes. Also notice the use of **state: latest** in Listing 12-3. This line ensures that the packages in the package group are installed if they have not been installed yet. If they have already been installed, they are updated to the latest version.

A new feature in RHEL 8 is the yum AppStream module. Modules as listed by the Linux **yum modules list** command can be managed with the Ansible yum module also. Working with yum modules is similar to working with yum package groups. In the example in Listing 12-4, the main difference is that a version number and the installation profile are included in the module name.

Listing 12-4   Installing Yum AppStream Modules with the Ansible yum Module

```
---
- name: installing an AppStream module
  hosts: ansible2
  tasks:
  - name: install or update an AppStream module
    yum:
      name: '@php:7.3/devel'
      state: present
```

> **NOTE** When using the yum module to install multiple packages, you can provide the **name** argument with a list of multiple packages. Alternatively, you can provide multiple packages in a loop. Of these solutions, using a list of multiple packages as the argument to **name** is always preferred. If multiple package names are provided in a loop, the module must execute a task for every single package. If multiple package names are provided as the argument to **name**, yum can install all these packages in one single task.

Managing Package Facts

When Ansible is gathering facts, package facts are not included. To include package facts as well, you need to run a separate task; that is, you need to use the package_facts module. Facts that have been gathered about packages are stored to the ansible_facts.packages variable. The sample playbook in Listing 12-5 shows how to use the package_facts module.

Listing 12-5 Using the package_facts Module to Show Package Details

```
---
- name: using package facts
  hosts: ansible2
  vars:
    my_package: nmap
  tasks:
  - name: install package
    yum:
      name: "{{ my_package }}"
      state: present
  - name: update package facts
    package_facts:
      manager: auto
  - name: show package facts for {{ my_package }}
    debug:
      var: ansible_facts.packages[my_package]
    when: my_package in ansible_facts.packages
```

As you can see, the package_facts module does not need much to do its work. The only argument used here is the **manager** argument, which specifies which package manager to communicate to. Its default value of **auto** automatically detects the appropriate package manager and uses that. If you want, you can specify the package manager manually, using any package manager such as yum or dnf. Listing 12-6 shows the output of running the Listing 12-5 playbook, where you can see details that are collected by the package_facts module.

Listing 12-6   Running **ansible-playbook listing125.yaml** Results

```
[ansible@control rhce8-book]$ ansible-playbook listing125.yaml

PLAY [using package facts] *******************************************

TASK [Gathering Facts] ***********************************************
ok: [ansible2]

TASK [install package] ***********************************************
ok: [ansible2]

TASK [update package facts] ******************************************
ok: [ansible2]

TASK [show package facts for my_package] ****************************
ok: [ansible2] => {
    "ansible_facts.packages[my_package]": [
        {
            "arch": "x86_64",
            "epoch": 2,
            "name": "nmap",
            "release": "5.el8",
            "source": "rpm",
            "version": "7.70"
        }
    ]
}

PLAY RECAP **********************************************************
ansible2                    : ok=4    changed=0    unreachable=0
failed=0    skipped=0    rescued=0    ignored=0
```

In Exercise 12-1 you can practice working with the different tools Ansible provides for module management.

Exercise 12-1   Managing Software Packages

1. Use your editor to create a new file with the name exercise121.yaml.

2. Write a play header that defines the variable **my_package** and sets its value to **virt-manager**:

```
---
- name: exercise121
  hosts: ansible2
  vars:
    my_package: virt-manager
  tasks:
```

3. Add a task that installs the package based on the name of the variable that was provided:

```
- name: install package
  yum:
    name: "{{ my_package }}"
    state: present
```

4. Add a task that gathers facts about installed packages:

```
- name: update package facts
  package_facts:
    manager: auto
```

5. As the last part of this exercise, add a task that shows facts about the package that you have just installed:

```
- name: show package facts for {{ my_package }}
  debug:
    var: ansible_facts.packages[my_package]
  when: my_package in ansible_facts.packages
```

6. Run the playbook using **ansible-playbook exercise121.yaml** and verify its output.

Using Modules to Manage Repositories and Subscriptions

To work with software packages, you need to make sure that repositories are accessible and subscriptions are available. In the previous section you learned how to write a playbook that enables you to access an existing repository. In this section you learn how to set up the server part of a repository if that still needs to be done. Also, you learn how to manage RHEL subscriptions using Ansible.

Setting Up Repositories

Most managed systems access the default repositories that are provided while installing the operating system. In some cases external repositories might not be accessible. If that happens, you need to set up a repository yourself. Before you can do that, however, it's important to know what a repository is. A repository is a directory that contains RPM files, as well as the repository metadata, which is an index that allows the repository client to figure out which packages are available in the repository.

Ansible does not provide a specific module to set up a repository. You must use a number of modules instead. Exactly which modules are involved depends on how you want to set up the repository. For instance, if you want to set up an FTP-based repository on the Ansible control host, you need to accomplish the following tasks:

- Install the FTP package.

- Start and enable the FTP server.

- Open the firewall for FTP traffic.

- Make sure the FTP shared repository directory is available.

- Download packages to the repository directory.

- Use the Linux **createrepo** command to generate the index that is required in each repository.

The playbook in Listing 12-7 provides an example of how this can be done.

Listing 12-7   Setting Up an FTP-based Repository

```
- name: install FTP to export repo
  hosts: localhost
  tasks:
  - name: install FTP server
    yum:
      name:
      - vsftpd
      - createrepo_c
      state: latest
  - name: start FTP server
    service:
      name: vsftpd
      state: started
      enabled: yes
```

```
  - name: open firewall for FTP
    firewalld:
      service: ftp
      state: enabled
      permanent: yes


- name: setup the repo directory
  hosts: localhost
  tasks:
  - name: make directory
    file:
      path: /var/ftp/repo
      state: directory
  - name: download packages
    yum:
      name: nmap
      download_only: yes
      download_dir: /var/ftp/repo
  - name: createrepo
    command: createrepo /var/ftp/repo
```

The most significant tasks in setting up the repository are the **download packages** and **createrepo** tasks. In the **download packages** task, the yum module is used to download a single package. To do so, the **download_only** argument is used to ensure that the package is not installed but downloaded to a directory. When you use the **download_only** argument, you also must specify where the package needs to be installed. To do this, the task uses the **download_dir** argument.

There is one disadvantage in using this approach to download the package, though: it requires repository access. If repository access is not available, the fetch module can be used instead to download a file from a specific URL.

Managing GPG Keys

To guarantee the integrity of packages, most repositories are set up with a GPG key. This enables the client to verify that packages have not been tampered with while transmitted between the repository server and client. For that reason, if packages are installed from a repository server on the Internet, you should always make sure that **gpgcheck: yes** is set while using the yum_repository module.

However, if you want to make sure that a GPG check is performed, you need to make sure the client knows where to fetch the repository key. To help with that, you can use the rpm_key module. You can see how to do this in Listing 12-8. Notice that the playbook in this listing doesn't work because no GPG-protected repository is available. Setting up GPG-protected repositories is complex and outside the scope of the EX294 objectives and for that reason is not covered here.

Listing 12-8   Using rpm_key to Fetch an RPM Key

```
- name: use rpm_key in repository access
  hosts: all
  tasks:
  - name: get the GPG public key
    rpm_key:
      key: ftp://control.example.com/repo/RPM-GPG-KEY
      state: present
  - name: set up the repository client
    yum_repository:
      file: myrepo
      name: myrepo
      description: example repo
      baseurl: ftp://control.example.com/repo
      enabled: yes
      gpgcheck: yes
      state: present
```

Managing RHEL Subscriptions

When you work with Red Hat Enterprise Linux, configuring repository access using the method described before is not enough. Red Hat Enterprise Linux works with subscriptions, and to be able to access software that is provided through your subscription entitlement, you need to set up managed systems to access these subscriptions.

TIP   Free developer subscriptions are available for RHEL as well as Ansible. Register yourself at https://developers.redhat.com and sign up for a free subscription if you want to test the topics described in this section on RHEL and you don't have a valid subscription yet.

To understand how to use the Ansible modules to register a RHEL system, you need to understand how to use the Linux command-line utilities. When you are managing subscriptions from the Linux command line, multiple steps are involved.

1. First, you use the **subscription-manager register** command to provide your RHEL credentials. Use, for instance, **subscription-manager register --username=yourname --password=yourpassword**.

2. Next, you need to find out which pools are available in your account. A pool is a collection of software channels available to your account. Use **subscription-manager list --available** for an overview.

3. Now you can connect to a specific pool using **subscription-manager attach --pool=***poolID*. Note that if only one subscription pool is available in your account, you don't have to provide the **--pool** argument.

4. Next, you need to find out which additional repositories are available to your account by using **subscription-manager repos --list**.

5. To register to use additional repositories, you use **subscription-manager repos --enable "repos name"**. Your system then has full access to its subscription and related repositories.

Two significant modules are provided by Ansible:

- **redhat_subscription:** This module enables you to perform subscription and registration in one task.

- **rhsm_repository:** This module enables you to add subscription manager repositories.

Listing 12-9 shows an example of a playbook that uses these modules to fully register a new RHEL 8 machine and add a new repository to the managed machine. Notice that this playbook is not runnable as such because important additional information needs to be provided. Exercise 12-3, later in the section titled "Implementing a Playbook to Manage Software," will guide you to a scenario that shows how to use this code in production.

Listing 12-9   Using Subscription Manager to Set Up Ansible

```
---
- name: use subscription manager to register and set up repos
  hosts: ansible5
  tasks:
  - name: register and subscribe ansible5
    redhat_subscription:
```

```
      username: bob@example.com
       password: verysecretpassword
       state: present
    - name: configure additional repo access
      rhsm_repository:
        name:
        - rh-gluster-3-client-for-rhel-8-x86_64-rpms
        - rhel-8-for-x86_64-appstream-debug-rpms
        state: present
```

In the sample playbook in Listing 12-9, you can see how the redhat_subscription and rhsm_repository modules are used. Notice that redhat_subscription requires a password. In Listing 12-9 the username and password are provided as clear-text values in the playbook. From a security perspective, this is very bad practice. You should use Ansible Vault instead. Exercise 12-3 will guide you through a setup where this is done.

In Exercise 12-2 you are guided through the procedure of setting up your own repository and using it. This procedure consists of two distinct parts. In the first part you set up a repository server that is based on FTP. Next, you write a second playbook that configures the clients with appropriate repository access, and after doing so, install a package.

Exercise 12-2   Setting Up a Repository

1. Use your editor to create the file exercise122-server.yaml.

2. Define the play that sets up the basic FTP configuration. Because all its tasks should be familiar to you at this point, you can enter all the tasks at once:

```
---
- name: install, configure, start and enable FTP
  hosts: localhost
  tasks:
  - name: install FTP server
    yum:
      name: vsftpd
      state: latest
  - name: allow anonymous access to FTP
    lineinfile:
```

```
        path: /etc/vsftpd/vsftpd.conf
        regexp: '^anonymous_enable=NO'
        line: anonymous_enable=YES
  - name: start FTP server
    service:
      name: vsftpd
      state: started
      enabled: yes
  - name: open firewall for FTP
    firewalld:
      service: ftp
      state: enabled
      immediate: yes
      permanent: yes
```

3. **Set up a repository directory.** Add the following play to the playbook. Notice the use of the download packages task, which uses the yum module to download a package without installing it. Also notice the createrepo task, which creates the repository metadata that converts the /var/ftp/repo directory into a repository.

```
- name: setup the repo directory
  hosts: localhost
  tasks:
  - name: make directory
    file:
      path: /var/ftp/repo
      state: directory
  - name: download packages
    yum:
      name: nmap
      download_only: yes
      download_dir: /var/ftp/repo
  - name: install createrepo package
    yum:
      name: createrepo_c
      state: latest
  - name: createrepo
    command: createrepo /var/ftp/repo
    notify:
    - restart_ftp
  handlers:
  - name: restart_ftp
    service:
```

```
      name: vsftpd
      state: restarted
```

4. Use the command **ansible-playbook exercise122-server.yaml** to set up the FTP server on control.example.com. If you haven't made any typos, you shouldn't encounter any errors.

5. Now that the repository server has been installed, it's time to set up the repository client. Use your editor to create the file exercise122-client.yaml and write the play header as follows:

```
---
- name: configure repository
  hosts: all
  vars:
    my_package: nmap
  tasks:
```

6. Add a task that uses the yum_repository module to configure access to the new repository:

```
- name: connect to example repo
  yum_repository:
    name: exercise122
    description: RHCE8 exercise 122 repo
    file: exercise122
    baseurl: ftp://control.example.com/repo/
    gpgcheck: no
```

7. After setting up the repository client, you also need to make sure that the clients know how to reach the repository server by addressing its name. Add the next task that writes a new line to /etc/hosts to make sure host name resolving on the clients is set up correctly:

```
- name: ensure control is resolvable
  lineinfile:
    path: /etc/hosts
    line: 192.168.4.200  control.example.com   control
- name: install package
  yum:
    name: "{{ my_package }}"
    state: present
```

8. If you are using the package_facts module, you need to remember to update it after installing new packages. Add the following task to get this done:

```
- name: update package facts
  package_facts:
    manager: auto
```

9. As the last task, just because it's fun, use the debug module together with the package facts to get information about the newly installed package:

```
- name: show package facts for {{ my_package }}
  debug:
     var: ansible_facts.packages[my_package]
  when: my_package in ansible_facts.packages
```

10. Use the command **ansible-playbook exercise122-client.yaml -e my_package= redis**. That's right; this command overwrites the my_package variable that was set in the playbook—just to remind you a bit about variable precedence.

Implementing a Playbook to Manage Software

In the previous sections you learned how to use different modules to manage software. In this section you apply this knowledge in a more advanced playbook example. You'll also find an advanced example like this in Chapters 13 through 15 so that you get the best possible preparation for the EX294 exam. To match the exam style of questions, the example is scenario based, and the assignment is formatted as a step-by-step exercise. As is the case for most exercises, the complete playbook discussed here is available in the GitHub repository at https://github.com/sandervanvugt/rhce8-book/exercise123.yaml.

To run this assignment on a RHEL 8 target, you need access to a valid RHEL 8 subscription. If you don't have a current subscription, you can request it from https://developers.redhat.com.

Exercise 12-3   Configuring a New RHEL Managed Node

Create a playbook that will fully automate the setup of a new RHEL host. To do this, you need a new host to be installed. For the new host, use the name ansible5 and the IP address 192.168.4.205, and ensure it is installed with RHEL (not CentOS). Write this playbook according to the following requirements:

■ Add the new host information to the inventory and /etc/hosts file on the control host.

■ Work with variables for the name of the host you want to set up.

■ Connect as user root to the new host. While running the playbook, run it with the appropriate option so that you will be prompted for the root password.

■ Set up the user ansible on the new host and make sure this user is a member of the group wheel.

■ Also set a password for user ansible using the playbook.

- Modify the sudoers file such that the user ansible can run root commands using sudo without having to enter a password.
- Automatically register the host with the RHEL Subscription Manager.
- Use Ansible Vault to provide the username and password in a secure way.
- Add the new host to the rh-gluster-3-client-for-rhel-8-x86_64-rpms repository and the rhel-8-for-x86_64-appstream-debug-rpms repository.
- Use tags so that you can run individual parts of the playbook.

1. On the control host, use **sudo yum install sshpass** to install the sshpass package. This package enables you to work with SSH passwords in a noninteractive way, and you need it to automate working with SSH passwords from a playbook environment.

2. To start, you need to set up the control host to include information about the new host. To make this playbook flexible, this playbook requires variables to be set from the command line because that is the only way to ensure that the variable is available in all of the plays. Using **vars_prompt** would have been an option, but variables that are set with **vars_prompt** apply only to the play in which they are set. To check that the variables were indeed passed as an argument to the **ansible-playbook** command, use the fail module as follows to check whether the variable **newhost** and the variable **newhostip** are provided as startup arguments. Create a file with the name exercise123.yaml as follows:

```
- name: add host to inventory
  hosts: localhost
  tasks:
  - fail:
      msg: "add the options -e newhost=hostname -e newhostip=ip.
ad.dr.ess and try again"
    when: (newhost is undefined) or (newhostip is undefined)
```

3. Write the next tasks for this first play. In these tasks, you want to make sure that the local inventory file and the /etc/hosts file are modified. To do this, the lineinfile module provides good service. Notice the use of the line the second time the lineinfile module is called. The line contains only variables, and for that reason the entire variable string must be between double quotes. Also, at the end of the play, include the **tags: addhost** line, which makes it easy to skip this task after it has run successfully in case it is needed to run the playbook again. Make sure to add the following text to complete the first play:

```
- name: add new host to inventory
  lineinfile:
    path: inventory
    state: present
```

```
          line: "{{ newhost }}"
  - name: add new host to /etc/hosts
    lineinfile:
      path: /etc/hosts
      state: present
      line: "{{ newhostip }}  {{ newhost}}"
  tags: addhost
```

4. At this point it's a good idea to test that all is going well so far. Use
    ansible-playbook -C exercise123.yaml and observe playbook output. It
    should fail because no arguments are provided on the command line. Use
    **ansible-playbook -C exercise123.yaml -e newhost=ansible5
    -e newhostip=192.168.4.205** and try again.

5. The first play is ready at this point, so it's time to configure the second play.
    This play is executed on the new host. The target host name is set to the
    variable **newhost**, which is defined while running the **ansible-playbook**
    command. Also notice that the **remote_user** and the **become** statements must
    be set because the default user ansible is not configured for privilege escalation
    yet. Write the play header for this second play as follows:

```
- name: configure a new RHEL host
  hosts: "{{ newhost }}"
  remote_user: root
  become: false
  tasks:
```

6. Now it's time to add the tasks as well as the tag to this play. In the tasks you
    need to make sure a user ansible exists and is a member of the group wheel.
    Next, you use the shell module to set a password for the user ansible. It's an ugly
    approach, but it works. In Chapter 13, "Managing Users," you'll learn how to
    do this in a much nicer way. As the next task you use the lineinfile module to
    modify the /etc/sudoers file and allow members of the group wheel to escalate
    permissions without entering a password. Add the tasks to do this as follows:

```
- name: configure user ansible
  user:
    name: ansible
    groups: wheel
    append: yes
    state: present
- name: set a password for this user
  shell: 'echo password | passwd --stdin ansible'
- name: enable sudo without passwords
```

```
    lineinfile:
      path: /etc/sudoers
      regexp: '^%wheel'
      line: '%wheel ALL=(ALL)   NOPASSWD: ALL'
      validate: /usr/sbin/visudo -cf %s
```

7. With this part you have set up the user ansible on the managed host, but one element is still missing: the user cannot log in with an SSH public/private key pair yet. In Chapter 13 you'll learn about a nice way to add the SSH public key to the remote user; for now you can do it in a quick-and-dirty way that will also work. Add the following lines to the playbook to conclude the second play:

```
- name: create SSH directory in user ansible home
  file:
    path: /home/ansible/.ssh
    state: directory
    owner: ansible
    group: ansible
- name: copy SSH public key to remote host
  copy:
    src: /home/ansible/.ssh/id_rsa.pub
    dest: /home/ansible/.ssh/authorized_keys
tags: setuphost
```

8. Feel free to test the second play at this point; it's better to filter out any errors now than to do it later. To test, use **ansible-playbook -C -k exercise123.yaml -e newhost=ansible5 -e newhostip=192.168.4.205**. Notice the use of the **-k** option, which prompts for the SSH password that user root in this play needs to set up the target host.

9. At this point your RHEL host should be ready for use. The only thing that is still missing is that it has not been registered against Red Hat Subscription Manager. To do this, you need your Red Hat credentials. Because these credentials are sensitive information, you should use Ansible Vault. So let's start creating the vault file and define the username and password variables in the Vault file. To create the Vault file, use **ansible-vault create exercise123-vault.yaml** and provide the following input, where you should use your real username and password and not *XXXXXXXXX*. Your rhsm_user name is the name (typically an email address) that you use to log in at redhat.com, and the rhsm_password is the password that you use with it. Also notice that for obvious security reasons, this file is NOT provided in the GitHub repository that comes with this book:

```
rhsm_user: XXXXXXXXXX
rhsm_password: XXXXXXXXXX
```

10. Now that you have created the Vault file, you can write the header for the third and last play in the file exercise123.yaml. The most important part of this header is the **vars_files** part, which refers to the Vault file:

```
- name: use subscription manager to register and set up repos
  hosts: "{{ newhost }}"
  vars_files:
  - exercise123-vault.yaml
  tasks:
```

11. At this point you can complete the playbook and add the remaining tasks:

```
- name: register and subscribe {{ newhost }}
  redhat_subscription:
    username: "{{ rhsm_user }}"
    password: "{{ rhsm_password }}"
    state: present
- name: configure additional repo access
  rhsm_repository:
    name:
    - rh-gluster-3-client-for-rhel-8-x86_64-rpms
    - rhel-8-for-x86_64-appstream-debug-rpms
    state: present
tags: registerhost
```

12. At this point the playbook is ready. Compare what you have written to the sample playbook exercise123.yaml that is in the GitHub repository and give it a try. To do so, use the **ansible-playbook -k --ask-vault-pass exercise123. yaml -e newhost=ansible5 -e newhostip=192.168.4.205** command. Everything should be running smoothly, but because this is a large playbook and it is very difficult to write it without typos right from the beginning, you might have to do a little bit of troubleshooting. To do so, I recommend that you use the tags that have been provided with the plays. If, after running the first and second plays successfully, the third play generates an error, you can run just that play again, using **ansible-playbook --tags=registerhost exercise123.yaml -e newhost=ansible5**. (Notice that this command doesn't use as many command-line options as the command you used just a minute ago because these parameters don't apply to the **registerhost** tag.)

Summary

In this chapter you learned how to work with software. You read about the different modules that are available for managing packages, as well as how to set up repositories and subscriptions. You also worked through an advanced scenario that implements a playbook to manage software.

Exam Preparation Tasks

As mentioned in the section "How to Use This Book" in the Introduction, you have a couple of choices for exam preparation: the exercises here, Chapter 16, "Final Preparation," and the exam simulation questions on the companion website.

Review All Key Topics

Review the most important topics in this chapter, noted with the Key Topics icon in the outer margin of the page. Table 12-4 lists a reference of these key topics and the page numbers on which each is found.

Table 12-4 Key Topics for Chapter 12

Key Topic Element	Description	Page Number
Table 12-2	Software Management Modules Overview	284
Table 12-3	yum_repository Key Arguments	285

Memory Tables

Print a copy of Appendix D, "Memory Tables" (found on the companion website), or at least the section for this chapter, and complete the tables and lists from memory. Appendix E, "Memory Tables Answer Key," also on the companion website, includes completed tables and lists to check your work.

Define Key Terms

Define the following key terms from this chapter, and check your answers in the glossary:

AppStream, GNU Privacy Guard (GPG), pool, subscription

Review Questions

1. Which Ansible module must be used to get information about software packages that are installed?

2. Which module is used to configure repository clients?

3. What line would you use in a playbook to install the Virtualization Host package group?

4. Which Linux command is used to generate repository metadata?

5. Which module can you use to download packages from a yum repository without installing them?

6. Which module can you use to get a file from a URL?

7. Which module would you use to import a GPG key from a yum repository?

8. Which module would you use to register a RHEL system with Red Hat Subscription Manager?

9. Which module would you use to add a repository that is offered through Red Hat Subscription Manager?

10. How do you provide a variable that can be used in all plays in a multiplay playbook?

End-of-Chapter Labs

In the end-of-chapter labs this time, you set up a configuration for managing playbooks.

Lab 12-1

Configure the control.example.com host as a repository server, according to the following requirements:

- Create a directory with the name /repo, and in that directory copy all packages that have a name starting with nginx.

- Generate the metadata that makes this directory a repository.

- Configure the Apache web server to provide access to the repository server. You just have to make sure that the DocumentRoot in Apache is going to be set to the /repo directory.

Lab 12-2

Write a playbook to configure all managed servers according to the following requirements:

- All hosts can access the repository that was created in Lab 12-1.

- Have the same playbook install the nginx package.

- Do NOT start the service. Use the appropriate module to gather information about the installed nginx package, and let the playbook print a message stating the name of the nginx package as well as the version.

This chapter covers the following subjects:

- Using Ansible Modules to Manage Users and Groups
- Managing SSH Connections
- Managing Encrypted Passwords
- Managing Users Advanced Scenario Exercise

## CHAPTER 13

Managing Users

The following RHCE exam objectives are covered in this chapter:

- ■ Use Ansible modules for system administration tasks that work with
  - ■ Users and groups

"Do I Know This Already?" Quiz

The "Do I Know This Already?" quiz allows you to assess whether you should read this entire chapter thoroughly or jump to the "Exam Preparation Tasks" section. If you are in doubt about your answers to these questions or your own assessment of your knowledge of the topics, read the entire chapter. Table 13-1 lists the major headings in this chapter and their corresponding "Do I Know This Already?" quiz questions. You can find the answers in Appendix A, "Answers to the 'Do I Know This Already?' Quizzes and Review Questions."

Table 13-1 "Do I Know This Already?" Section-to-Question Mapping

Foundation Topics Section	Questions
Using Ansible Modules to Manage Users and Groups	1–3
Managing SSH Connections	4–6
Managing Encrypted Passwords	7–9
Managing Users Advanced Scenario Exercise	10

1. Which Ansible module would you use to manage the SSH known hosts file for existing or new users?

   a. lineinfile

   b. ssh_key

   c. ssh_config

   d. known_hosts

2. Which arguments must be used with the user module to make an existing user a member of additional groups without overwriting any current group assignments? (Choose two.)

   a. **group**

   b. **groups**

   c. **append**

   d. **newgroups**

3. Which Ansible modules can you use to manage the sudoers configuration file? (Choose two.)

   a. lineinfile

   b. template

   c. sudoers

   d. sudo

4. Which module can you use to manage a server's SSH public key?

   a. authorized_key

   b. authorized_hosts

   c. known_keys

   d. known_hosts

5. What should you use to look up a specific file and copy that file over to the managed host?

   a. The copy module

   b. The lookup module

   c. The copy plug-in

   d. The lookup plug-in

6. Which of the following restrictions applies to the authorized_keys module?

   a. It cannot read files from a hidden directory.

   b. It works only for the default Ansible user.

   c. It needs permission mode to be set to 644 on the target file.

   d. It doesn't work from a sudo shell.

7. An encrypted password as stored in /etc/shadow consists of different parts. Which of the following is not one of them?

   a. The hashing algorithm that was used

   b. The random salt that was used to encrypt the password

   c. The username

   d. The encrypted hash of the user password

8. Different solutions can be used to generate an encrypted password for use by the Ansible user module. Which of the following is not one of them?

   a. Use the shell module with the **passwd --stdin** command to store the encrypted password in a variable.

   b. Use the command module with the **passwd --stdin** command to store the encrypted password in a variable.

   c. Use an ad hoc command with the debug module to generate the encrypted password string.

   d. Create a task that uses the debug module to generate the encrypted password string.

9. When you're working with encrypted passwords in playbooks, there must be some way to ensure that security is guaranteed. Which of the following solutions is best?

   a. Store the password in a Vault file.

   b. Have the playbook prompt for the password to be used.

   c. Store the password in a file that is accessible by the root user only.

   d. Use an inventory variables file to read the password.

10. What is the best way to create multiple user accounts?

   a. Use loop to iterate over a list of users.

   b. Define the users in a variable and use loop to iterate over that variable.

   c. Define a variables file, in which the users are defined as a list, and use loop from the playbook to iterate over that.

   d. Use vars_prompt to have the playbook prompt for variable names to be used.

Foundation Topics

Using Ansible Modules to Manage Users and Groups

To manage users on Ansible, different tasks are involved. To begin with, there is the management of the user and group accounts and their direct properties. This includes management of sudo privilege escalation also because the new user may need to be configured to run tasks with privilege escalation. Setting up SSH connections and setting user passwords are different topics that require attention.

Modules Overview

Different modules are involved for managing users, groups, and their most important properties. Table 13-2 provides an overview.

Table 13-2   Managing Users and Groups Modules Overview

Module	Description
user	Manages users and their base properties
group	Manages groups and their properties
pamd	Manages advanced authentication configuration through Linux Pluggable Authentication Modules (PAM)
known_hosts	Manages SSH known hosts
authorized_key	Copies a user authorized key to a managed host
lineinfile	Modifies configuration files

Managing Users and Groups

Managing users and groups is a pretty straightforward procedure in which you use the user and group modules to set the properties that are required for user accounts. Listing 13-1 provides an example.

Listing 13-1   Managing Users and Groups

```
---
- name: creating a user and group
  hosts: ansible2
  tasks:
  - name: setup the group account
    group:
```

```
    name: students
    state: present
- name: setup the user account
  user:
    name: anna
    create_home: yes
    groups: wheel,students
    append: yes
    generate_ssh_key: yes
    ssh_key_bits: 2048
    ssh_key_file: .ssh/id_rsa
```

When you use the user module, many options are available. Most of them speak for themselves; however, just two arguments need attention, and they are **group** and **groups**. The **group** argument is used to specify the primary group of the user. By default, when you are creating a new user, a new group is created with the name of that user, and that group is set as the primary group. The **groups** argument is used to make the user a member of additional groups. While using the **groups** argument for existing users, make sure to include the **append** argument as well. Without **append**, all current secondary group assignments are overwritten.

Also notice that the user module has some options that cannot normally be managed with the Linux **useradd** command. As shown in Listing 13-1, the module can also be used to generate an SSH key and specify its properties.

Managing sudo

When you're setting up new user accounts on Ansible, some of these users may require sudo privileges to be set up. Because no Ansible module specifically targets managing a sudo configuration, you need to use generic Ansible modules instead. There are two options. First, you can use the template module to create a sudo configuration file in the directory /etc/sudoers.d. Using such a file is recommended because the file is managed independently, and as such, there is no risk it will be overwritten by an RPM update. The alternative is to use the lineinfile module to manage the /etc/sudoers main configuration file directly.

In Listings 13-2, 13-3, and 13-4 you can see a playbook construction where users are created and added to a sudo file that is generated from a template. To split static code from the dynamic site-specific settings, the playbook in Listing 13-4 makes use of two variable files shown in Listing 13-2.

Listing 13-2   Variables for Managing sudo

```
[ansible@control rhce8-book]$ cat vars/sudo
sudo_groups:
  - name: developers
    groupid: 5000
    sudo: false
  - name: admins
    groupid: 5001
    sudo: true
  - name: dbas
    groupid: 5002
    sudo: false
  - name: sales
    groupid: 5003
    sudo: true
  - name: account
    groupid: 5004
    sudo: false
[ansible@control rhce8-book]$ cat vars/users
users:
  - username: linda
    groups: sales
  - username: lori
    groups: sales
  - username: lisa
    groups: account
  - username: lucy
    groups: account
```

As you can see, the vars/users file defines users and the groups they should be a member of. Apart from that, the vars/sudo file defines new groups and, for each of these groups, sets a sudo parameter, which will be used in the template file shown in Listing 13-3.

Listing 13-3   Template File for Managing sudo

```
{% for item in sudo_groups %}
{% if item.sudo %}
%{{ item.name}} ALL=(ALL:ALL) NOPASSWD:ALL
{% endif %}
{% endfor %}
```

In the template file in Listing 13-3, a **for** loop is used to walk through all items that have been defined in the **sudo_groups** variable in the vars/sudo file. Next, for each of these groups an **if** statement is used to check the value of the Boolean variable sudo. If this variable is set to the Boolean value true, the group is added as a sudo group to the /etc/sudoers.d/sudogroups file.

Listing 13-4   Managing sudo

```
---
- name: configure sudo
  hosts: ansible2
  vars_files:
    - vars/sudo
    - vars/users
  tasks:
  - name: add groups
    group:
      name: "{{ item.name }}"
    loop: "{{ sudo_groups }}"
  - name: add users
    user:
      name: "{{ item.username }}"
      groups: "{{ item.groups }}"
    loop: "{{ users }}"
  - name: allow group members in sudo
    template:
      src: listing133.j2
      dest: /etc/sudoers.d/sudogroups
      validate: 'visudo -cf %s'
      mode: 0440
```

The playbook in Listing 13-4 uses the variables as well as the template file to create the users and the sudoers configuration. The result is written to the relevant configuration files on the managed hosts, such that a sudo configuration is automatically created. In Exercise 13-1 you practice managing users and groups.

Exercise 13-1   Managing Users and Groups

1. Use **mkdir host_vars** to create the host_vars directory.

2. Use your editor to create the file host_vars/ansible1 and give it the following contents:

```
users:
- username: zeina
```

```
      groups: admins
    - username: marlet
      groups: admins
    - username: victoria
      groups: students
    - username: emma
      groups: students
```

3. Create the file exercise131.yaml and write the following play header:

```
---
- name: create user accounts
  hosts: ansible1
  tasks:
```

4. Continue and add the first task that will create required groups:

```
- name: create groups
  group:
    name: "{{ item.groups }}"
    state: present
  loop: "{{ users }}"
```

5. Add a task to create user accounts:

```
- name: create users
  user:
    name: "{{ item.username }}"
    group: "{{ item.groups }}"
  loop: "{{ users }}"
```

6. Create the file exercise131.j2 as a Jinja2 template and make sure it has the following contents:

```
{{ item.groups }} ALL=(ALL:ALL) NOPASSWD:ALL
```

7. Add the last task, which generates the template file to the exercise131.yaml file:

```
- name: allow group members in sudo
  template:
    src: exercise131.j2
    dest: /etc/sudoers.d/sudogroups
    validate: 'visudo -cf %s'
    mode: 0440
  loop: "{{ users }}"
```

8. Use the command **ansible-playbook exercise131.yaml** and verify the playbook is working as expected.

Managing SSH Connections

While creating users, you might also have to set up SSH keys. In Chapter 12, "Managing Software with Ansible," you saw an example where a complete host was set up to be managed by Ansible. In that example the copy module was used to copy over an SSH public key to the target user account, which allowed for password-less SSH login to the remote host as this user. The main topic in this section is how to provide SSH keys for new users in such a way that users are provided with SSH keys without having to set them up themselves. To do this, you use the authorized_key module together with the **generate_ssh_key** argument to the user module.

Understanding SSH Connection Management Requirements

Before we look at setting up SSH keys, let me quickly summarize how SSH keys are used in the communication process between a user and an SSH server. The following list provides a simplified overview of the procedure when a user logs in to an SSH server:

1. The user initiates a session with an SSH server.

2. The server sends back an identification token that is encrypted with the server's private key to the user.

3. The user uses the server's public key fingerprint, which is stored in the ~/.ssh/known_hosts file to verify the identification token.

4. If no public key fingerprint was stored yet in the ~/.ssh/known_hosts file, the user is prompted to store the remote server identity in the ~/.ssh/known_hosts file. At this point there is no good way to verify whether the user is indeed communicating with the intended server.

5. After establishing the identity of the remote server, the user can either send over a password or generate an authentication token that is based on the user's private key.

6. If an authentication token that was based on the user's private key is sent over, this token is received by the server, which tries to match it against the user's public key that is stored in the ~/.ssh/authorized_keys file.

7. After the incoming authentication token to the stored user public key in the authorized_keys file is matched, the user is authenticated. If this authentication fails and password authentication is allowed, password authentication is attempted next.

In the authentication procedure, two key pairs play an important role. First, there is the server's public/private key pair, which is used to establish a secure connection.

To manage the host public key, you can use the Ansible known_hosts module. Next, there is the user's public/private key pair, which the user uses to authenticate. To manage the public key in this key pair, you can use the Ansible authorized_key module.

Using the Lookup Plug-in

When you're working with SSH public keys, the lookup plug-in plays an important role. Ansible comes with a number of plug-ins to add to the Ansible core functionality. The lookup plug-in enables Ansible to access data from outside sources. You can use it to read the file system, for instance, or to contact external datastores and services.

Operations that are performed by a plug-in run on the Ansible control host, and the result of the plug-in work is typically stored in variables or templates. In the case of handling SSH keys, the lookup plug-in comes in handy to find items in the file system. Listing 13-5 shows a simple example where the lookup plug-in is used to set the value of a variable to the contents of a file.

Listing 13-5 Setting Variable Value to File Contents with the Lookup Plug-in

```
---
- name: simple demo with the lookup plugin
  hosts: localhost
  vars:
    file_contents: "{{lookup('file', '/etc/hosts')}}"
  tasks:
  - debug:
      var: file_contents
```

Setting Up SSH User Keys

To use SSH to connect to a user account on a managed host, using a user account from the control host, you might want to copy over the local user public key to the remote user ~/.ssh/authorized_keys file. If the target authorized_keys file just has to contain one single key, you could use the copy module to copy it over. If, however, you want to manage multiple keys in the remote user authorized_keys file, you're better off using the authorized_key module. In essence, this module is simple to use.

In the example in Listing 13-6, you can see how the authorized_key module is used to copy the authorized_key for user ansible. As the input source, the file /home/ansible/.ssh/id_rsa.pub is used. The lookup plug-in is used to refer to the file contents that should be used.

Listing 13-6 Using the authorized_key Module

```
---
- name: authorized_key simple demo
  hosts: ansible2
  tasks:
  - name: copy authorized key for ansible user
    authorized_key:
      user: ansible
      state: present
      key: "{{ lookup('file', '/home/ansible/.ssh/id_rsa.pub') }}"
```

If you understand how Listing 13-6 works, it's easy to enhance that code such that it will do the same for multiple users. Listing 13-7 shows the contents of two variable include files, which are applied in the playbook in Listing 13-8.

Listing 13-7 Variable Files Used in Listing 13-8

```
[ansible@control rhce8-book]$ cat vars/users
---
users:
  - username: linda
    groups: sales
  - username: lori
    groups: sales
  - username: lisa
    groups: account
  - username: lucy
    groups: account
[ansible@control rhce8-book]$ cat vars/groups
---
usergroups:
  - groupname: sales
  - groupname: account
```

Listing 13-8   Using the authorized_key Module with the Lookup Plug-in

```
---
- name: configure users with SSH keys
  hosts: ansible2
  vars_files:
    - vars/users
    - vars/groups
  tasks:
  - name: add groups
    group:
      name: "{{ item.groupname }}"
    loop: "{{ usergroups }}"
  - name: add users
    user:
      name: "{{ item.username }}"
      groups: "{{ item.groups }}"
    loop: "{{ users }}"
  - name: add SSH public keys
    authorized_key:
      user: "{{ item.username }}"
      key: "{{ lookup('file', 'files/'+ item.username +
'/id_rsa.pub') }}"
    loop: "{{ users }}"
```

The most interesting new part in Listing 13-8 is the authorized_key module, which is set up to work on **item.username**, using a **loop** on the **users** variable. This construction enables the playbook to apply to each user. Notice that the id_rsa.pub files that have to be copied over are expected to exist in the files directory, which exists in the current project directory.

Copying over the user public keys to the project directory is a solution for an important problem that's difficult to deal with: the authorized_keys module cannot read files from a hidden directory. It would be much nicer to use **key: "{{ lookup('file', '/home/' + item.username + '.ssh/id_rsa.pub') }}"**, but that doesn't work. For that reason, to get it working anyway, you need to apply a workaround. You apply this workaround in the sample playbook in Exercise 13-2. Before you work on the exercise, though, let's look at what exactly you are going to do in this exercise.

In the first task (see Listing 13-9), you create a local user, including an SSH key. Because an SSH key should include the name of the user and host that it applies to, you need to use the **generate_ssh_key** argument, as well as the **ssh_key_comment** argument to write the correct comment into the public key. Without this content, the key will have generic content and not be considered a valid key.

Listing 13-9 Creating the User with SSH Key

```
- name: create the local user, including SSH key
  user:
    name: "{{ username }}"
    generate_ssh_key: true
    ssh_key_comment: "{{ username }}@{{ ansible_fqdn }}"
```

After creating the SSH keys this way, you aren't able to fetch the key directly from the user home directory. To fix that problem, you create a directory with the name of the user in the project directory and copy the user public key from there by using the shell module. You can see the sample code to do this in Listing 13-10.

Listing 13-10 Copying the User SSH Public Key to a Location from Which It Can Be Copied

```
- name: create a directory to store the file
  file:
    name: "{{ username }}"
    state: directory
- name: copy the local user ssh key to temporary {{ username }} key
  shell: 'cat /home/{{ username }}/.ssh/id_rsa.pub > {{ username }}/
id_rsa.pub'
- name: verify that file exists
  command: ls -l {{ username }}/
```

Next, in the second play you create the remote user and use the authorized_key module to copy the key from the temporary directory to the new user home directory. As mentioned, Exercise 13-2 guides you through all these steps.

In this playbook, you first create a local user, including the SSH key.

Exercise 13-2   Managing Users with SSH Keys

1. Use your editor to create the file exercise132.yaml and write the header of the first play, which creates a user on localhost:

    ```
    ---
    - name: prepare localhost
      hosts: localhost
      tasks:
    ```

2. Write the first task, which creates the user on localhost. Notice that the variable **{{ username }}** is used. When running the playbook later, you'll need to make sure this variable has a value, for instance, by using the argument

-e username=sharon while running the playbook. In the user module, you use the appropriate arguments to create the SSH public/private key pair according to the required format:

```
- name: create the local user, including SSH key
  user:
    name: "{{ username }}"
    generate_ssh_key: true
    ssh_key_comment: "{{ username }}@{{ ansible_fqdn }}"
```

3. You need to make sure the public key is copied to a directory where it can be accessed. The following three tasks do this:

```
- name: create a directory to store the file
  file:
    name: "{{ username }}"
    state: directory
- name: copy the local user ssh key to temporary {{ username }}
key
    shell: 'cat /home/{{ username }}/.ssh/id_rsa.pub > {{ username
}}/id_rsa.pub'
- name: verify that file exists
    command: ls -l {{ username }}/
```

4. At this point, the user public SSH key is created and accessible, and you can write the second play. This second play uses the user module to create the user, as well as the authorized_key module to fetch the key from localhost and copy it to the .ssh/authorized_keys file in the remote user home directory:

```
- name: setup remote host
  hosts: ansible1
  tasks:
  - name: create remote user, no need for SSH key
    user:
      name: "{{ username }}"
  - name: use authorized_key to set the password
    authorized_key:
      user: "{{ username }}"
      key: "{{ lookup('file', './'+ username +'/id_rsa.pub') }}"
```

5. At this point, use the command **ansible-playbook exercise132.yaml -e username=radha** to create the user radha with the appropriate SSH keys.

6. To verify it has worked, use **sudo su - radha** on the control host, and type the command **ssh ansible1**. You should be able to log in without entering a password.

Managing Encrypted Passwords

When managing users in Ansible, you probably want to set user passwords as well. The challenge is that you cannot just enter a password as the value to the **password:** argument in the user module because the user module expects you to use an encrypted string.

Understanding Encrypted Passwords

When a user creates a password, it is encrypted. The hash of the encrypted password is stored in the /etc/shadow file, a file that is strictly secured and accessible only with root privileges. The string looks like $6$237687687/$9809erhb8oyw48oih290u09. In this string are three elements, which are separated by $ signs:

- The hashing algorithm that was used

- The random salt that was used to encrypt the password

- The encrypted hash of the user password

When a user sets a password, a random salt is used to prevent two users who have identical passwords from having identical entries in /etc/shadow. The salt and the unencrypted password are combined and encrypted, which generates the encrypted hash that is stored in /etc/shadow. Based on this string, the password that the user enters can be verified against the password field in /etc/shadow, and if it matches, the user is authenticated.

Generating Encrypted Passwords

When you're creating users with the Ansible user module, there is a password option. This option is not capable of generating an encrypted password. It expects an encrypted password string as its input. That means an external utility must be used to generate an encrypted string. This encrypted string must be stored in a variable to create the password. Because the variable is basically the user password, the variable should be stored securely in, for example, an Ansible Vault secured file.

To generate the encrypted variable, you can choose to create the variable before creating the user account. Alternatively, you can run the command to create the variable in the playbook, use **register** to write the result to a variable, and use that to create the encrypted user. If you want to generate the variable beforehand, you can use the following ad hoc command:

```
ansible localhost -m debug -a "msg={{ 'password' | password_
hash('sha512','myrandomsalt') }}"
```

This command generates the encrypted string as shown in Listing 13-11, and this string can next be used in a playbook. An example of such a playbook is shown in Listing 13-12.

Listing 13-11   Generating the Encrypted Password String

```
[ansible@control ~]$ ansible localhost -m debug -a "msg={{ 'password'
| password_hash('sha512','myrandomsalt') }}"
localhost | SUCCESS => {
    "msg": "$6$myrandomsalt$McEB.xAVUWe0./6XqZ8n/7k9VV/
Gxndy9nIMLyQAiPnhyBoToMWbxX2vA4f.Uv9PKnPRaYUUc76AjLWVAX6U10"
}
```

Listing 13-12   Sample Playbook That Creates an Encrypted User Password

```
---
- name: create user with encrypted password
  hosts: ansible2.example.com
  vars:
    password: "$6$myrandomsalt$McEB.xAVUWe0./6XqZ8n/7k9VV/
Gxndy9nIMLyQAiPnhyBoToMWbxX2vA4f.Uv9PKnPRaYUUc76AjLWVAX6U10"
  tasks:
  - name: create the user
    user:
      name: anna
      password: "{{ password }}"
```

The method that is used here works but is not elegant. First, you need to generate the encrypted password manually beforehand. Also, the encrypted password string is used in a readable way in the playbook. By seeing the encrypted password and salt, it's possible to get to the original password, which is why the password should not be visible in the playbook in a secure environment.

In Exercise 13-3 you create a playbook that prompts for the user password and that uses the debug module, which was used in Listing 13-11 inside the playbook, together with register, so that the password no longer is readable in clear text. Before looking at Exercise 13-3, though, let's first look at an alternative approach that also works.

EXAM TIP The procedure to use encrypted passwords while creating user accounts is documented in the Frequently Asked Questions from the Ansible documentation. Because the documentation is available on the exam, make sure you know where to find this information! Search for the item "How do I generate encrypted passwords for the user module?"

Using an Alternative Approach

As has been mentioned on multiple occasions, in Ansible often different solutions exist for the same problem. And sometimes, apart from the most elegant solution, there's also a quick-and-dirty solution, and that counts for setting a user-encrypted password as well. Instead of using the solution described in the previous section, "Generating Encrypted Passwords," you can use the Linux command **echo password | passwd --stdin** to set the user password. Listing 13-13 shows how to do this. Notice this example focuses on how to do it, not on security. If you want to make the playbook more secure, it would be nice to store the password in Ansible Vault.

Listing 13-13   Setting the User Password: Alternative Solution

```
---
- name: create user with encrypted password
  hosts: ansible3
  vars:
    password: mypassword
    user: anna
  tasks:
  - name: configure user {{ user }}
    user:
      name: "{{ user }}"
      groups: wheel
      append: yes
      state: present
  - name: set a password for {{ user }}
    shell: 'echo {{ password }} | passwd --stdin {{ user }}'
```

Exercise 13-3   Creating Users with Encrypted Passwords

1. Use your editor to create the file exercise133.yaml.

2. Write the play header as follows:

```
---
- name: create user with encrypted password
  hosts: ansible3
  vars_prompt:
  - name: passw
    prompt: which password do you want to use
  vars:
    user: sharon
  tasks:
```

3. Add the first task that uses the debug module to generate the encrypted password string and register to store the string in the variable **mypass**:

```
- debug:
    msg: "{{ '{{ passw }}'| password_
hash('sha512','myrandomsalt') }}"
  register: mypass
```

4. Add a debug module to analyze the exact format of the registered variable:

```
- debug:
    var: mypass
```

5. Use **ansible-playbook exercise133.yaml** to run the playbook the first time so that you can see the exact name of the variable that you have to use. This code shows that the **mypass.msg** variable contains the encrypted password string (see Listing 13-14).

Listing 13-14   Finding the Variable Name Using debug

```
TASK [debug] ********************************************************
**************
ok: [ansible2] => {
    "mypass": {
      "changed": false,
        "failed": false,
        "msg": "$6$myrandomsalt$Jesm4QGoCGAny9ebP85apmh0/
uUXrjOlouYb03leLoOWSDy/imjVGmcODhrpIJZtOrz.GBp9pZYpfm0SU2/PO."
    }
}
```

6. Based on the output that you saw with the previous command, you can now use the user module to refer to the password in the right way. Add the following task to do so:

```
- name: create the user
  user:
    name: "{{ user }}"
    password: "{{ mypass.msg }}"
```

7. Use **ansible-playbook exercise133.yaml** to run the playbook and verify its output.

Managing Users Advanced Scenario Exercise

It's time to work on an advanced scenario now. Exercise 13-4 includes a step-by-step procedure that guides you through the process of setting up a complex playbook. In this procedure I tried to give you practical guidelines on how to approach such a complex task on the exam, including the part where you may change your mind because you have realized there is a more efficient method. It is important to read the steps carefully because some improvements will be applied while working on this procedure.

WARNING   This exercise is written such that you can learn from errors that are made. In early steps, some configuration is created that will be optimized later. I purposely used this approach, and you are advised to closely follow the steps in the exercise before investigating the final solution in the exercise134.yaml playbook that is provided in the book GitHub repository.

Exercise 13-4   Setting Up Ansible Users

In this exercise you create a few Ansible users. The users need to be created on the Ansible control host as well as on the managed hosts, and after running the playbook, any user created on the localhost must be able to log in using SSH keys to the corresponding user account on the remote host without having to enter a password. Make sure that the setup meets the following requirements:

- Create users sharon, blair, ashley, and ahmed.

- Users sharon and blair are members of the group admins; users ashley and ahmed are members of the group students.

- On the managed hosts, members of the group admins should have sudo privileges to run any command they want.

- All users must be configured with the default password "password".

1. This time you're going to use a different approach and set up the framework of the playbook first. This is a good approach to start the development of more complex playbooks and minimizes chances that you miss anything in the playbook. To do so, use your editor to create a file with the name exercise134.yaml, and define the play headers and the names and modules you intend to use for each of the tasks according to the following example:

```
---
- name: create users on localhost
  hosts: localhost
  tasks:
  - name: create groups
    groups:
  - name: create users
    user:
- name: create users on managed hosts
  hosts: ansible2
  tasks:
  - name: create groups
    groups:
  - name: create users
    users:
  - name: copy authorized keys
    authorized_key:
  - name: modify sudo configuration
    template:
```

2. Now that you have defined the global structure, you can start filling it in with details. Begin with the first play, which should start with the creation of the user accounts. In this play, users and groups need to be created. To start with, focus on the basic setup and fill it in with additional details later:

```
---
- name: create users on localhost
  hosts: localhost
  vars:
    users:
    - username: sharon
      groups: admins
    - username: blair
      groups: admins
    - username: ashley
      groups: students
```

```
    - username: ahmed
      groups: students
  tasks:
  - name: create groups
    groups:
      name: "{{ item.groups }}"
      state: present
    loop: "{{ users }}"
  - name: create users
    user:
      name: "{{ item.username }}"
      groups: "{{ item.groups }}"
    loop: "{{ users }}"
```

3. Because you're in for a big project this time, now is a good moment to give it a try. To do so, temporarily comment out the entire second play and run the playbook in check mode by using **ansible-playbook -C exercise134.yaml**. If you typed the exact text listed in step 2, you get an error at the line where the groups module is referred to. That's right—there is no groups module; the name is group. Correct this and run the playbook again in check mode. Notice that in check mode you might get false errors. Just double-check, and if you're convinced you've done it right, ignore the error. Notice that it also doesn't really hurt if you just run the playbook. Any later modifications will be added to the configuration anyway.

4. Now you're ready to complete the first play by adding the remaining tasks to it. To do so, you still have to do two things, both of which must be done on the user module: you need to set the user password, and you need to create an SSH key pair. To generate the password, you need to generate an encrypted string that can be used as an argument to the user module **password** argument. To generate this string, use an ad hoc command: **ansible localhost -m debug -a "msg={{ 'password' | password_hash('sha512', 'mysalt') }}"**. Just copy the crypto string this generates (it starts with 6) and use that in the next step.

5. Complete the user task in the first play with the **generate_ssh_key** and **password** arguments. The complete task looks as follows:

```
  - name: create users
    user:
      name: "{{ item.username }}"
      groups: "{{ item.groups }}"
      generate_ssh_key: yes
      password: $6$mysalt$khiuhihrb8y349hwbohbuoehr8bhqohoibhro8b
ohoiheoi
```

```
    loop: "{{ users }}"
  tags: setuplocal
```

Notice the use of **tags: setuplocal** on the last line; this tag makes it easier to run specific parts of the playbook only, which can be convenient later in the setup procedure. You might want to run the playbook now by using **ansible-playbook exercise134.yaml --tags=setuplocal**.

6. At this point the local part of the setup seems to be done, so you can work on the second play. You should start by observing what you're trying to do. In the second play, a couple of tasks are exactly the same as in the first play. Because just repeating the same stuff again wouldn't be very efficient, you can create some imports instead and move the existing code to a file that will be imported. To start with, create the exercise134-vars.yaml file and give it the following contents:

```
---
users:
- username: sharon
  groups: admins
- username: blair
  groups: admins
- username: ashley
  groups: students
- username: ahmed
  groups: students
```

7. Create the exercise134-tasks.yaml file and give it the following contents:

```
- name: create groups
  group:
    name: "{{ item.groups }}"
    state: present
  loop: "{{ users }}"
- name: create users
  user:
    name: "{{ item.username }}"
    groups: "{{ item.groups }}"
    generate_ssh_key: yes
    ssh_key_comment: "{{ item.username }}@{{ ansible_fqdn }}"
    password: $6$mysalt$khiuhihrb8y349hwbohbuoehr8bhqohoibhro8b
ohoiheoi
  loop: "{{ users }}"
```

8. Now it's time to rewrite the playbook in exercise134.yaml so that the entire playbook looks as follows (note that the last two tasks still need to be defined):

```
---
- name: create users on localhost
  hosts: localhost
  vars_files:
  - exercise134-vars.yaml
  tasks:
  - name: include user and group setup
    import_tasks: exercise134-tasks.yaml
  tags: setuplocal

- name: create users on managed hosts
  hosts: ansible2
  vars_files:
  - exercise134-vars.yaml
  tasks:
  - name: include user and group setup
    import_tasks: exercise134-tasks.yaml
  - name: copy authorized keys
    authorized_key:
  - name: modify sudo configuration
    template:
```

9. You can work on the copy authorized keys task at this point. Because the users were created on localhost and each user has its own SSH key pair, this step appears to be fairly easy. The challenge in this task is the use of the lookup plug-in. Complete the authorized_key task such that the second play looks as follows:

```
- name: create users on managed hosts
  hosts: ansible2
  vars_files:
  - exercise134-vars.yaml
  tasks:
  - name: include user and group setup
    import_tasks: exercise134-tasks.yaml
  - name: copy authorized keys
    authorized_key:
      user: "{{ item.username }}"
      key: "{{ lookup('file', '/home/'+ item.username + '/.ssh/
id_rsa.pub') }}"
    loop: "{{ users }}"
#  - name: modify sudo configuration
  tags: setupremote
```

10. Because you can easily make an error while using the lookup plug-in, it's a good idea to run the second play by using **ansible-playbook exercise134.yaml --tags=setupremote**. Notice that this play works only if the first play has been executed successfully. And oops! That doesn't work out well! You can see the error shown in Listing 13-15. This error is generated because the authorized_keys module cannot access the id_rsa.pub file directly from the hidden .ssh directory in the user home directory.

Listing 13-15   Task 10 Error Output

```
TASK [copy authorized keys] ****************************************
[WARNING]: Unable to find '/home/laksmi/id_rsa.pub' in expected
paths (use -vvvvv to see paths)
fatal: [ansible3]: FAILED! => {"msg": "An unhandled exception
occurred while running the lookup plugin 'file'. Error was a <class
'ansible.errors.AnsibleError'>, original message: could not locate
file in lookup: /home/laksmi/id_rsa.pub"}
```

11. To fix the error that occurred in step 10, you must first rewrite the first play with the solution discussed in the earlier section "Managing SSH Connections." The following code shows the entire first play, with the modifications you need to make applied after the **import_tasks:** statement:

```
---
- name: create users on localhost
  hosts: localhost
  vars_files:
  - exercise134-vars.yaml
  tasks:
  - name: include user and group setup
    import_tasks: exercise134-tasks.yaml
  - name: create a directory to store the key file
    file:
      name: "{{ item.username }}"
      state: directory
    loop: "{{ users }}"
  - name: copy the local user ssh key to temporary {{ item.
username }} key
    shell: 'cat /home/{{ item.username }}/.ssh/id_rsa.pub > {{
item.username }}/id_rsa.pub'
    loop: "{{ users }}"
```

```
   - name: verify that file exists
     command: ls -l {{ item.username }}/
     loop: "{{ users }}"
 tags: setuplocal
```

12. In the current second play, change the task "copy authorized keys" to copy the authorized key from the temporary directory to which it was copied in the first play. The new "copy authorized keys" task should look as follows:

```
- name: copy authorized keys
  authorized_key:
    user: "{{ item.username }}"
    key: "{{ lookup('file', './'+ item.username +'/id_rsa.pub') }}"
  loop: "{{ users }}"
```

13. Now it's time to configure the sudo file in the /etc/sudoers.d/directory. Do this at the end of the second play in the exercise134.yaml playbook. While you've been setting up the rough structure of the playbook so far, using the template module has been suggested. But the fact is that the file that needs to be created is simple and straightforward, and just needs to contain the line **%admins ALL=(ALL:ALL) NOPASSWD:ALL**. Because this is a simple task, you don't need to use the template module. Just use the copy module instead, such that after the authorized_key task, only the following task is included:

```
- name: copy sudoers file
  copy:
    content: '%admins ALL=(ALL:ALL) NOPASSWD:ALL'
    dest: /etc/sudoers.d/admins
```

14. Before running the playbook, you may verify what you have typed with the sample playbook in the GitHub repository at https://github.com/sandervanvugt/rhce8-book/exercise134.yaml.

15. At this point, you can run the playbook by using **ansible-playbook exercise134.yaml**, and you should encounter no errors.

16. To verify that all works well, on the control host, type **sudo su - ahmed**, and once in a shell as user ahmed, type **ssh ansible2**. Ansible should let the user in without asking for a password.

Summary

In this chapter you learned how to manage users. Although setting up users seems to be an easy task, some related tasks make it challenging anyway. In this chapter you learned how to handle these tasks. You should now be able to create user and group accounts, manage SSH authorized keys, handle encrypted passwords, and manage related sudo configuration.

Exam Preparation Tasks

As mentioned in the section "How to Use This Book" in the Introduction, you have a couple of choices for exam preparation: the exercises here, Chapter 16, "Final Preparation," and the exam simulation questions on the companion website.

Review All Key Topics

Review the most important topics in this chapter, noted with the Key Topics icon in the outer margin of the page. Table 13-3 lists a reference of these key topics and the page numbers on which each is found.

Table 13-3   Key Topics for Chapter 13

Key Topic Element	Description	Page Number
List	Simplified overview of the procedure when a user logs in to an SSH server	313

Memory Tables

Print a copy of Appendix D, "Memory Tables" (found on the companion website), or at least the section for this chapter, and complete the tables and lists from memory. Appendix E, "Memory Tables Answer Key," also on the companion website, includes completed tables and lists to check your work.

Define Key Terms

Define the following key terms from this chapter, and check your answers in the glossary:

authorized_keys, hash, hashing algorithm, PAM, plug-in, public key fingerprint, random salt

Review Questions

1. Which module would you use to modify the sudo configuration?

2. Which module can you use to extend the standard Linux authentication procedure?

3. Which module can you use to manage SSH known hosts?

4. Which argument would you use to the user module to specify primary group membership?

5. Which argument would you use to the user module to manage secondary group membership?

6. What is the name of the plug-in that is commonly used with the authorized_keys module to find a specific file name?

7. When you're creating an SSH key pair while creating a user with the ansible user module, which additional argument must be used to ensure the name of the user is included in the public key file?

8. What is a major limitation to the authorized_keys module?

9. Which two methods exist to generate an encrypted password hash?

10. When using the **passwd --stdin** method to generate an encrypted password, which Ansible module must be used?

End-of-Chapter Lab

In this end-of-chapter lab, you apply what you have learned in this chapter.

Lab 13-1

Write a playbook that creates users according to the following specifications:

- Create users kim, christina, kelly, and bill.
- Users kim and kelly must be members of the profs group; users christina and bill are members of the students group.
- While creating the users, set the encrypted password to "password".
- Ensure that members of the group profs have sudo privileges.

This chapter covers the following subjects:

- Managing Services
- Managing the Boot Process
- Managing the Boot Process and Services Advanced Exercise

## CHAPTER 14

Managing Services and the Boot Process

The following RHCE exam objectives are covered in this chapter:

- Use Ansible Modules for System Administration Tasks that work with

    - Services

    - Scheduled tasks

"Do I Know This Already?" Quiz

The "Do I Know This Already?" quiz allows you to assess whether you should read this entire chapter thoroughly or jump to the "Exam Preparation Tasks" section. If you are in doubt about your answers to these questions or your own assessment of your knowledge of the topics, read the entire chapter. Table 14-1 lists the major headings in this chapter and their corresponding "Do I Know This Already?" quiz questions. You can find the answers in Appendix A, "Answers to the 'Do I Know This Already?' Quizzes and Review Questions."

Table 14-1 "Do I Know This Already?" Section-to-Question Mapping

Foundation Topics Section	Questions
Managing Services	1–6
Managing the Boot Process	7–9
Managing the Boot Process and Services Advanced Exercise	10

1. Which module should you use to mask a service?

    a. service

    b. systemd

    c. upstart

    d. init

2. Which statement about service facts is true?

   a. Facts about services are not gathered by default.

   b. The systemd module gathers facts about services; the service module does not.

   c. The service module gathers facts about services; the systemd module does not.

   d. You use the setup module to gather facts about services.

3. You want to use Ansible to manage a task that should be started once. Your play should be compatible to BSD init systems, as well as to systems using systemd as their init system. Which module should you use?

   a. service

   b. cron

   c. run

   d. at

4. Which of the following arguments are specific to the systemd module and do not occur in the service module? (Choose two.)

   a. mask

   b. enabled

   c. started

   d. daemon_reload

5. Which of the following need to be defined using the Ansible cron module in a task that is intended to remove a cron job? (Choose two.)

   a. time

   b. user

   c. name

   d. state

6. You are using the Ansible cron module to run a cron task with a name that has been used by another cron task. What will happen?

   a. The playbook will generate an error, and nothing will change.

   b. The new task will be added to the list of tasks.

   c. The new task will overwrite the old task.

   d. The playbook will show an ok status and do nothing because a task with the specified name already exists.

7. Which module do you use to change the default systemd target that a managed host should start in?

   a. systemd

   b. file

   c. command

   d. target

8. Which module can you use to manage a system restart from a playbook?

   a. systemd

   b. power

   c. reboot

   d. restart

9. The reboot module uses multiple options to specify timeouts to be respected. Which of the following is used to define how long Ansible should try to reconnect to the rebooted host?

   a. connect_timeout

   b. post_reboot_delay

   c. pre_reboot_delay

   d. reboot_timeout

10. You want to use the cron module to write the current time to a file. Which notation do you need to use? (Choose two.)

    a. **job: echo rebooted at {{ ansible_facts['date_time']['time'] }} >> /tmp/rebooted**

    b. **job: echo rebooted at {{ ansible_date_time.time }} >> /tmp/rebooted**

    c. **job: echo rebooted at $(date) >> /tmp/rebooted**

    d. **job: echo rebooted at 'date' >> /tmp/rebooted**

Foundation Topics

Managing Services

Services can be managed in many ways. You can manage systemd services, but Ansible also allows for management of tasks using Linux cron and at. Apart from that, you can use Ansible to manage the desired systemd target that a managed system should be started in, and it can reboot running machines. Table 14-2 gives an overview of the most significant modules for managing services.

Table 14-2   Modules Related to Service Management

Module	Use
service	Works for multiple init systems, including BSD init, upstart, and systemd; a generic module that allows for services
service_facts	Gathers facts for services started by BSD init, upstart, or systemd
cron	Uses the Linux cron service to schedule services
at	Uses the Linux at service to run services one time only
system	Manages systemd specific service properties; does have overlap with the service module
reboot	Reboots managed hosts

Managing Systemd Services

Throughout this book you have used the service module a lot. This module enables you to manage services, regardless of the init system that is used, so it works with System-V init, with Upstart, as well as systemd. In many cases, you can use the service module for any service-related task.

If systemd specifics need to be addressed, you must use the systemd module instead of the service module. Such systemd-specific features include **daemon_reload** and **mask**. The **daemon_reload** feature forces the systemd daemon to reread its configuration files, which is useful after applying changes (or after editing the service files directory, without using the Linux **systemctl** command). The **mask** feature marks a systemd service in such a way that it cannot be started, not even by accident. The systemd module also offers common service management options that are offered by the service module as well. Listing 14-1 shows an example where the systemd module is used to manage services.

Listing 14-1 Using systemd Module Features

```
---
- name: using systemd module to manage services
  hosts: ansible2
  tasks:
  - name: enable service httpd and ensure it is not masked
    systemd:
      name: httpd
      enabled: yes
      state: started
      masked: no
      daemon_reload: yes
```

Given the large amount of functionality that is available in systemd, the functions that are offered by the systemd services are a bit limited, and for many specific features, you must use generic modules such as file and command instead. An example is setting the default target, which is done by creating a symbolic link using the file module.

Managing cron Jobs

The cron module can be used to manage cron jobs. A Linux cron job is a task that is periodically executed by the Linux crond daemon at a specific time. The cron module can manage jobs in different ways:

- Write the job directly to a user's crontab

- Write the job to /etc/crontab or under the /etc/cron.d directory

- Pass the job to anacron so that it will be run once an hour, day, week, month, or year without specifically defining when exactly

If you are familiar with Linux cron, using the Ansible cron module is straightforward. Listing 14-2 shows an example that runs the **fstrim** command every day at 4:05 and at 19:05.

Listing 14-2 Running a cron Job

```
---
- name: run a cron job
  hosts: ansible2
  tasks:
```

```
- name: run a periodic job
  cron:
    name: "run fstrim"
    minute: "5"
    hour: "4,19"
    job: "fstrim"
```

As a result of this playbook, a crontab file is created for user root. To create a crontab file for another user, you can use the **user** attribute. Notice that while managing cron jobs using the cron module, a **name** attribute is specified. This attribute is required for Ansible to manage the cron jobs and has no meaning for Linux crontab itself. If, for instance, you later want to remove a cron job, you must use the name of the job as an identifier.

Listing 14-3 shows a sample playbook that removes the job that was created in Listing 14-2. Notice that it just specifies **state: absent** as well as the name of the job that was previously created; no other parameters are required.

Listing 14-3   Removing a cron Job Using the **name** Attribute

```
---
- name: run a cron job
  hosts: ansible2
  tasks:
  - name: run a periodic job
    cron:
      name: "run fstrim"
      state: absent
```

Managing at Jobs

Whereas you use Linux cron to schedule tasks at a regular interval, you use the Linux at solution to manage tasks that need to run once only. To interface with Linux at, the Ansible at module is provided. Table 14-3 gives an overview of the arguments it takes to specify how the task should be executed.

Table 14-3   at Module Arguments Overview

Argument	Use
command	Specifies the command that needs to be executed
units	Indicates the units (minute, hour, day, week) to identify the time in the future when the task must be executed

Argument	Use
count	Specifies the number of units to execute the task at
script_file	Indicates the name of a script that needs to be executed
state	Uses **added** or **deleted** as state to either add or delete a specific command
unique	Set to yes to ensure a specific job is started once only

The most important point to understand when working with at is that it is used to define how far from now a task has to be executed. This is done using **count** and **units**. If, for example, you want to run a task five minutes from now, you specify the job with the arguments **count: 5** and **units: minutes**. Also notice the use of the **unique** argument. If set to yes, the task is ignored if a similar job is scheduled to run already. Listing 14-4 shows an example.

Listing 14-4   Running Commands in the Future with at

```
---
- name: run an at task
  hosts: ansible2
  tasks:
    - name: run command and write output to file
      at:
        command: "date > /tmp/my-at-file"
        count: 5
        units: minutes
        unique: yes
        state: present
```

In Exercise 14-1 you practice your skills working with the cron module.

Exercise 14-1   Managing cron Jobs

1. Use your editor to create the playbook exercise141-1.yaml and give it the following contents:

```
---
- name: run a cron job
  hosts: ansible2
  tasks:
    - name: run a periodic job
      cron:
```

```
     name: "run logger"
     minute: "0"
     hour: "5"
     job: "logger IT IS 5 AM"
```

2. Use **ansible-playbook exercise141-1.yaml** to run the job.

3. Use the command **ansible ansible2 -a "crontab -l"** to verify the cron job has been added. The output should look as follows:

```
ansible2 | CHANGED | rc=0 >>
#Ansible: run logger
0 5 * * * logger IT IS 5 AM
```

4. Create a new playbook with the name exercise141-2 that runs a new cron job but uses the same name:

```
---
- name: run a cron job
  hosts: ansible2
  tasks:
  - name: run a periodic job
    cron:
      name: "run logger"
      minute: "0"
      hour: "6"
      job: "logger IT IS 6 AM"
```

5. Run this new playbook by using **ansible-playbook exercise141-2.yaml**. Notice that the job runs with a **changed** status.

6. Repeat the command **ansible ansible2 -a "crontab -l"**. This shows you that the new cron job has overwritten the old job because it was using the same name. Here is something important to remember: all cron jobs should have a unique name!

7. Write the playbook exercise141-3.yaml to remove the cron job that you just created:

```
---
- name: run a cron job
  hosts: ansible2
  tasks:
  - name: run logger
    cron:
      name: "run logger"
      state: absent
```

8. Use **ansible-playbook exercise141-3.yaml** to run the last playbook. Next, use **ansible ansible2 -a "crontab -l"** to verify that the cron job was indeed removed.

Managing the Boot Process

Managing the boot process with Ansible is a bit disappointing because Ansible offers no specific modules to do so. As a result, you must use generic modules instead, like the file module to manage the systemd boot targets or the lineinfile module to manage the GRUB configuration. What Ansible does offer, however, is the reboot module, which enables you to reboot a host and pick up after the reboot at the exact same location. The next two sections describe how to do this.

Managing Systemd Targets

Managing the default target that a host should start in is a common task in Ansible. However, the systemd module has no options to manage this setting, and no other option to manage it is available. For that reason, you must fall back to a generic option instead.

If you need to manage the default systemd target, a file with the name /etc/systemd/system/default.target has to exist as a symbolic link to the desired default target. See, for instance, Listing 14-5, where the output of the Linux **ls -l** command is used to show the current configuration.

Listing 14-5 Showing the Default Systemd Target

```
[ansible@control rhce8-book]$ ls -l /etc/systemd/system/default.target
lrwxrwxrwx. 1 root root 37 Mar 23 05:33 /etc/systemd/system/default.
target -> /lib/systemd/system/multi-user.target
```

Because Ansible itself doesn't have any module to specifically set the default.target, you must use a generic module. In theory, you could use either the command module or the file module, but because the file module is a more specific module to generate the symbolic link, you should use the file module. Listing 14-6 shows how to manage the boot target.

Listing 14-6 Managing the Default Boot Target

```
---
- name: set default boot target
  hosts: ansible2
  tasks:
    - name: set boot target to graphical
      file:
        src: /usr/lib/systemd/system/graphical.target
        dest: /etc/systemd/system/default.target
        state: link
```

Rebooting Managed Hosts

In some cases, a managed host needs to be rebooted while running a playbook. To do so, you can use the reboot module. This module uses several arguments to restart managed nodes. To verify the renewed availability of the managed hosts, you need to specify the **test_command** argument. This argument specifies an arbitrary command that Ansible should run successfully on the managed hosts after the reboot. The success of this command indicates that the rebooted host is available again.

Equally useful while using the reboot module are the arguments that relate to timeouts. The reboot module uses no fewer than four of them:

- **connect_timeout:** The maximum seconds to wait for a successful connection before trying again

- **post_reboot_delay:** The number of seconds to wait after the **reboot** command before trying to validate the managed host is available again

- **pre_reboot_delay:** The number of seconds to wait before actually issuing the reboot

- **reboot_timeout:** The maximum seconds to wait for the rebooted machine to respond to the **test** command

When the rebooted host is back, the current playbook continues its tasks. This scenario is shown in the example in Listing 14-7, where first all managed hosts are rebooted, and after a successful reboot is issued, the message "successfully rebooted" is shown. Listing 14-8 shows the result of running this playbook. In Exercise 14-2 you can practice rebooting hosts using the reboot module.

Listing 14-7 Rebooting Managed Hosts

```
---
- name: reboot all hosts
  hosts: all
  gather_facts: no
  tasks:
  - name: reboot hosts
    reboot:
      msg: reboot initiated by Ansible
      test_command: whoami
  - name: print message to show host is back
    debug:
      msg: successfully rebooted
```

Listing 14-8   Verifying the Success of the reboot Module

```
[ansible@control rhce8-book]$ ansible-playbook listing147.yaml

PLAY [reboot all hosts] ********************************************

TASK [reboot hosts] ***********************************************
changed: [ansible2]
changed: [ansible1]
changed: [ansible3]
changed: [ansible4]
changed: [ansible5]

TASK [print message to show host is back] ************************
ok: [ansible1] => {
    "msg": "successfully rebooted"
}
ok: [ansible2] => {
    "msg": "successfully rebooted"
}
ok: [ansible3] => {
    "msg": "successfully rebooted"
}
ok: [ansible4] => {
    "msg": "successfully rebooted"
}
ok: [ansible5] => {
    "msg": "successfully rebooted"
}

PLAY RECAP ********************************************************
ansible1                     : ok=2       changed=1     unreachable=0
failed=0     skipped=0      rescued=0    ignored=0
ansible2                     : ok=2       changed=1     unreachable=0
failed=0     skipped=0      rescued=0    ignored=0
ansible3                     : ok=2       changed=1     unreachable=0
failed=0     skipped=0      rescued=0    ignored=0
ansible4                     : ok=2       changed=1     unreachable=0
failed=0     skipped=0      rescued=0    ignored=0
ansible5                     : ok=2       changed=1     unreachable=0
failed=0     skipped=0      rescued=0    ignored=0
```

Exercise 14-2   Managing Boot State

1. As a preparation for this playbook, so that it actually changes the default boot target on the managed host, use **ansible ansible2 -m file -a "state=link src=/usr/lib/systemd/system/graphical.target dest=/etc/systemd/system/default.target"**.

2. Use your editor to create the file exercise142.yaml and write the following playbook header:

   ```
   ---
   - name: set default boot target and reboot
     hosts: ansible2
     tasks:
   ```

3. Now you set the default boot target to multi-user.target. Add the following task to do so:

   ```
   - name: set default boot target
     file:
       src: /usr/lib/systemd/system/multi-user.target
       dest: /etc/systemd/system/default.target
       state: link
   ```

4. Complete the playbook to reboot the managed hosts by including the following tasks:

   ```
   - name: reboot hosts
     reboot:
       msg: reboot initiated by Ansible
       test_command: whoami
   - name: print message to show host is back
     debug:
       msg: successfully rebooted
   ```

5. Run the playbook by using **ansible-playbook exercise142.yaml**.

6. Test that the reboot was issued successfully by using **ansible ansible2 -a "systemctl get-default"**.

Managing the Boot Process and Services Advanced Exercise

The advanced exercise, 14-3, is a relatively easy task this time. You are guided through the procedure of creating a playbook that runs a command before the reboot, schedules a cron job at the next reboot, and, using that cron job, ensures that after rebooting a specific command is used as well. To make sure you see what happens when, you work with a temporary file to which lines are added.

Exercise 14-3   Managing the Boot Process and Services

1. Use your editor to create the file exercise143.yaml and write the playbook header as follows:

```
---
- name: exercise143
  hosts: ansible2
  tasks:
```

2. Write the first task. This task is not really functional but enables you to check what is happening in the remaining tasks in the playbook. In this task, you use the lineinfile module to add a line to the end of the check file /tmp/rebooted. Notice how the time, including a second indicator, is written using two Ansible facts. It's required to operate this way because not one single fact has the time in an hh:mm:ss format. Write this task code as follows:

```
- name: add a line to file before rebooting
  lineinfile:
    create: true
    state: present
    path: /tmp/rebooted
    insertafter: EOF
    line: rebooted at {{ ansible_facts['date_time']['time'] }}:{{ ansible_facts['date_time']['second'] }}
```

3. At this point, you can add a cron job that runs at reboot. The job that runs will add a message to the /tmp/rebooted file, and to make sure that it is working correctly, you use bash shell command substitution to print the results of the Linux **date** command. Notice that this is possible in the cron module because commands are executed by a bash shell, but it's not possible in the previous task that uses the lineinfile module because in that task the commands are not processed by a shell. Now add the task as follows:

```
- name: run a cron job on reboot
  cron:
    name: "run on reboot"
    state: present
    special_time: reboot
    job: "echo rebooted at $(date) >> /tmp/rebooted"
```

4. Add another task that uses the reboot module to reboot the managed host:

```
- name: reboot managed host
  reboot:
    msg: reboot initiated by Ansible
    test_command: whoami
```

```
   - name: show reboot success
     debug:
       msg: just rebooted successfully
```

5. Now that the playbook is complete, you can run it by using **ansible-playbook exercise143.yaml**. Notice that it needs a minute because it has to wait until the target host is back. When it is back, use **ansible ansible2 -a "cat /tmp/ rebooted"**. You then see that both reboot messages are written, and there is about 30 seconds between the pre-reboot and the post-reboot commands.

Summary

In this chapter you learned how to manage tasks. In the first section you read how to manage tasks using systemd, cron, and at, using the corresponding Ansible modules. In the second section you read how to manage the default systemd target as well as system reboots.

Exam Preparation Tasks

As mentioned in the section "How to Use This Book" in the Introduction, you have a couple of choices for exam preparation: the exercises here, Chapter 16, "Final Preparation," and the exam simulation questions on the companion website.

Review All Key Topics

Review the most important topics in this chapter, noted with the Key Topics icon in the outer margin of the page. Table 14-4 lists a reference of these key topics and the page numbers on which each is found.

Table 14-4   Key Topics for Chapter 14

Key Topic Element	Description	Page Number
Table 14-2	Modules Related to Service Management	336
List	Different ways in which the cron module can manage jobs	337
List	reboot arguments	342

Memory Tables

Print a copy of Appendix D, "Memory Tables" (found on the companion website), or at least the section for this chapter, and complete the tables and lists from memory. Appendix E, "Memory Tables Answer Key," also on the companion website, includes completed tables and lists to check your work.

Define Key Terms

Define the following key terms from this chapter, and check your answers in the glossary:

anacron, init system

Review Questions

1. Which Ansible module should you use to print facts about systemd services?

2. You want to write a generic playbook that works on Ubuntu as well as Red Hat to start the vsftpd service. Which Ansible module should you use?

3. Which argument must be used with the cron module to allow cron jobs to be managed by Ansible?

4. Which module should you use to set the default systemd target that is entered at startup?

5. Which argument should you use with the cron module to schedule a job to happen immediately after system restart?

6. Which arguments to the at module should you use to specify time in minutes from now?

7. Which argument to the reboot module should you use to define how to check whether a rebooted node is back?

8. Which argument to the reboot module should you use to specify the maximum amount of time that Ansible should wait for the rebooted node to return before generating a failure?

9. Which argument to the at module should you use to have at run a script file?

10. Why can't you use bash command substitution to work with the result of a command in the lineinfile module?

End-of-Chapter Lab

In this end-of-chapter lab, you combine the use of cron and reboot.

Lab 14-1

Write a playbook according to the following specifications:

- The cron module must be used to restart your managed servers at 2 a.m. each weekday.

- After rebooting, a message must be written to syslog, with the text "CRON initiated reboot just completed."

- The default systemd target must be set to multi-user.target.

- The last task should use service facts to show the current version of the cron process.

This chapter covers the following subjects:

- Discovering Storage-Related Facts
- Managing Partitions and LVM
- Configuring Storage Advanced Exercise

## CHAPTER 15

Managing Storage

The following RHCE exam objectives are covered in this chapter:

- Use Ansible modules for system administration tasks that work with
  - Storage devices

"Do I Know This Already?" Quiz

The "Do I Know This Already?" quiz allows you to assess whether you should read this entire chapter thoroughly or jump to the "Exam Preparation Tasks" section. If you are in doubt about your answers to these questions or your own assessment of your knowledge of the topics, read the entire chapter. Table 15-1 lists the major headings in this chapter and their corresponding "Do I Know This Already?" quiz questions. You can find the answers in Appendix A, "Answers to the 'Do I Know This Already?' Quizzes and Review Questions."

Table 15-1 "Do I Know This Already?" Section-to-Question Mapping

Foundation Topics Section	Questions
Discovering Storage-Related Facts	1–4
Managing Partitions and LVM	5–9
Configuring Storage Advanced Exercise	10

1. Which module should you use to manage partitions in a scripted way?
    a. fdisk
    b. gpart
    c. gdisk
    d. parted

2. Which Ansible module should you use to manage the extent size used in LVM?

   a. lvpv

   b. lvg

   c. lvm

   d. lvol

3. When using Ansible facts, what should you look for to get information about discovered disks?

   a. **ansible_disks**

   b. **ansible_devices**

   c. **ansible_mounts**

   d. **ansible_device_links**

4. What can you use to set a variable inside a task, based on discovered Ansible facts?

   a. **set**

   b. **set_vars**

   c. **vars**

   d. **set_facts**

5. On a disk you already have one partition with a size of 2 GiB. You want to create a second partition with a size of 2 GiB. Which of the following arguments to the parted module must be used? (Choose all that apply.)

   a. **part_end: 2GiB**

   b. **part_end: 4GiB**

   c. **part_start: 2GiB**

   d. **part_start: 1MiB**

6. Which argument must be used in the parted module to create GPT partitions?

   a. **label: gpt**

   b. **type: gpt**

   c. **table: gpt**

   d. **state: gpt**

7. Which of the following is set to write a file system label using the filesystem module?

   a. **opts: label=mylabel**

   b. **label: mylabel**

   c. **fslabel: mylabel**

   d. **setopts: label=mylabel**

8. Which of the following ensures that a file system is mounted now and added persistently to /etc/fstab?

   a. **state: mounted**

   b. **state: present**

   c. **state: mounted, fstab: yes**

   d. **state: present, fstab: yes**

9. Which module do you use to enable swap space?

   a. swap

   b. mount

   c. command

   d. filesystem

10. You have a value that is presented as a float type. What do you need to do before you can compare its size to an expected size?

    a. Use the int filter.

    b. Nothing; floats can be used in tests.

    c. Put the variable name between double quotes.

    d. Put the variable name between single quotes.

Foundation Topics

Discovering Storage-Related Facts

To work with storage in an Ansible environment, you need to know which devices exist on the managed nodes. A wide range of storage devices is available, and you probably need to run conditionals based on the specific device type. Once the device type is successfully discovered, you can continue to manage your storage devices by using one of the multiple storage-related modules. Table 15-2 shows a list of modules that are discussed in this chapter. Many other vendor-dependent storage management modules are available as well; you can use **ansible-doc -l** to search for specific vendors.

Table 15-2 Modules for Managing Storage

Module	Use
parted	Manages partitions in a scripted way
lvg	Manages LVM volume groups
lvol	Manages LVM logical volumes
filesystem	Manages file systems on storage devices
mount	Mounts storage devices that have been configured with a file system
vdo	Interfaces the new VDO storage layer that is available in RHEL 8

The challenge in writing playbooks that deal with storage is that so many storage devices could be used and different device names can be used for them. So, to make sure that your playbook is applied to the right devices, you first need to find which devices are available on your managed system. After you find them, you can use conditionals to make sure that tasks are executed on the right devices.

Using Storage-Related Facts

Facts about storage are gathered automatically when the setup module is collecting facts about the managed machines. Relevant information is stored in different facts; Table 15-3 gives an overview.

Table 15-3 Storage-Related Facts

Fact	Use
ansible_devices	Shows all available storage devices, including additional device information
ansible_device_links	Shows storage devices from different perspectives, including information on how to access the storage device
ansible_mounts	Shows mount points, including information about the device that is mounted on a specific location

To request specific information about these facts, you can use the **ansible -m setup** command with a filter. For instance, use **ansible ansible1 -m setup -a 'filter= ansible_device'** to find generic information about storage devices. Listing 15-1 shows a part of the result of this command.

Listing 15-1 Discovering Storage Facts Using **ansible -m setup**

```
[ansible@control rhce8-book]$ ansible ansible1 -m setup -a
'filter=ansible_devices'
ansible1 | SUCCESS => {
    "ansible_facts": {
        "ansible_devices": {
            ...
            "sda": {
                "holders": [],
                "host": "SCSI storage controller: Broadcom / LSI
53c1030 PCI-X Fusion-MPT Dual Ultra320 SCSI (rev 01)",
                "links": {
                    "ids": [],
                    "labels": [],
                    "masters": [],
                    "uuids": []
                },
                "model": "VMware Virtual S",
                "partitions": {
                    "sda1": {
                        "holders": [],
                        "links": {
                            "ids": [],
                            "labels": [],
```

```
                                    "masters": [],
                                    "uuids": [
                                        "7acd65d6-115f-499f-a02f-
90364a18b9fc"
                                    ]
                                },
                                "sectors": "2097152",
                                "sectorsize": 512,
                                "size": "1.00 GB",
                                "start": "2048",
                                "uuid":
"7acd65d6-115f-499f-a02f-90364a18b9fc"
                            },
                            "sda2": {
                                "holders": [
                                    "cl-swap",
                                    "cl-root"
                                ],
                                "links": {
                                    "ids": [
                                        "lvm-pv-uuid-vswoyx-HihU-cRqK-2tvx-
aesr-SXAR-YY1lLL"
                                    ],
                                    "labels": [],
                                    "masters": [
                                        "dm-0",
                                        "dm-1"
                                    ],
                                    "uuids": []
                                },
                                "sectors": "39843840",
                                "sectorsize": 512,
                                "size": "19.00 GB",
                                "start": "2099200",
                                "uuid": null
                            }
                        },
                        "removable": "0",
                        "rotational": "1",
                        "sas_address": null,
                        "sas_device_handle": null,
```

```
                    "scheduler_mode": "mq-deadline",
                    "sectors": "41943040",
                    "sectorsize": "512",
                    "size": "20.00 GB",
                    "support_discard": "0",
                    "vendor": "VMware,",
                    "virtual": 1
                },
                "sr0": {
...

                }
            },
            "discovered_interpreter_python": "/usr/libexec/
platform-python"
        },
        "changed": false
}
```

NOTE The **filter** argument to the setup module uses a shell-style wildcard to search for matching items and for that reason can search in the highest-level facts, such as **ansible_devices**, but it is incapable of further specifying what is searched for. For that reason, in the **filter** argument to the setup module, you cannot use a construction like **ansible ansible1 -m setup -a "filter=ansible_devices.sda"**, which is common when looking up the variable in conditional statements.

Using Storage-Related Facts in Conditional Statements

When you want to work with storage devices in Ansible playbooks, just gathering facts is not enough. It's important that these facts can be used in conditional statements. There are different ways in which these conditional statements can be formulated. You can, for instance, use the assert module to show an error message if a device does not exist and to perform a task if the device exists. For an easier solution, you can also use a **when** statement to look for the existence of a device. The advantage of using the assert module is that an error message can be printed if the condition is not met.

Listing 15-2 shows where the assert module is used; Listing 15-3 shows the result of running this playbook.

IMPORTANT   For the labs and demos in this chapter, it is important that nodes ansible2 and ansible3 are configured with an additional disk device. Add node ansible3 if you haven't done that yet. If this is not the case yet, configure your virtual machines such that they do show a second disk device. The examples use the /dev/sdb device name. If your host uses different device names, such as /dev/vdb in a KVM virtual machine, it is important to change the examples in this chapter and in the GitHub repository accordingly. Or you can apply the solution that is shown in Exercise 15-1 to dynamically detect device names.

Listing 15-2   Using assert to Run a Task Only If a Device Exists

```
---
- name: search for /dev/sdb continue only if it is found
  hosts: all
  vars:
    disk_name: sdb
  tasks:
  - name: abort if second disk does not exist
    assert:
      that:
        - "ansible_facts['devices']['{{ disk_name }}'] is defined"
      fail_msg: second hard disk not found
  - debug:
      msg: "{{ disk_name }} was found, lets continue"
```

Listing 15-3   ansible-playbook listing152.yaml Result

```
[ansible@control rhce8-book]$ ansible-playbook listing152.yaml

PLAY [search for /dev/sdb continue only if it is found] *************

TASK [Gathering Facts] *********************************************
ok: [ansible2]
ok: [ansible1]
ok: [ansible3]
ok: [ansible4]
ok: [ansible5]

TASK [abort if second disk does not exist] *************************
```

```
fatal: [ansible1]: FAILED! => {
    "assertion": "ansible_facts['devices']['sdb'] is defined",
    "changed": false,
    "evaluated_to": false,
    "msg": "second hard disk not found"
}
ok: [ansible2] => {
    "changed": false,
    "msg": "All assertions passed"
}
ok: [ansible3] => {
    "changed": false,
    "msg": "All assertions passed"
}
fatal: [ansible4]: FAILED! => {
    "assertion": "ansible_facts['devices']['sdb'] is defined",
    "changed": false,
    "evaluated_to": false,
    "msg": "second hard disk not found"
}
fatal: [ansible5]: FAILED! => {
    "assertion": "ansible_facts['devices']['sdb'] is defined",
    "changed": false,
    "evaluated_to": false,
    "msg": "second hard disk not found"
}


TASK [debug] ********************************************************
ok: [ansible2] => {
    "msg": "sdb was found, lets continue"
}
ok: [ansible3] => {
    "msg": "sdb was found, lets continue"
}


PLAY RECAP **********************************************************
ansible1                       : ok=1      changed=0    unreachable=0
failed=1     skipped=0     rescued=0     ignored=0
ansible2                       : ok=3      changed=0    unreachable=0
failed=0     skipped=0     rescued=0     ignored=0
ansible3                       : ok=3      changed=0    unreachable=0
failed=0     skipped=0     rescued=0     ignored=0
```

```
ansible4                        : ok=1    changed=0    unreachable=0
failed=1     skipped=0    rescued=0    ignored=0
ansible5                        : ok=1    changed=0    unreachable=0
failed=1     skipped=0    rescued=0    ignored=0
```

To make sure partitioning operations are handled the right way, you must detect which devices are used. Some managed hosts have more than one disk device, so sometimes you interface a /dev/sda, but at other times it might be a /dev/vda for a KVM virtual disk or a /dev/nvme0n1 for an NVME disk device. To do so, you must write a playbook that first finds out the name of the disk device and puts that in a variable that you can work with further on in the playbook. The **set_fact** argument comes in handy to do so. You can use it in combination with a **when** conditional statement to store a detected device name in a variable. In Listing 15-4 you can see what that looks like, and in Exercise 15-1 you practice this approach.

Listing 15-4   Storing the Detected Disk Device Name in a Variable

```
---
- name: define variable according to diskname detected
  hosts: all
  tasks:
  - ignore_errors: yes
    set_fact:
      disk2name: sdb
    when: ansible_facts['devices']['sdb']
```

Exercise 15-1   Working with Different Device Names

1. Use your editor to create the file exercise151.yaml and write the play header as follows:

    ```
    ---
    - name: define variable according to diskname detected
      hosts: all
      tasks:
    ```

2. Add the first task to set the variable **disk2name** to the value **sdb** if an sdb device is detected in Ansible facts. Notice that ignore_errors:yes is used because you need this playbook to continue until it has scanned all possible disk devices.

    ```
    - ignore_errors: yes
      set_fact:
    ```

```
      disk2name: sdb
  when: ansible_facts['devices']['sdb']
```

3. Repeat this by creating a task for any other second disk device you might detect. (You can change this according to devices found on your system, so use vdb if you're on a KVM virtual machine.)

```
- ignore_errors: yes
  set_fact:
    disk2name: nvme0n2
  when: ansible_facts['devices']['nvme0n2']
```

4. In case there is no second disk, the playbook needs to stop executing on that specific host. The fail module is an excellent module to realize this. Do this by adding the next task:

```
- name: getting out if there is no second disk
  fail:
    msg: there is no second disk
  when: disk2name is not defined
```

5. As the last element, add a debug task to show how the second disk device was found if it was found.

```
- name: showing this only for hosts with a second disk
  debug:
    msg: continuing with {{ disk2name }}
```

6. If possible, before running the playbook, you might want to consider adding another node that has a second disk device that is not /dev/sdb. If, for instance, you install a RHEL 8 virtual machine in VMware Workstation or Fusion, it enables you to configure NVME disk devices. Alternatively, you can fall back on IDE devices, which show as /dev/hda and /dev/hdb. Run the playbook by using **ansible-playbook exercise151.yaml**. In Listing 15-5 you can see what the playbook output might look like.

Listing 15-5 Running **ansible-playbook exercise151.yaml** Output

```
[ansible@control rhce8-book]$ ansible-playbook exercise151.yaml

PLAY [define variable according to diskname detected debug test] ****

TASK [Gathering Facts] ********************************************
ok: [ansible2]
ok: [ansible1]
```

```
ok: [ansible3]
ok: [ansible4]
ok: [ansible5]
ok: [ansible6]


TASK [set_fact] ********************************************************
fatal: [ansible1]: FAILED! => {"msg": "The conditional check 'ansible_
facts['devices']['sdb']' failed. The error was: error while evaluating
conditional (ansible_facts['devices']['sdb']): 'dict object' has no
attribute 'sdb'\n\nThe error appears to be in '/home/ansible/rhce8-
book/exercise151.yaml': line 5, column 5, but may\nbe elsewhere in
the file depending on the exact syntax problem.\n\nThe offending line
appears to be:\n\n  tasks:\n  - ignore_errors: yes\n    ^ here\n"}
...ignoring
ok: [ansible2]
ok: [ansible3]
fatal: [ansible4]: FAILED! => {"msg": "The conditional check 'ansible_
facts['devices']['sdb']' failed. The error was: error while evaluating
conditional (ansible_facts['devices']['sdb']): 'dict object' has no
attribute 'sdb'\n\nThe error appears to be in '/home/ansible/rhce8-
book/exercise151.yaml': line 5, column 5, but may\nbe elsewhere in
the file depending on the exact syntax problem.\n\nThe offending line
appears to be:\n\n  tasks:\n  - ignore_errors: yes\n    ^ here\n"}
...ignoring
fatal: [ansible5]: FAILED! => {"msg": "The conditional check 'ansible_
facts['devices']['sdb']' failed. The error was: error while evaluating
conditional (ansible_facts['devices']['sdb']): 'dict object' has no
attribute 'sdb'\n\nThe error appears to be in '/home/ansible/rhce8-
book/exercise151.yaml': line 5, column 5, but may\nbe elsewhere in
the file depending on the exact syntax problem.\n\nThe offending line
appears to be:\n\n  tasks:\n  - ignore_errors: yes\n    ^ here\n"}
...ignoring
fatal: [ansible6]: FAILED! => {"msg": "The conditional check 'ansible_
facts['devices']['sdb']' failed. The error was: error while evaluating
conditional (ansible_facts['devices']['sdb']): 'dict object' has no
attribute 'sdb'\n\nThe error appears to be in '/home/ansible/rhce8-
book/exercise151.yaml': line 5, column 5, but may\nbe elsewhere in
the file depending on the exact syntax problem.\n\nThe offending line
appears to be:\n\n  tasks:\n  - ignore_errors: yes\n    ^ here\n"}
...ignoring


TASK [set_fact] ********************************************************
fatal: [ansible1]: FAILED! => {"msg": "The conditional check
'ansible_facts['devices']['nvme0n2']' failed. The error was: error
while evaluating conditional (ansible_facts['devices']['nvme0n2']):
'dict object' has no attribute 'nvme0n2'\n\nThe error appears to
be in '/home/ansible/rhce8-book/exercise151.yaml': line 9, column
5, but may\nbe elsewhere in the file depending on the exact syntax
```

```
problem.\n\nThe offending line appears to be:\n\n    when: ansible_
facts['devices']['sdb']\n  - ignore_errors: yes\n     ^ here\n"}
...ignoring
fatal: [ansible2]: FAILED! => {"msg": "The conditional check
'ansible_facts['devices']['nvme0n2']' failed. The error was: error
while evaluating conditional (ansible_facts['devices']['nvme0n2']):
'dict object' has no attribute 'nvme0n2'\n\nThe error appears to
be in '/home/ansible/rhce8-book/exercise151.yaml': line 9, column
5, but may\nbe elsewhere in the file depending on the exact syntax
problem.\n\nThe offending line appears to be:\n\n    when: ansible_
facts['devices']['sdb']\n  - ignore_errors: yes\n     ^ here\n"}
...ignoring
fatal: [ansible3]: FAILED! => {"msg": "The conditional check
'ansible_facts['devices']['nvme0n2']' failed. The error was: error
while evaluating conditional (ansible_facts['devices']['nvme0n2']):
'dict object' has no attribute 'nvme0n2'\n\nThe error appears to
be in '/home/ansible/rhce8-book/exercise151.yaml': line 9, column
5, but may\nbe elsewhere in the file depending on the exact syntax
problem.\n\nThe offending line appears to be:\n\n    when: ansible_
facts['devices']['sdb']\n  - ignore_errors: yes\n     ^ here\n"}
...ignoring
fatal: [ansible4]: FAILED! => {"msg": "The conditional check
'ansible_facts['devices']['nvme0n2']' failed. The error was: error
while evaluating conditional (ansible_facts['devices']['nvme0n2']):
'dict object' has no attribute 'nvme0n2'\n\nThe error appears to
be in '/home/ansible/rhce8-book/exercise151.yaml': line 9, column
5, but may\nbe elsewhere in the file depending on the exact syntax
problem.\n\nThe offending line appears to be:\n\n    when: ansible_
facts['devices']['sdb']\n  - ignore_errors: yes\n     ^ here\n"}
...ignoring
fatal: [ansible5]: FAILED! => {"msg": "The conditional check
'ansible_facts['devices']['nvme0n2']' failed. The error was: error
while evaluating conditional (ansible_facts['devices']['nvme0n2']):
'dict object' has no attribute 'nvme0n2'\n\nThe error appears to
be in '/home/ansible/rhce8-book/exercise151.yaml': line 9, column
5, but may\nbe elsewhere in the file depending on the exact syntax
problem.\n\nThe offending line appears to be:\n\n    when: ansible_
facts['devices']['sdb']\n  - ignore_errors: yes\n     ^ here\n"}
...ignoring
ok: [ansible6]


TASK [getting out if there is no second disk] ************************
fatal: [ansible1]: FAILED! => {"changed": false, "msg": "there is no
second disk"}
skipping: [ansible2]
skipping: [ansible3]
fatal: [ansible4]: FAILED! => {"changed": false, "msg": "there is no
second disk"}
```

```
fatal: [ansible5]: FAILED! => {"changed": false, "msg": "there is no
second disk"}
skipping: [ansible6]

TASK [showing this is only for hosts with a second disk] *************
ok: [ansible2] => {
    "msg": "continuing with sdb"
}
ok: [ansible3] => {
    "msg": "continuing with sdb"
}
ok: [ansible6] => {
    "msg": "continuing with nvme0n2"
}


PLAY RECAP ***********************************************************
ansible1                     : ok=3      changed=0      unreachable=0
failed=1      skipped=0      rescued=0      ignored=2
ansible2                     : ok=4      changed=0      unreachable=0
failed=0      skipped=1      rescued=0      ignored=1
ansible3                     : ok=4      changed=0      unreachable=0
failed=0      skipped=1      rescued=0      ignored=1
ansible4                     : ok=3      changed=0      unreachable=0
failed=1      skipped=0      rescued=0      ignored=2
ansible5                     : ok=3      changed=0      unreachable=0
failed=1      skipped=0      rescued=0      ignored=2
ansible6                     : ok=4      changed=0      unreachable=0
failed=0      skipped=1      rescued=0      ignored=1
```

Managing Partitions and LVM

After detecting the disk device that needs to be used, you can move on and start creating partitions and logical volumes. The following sections explain how to partition a disk using the parted module, how to work with the lvg and lvol modules to manage LVM logical volumes, how to create file systems using the filesystem module and mount them using the mount module, and finally, how to manage swap storage.

Creating Partitions

If you need to manage partitions, Ansible provides the parted module. Because this module has a few options that are not really intuitive, Table 15-4 provides an overview. Listing 15-6 shows a playbook that uses this module.

Table 15-4 parted Options

Option	Use
name	Is required for GPT partitions; specifies a unique name assigned to the partition
label	Specifies the type of partition that should be created: **msdos** is the default (and used on MBR disks); **gpt** is used to create GPT partitions
device	Indicates the device on which the partition should be created
number	Specifies the partition number
state	Uses **present** to create and **absent** to remove a partition
part_start	Indicates the starting partition, expressed as an offset from the beginning of the disk
part_end	Specifies where to end the partition, expressed as an offset from the beginning of the disk
flags	Sets specific partition properties, such as the LVM partition type

Listing 15-6 Creating Partitions with parted

```
---
- name: create storage
  hosts: ansible2
  tasks:
  - name: create new partition
    parted:
      name: files
      label: gpt
      device: /dev/sdb
      number: 1
      state: present
      part_start: 1MiB
      part_end: 2GiB
  - name: create another new partition
    parted:
      name: swap
      label: gpt
      device: /dev/sdb
      number: 2
      state: present
      part_start: 2GiB
      part_end: 4GiB
      flags: [ lvm ]
```

Working with the parted module is not always intuitive. Let's look at the contents of the playbook in Listing 15-6 for an example. The first argument to the parted module is **name**. If the partition is created as an MBR partition, this argument is not required. If you want to create a GPT partition, however, a name must be specified.

The next item you should notice is **label**. This argument is used to set the partition table type, not the file system label. File system labels are a property of the file system and for that reason are set using the filesystem module.

Next, there is the size specification. When you use parted, sizes are indicated as an offset from the start of a disk. To create partitions, you should use **part_start** as well as **part_end**. If these arguments are not used, the partition starts at 0% and ends at 100% of the available disk space. When you specify **part_start**, the first couple of bytes on a disk are used for metadata storage, so you cannot start a partition at the beginning of a disk. That's why you see the first partition starts at 1 MiB. Also notice the second partition, where **part_start** is set to 2 GiB. You need to enter this because the parted module is not smart enough to figure out that the next partition should be created after already existing partitions.

Finally, there is the **flags** argument. This argument sets the partition type and is required if you want to create an LVM partition type.

Managing Volume Groups and LVM Logical Volumes

If you need to manage LVM logical volumes, the lvg module is available for managing LVM volume groups, and the lvol module is available for managing LVM logical volumes. Creating a volume group is relatively easy: you use the **vg** argument to set the name of the volume group and the **pvs** argument to identify the physical volume (which is often a partition or a disk device) on which the volume group needs to be created. Also you might have to specify the **pesize** to refer to the size of the physical extents. Listing 15-7 shows a task that creates a volume group. (Listing 15-7 and some of the following listings show only the tasks that you should include, not the complete playbook!)

Listing 15-7   Creating an LVM Volume Group

```
- name: create a volume group
  lvg:
    vg: vgdata
    pesize: "8"
    pvs: /dev/sdb1
```

After you create an LVM volume group, you can create LVM logical volumes. When you're creating logical volumes, a wide range of options is available. Table 15-5 gives an overview of some of the most useful options, and Listing 15-8 shows a task that creates an LVM logical volume.

Table 15-5 lvol Common Options

Option	Use
lv	Specifies the name of the logical volume.
pvs	Indicates a comma-separated list of physical volumes. If the PV is a partition, make sure it has the **lvm** option set.
resizefs	Indicates that the underlying file system must be resized automatically when the logical volume is resized.
size	Specifies the size of the logical volume.
snapshot	Specifies a name if this logical volume is a snapshot.
vg	Indicates the name of the volume group in which the logical volume should be created.

Listing 15-8 Creating an LVM Logical Volume

```
- name: create a logical volume
  lvol:
    lv: lvdata
    size: 100%FREE
    vg: vgdata
```

Creating and Mounting File Systems

After creating the block device layer of the storage setup, you must put a file system on top of it. Ansible provides the filesystem module to do so. This module supports creating as well as resizing file systems. Table 15-6 gives an overview of its most common options.

Table 15-6 filesystem Common Options

Option	Use
dev	Indicates the block device name.
fstype	Specifies the file system type. All common Linux file systems are supported.
opts	Identifies options that should be passed to the underlying Linux **mkfs** command.
resizefs	Extends the file system if set to **yes**. The file system will be extended to the current block size.

The filesystem module has a relatively limited number of options. The reason is that all options are passed directly to the underlying Linux **mkfs** command, and they are specified using the **opts** argument. Listing 15-9 shows how to create a file system.

Listing 15-9   Creating an XFS File System

```
- name: create an XFS filesystem
  filesystem:
    dev: /dev/vgdata/lvdata
    fstype: xfs
```

After the file system is created, it can be mounted. To mount file systems, you use the mount module. Table 15-7 shows common options to this module, and Listing 15-10 shows a task that mounts a file system.

Table 15-7   mount Module Common Options

Option	Use
fstype	Specifies the file system type. Notice the **fstype** is not automatically detected.
path	Indicates the directory where the file system must be mounted.
src	Specifies the device that should be mounted.
state	Specifies the current mount state. Use **mounted** to actively mount the device now, as well as through fstab. Use **present** to set in /etc/fstab but not to mount it now.

Listing 15-10   Using the mount Module to Mount a File System

```
- name: mount the filesystem
  mount:
    src: /dev/vgdata/lvdata
    fstype: xfs
    state: mounted
    path: /mydir
```

Configuring Swap Space

Swap space can be a useful addition in systems that have a shortage of memory. Swap space is emulated memory that is allocated on disk. To set up swap space, you must first format a device as swap space and next mount the swap space. To format a device as swap space, you use the filesystem module. There is no specific Ansible module to activate the swap space, so you use the command module to run the Linux **swapon** command.

Because adding swap space is not always required, it can be done in a conditional statement. In the statement, use the **ansible_swaptotal_mb** fact to discover how much swap is actually available. If that amount falls below a specific threshold, the swap space can be created and activated. Listing 15-11 shows an example where a conditional check is performed, and additional swap space is configured if the current amount of swap space is lower than 256 MiB.

Listing 15-11   Setting Up Swap Space

```
---
- name: configure swap storage
  hosts: ansible2
  tasks:
  - name: setup swap
    block:
    - name: make the swap filesystem
      filesystem:
        fstype: swap
        dev: /dev/sdb1
    - name: activate swap space
      command: swapon /dev/sdb1
    when: ansible_swaptotal_mb < 256
```

Now that you know how to manage storage with Ansible, you can practice these skills in Exercise 15-2, which guides you through the complete procedure of setting up storage devices.

Exercise 15-2   Setting Up Storage

1. Use your editor to create the file exercise152.yaml and write the playbook header as follows:

```
---
- name: create storage
  hosts: ansible2
  tasks:
```

2. Write the first task to set up a GPT partition on /dev/sdb:

```
- name: create new partition
  parted:
```

```
    name: files
    label: gpt
    device: /dev/sdb
    number: 1
    state: present
    part_start: 1MiB
    part_end: 2GiB
```

3. Create a second partition for use as an LVM physical volume:

```
- name: create another new partition
  parted:
    name: swap
    label: gpt
    device: /dev/sdb
    number: 2
    state: present
    part_start: 2GiB
    part_end: 4GiB
    flags: [ lvm ]
```

4. Continue with the next task, which sets up an LVM volume group:

```
- name: create a volume group
  lvg:
    vg: vgdata
    pesize: "8"
    pvs: /dev/sdb2
```

5. Add a task that creates a logical volume within the volume group:

```
- name: create a logical volume
  lvol:
    lv: lvdata
    size: 100%FREE
    vg: vgdata
```

6. On top of the logical volume, create an XFS file system:

```
- name: create an XFS filesystem
  filesystem:
    dev: /dev/vgdata/lvdata
    fstype: xfs
```

7. Mount the file system:

```
- name: mount the filesystem
  mount:
    src: /dev/vgdata/lvdata
```

```
            fstype: xfs
            state: mounted
            path: /data
```

8. This concludes the setup of the LVM storage. Now add a block that creates and activates swap space, but only if the current amount of swap space as detected in the Ansible facts is smaller than 256 MiB. Notice the indentation; the tasks within the block are indented one level deeper:

```
- name: setup swap
  block:
  - name: make the swap filesystem
    filesystem:
       fstype: swap
       dev: /dev/sdb1
  - name: activate swap space
    command: swapon /dev/sdb1
  when: ansible_swaptotal_mb < 256
```

9. Before running this playbook, run an ad hoc command to ensure that /dev/sdb on the target host is empty:

```
ansible ansible2 -a "dd if=/dev/zero of=/dev/sdb bs=1M count=10"
```

10. Just to make sure that you don't get any errors about partitions that are in use, also reboot the target host:

```
ansible ansible2 -m reboot
```

11. Run the playbook by using **ansible-playbook exercise152.yaml**. You should see no problems.

12. Run the playbook again. Notice that at this point you get an error on the task [create a logical volume]. The reason is that this task was not written in an idempotent way. The reason for the lack of idempotency is that the size is specified as 100%FREE, which is a relative value, not an absolute value. This value works the first time you run the playbook, but it does not the second time you run the playbook. Because no free space is available, the LVM layer interprets the task as if you wanted to create a logical volume with a size of 0 MiB and will complain about that. To ensure that plays are written in an idempotent way, make sure that you use absolute values, not relative values!

Configuring Storage Advanced Exercise

It's time again for an advanced exercise. Exercise 15-3 is probably the most advanced exercise of all the exercises in this book, so make sure to take your time to understand all that is covered. To work on this exercise, you need managed machines with an additional disk device: add a 10 GB second disk to host ansible2 and a 5 GB second disk to host ansible3. The exercise assumes the name of the second disk is /dev/sdb; if a different disk name is used in your configuration, change this according to your specifications.

Exercise 15-3   Setting Up an Advanced Storage Solution

In this exercise you need to set up a storage solution that meets the following requirements:

- Tasks in this playbook should be executed only on hosts where the device /dev/sdb exists.
- If no device /dev/sdb exists, the playbook should print "device sdb not present" and stop executing tasks on that host.
- Configure the device with one partition that includes all available disk space.
- Create an LVM volume group with the name vgfiles.
- If the volume group is bigger than 5 GB, create an LVM logical volume with the name lvfiles and a size of 6 GB. Note that you must check the LVM volume group size and not the /dev/sdb1 size because in theory you could have multiple block devices in a volume group.
- If the volume group is equal to or smaller than 5 GB, create an LVM logical volume with the name lvfiles and a size of 3 GB.
- Format the volume with the XFS file system.
- Mount it on the /files directory.

WARNING!   This exercise will fail if any previously configured storage devices are allocated to /dev/sdb. Make sure you wipe /dev/sdb before continuing, and also verify there are no references to storage devices created earlier in this chapter in /etc/fstab.

1. Because this is going to be a bigger playbook, it's wise to split development into different parts so that the different parts can be tested individually. If this were a task on the EX294 exam, it would be smart to start with the most challenging task and write it in a small playbook so that it could run independently. The reason is time management: if you can't configure the challenging task, it doesn't make sense to spend your time on other tasks. With this point in mind, let's focus on the condition where you need to check the size of the volume group. It might not be the best idea to start working on all tasks that are required to get you testing the volume group that needs to be created. You can, however, write a test that works on a default volume group, and that is what you're going to do first, using the name of the default volume group on CentOS 8, which is "cl" (rhel if you're using RHEL 8). The purpose is to test

the constructions, which is why it doesn't really matter that the two tasks have overlapping **when** statements. So create a file with the name exercise153-dev1.yaml and give it the following contents:

```
---
- name: get vg sizes
  hosts: all
  tasks:
  - name: find small vgroup sizes
    debug:
      msg: volume group smaller than or equal to 20G
    when:
    - ansible_facts['lvm']['vgs']['cl'] is defined
    - ansible_facts['lvm']['vgs']['cl']['size_g'] <= 20.00
  - name: find large vgroup size
    debug:
      msg: volume group larger than or equal to 19G
    when:
    - ansible_facts['lvm']['vgs']['cl'] is defined
    - ansible_facts['lvm']['vgs']['cl']['size_g'] >= 19.00
```

2. Run the playbook by using **ansible-playbook exercise153-dev1.yaml**. You'll notice that it fails with the errors shown in Listing 15-12.

Listing 15-12   exercise153-dev1.yaml Failure Message

```
TASK [find small vgroups sizes] ************************************
****************
fatal: [ansible1]: FAILED! => {"msg": "The conditional check
'ansible_facts['lvm']['vgs']['cl']['size_g'] <= 20.00' failed. The
error was: Unexpected templating type error occurred on ({% if
ansible_facts['lvm']['vgs']['cl']['size_g'] <= 20.00 %} True {%
else %} False {% endif %}): '<=' not supported between instances
of 'AnsibleUnsafeText' and 'float'\n\nThe error appears to be in '/
home/ansible/rhce8-book/exercise153-dev1.yaml': line 5, column 5,
but may\nbe elsewhere in the file depending on the exact syntax
problem.\n\nThe offending line appears to be:\n\n  tasks:\n    -
name: find small vgroups sizes\n      ^ here\n"}
fatal: [ansible2]: FAILED! => {"msg": "The conditional check
'ansible_facts['lvm']['vgs']['cl']['size_g'] <= 20.00' failed. The
error was: Unexpected templating type error occurred on ({% if
ansible_facts['lvm']['vgs']['cl']['size_g'] <= 20.00 %} True {%
else %} False {% endif %}): '<=' not supported between instances
of 'AnsibleUnsafeText' and 'float'\n\nThe error appears to be in '/
home/ansible/rhce8-book/exercise153-dev1.yaml': line 5, column 5,
but may\nbe elsewhere in the file depending on the exact syntax
problem.\n\nThe offending line appears to be:\n\n  tasks:\n    -
name: find small vgroups sizes\n      ^ here\n"}
```

```
fatal: [ansible3]: FAILED! => {"msg": "The conditional check
'ansible_facts['lvm']['vgs']['cl']['size_g'] <= 20.00' failed. The
error was: Unexpected templating type error occurred on ({% if
ansible_facts['lvm']['vgs']['cl']['size_g'] <= 20.00 %} True {%
else %} False {% endif %}): '<=' not supported between instances
of 'AnsibleUnsafeText' and 'float'\n\nThe error appears to be in '/
home/ansible/rhce8-book/exercise153-dev1.yaml': line 5, column 5,
but may\nbe elsewhere in the file depending on the exact syntax
problem.\n\nThe offending line appears to be:\n\n  tasks:\n   -
name: find small vgroups sizes\n      ^ here\n"}
fatal: [ansible4]: FAILED! => {"msg": "The conditional check
'ansible_facts['lvm']['vgs']['cl']['size_g'] <= 20.00' failed. The
error was: Unexpected templating type error occurred on ({% if
ansible_facts['lvm']['vgs']['cl']['size_g'] <= 20.00 %} True {%
else %} False {% endif %}): '<=' not supported between instances
of 'AnsibleUnsafeText' and 'float'\n\nThe error appears to be in '/
home/ansible/rhce8-book/exercise153-dev1.yaml': line 5, column 5,
but may\nbe elsewhere in the file depending on the exact syntax
problem.\n\nThe offending line appears to be:\n\n  tasks:\n   -
name: find small vgroups sizes\n      ^ here\n"}
skipping: [ansible5]
skipping: [ansible6]


TASK [find large vgroups sizes] *************************************
****************
skipping: [ansible5]
skipping: [ansible6]
```

3. As you can see in the errors in Listing 15-12, there are two problems in the playbook. The first problem is that there is no **ignore_errors** in the failing play, which means that only hosts that haven't failed will reach the next task. The second error is the "Unexpected templating error". The playbook in its current form is trying to perform a logical test to compare the value of two variables that have an incompatible variable type. The Ansible fact has the type "Ansible-UnsafeText", and the value of 20.00 is a float, not an integer. To make this test work, you must force the type of both variables to be set to an integer. Now write **exercise153-dev2.yaml** where this is happening; notice the use of the filter **int**, which is essential for the success of this playbook:

```
---
- name: get vg sizes
  ignore_errors: yes
  hosts: all
  tasks:
  - name: set vgroup sizes in variables
    set_fact:
```

```
        vgsize: "{{ ansible_facts['lvm']['vgs']['cl']['size_g'] |
int }}"
    - name: debug this
      debug:
        msg: the value of vgsize is {{ vgsize }}
    - name: testing big vgsize value
      debug:
        msg: the value of vgsize is bigger than 18
      when: vgsize | int > 18
    - name: testing small vgsize value
      debug:
        msg: the value of vgsize is smaller than 20
      when: vgsize | int <= 20
```

4. Run this playbook. You'll notice it skips and ignores some tasks but doesn't fail
   anywhere, which means that this playbook—although absolutely not perfect—is
   usable as an example to test the size of the vgfiles volume group later in this
   exercise.

5. Now that you've tested the most complex part of the assignment, you can
   start writing the rest of the playbook. Do this in a new file with the name
   exercise153.yaml. Because this playbook has quite a few tasks to accomplish,
   it might be smart to define the rough structure and ensure that all elements
   that are needed later are at least documented so that you can later work out
   the details. So let's start with the first part, where the play header is defined, as
   well as the rough structure. This is the moment where you still have the global
   overview of all the tasks in this requirement, so you need to make sure you
   won't forget about them later, which is a real risk if you've been into the details
   too much for too long.

```
---

- name: set up hosts that have an sdb device
  hosts: all
  tasks:
  - name: getting out with a nice failure message if there is no
second disk
      # fail:
      debug:
        msg: write a nice failure message and a when test here
      # when: something
  - name: create a partition
    #parted
    debug:
      msg: creating the partition
```

```
    - name: create a volume group
      #lvg:
      debug:
        msg: creating the volume group
    - name: get the vg size and store it in a variable
      #set_fact:
      debug:
        msg: storing variable as an integer
    - name: create an LVM on big volume groups
      #lvol:
      debug:
        msg: use when statement to create 6g lvol if vsize > 5
    - name: create an LVM on small volume groups
      #lvol:
      debug:
        msg: use when statement to create 3g lvol if vsize <= 5
    - name: formatting the XFS filesystem
      # filesystem
      debug:
        msg: creating the filesystem
    - name: mounting /dev/vgfiles/lvfiles
      # mount:
      debug:
        msg: mounting the volume
```

6. The advantage of a generic structure like the one you just defined is that you can run a test at any moment. Now it's time to fill it in. Start with the play header and then check whether /dev/sdb is present on the managed system:

```
---
- name: setup up hosts that have an sdb device
  hosts: all
  tasks:
  - name: getting out with a nice failure message if there is no
second disk
    fail:
      msg: there is no second disk
    when: ansible_facts['devices']['sdb'] is not defined
```

7. At this point I recommend you run a test to see that the playbook really does skip all hosts that don't have a second disk device. Use **ansible-playbook exercise153.yaml** to do so and observe that you see a lot of skipping messages in the output. You should also see that hosts that don't have a second disk device generate a failure.

8. If all is well so far, you can continue to create the partition and create the logical volume group as well. Here are the tasks you need to enter. Notice that no size is specified at any point, which means that the partition and the volume group will be allowed to grow up to the maximum size.

```
- name: create a partition
  parted:
    device: /dev/sdb
    number: 1
    state: present
- name: create a volume group
  lvg:
    pvs: /dev/sdb1
    vg: vgfiles
```

9. At this point you can insert the part where you save the volume group size into a variable, which can be used in the **when** statement that will occur in one of the next tasks. Also, because it's good to check a lot while you are writing a complex playbook, use the debug module to verify the results.

```
- name: get vg size and convert to integer in new variable
  set_fact:
    vgsize: "{{ ansible_facts['lvm']['vgs']['vgfiles']['size_g']
| int }}"
- name: show vgsize value
  debug:
    var: "{{ vgsize }}"
```

10. After this important step, it's time to run a test. If you need it, you can find a sample playbook of the state so far named exercise153-step9.yaml in the GitHub repository at https://github.com/sandervanvugt/rhce8-book, but it's obviously much better and recommended to run your own code! So use **ansible-playbook exercise153.yaml** to verify what you've got so far. Notice that you *must* make sure to run it on hosts that don't have any configuration yet. If a configuration already exists, that will most likely give you false positives! If you want to make sure all is clean, use **ansible all -a "dd if=/dev/zero of=/dev/ sdb bs=1M count=10"** to wipe the /dev/sdb devices on your managed hosts. Also check there are no references in /etc/fstab to storage devices you have created earlier in this chapter. Next, use **ansible all -m reboot** to to reboot all of them before you test. The purpose is that at this point you see the error message shown in Listing 15-13. Before moving on to the next step, try to understand what is going wrong.

Listing 15-13 Error Message After Exercise 15-3 Step 10

```
TASK [get vg size and convert to integer in new variable]
*******************************
fatal: [ansible2]: FAILED! => {"msg": "The task includes an option
with an undefined variable. The error was: 'dict object' has no
attribute 'vgfiles'\n\nThe error appears to be in '/home/ansible/
rhce8-book/exercise153-step9.yaml': line 18, column 5, but may\nbe
elsewhere in the file depending on the exact syntax problem.\n\nThe
offending line appears to be:\n\n        vg: vgfiles\n  - name: get
vg size and convert to integer in new variable\n    ^ here\n"}
fatal: [ansible3]: FAILED! => {"msg": "The task includes an option
with an undefined variable. The error was: 'dict object' has no
attribute 'vgfiles'\n\nThe error appears to be in '/home/ansible/
rhce8-book/exercise153-step9.yaml': line 18, column 5, but may\nbe
elsewhere in the file depending on the exact syntax problem.\n\nThe
offending line appears to be:\n\n        vg: vgfiles\n  - name: get
vg size and convert to integer in new variable\n    ^ here\n"
```

11. As you can see, the variable that you are trying to use has no value yet. And that is for the simple reason that fact gathering is required to set the variable, and fact gathering is happening at the beginning of the playbook. At this point, you need to add a task that runs the setup module right after creating the volume group, and then you can try again. In the output you have to look at the [show vgsize value] task, which should look all right now, and everything after that can be ignored. See exercise153-step11.yaml in the GitHub repository if you need the complete example.

```
# skipping first part of the playbook in this listing
- name: create a volume group
  lvg:
    pvs: /dev/sdb1
    vg: vgfiles
- name: run the setup module so that we can use updated facts
  setup:
- name: get vg size and convert to integer in new variable
  set_fact:
    vgsize: "{{ ansible_facts['lvm']['vgs']['vgfiles']['size_g']
| int }}"
- name: show vgsize value
  debug:
    var: "{{ vgsize }}"
```

12. Assuming that all went well, you can now add the two conditional tests, where according to the **vgsize** value, the lvol module is used to create the logical volumes:

```
- name: create an LVM on big volume groups
  lvol:
     vg: vgfiles
     lv: lvfiles
     size: 6g
  when: vgsize | int > 5
- name: create an LVM on small volume groups
  lvol:
     vg: vgfiles
     lv: lvfiles
     size: 3g
  when: vgsize | int <= 5
```

13. Add the tasks to format the volumes with the XFS file system and mount them:

```
- name: formatting the XFS filesystem
  filesystem:
     dev: /dev/vgfiles/lvfiles
     fstype: xfs
- name: mounting /dev/vgfile/lvfiles
  mount:
     path: /file
     state: mounted
     src: /dev/vgfiles/lvfiles
     fstype: xfs
```

14. That's all! The playbook is now ready for use. Run it by using **ansible-playbook exercise153.yaml** and verify its output.

15. Use the ad hoc command **ansible ansible2,ansible3 -a "lvs"** to show LVM logical volume sizes on the machines with the additional hard drive. You should see that all has worked out well and you are done!

Summary

In this chapter you learned how to work with storage. Setting up storage is an important task that you need to consider carefully because so many things can go wrong while trying to set it up! You first learned how to use Ansible facts to discover facts about your current storage configuration. After that you learned how to set up storage devices using the appropriate modules. You also worked through one of the most advanced playbook examples in this book, so you are getting close to being ready for the exam!

Exam Preparation Tasks

As mentioned in the section "How to Use This Book" in the Introduction, you have a couple of choices for exam preparation: the exercises here, Chapter 16, "Final Preparation," and the exam simulation questions on the companion website.

Review All Key Topics

Review the most important topics in this chapter, noted with the Key Topics icon in the outer margin of the page. Table 15-8 lists a reference of these key topics and the page numbers on which each is found.

Table 15-8   Key Topics for Chapter 15

Key Topic Element	Description	Page Number
Table 15-3	Storage-Related Facts	355
Table 15-4	parted Options	365
Table 15-5	lvol Common Options	367
Table 15-6	filesystem Common Options	367
Table 15-7	mount Module Common Options	368

Memory Tables

Print a copy of Appendix D, "Memory Tables" (found on the companion website), or at least the section for this chapter, and complete the tables and lists from memory. Appendix E, "Memory Tables Answer Key," also on the companion website, includes completed tables and lists to check your work.

Define Key Terms

There are no terms for this chapter.

Review Questions

1. Which Ansible fact can you use to get an overview of current mounts?

2. You need to write a playbook that generates an error if a device does not exist. Which two modules can you use for this purpose?

3. Which module do you use to create partitions?

4. Which parted option can you use to specify that it should use GPT partitions?

5. Which parted option do you use to set the lvm partition type?

6. You want to use the parted module to create a partition on a disk that already has a 2 GB partition. Which option should you use to ensure the partition starts at the right location?

7. Which module would you use to manage LVM volume groups?

8. Why should you avoid using **size: 100%FREE** when using the lvol module to create an LVM volume that uses all available disk space in the volume group?

9. Which option do you use with the mount module to specify the device that you want to mount?

10. Which value must be assigned to the mount module **state** argument to ensure the device is mounted now but also mounted persistently through /etc/fstab?

End-of-Chapter Lab

In this chapter you worked on many advanced storage tasks. Now you're going to write a playbook to clean up the hosts from all that you've done in the exercises in this chapter.

Lab 15-1

Write a playbook that cleans up the second hard disks on all hosts that have been modified in this chapter.

## CHAPTER 16

Final Preparation

Congratulations! You made it through the book, and now it's time to finish getting ready for the exam. This chapter helps you get ready to take and pass the exam. In this chapter, you learn more about the exam process and how to register for the exam. You also get some useful tips that help you avoid some common pitfalls while taking the exam.

Generic Tips

In this section, you get some generic tips about the exam. You learn how to verify your exam readiness, how to register for the exam, and what to do on the exam.

Verifying Your Readiness

Register for the exam only when you think that you are ready for it. This book contains a lot of material to help you verify your exam readiness. To start with, you should be able to answer all the "Do I Know This Already?" questions, which you find at the beginning of each chapter. You should also have completed all the exercises in the chapters successfully. At the end of each chapter, you can find the end-of-chapter labs. These are the first real way of testing your readiness. The end-of-chapter lab questions are formulated in the same way as you might expect the real exam questions to be, so they are a good way of finding out whether you are ready for the exam.

Now that you have worked through all the material in this book, you are ready for the test exams in this chapter. Make sure that you can perform all the tests in the test exams before you register for the exam.

No sample answers are provided for the test exams, and that is on purpose. On the real exams, nobody tells you what you've done wrong if you fail on specific tasks. You should be able to find out yourself whether you have performed specific tasks successfully. If you are in doubt about specific tasks, chances are that you are just not ready for these tasks. The idea is that you should make sure that you feel comfortable with the exam topics. And if you are, you'll be able to verify the playbooks that you've written.

Registering for the Exam

There are two ways of taking the RHCE exam. You can either take it as a classroom exam or as a kiosk exam. The classroom exam is typically on Friday only, and it is offered primarily by Red Hat to provide an exam at the end of a course. Therefore, most of the people who are with you in the exam classroom have taken four days of training before taking the exam, and for that reason, classroom exam availability is limited.

For a long time, the classroom exam was the only way to take the exam. For some time now, though, Red Hat has provided kiosk exams too. A kiosk exam is an individual exam, where you work through the exam tasks on a kiosk computer. This monitored computer is in a booth in an exam center, where you are monitored through multiple cameras while working on the exam tasks. The good things about a kiosk exam are that it is individual and that you schedule the exam time and place yourself at your convenience.

Since very recently, Red Hat is also starting to offer exams that can be taken from home. At the moment this book was finished, the home exams were still in an experimental stage. Consult https://redhat.com/training for more details and the latest news about this new way to take the exams.

You can register for the exam through redhat.com or through a training company. It does not really matter where you buy it because you end up at the same exam anyway. It might be easier, though, to get a discount while booking through a local training company. Booking through Red Hat is faster normally because you have direct access to Red Hat. Notice that specific policies may apply to specific countries, and not all options may be available in your area.

If you book a classroom exam, you get an invitation for the time and date the exam is scheduled. If you book a kiosk exam, you get a voucher code that you can use to book the exam venue, time, and date yourself.

On Exam Day

Make sure to bring appropriate identification to the exam. To be allowed to take the exam, you need an approved government ID. Normally, a passport or driver's license will do; other types of proof may be accepted in your country as well. Do not forget it; without ID, you will not be allowed to take the exam.

Also make sure you are on time. It is a good idea to arrive half an hour before the exam's scheduled starting time. If you are late, you will normally be allowed access to the exam, but you will not get extra time. So, just make sure that you are on time.

After proving your identity, you are introduced to the exam environment. Because of the nondisclosure agreement that every test-taker signs with Red Hat, I cannot tell you in detail what the exam environment looks like. I can tell you, though, that there will be an environment in which you have to work. Depending on the exam you are taking, this consists of one or more servers. There is also a list of tasks that have to be performed. Work your way through the tasks, read all well, and you will pass the exam.

During the Exam

The tasks that you have to work on during the exam are not necessarily presented in the most logical order. Therefore, it is a good idea to start reading through all the tasks before you start working on the first assignment. While reading through all the tasks, you can decide which is the best order to create the configurations needed. Determine the best possible order for yourself because it may not be obvious.

Another important tip is to read carefully. Not many people know how to read carefully anymore, and you are probably among those people. IT administrators are very skilled in scanning web pages to retrieve the information that they need. That skill will not help you on the exam. Reading skills will. I cannot stress that point enough. According to my estimate, 40 percent of all people who fail the exam fail because they do not read (they scan instead). So, let me give you some tips on how to read the exam questions:

- If English is not your native language, or if you master one or more additional languages, you can switch the language in which questions are presented. Maybe the English language question is not clear to you, but the question translated in another language is. So, if in doubt, read the translation as well.

- The English language questions are the most used and best scanned questions. Exam questions are perfect because Red Hat has made a tremendous effort to make them perfect. Given the fact that most of the exam candidates work on English language questions, the quality of English language questions is the best. You are free to use translated questions, but you should use the English language questions as your primary source.

- To make sure that you do not miss anything, make a task list for each question. You can open a document on the exam host computer to take notes. Use it to make a short list of tasks that you have to accomplish and work on them one by one. This approach helps you to concentrate on what the exam question is actually asking.

- After you have worked on all assignments, go have a cup of coffee (you are allowed to take breaks during the exam). When you return, read all questions again to make sure that you did not miss anything. Taking a small break is important; it allows you to take distance from the exam, after which you will read the questions as if it is the first time that you have seen them.

Another important part of the exam is the order in which you work on the assignments. Even though I cannot talk about specific exam content, some topics need to be fixed before other topics. Make sure that you deal with those topics first. If you do not, fixing the other assignments will be more difficult or impossible.

The Nondisclosure Agreement

The RHCE certification is one of the most sought-after certifications that currently exist in IT. It represents a real value because the person who takes the RHCE exam has worked through a list of realistic assignments and knows how to do the job. It is in everybody's interest to help maintain this high value. The nondisclosure agreement is an important part of that.

The RHCE exam still represents real skills because the content of these exams is not publicly available. Please help keep these exams valuable by not talking about questions that you saw on your exam. A person who knows which questions are asked will have an easier exam than you did, which means that the certificate value will diminish, which will also make your effort less valuable. So, please help protect what you have worked so hard for and do not talk about exam content to anyone.

Practice Exam A

To work through this exam, you need a total of five servers that are running RHEL 8 or CentOS 8. One server needs to be configured as the control host; the other four servers need to be configured as managed servers, using the names ansible1.example.com through ansible4.example.com. The IP addresses used on the managed servers are not important; you can pick anything that matches your configuration. Make sure the servers meet the following requirements:

- 1 GB of RAM.

- A primary disk /dev/sda with a size of 20 GB.

- Only on ansible1 and ansible2, a secondary disk /dev/sdb with a size of 5 GB.

- The root user account configured with the password "password" on each of the servers.

- The control server with a user account "ansible." SSH public and private keys have been generated for this user. No further configuration has been done yet.

In the assignments in this exam, you must create scripts and YAML files. Make sure that all these scripts are stored in the directory /home/ansible unless specified otherwise.

Common Tasks

1. Configure the control host with a static inventory, as well as the ansible. cfg configuration file. In the static inventory, configure the following host groups:

   a. Group "test" with ansible1 as a member
   b. Group "dev" with ansible2 as a member
   c. Group "prod" with ansible3 and ansible4 as members
   d. Group "servers" with groups dev and prod as members
   e. Ensure that hosts can be reached through their FQDN and also by using the short name (so ansible1.example.com as well as ansible1)

2. Create a playbook with the name setupreposerver.yml to set up the control host as a repository host. Make sure this host meets the following requirements, which must be done by the playbook:

   a. The RHEL 8 installation ISO is loop-mounted on the directory /var/ftp/repo.

   b. The firewalld service is disabled.

   c. The vsftpd service is started as well as enabled, and it allows anonymous user access to the /var/ftp/repo directory.

3. Create a Bash script that configures the managed servers as repository clients to the repository server that you set up in the previous task. This script must use ad hoc commands and perform the following tasks:

   a. Disable any currently existing repository.

   b. Enable access to the BaseOS repository on control.example.com.

   c. Enable access to the AppStream repository on control.example.com.

4. Create a Bash script with the name setuphosts.sh that uses ad hoc commands to complete configuration on the managed servers. This includes

   a. Installing Python

   b. Creating a user with the name "ansible"

   c. Creating a sudo configuration that allows user ansible to run tasks with root privileges

   d. Using an ad hoc command to call the appropriate module to test connectivity to the remote hosts

Exam A Specific Tasks

1. Write a playbook that installs software packages:

   a. Nmap and wireshark on servers in the groups dev, test, and prod.

   b. All packages from the package group "Virtualization Host" on the group prod.

   c. Servers in the group prod must be fully updated.

2. Create a playbook that configures an LVM logical volume with the name lvdata in the volume group vgdata, according to the following requirements:

    a. Only on servers that have a second disk available, the volume group vgdata should be created.

    b. If no second hard disk is available, the playbook should print "no second disk available" and do nothing.

3. Create a playbook with the name report.yml that generates a file on the ansible control server. The file should have the name hwtemplate.txt and the following contents:

```
NAME=
IPADDRESS=
DISKS=
SECOND_DISK_NAME=
```

Use this file to generate a report on the managed servers. To do so, copy the file to /root/report.txt, and have your playbook modify it, but do not overwrite current settings. Apply the following requirements:

    a. NAME= gets the FQDN of the managed host as argument.
    b. IPADDRESS= gets the IP address of the managed host.
    c. DISKS= gets the names of all disk devices on your computer.
    d. If the host has a second hard disk, SECOND_DISK_NAME should get the name of that DISK. If the managed host has no second hard disk, the playbook should set SECOND_DISK_NAME=NONE.

4. Create a Vault-encrypted file with the name pass.txt. This file should set the variable devpass to the value password and the variable prodpass to the value secret. Set the Vault password required to access this file to vaultpass. Also create a Vault password file with the name vaultpass.txt that can be used to automatically enter this password such that no further action is required when accessing the Vault-encrypted files.

   After creating the Vault-encrypted file, change the Vault password to myvault-pass and ensure it still can be used automatically.

5. Use the RHEL system role that manages time in a playbook with the name time.yml. Ensure that control.example.com is used as the time server and set the appropriate parameter that allows changing time even if a large difference exists between time on the managed machine and time on the time server. At the end of the playbook, verify that time is synchronized. If this is not the case, the playbook should print the text "time could not be synchronized."

6. Configure a playbook with the name runwebserver.yml that meets the following requirements. Ensure that the web server contents are accessible from other machines.

   a. Create a file /webcontent/index.html that contains the text "welcome to this webserver. The server is managed by USERNAME."

   b. Use a variable to set USERNAME to julie. The variable should be set by using inclusion of a file that is created for servers in the group prod only.

   c. Create a symbolic link in /var/www/html/index.html that links to the file /webcontent/index.html and ensure the contents of this file are visible from remote hosts.

Practice Exam B

To work through this exam, you need a total of five servers that are running RHEL 8 or CentOS 8. One server needs to be configured as the control host; the other four servers need to be configured as managed servers, using the names ansible1.example.com through ansible4.example.com. The IP addresses used on the managed servers are not important; you can pick anything that matches your configuration. Make sure the servers meet the following requirements:

- 1 GB of RAM.

- A primary disk /dev/sda with a size of 20 GB.

- Only on ansible1 and ansible2, a secondary disk /dev/sdb with a size of 5 GB.

- The root user account configured with the password "password" on each of the servers.

- The control server with a user account "ansible." SSH public and private keys have been generated for this user. No further configuration has been done yet.

In the assignments in this exam, you must create scripts and YAML files. Make sure that all these scripts are stored in the directory /home/ansible unless specified otherwise.

Common Tasks

1. Configure the control host with a static inventory, as well as the ansible. cfg configuration file. In the static inventory, configure the following host groups:

   a. Group "test" with ansible1 as a member

   b. Group "dev" with ansible2 as a member

   c. Group "prod" with ansible3 and ansible4 as members

   d. Group "servers" with groups dev and prod as members

Ensure that hosts can be reached through their FQDN and also by using the short name (so ansible1.example.com as well as ansible1).

2. Create a playbook with the name setupreposerver.yml to set up the control host as a repository host. Make sure this host meets the following requirements, which must be done by the playbook:

   a. The RHEL 8 installation ISO is loop-mounted on the directory /var/ftp/repo.

   b. The firewalld service is disabled.

   c. The vsftpd service is started as well as enabled, and it allows anonymous user access to the /var/ftp/repo directory.

3. Create a Bash script that configures the managed servers as repository clients to the repository server that you set up in the previous task. This script must use ad hoc commands and perform the following tasks:

   a. Disable any currently existing repository.

   b. Enable access to the BaseOS repository on control.example.com.

   c. Enable access to the AppStream repository on control.example.com.

4. Create a Bash script with the name setuphosts.sh that uses ad hoc commands to complete configuration on the managed servers. This includes

   a. Installing Python

   b. Creating a user with the name "ansible"

   c. Creating a sudo configuration that allows user ansible to run tasks with root privileges

   d. Using an ad hoc command to call the appropriate module to test connectivity to the remote hosts

Exam B Specific Tasks

1. Write a playbook that installs a vsftpd server:

   a. The latest version of the software package should be installed.

   b. The service should be started and enabled.

   c. A port in the firewall must be opened for this service.

   d. A file must be created with the name /var/ftp/pub/README.txt, containing the text "welcome to the vsftpd service."

2. Create a playbook that installs software on the managed host, according to the following requirements:

   a. Custom facts with the names package1 and package2 are available on host ansible2 and not on other hosts.

   b. The value of package1 is set to smb; the value of package2 is set to mariadb-server.

   c. Write a playbook that pushes these custom facts to host ansible2.

   d. Write another playbook that installs and enables the packages.

   e. Write a script with the name mypackages.sh, which uses package fact gathering to show the properties of only the packages that were just installed. Write the output of this script to the file packages-out.txt in the current directory on the control host.

3. Write a playbook that creates a user with the name anna and meets the following requirements:

   a. The password is set to "secret." Ensure that the password is set properly hashed (and not as a plain-text value, which won't work).

   b. Enable full administrative access through sudo for this user.

4. Write a playbook that changes SELinux mode to permissive on host ansible3. If the mode is changed successfully, the target host should be rebooted after waiting for 30 seconds. If no change is made, the playbook should print the message "no change was made."

5. Apply Ansible optimization in the following way:

   a. While processing playbooks, it should be possible to process no more than two hosts simultaneously.

   b. While processing the playbook, all tasks should be executed on two hosts, before continuing with the next group of two hosts.

6. Write an Ansible playbook that meets the following requirements:

   a. Host group variables are used to set the variable username=mandie groupname=profs on hosts in the group dev, and username=chantal and groupname=students on hosts in the group prod.

   b. The passwords for the users should be obtained from an Ansible Vault-encrypted file. The Vault file is protected with the password vaultpw. The user passwords are set to userpw. You do not need to apply additional encryption to the user passwords.

Answers to the "Do I Know This Already?" Quizzes and Review Questions

Chapter 1

"Do I Know This Already?" Quiz

1. **A and C.** Managing Windows with a Bash shell script simply doesn't work. This is just one example that makes answer A true. Apart from that, it is difficult to guarantee that shell scripts will always produce the same result if the configuration on the managed machine changes.

2. **B.** In releasing, the new software is made available. To have it working as it should, configuration comes next to ensure that the systems where the software is running conform to expectations.

3. **D.** Putting the infrastructure as code configuration files in a CVS has many advantages, including all the features mentioned in the answers to this question.

4. **C.** Although Red Hat Satellite does take care of some automation tasks, it cannot be considered a complete automation utility because it lacks specific features.

5. **B and C.** Most alternative solutions need an agent and use a more complex format to create configurations. Ease of configuration and the ability to manage assets without the need to install an agent are two major advantages of Ansible.

6. **A.** Ansible uses native remote access to managed devices. Often this is SSH. On Windows, Windows Remote Management (WinRM) is the default, and on network devices API access can be used. Agents are never required.

7. **C.** AWX is the open-source project that has a web interface which allows you to manage Ansible in large environments. Red Hat offers Ansible Tower as the commercial version of AWX, adding a support license to it.

8. **C.** Although answer D is not strictly wrong, answer C is better because it is about making just the changes that are needed to reach the desired state.

9. C. Ansible can perfectly push configurations to a bare-metal server that has performed a PXE-boot with the help of another system, but Ansible itself is not capable of performing a PXE-boot.

10. A. Ansible started as a solution for configuration management, and that is the reason most people still use it. Ansible can be used in other scenarios as well, but configuration management still is its core function.

Chapter 2

"Do I Know This Already?" Quiz

1. B and D. Ansible commands are executed as Python scripts on the managed nodes. To push the Python scripts to the managed nodes, SSH access is required.

2. B and C. As Python 3 has become the default Python version in RHEL 8, Ansible, if installed on RHEL 8, is based on Python 3 also. Ansible needs Python to be installed on managed nodes in order to run the Ansible scripts on these hosts.

3. B. Even if working with SSH key-based login is recommended, it is not mandatory. Password-based login is also supported.

4. A. Password-less privilege escalation is convenient but not mandatory.

5. C. Even if having 20 GB disk space or more is advised, Ansible itself really doesn't need much disk space.

6. D. Ansible can be installed using the python-pip installer. Using the Java installer is not an option because Ansible is not related to Java at all.

7. C. There must be some way to run configuration tasks that require administrator privileges, and that is using root execution through sudo.

8. B. In all installation patterns, Python 3 is installed by default, so it doesn't have to be installed separately.

9. A. Ansible needs access to SSH and that's all. No further agents need additional configuration.

10. C. To access a remote host using public/private keys, the public key of the user must be on the remote host, not the private key as suggested in answer B.

Review Questions

1. Add the Ansible repository provided by Red Hat using subscription-manager and install Ansible from there.

2. A dedicated user account needs to be created on the host, and sudo privilege escalation needs to be set up. Also, the user must be able to log in to the managed host using SSH.

3. Python pip

4. No agents are needed; you just need the SSH service to be running and accessible.

5. AWX

6. Configure passphrases, and cache the passphrases using **ssh-agent** and **ssh-add**.

7. /etc/sudoers.d/

8. Use the raw module (discussed later).

9. By default, the Ansible control node generates a Python script. This script is sent over an SSH connection to the managed host and executed there. Ansible can be used to manage devices that don't have a Python stack. In that case, Ansible sends native code to the managed device, and no Python installation is required.

10. Use Ansible Tower, which allows passwords to be kept in a secured cache.

Chapter 3

"Do I Know This Already?" Quiz

1. A. Ansible does not look for an inventory file in the current directory. If no inventory file is specified, Ansible looks at the /etc/ansible/hosts file as the default file to be used.

2. C. If no inventory file can be used, Ansible uses localhost as the default target host.

3. D. The default location where Ansible looks for an inventory is /etc/ansible/hosts.

4. B. Even if most dynamic inventory scripts are written in Python, this is not a formal requirement.

5. C. When a directory name is specified as the inventory, all files in that directory are considered as inventory files. Notice that dynamic inventory scripts must all have the execute permission.

6. A. Defining host variables in inventory was common practice but now is considered deprecated. Host variables should be defined in the host_vars and group_vars directories.

7. D. Privilege escalation parameters can be specified in the ansible.cfg file, in individual plays, or at the command line. It is not possible to specify privilege escalation parameters in the inventory file.

8. C. To make it easy to manage diverse Ansible projects, you should store inventory files in big environments in the project directory, where playbooks used to accomplish a specific task are also stored. Alternatively, you can use Ansible Tower for this purpose, but using Tower is absolutely not a requirement.

9. B. The remote_user setting specifies the host name of the user that is used to connect to the remote host.

10. A. The host_key_checking parameter can be used to specify whether or not the validity of SSH host keys should be verified.

Review Questions

1. You don't have to use any syntax. The group named all is defined as a default group.

2. Anything you want. There is no name requirement for an inventory file.

3. /etc/ansible/hosts

4. [linux:children]

    web

    file

5. **--list** and **--host**

6. web[001:010]

7. ungrouped

8. **ansible-inventory -i inventory --graph**

9. There is no **--list-hosts** option. Use either **--list** or **--host <hostname>**.

10. become_method

Chapter 4

"Do I Know This Already?" Quiz

1. A. To repeat tasks in a consistent way, use a playbook. Ad hoc commands work with command-line arguments and are not as easy to run again in exactly the same way as tasks that are executed through playbooks.

2. C. If no module is specified in an ad hoc command, the default command module is used. This module, however, cannot work with shell features such as pipes. Use the shell module instead.

3. D. Ansible is idempotent, which means Ansible compares the desired state in the ad hoc command or playbook with the current state of the managed host. If the current state matches the desired state, no changes are applied.

4. B. Shell redirection is a shell feature, and shell features are not supported by the command module. Optionally, the raw module could be used as well, but because the shell module is more specific, use the shell module instead.

5. C. The raw module is the only module that enables you to run commands on managed nodes that don't have Python installed.

6. B. In an environment with multiple Linux distributions, you should use the package module. Use the distribution-specific module only if you're managing just that specific distribution.

7. D. The Ansible ping module tests whether a target host is in a manageable state. It tests not only connectivity but also whether Python has been set up correctly.

8. C. The **ansible-doc -l** command produces a list of modules that are installed.

9. C. Use **ansible-doc -s** to get a list of module arguments in playbook-compatible format.

10. C. The Ansible documentation website groups modules into specific functional categories. One of them is the system modules category, in which you can find a list of modules that can be used for a wide range of system administration tasks.

Review Questions

1. To perform quick checks and to perform initial setup of hosts

2. The raw module

3. The best way to get information about installed packages is to use the yum module because in Ansible using the most specific module is recommended. However, you can run this command as an argument to the shell module also.

4. Absolutely! On the exam only the result is evaluated, and as long as you obtain that result with Ansible, there's nothing wrong with that.

5. name=, state=, and enabled=

6. The SEE ALSO section contains information about related modules.

7. Look at the first line of the documentation for the module; it contains the location of the Python script this module is using.

8. The script doesn't have the execute permission set.

9. You would edit the /etc/ansible/ansible.cfg file.

10. Look at the EXAMPLES section in the output of **ansible-doc**, or use **ansible-doc -s**, followed by the name of the module you want to investigate.

Chapter 5

"Do I Know This Already?" Quiz

1. C. Playbooks should start with --- to indicate the start of the playbook.

2. D. Using the **become** parameter in the play header is optional. If it is not specified, the default parameter from the ansible.cfg is used.

3. A and C. Indentation is a mandatory element in a playbook that is used to identify relationships between parent and child objects. Only spaces can be used, no tabs.

4. C and D. There is no easy way to undo changes applied by a playbook. The only way is to write a playbook that does exactly the opposite.

5. B. A task that has modified the managed system shows "changed." Tasks that do not require a modification show "ok."

6. C. YAML lists are supported by specific modules only. The yum module works with YAML lists; the service module does not.

7. A. If a value contains text to be written to a destination file, you should use the | sign in a key:| syntax to indicate that newlines in the following lines must be maintained.

8. D. A dry run shows the result of tasks on managed hosts. To trigger a dry run, use the **-C** option.

9. B. Configuring a multiplay playbook makes sense if there is a clear relation between the different plays. If there is no direct relation between the plays, in most cases it is better to run separate playbooks because they are easier to manage independently.

10. C. Using multiplay playbooks has many benefits, but scheduling plays independently is not one of them.

Review Questions

1. Use **-vvvv**. Notice that **-vvvvv** can also be used but has a meaning only while managing Windows machines.

2. Spaces

3. Use **ansible-playbook --syntax-check**.

4. The uri module

5. The copy module; other modules can be used as well but are not discussed in this chapter. The lineinfile or blockinfile modules are a much better choice as they can also edit existing files. You'll learn more about them in Chapter 8.

6. The > sign is used in front of a string of text that needs to be copied to a target file. The > sign does not keep newline characters in the text, and that is useful for readability.

7. Multiple playbooks should be used if there is no direct logical relation between the different plays in the playbooks.

8. OK

9. Four times, because playbooks, by default, also run fact gathering on managed hosts as a task

10. 200

Chapter 6

"Do I Know This Already?" Quiz

1. D. When the output starts with a variable value, it must be placed between double quotes. Although answer A seems correct, variables that have a name starting with ansible_ are normally used to refer to Ansible facts. That makes answer D a better answer than answer A.

2. B. To gather facts, you use the setup module.

3. A. In Ansible versions since 2.5, all variables are stored in a dictionary variable with the name ansible_facts, which makes answers A and B the better choices. To refer to variables, the method that uses square brackets is the preferred method.

4. B. Custom facts can be provided as a static file or as a dynamic file. When you use a static custom facts file, it is not necessary that these files are executable.

5. C. The variable name my_file1 is the only one that contains letters, numbers, and underscores and does start with a letter.

6. D. There is no variables key that can be used in a play header. The name of the key is vars.

7. A. The hostvars variable is a magic variable that contains many settings that apply to the managed host.

8. B. You can use the **ansible-vault rekey** command to change passwords on Ansible Vault-encrypted files.

9. B. To interactively prompt for a password, you can use the **--ask-vault-pass** option, but it prompts once only, which doesn't work if multiple encrypted

files are included where each has a different password. In that case, use the **--vault-id @prompt** option.

10. C. You can use the **register** parameter in a task to store the standard output generated by a command in a multivalued variable.

Review Questions

1. Custom facts must be stored in the /etc/ansible/facts.d directory. The name of the file that stores the fact must end in the .fact extension.

2. The setup module is used to trigger fact gathering.

3. You must change a parameter in ansible.cfg, and you must enable a plug-in that allows facts to be cached for a specific period.

4. Include **vars_files:** in the play header.

5. In the current project directory, create a directory with the name group_vars. In that directory, create a file with the name of the host group to which the variables should be applied, and define the variables there. No further action is required in the playbook; the variables are included automatically.

6. Use an array; loops cannot be applied to variables in a dictionary.

7. The hostvars magic variable contains all settings that apply to a specific host.

8. Use **ansible-vault rekey filename**.

9. In the project directory, create a directory group_vars. In that directory, create a subdirectory with the name of the host group, and in there, create a file with the name vars, which contains regular variables, and a file with the name vault, which contains Vault-encrypted variables.

10. To show any variable in a playbook, you can use the debug module. In this module use **var: "{{ cmd_result.rc }}"** to show the exit code of the command.

Chapter 7

"Do I Know This Already?" Quiz

1. D. To iterate over any list of values, use **loop**. In Ansible 2.5 and earlier, **with_items** was used instead, but that syntax is now deprecated.

2. B. When using variables in a **when** statement, you don't have to put the variable names between double brackets.

3. B. To test the value of a Boolean variable, you just need to mention the name of the variable.

4. D. To test a variable for a specific value, you must use **==**. In a string test, the value must be placed between double quotes. Without double quotes, it is interpreted as an integer.

5. C. To test a variable for a specific value, you must use **==**. If the value is a numeric value, it cannot be placed between double quotes.

6. C. Use **vars_prompt** in a playbook to ask a user to provide a value for a specific variable.

7. A. To activate a handler, use the **notify** statement, with the name of the handler that should be activated as its argument.

8. C. A handler will run only if the task that's calling it results in a changed status.

9. A and B. If a task in a playbook fails, playbook execution normally stops. Override this by using **ignore_errors**. Next, use **force_handlers** to ensure that the handler will run, despite the failing task.

10. C. You can use the fail module to configure a specific error message that should be shown on task failure.

Review Questions

1. The name is **item**.

2. You cannot loop over values in a dictionary. If you need this capability anyway, use the dict2items filter.

3. Use **when**.

4. Just use **when myvar**; nothing else is needed.

5. **when myvar == "myvalue"**

6. Use **myvar in mypackages**.

7. Use **(var1 == "value1" and var2 == "value2") or (var3 == "value3" and var4 == "value4")**.

8. Use **when: cmd_out.stdout.find('error') != -1**.

9. Use **ignore_errors** in the play.

10. Use **any_errors_fatal**.

Chapter 8

"Do I Know This Already?" Quiz

1. A. You can use the stat module to request information about file properties, including the current permission mode.

2. C. You can use the lineinfile module to replace a specific line of text in a file. You can use the blockinfile module for this purpose as well, but because it's more complex in use, it is better to use the lineinfile module if only one line needs to be modified.

3. C. The permission mode is written to the variable **st.stat.mode**. This variable contains a string, so you should use a string test operator, which is why the value is between single quotes.

4. D. In the lineinfile module, you use the **regexp** statement to look for a regular expression. To indicate that the line should start with the identified text, the regex should start with a ^.

5. B. The file module cannot be used to copy a line of text into a file. Use the lineinfile module instead.

6. D. You can use the fetch module to copy a file from a managed node to the control host.

7. A. You can use the file module to set SELinux file properties, but any property that is set with the file module is not applied persistently in the SELinux policy. Use sefcontext instead.

8. A. Ansible does not offer a specific module to restore context. Use the command module to run the **restorecon** command.

9. C. To work on variable contents within a template, use Ansible filters.

10. B. You can use the hostvars magic variable to process facts that were discovered on specific hosts.

Review Questions

1. Use acl.

2. Use lineinfile and replace.

3. Use stat.

4. You can create new files or directories, create links, remove files, and set permissions and ownership.

5. Use synchronize.

6. It writes changes to the file system and not to the policy. Use sefcontext instead.

7. Use seboolean.

8. The task that triggers the handler has not changed anything.

9. Use {# **comment line** #}.

10. It can include a line if a specific condition is true. It is mainly used to work on Boolean variables.

Chapter 9

"Do I Know This Already?" Quiz

1. A. Role variables can be stored in the defaults directory or in the vars directory. Variables in defaults may be overwritten from a playbook; variables in the vars directory are not supposed to be overwritten.

2. D. The /usr/share/ansible/roles directory is used for storing roles that are installed from RPM packages. Custom roles should not be stored here.

3. C. Community-provided roles can be found on Ansible Galaxy.

4. D. Normally, handlers in a play always run after the tasks in a play. To have tasks run after the handlers, include them in a post_tasks section.

5. B. Role dependencies should be defined in the meta/main.yml file. This file is a part of the role hierarchy.

6. C. The **ansible-galaxy init** command sets up the directory structure that is needed to create a custom inventory.

7. B. You can use a requirements file to install Ansible Galaxy roles before using them from the command line. Use **ansible-galaxy install -r filename** to install this file.

8. A. The EL platform ensures that roles will be found that can be used on RHEL as well as CentOS.

9. A. You use the **iburst** attribute of the **timesync_ntp_servers** variable to specify whether fast synchronization should happen.

10. B and D. You use the **selinux_fcontext** variable to define the file context that should be set on a target. Also, you must set the **selinux_restore_dirs** variable to the name of the directory where the **selinux_fcontext** is applied to ensure that the **restorecon** command will be applied to that directory.

Review Questions

1. Configure the **roles_dir** setting in ansible.cfg.

2. In the defaults directory

3. The meta/main.yml file

4. In ~/.ansible/roles

5. Use **pre_tasks**.

6. Use **post_tasks**.

7. Use **ansible-galaxy init**.

8. Define a requirements file and run it using **ansible-galaxy install -r requirementsfile.yml**.

9. Look up the sample files and other documentation in /usr/share/doc/rhel-system-roles.

10. Look at variables. To instruct a RHEL System Role what to do, in most cases you just have to write a simple playbook that defines variables and calls the System Role.

Chapter 10

"Do I Know This Already?" Quiz

1. A. When using a wildcard in a host name pattern, you must place the entire pattern between single quotation marks.

2. D. If an external system is available to store host names, a dynamic inventory script can be used to query these host names. There is no limitation to which systems can be used.

3. D. The **ansible-inventory** command does not have an **--all** option.

4. A. Many dynamic inventory scripts are written in Python, but this is not a requirement.

5. D. To make sure one group of hosts is fully processed before moving over to the next group of hosts, use the **serial** keyword in the play header.

6. A and B. To increase the number of hosts on which tasks can run simultaneously, use the **forks** option. This option can be set in ansible.cfg or using the **--forks** parameter while starting the play with the **ansible-playbook** command.

7. B. An include ensures that code is processed when the specific contents are reached and is a dynamic process. Notice that roles can be included as well.

8. B. Use **import_tasks** to statically import a task file. The file is imported before any of the tasks are processed.

9. D. You can use conditional statements to ensure that tasks run only if a specific condition is true. Due to the dynamic nature of includes, you cannot do anything that requires the result of the include to be there while performing the specific operation.

10. C. Because **import_tasks** happens before the tasks are actually executed, they are a part of the playbook from the moment the task is started, and **ansible-playbook --start-at-task** can be used without any issues.

Review Questions

1. Use **web,&file** or **&web,file**.

2. **--list** and **--host <hostname>**

3. You use an .ini file.

4. Use **ansible-inventory --graph**.

5. Use **-f 10** to specify the number of forks.

6. Use **serial: 3** in the playbook header.

7. Use **include_tasks**. Using **import_tasks** statically includes the tasks before the playbook is executed.

8. Use a variable include file.

9. The **ansible-playbook --list-tasks** command doesn't work on dynamically included task files. Use statically imported task files instead.

10. Importing playbooks is recommended in complex projects, where a main site playbook is used, to import complete procedures that are written as separate playbooks.

Chapter 11

"Do I Know This Already?" Quiz

1. B. When you run an Ansible command, it either works or it doesn't. If the command doesn't work out well, the output is written to the STDOUT and can easily be analyzed from there. Collecting a history of all Ansible command output in a log file wouldn't add very much helpful information.

2. C. You should use the **--check** option to ensure that modifications are shown but not written. You must add the **--diff** option to that command to see which modifications would be written by the template module.

3. B. If a task is not executed because the requirement in a conditional was not met, you see "skipped" in the playbook results.

4. B. When tasks are dynamically executed, it is not known right from the beginning what exactly will be executed.

5. C. You use the assert module to check whether an expected result is present but otherwise fails. In both cases, it can be used to write easy-to-understand failure messages.

6. A. The uri module shows values that are returned by web services or RESTful APIs.

7. D. You use the stat module to show file properties.

8. C and D. To run a task that is configured with the **debug** and **never** tags, you must specifically mention the **debug** or the **never** tag. However, you also need to run all other tasks, which is done by referring to them using either the **all** or **untagged** tags (depending on how tags are used on the other tasks).

9. D. You use the ping module to test IP connectivity, accessibility of the SSH service, sudo configuration, and availability of a Python stack.

10. C. The error "Missing sudo password" indicates that sudo could not be used successfully. The most likely explanation is that the remote_user has not been configured to run sudo commands without entering a password. Check your Linux sudo configuration.

Review Questions

1. Set **check_mode: no** as an argument to the task.

2. rescued

3. **log_path**

4. uri

5. fail

6. assert

7. Use the int filter.

8. never

9. You need to call this tag specifically using **ansible-playbook --tags all,debug**.

10. **ansible all -m ping**

Chapter 12

"Do I Know This Already?" Quiz

1. D. To set up access to a yum repository, you should use the yum_repository module. There is no generic repository module.

2. B. By default, Ansible does not collect information about packages. You should use the package_facts module to collect this information.

3. A. You can use the **file** argument with the yum_repository module to specify the name of the repository file that will be created.

4. C. While you are managing AppStream modules with yum, the module name must start with an at sign (@), and the entire string must be placed between single quotation marks.

5. C. You use **state: latest** to update installed packages to the latest version that is available or install packages if they haven't been installed yet. If you combine this with **name:** `'*'`, all currently installed packages are updated.

6. B. To create repository metadata, you need the Linux **createrepo** command. No Ansible module runs this command, so you have to use the command module.

7. D. To specify where downloaded packages are stored, the **download_only** argument requires you to use the **download_dir** argument to specify the package download directory.

8. A and B. After you register RHEL with the redhat_subscription module, you use the rhsm_repository module to register to repositories that are offered through Red Hat Subscription Manager. Other repositories can be addressed using yum_repository.

9. D. Variables that are set with the **-e** command-line option apply to all plays in the playbook. The other option is to set a **host_groups** variable, but because in this case the variable is used to add a new host, that approach does not work.

10. B and C. When **vars_prompt** prompts for the values of variables, the user input is not written to the screen and also not stored in history, which makes it a secure way to provide these sensitive values. Using Ansible Vault also provides a secure way. Answer D is a bad response because the variable is readable from Linux shell history. Answer A is even worse because the variables are readable from the playbook file.

Review Questions

1. package_facts

2. yum_repository

3. name: `'@Virtualization Host'`

4. **createrepo**

5. Use the yum module's **download_only** argument together with the **download_dir** argument to specify in which directory the packages must be installed.

6. fetch

7. rpm_key

8. redhat_subscription

9. rhsm_repository

10. Pass the variable as an argument to the **ansible-playbook** command using **-e varname**.

Chapter 13

"Do I Know This Already?" Quiz

1. D. You use the known_hosts module to manage known hosts settings for users.

2. B and C. To make a user a member of secondary groups, use the **groups** argument. To ensure that current group assignments are not overwritten, add the **append** option.

3. A and B. Ansible offers no modules that are specifically developed to manage sudoers configuration files, so you must use the generic lineinfile or template modules. If either of these modules is used on the /etc/sudoers file, don't forget to use the **verify** option to have the Linux **visudo** command verify that no errors occurred while modifying the file.

4. D. You use the authorized_key module to manage user SSH public keys. You use the known_host module to manage server public keys in the known_hosts file of the managed hosts.

5. D. You can use the lookup plug-in to dynamically look up values and work with them. Notice that lookup is not a module but a plug-in.

6. A. The authorized_keys module cannot read files from a hidden directory, and for that reason, the id_rsa.pub file needs to be copied or moved to a location where the module is allowed to read it.

7. C. The encrypted password as stored in /etc/shadow consists of the hashing algorithm, the random salt, and the encrypted hash of the user password. Username is not a part of the string.

8. B. You cannot use the command module with the **passwd --stdin** command because this command gets its input from a pipe and shell pipes don't work in the command module.

9. A. In all cases, if the highest level of security is required, Ansible Vault is the only option.

10. C. To maintain flexibility, store the users in a variable, and to implement separation according to function, define that variable in an include file.

Review Questions

1. Use lineinfile; no module specifically targets sudo configuration.

2. Use pamd.

3. Use known_hosts.

4. Use group.

5. Use groups.

6. lookup

7. **ssh_key_comment**

8. It cannot read public keys from a hidden directory.

9. Use **passwd --stdin** in the shell module, or use the debug module together with the **password_hash** function.

10. shell

Chapter 14

"Do I Know This Already?" Quiz

1. B. You should use the systemd module to mask a service because masking services is specific to systemd services.

2. A. Service properties are not discovered when the setup module is run to gather facts. Use the service_facts module instead.

3. D. The at module interfaces Linux at to run tasks once.

4. A and D. The **mask** and **daemon_reload** options are specific to the systemd module because they address features unique to the systemd service manager.

5. C and D. To remove a cron job, you need to mention its name as well as its state: absent.

6. C. Ansible uses the name of cron tasks as the unique key to manage the task. If a task with the specified name already exists, Ansible overwrites it and the playbook itself shows a changed status.

7. B. The Ansible systemd module does not manage the default target. Use the file module instead to manually create the symbolic link that manages the systemd target.

8. C. You can use the Ansible reboot module to restart a managed node from a playbook and continue the playbook once the managed host is back.

9. D. The reboot_timeout option specifies the number of seconds to wait for the machine to reboot and respond to the test command. By default, it is set to 600 seconds.

10. C and D. Commands that are executed in the cron module are executed by a shell, so you should use shell command substitution. Using facts is not an option because they show the time of fact gathering, not the time the module was actually executed.

Review Questions

1. Use the service_facts module.

2. Use the service module. You could use the systemd module as well, but it doesn't work on older servers where other service managers are used.

3. Use the **name** argument. Notice that this argument writes a name to the cron comments field and has no meaning to Linux cron but is essential to the Ansible cron module.

4. Use the file module because you have to create a symbolic link.

5. Use **special_time**.

6. Use **units** to set the units to minutes; use **count** to specify the number of minutes.

7. **test_command**

8. **reboot_timeout**

9. **script_file**

10. Because tasks executed are not executed in a Bash shell

Chapter 15

"Do I Know This Already?" Quiz

1. D. You use the parted module to manage partitions and their properties.

2. B. Extents are a property of the LVM volume group. To manage the LVM volume group, you use the lvg module.

3. B. The **ansible_devices** option gives access to a list of all discovered devices, including their properties.

4. D. To set a variable within a task, you can use **set_facts**. The variable from then on will be available as an Ansible local fact.

5. B and C. When using parted to create partitions, you must specify the partition size as an offset from the beginning of the disk by using the **part_start** as well as the **part_end** arguments. So if a 2 GiB partition already exists, **part_start** must be set to 2 GiB so that the partition will start right after the already existing partition. The **part_end** argument should be 2 GiB after that, so **part_end** must be set to 4 GiB.

6. A. The parted **label** argument is not about file system labels (which are set at the file system level); it's about the partition table type, so you need **label: gpt** to create GPT-type partitions.

7. A. The filesystem module uses a generic **opts** argument to pass arguments to the underlying Linux **mkfs** command.

8. A. You use **state: mounted** to mount a device now and it will also add a line to /etc/fstab to mount it persistently. Notice that the mount module has no **fstab** argument.

9. C. There is no module for activating swap space. You use the command module instead.

10. A. You cannot perform a size-related test on a float; it needs to be converted to an integer. You can use the int filter to do so.

Review Questions

1. ansible_mounts

2. Use assert and fail.

3. parted

4. **label: gpt**

5. **flags: lvm**

6. **part_start: 2GiB**

7. lvg

8. It is not idempotent. The next time you run the same module, it will see the **100%FREE** requirement as a requirement that isn't met yet, so it will try to apply the new configuration, which will fail because no more space is available in the volume group.

9. **src: devicename**

10. **state: mounted**

Getting Started with Ansible Tower

In this book you've learned how to work with Ansible from the command line, or Ansible Engine as Red Hat refers to it. Although working with Ansible from the command line offers you all that you may ever need, there is an alternative that enables you to manage Ansible from a web-based environment. This solution is known as Ansible Tower. You won't find one single question about Ansible Tower on the exam, but the solution is too important to completely ignore it, which is why in this appendix I introduce you to working with Ansible Tower. This appendix covers the following topics:

- Understanding Ansible Tower

- Installing Ansible Tower

- Installing AWX

- Managing Nodes with Ansible Tower

- Understanding Ansible Tower Core Components

- Running a Project in Ansible Tower

Understanding Ansible Tower

Ansible Tower offers a web-based environment to manage Ansible in large environments. From this dashboard you can easily get an overview of the current status of Ansible, the job activity, and the success and failure of recent jobs. It offers other benefits as well:

- **Workflow design:** Using Ansible Tower workflows enables you to model complex processes in Ansible Tower. Different playbooks can be connected together and use different inventories as well as different credentials to run the playbooks.

- **Activity logging:** Ansible Tower provides activity logging. You can easily find out which user ran which job at what specific time.

- **Scalability:** You can build clusters with Ansible Tower. In a cluster, up to 20 cluster nodes can work together to provide Ansible control node functionality in a scalable way and service up to 200,000 nodes.

- **Notifications:** Ansible Tower can be configured to send notifications to specific users.

- **Scheduling:** In Ansible Tower you are able to schedule jobs to run at a specific time.

- **Integrated inventory:** In Ansible Tower, multiple sources of inventory can be used and presented as one big inventory, no matter where the inventory hosts come from.

- **Self-service:** Using Ansible Tower makes it easy to delegate jobs to specific users. Ansible Tower enables you to create user accounts and grant specific Tower users permissions to specific jobs.

- **Remote execution:** The Ansible Tower run command interface provides an easy-to-use interface for remote command execution, which in fact runs ad hoc commands on selected nodes.

- **REST API and Tower CLI tool:** Apart from the web interface, Ansible Tower provides a REST API and the towercli command-line tool, which allows users to address the API directly without using the web interface.

Ansible Tower is a Red Hat product that comes with an enterprise license for updates and support. You can request a limited evaluation version of Tower at ansible.com, or you can use the open-source upstream project AWX instead.

Once they are configured, there is no difference between Tower and AWX. The setup procedure for both solutions is quite different, which is why the following sections contain instructions for setting up both environments. To install either solution, you need a dedicated node that meets the following requirements:

- 4 GB RAM (8 GB recommended)

- 2 vCPUs

- 20 GB disk space, much more when used to manage many nodes

- RHEL 7 or 8

The managed machines have no specific requirements. Even when used with Ansible Tower, Ansible is still agentless, which means that normal access mechanisms are used for the managed machines.

Installing Ansible Tower

To install the Ansible Tower software, you need to obtain a free evaluation version from www.ansible.com. This installation version gives access to a tarball, as well as a license. You can use the Ansible Tower license with your current Red Hat account or use a license file. The following procedure explains how to install Ansible Tower on a virtual machine that has CentOS 8.x installed.

1. Go to https://ansible.com/products/tower and request access to the free evaluation of Ansible Tower.

2. Store the tarball containing the Ansible software in your home directory. The name of the tarball should be ansible-tower-setup-latest.tar.

3. Use **tar xvf ansible-tower-setup-latest.tar** to extract the tar archive to the current directory.

4. Use **cd ansible[Tab]** to change into the directory that was created by extracting the tarball.

5. Type **vim inventory** to open the inventory file that is provided. Make sure to set your passwords as follows:

```
admin_password='password'
pg_password='password'
rabbitmq_password='password'
```

6. Run the setup.sh file by using **sudo ./setup.sh**. Completion will take about 15 minutes.

7. When setup is complete, access the Ansible Tower main web page, using https://localhost. Log in with the provided credentials.

8. You now see a screen where you are prompted for a license (see Figure B-1). There are three options to access the license:

   ■ If you don't have a license, click the **Request License** link to request one.

   ■ If you have a license file, use the **Browse** button to browse to the location of that file.

   ■ If your current Red Hat ID is entitled to use a license, log in using your Red Hat username and password.

FIGURE B-1   Entering License Details

9. After entering the license details, click the check box to agree with the license conditions and click **Submit**. This gives you access to the Ansible Tower web page.

Installing AWX

The installation of AWX is very different. AWX is provided as a container in Open-Shift, Kubernetes, or Docker-Compose. Of these methods, the Docker-Compose method is the most accessible method because it doesn't require a complete container orchestration platform like OpenShift or Kubernetes to be set up. For that reason, in this procedure you learn how to set up AWX on top of Docker-Compose. Make sure you use a dedicated system for installing AWX (so don't try to run it on the machine where you just installed Ansible Tower).

1. Use **sudo systemctl disable --now firewalld** to disable the firewall—not because you have to, but just because it makes it easier to get started with AWX.

2. Disable SELinux by using **sudo setenforce 0**. Make this persistent as well by including the line **SELINUX=disabled** in the /etc/sysconfig/selinux configuration file.

3. Install the EPEL repository using **sudo yum install epel-release**.

4. Install Ansible using **sudo yum install ansible**.

5. After installing Ansible, clone the AWX GitHub repository by using **git clone https://github.com/ansible/awx**.

6. Now you need to install some supporting packages. To do so, use **sudo yum install yum-utils device-mapper-persistent-data lvm2**.

7. Add the Docker repository by using **sudo yum config-manager --add-repo https://download.docker.com/linux/centos/docker-ce.repo**.

8. Remove the default CentOS/RHEL 8 container management tool podman by using **sudo yum remove podman -y**.

9. Install the Docker Community Edition Software by using **sudo yum install docker-ce docker-ce-cli containerd.io --nobest -y**.

10. Enable the Docker daemon. To do so, use **sudo systemctl enable --now docker**.

11. Make your current user account a member of the group docker. Use **sudo usermod -aG $(whoami)**.

12. Make your new group membership effective by using **newgrp docker**.

13. Create a symbolic link to start Python. Use **sudo ln -s /usr/bin/python3 /usr/bin/python**.

14. Install the Docker compose software. Use **sudo pip3 install docker-compose**.

15. Edit ~/awx/installer/inventory and ensure it contains the line **pg_admin_password=password**. Look up the existing pg_admin_password line and remove the comment sign to ensure it is at the right location in the file.

16. Start the installer. First, use **cd ~/awx/installer** to get into the right directory, and from there, type **ansible-playbook -i inventory install.yml** to start the installation.

17. After completing the installation, type **docker ps** to verify that the Docker containers have been started.

18. Use **docker logs -f awx_task** and make sure it shows completed. This process can take about five minutes.

19. After the task is complete, access the AWX web page at http://localhost. Log in using the username **admin** and the password **password**.

At this point you should have access to the main web page in either AWX or Ansible Tower. In the following sections you learn how to start performing your management tasks from there.

Managing Nodes with Ansible Tower

To manage machines with Ansible Tower, you must do something to reach out to these machines. Because Ansible Tower is still Ansible, there is no fundamental difference in how you reach out to the managed machines from Ansible Tower:

- You need to set up name resolution for managed machines.

- You must ensure that the managed machines are running an SSH process that is accessible through the firewall.

- You need a user account with sudo privileges.

- You need to set up a password and SSH keys.

If you're reading this appendix after working through the other chapters in this book, setting up Tower is easy. It consists of the following tasks, which are all executed on the Tower node:

- Create an ansible user.

- Use **ssh-keygen** to generate an SSH key pair.

- Use **ssh-copy-id** to copy the public key to the managed machines.

Because the managed hosts were set up previously, no additional configuration is required. If you still need to set up the managed hosts, read Chapter 2, "Installing Ansible," for more information about that procedure. You don't need to configure an inventory or an ansible.cfg file; this functionality is taken over by Ansible Tower.

Understanding Ansible Tower Core Components

To work with Ansible Tower, you use a few key resources. Working with Ansible Tower means you need to be able to configure these key resources the appropriate way. Let's start with an overview:

- **Organization:** In Ansible Tower, an organization is a collection of managed devices. Notice that in the evaluation version of Ansible Tower, only one organization is available.

- **Users:** Different users can be created, and RBAC can be configured for these users.

- **Inventories:** Inventories are the managed servers. They can be created statically or dynamically.

- **Credentials:** Credentials are what you need to log in to a managed machine. They typically consist of the Ansible control node user account, including SSH public key and sudo privileges.

- **Project:** A project is a collection of playbooks that is obtained from a certain location, such as GitHub.

- **Template:** A template is a job definition with all of its parameters. Jobs must be launched and scheduled from the template.

Running a Project in Ansible Tower

Now that you know which elements are required for working with Ansible Tower, let's set up a project in Tower. To get started with this project, you need to make sure that some Ansible managed machines are available. The machines you used throughout this book will do fine, or you can install new machines. Just make sure that on the managed machines you have set up a dedicated Ansible user account, and this user account is configured for sudo privilege escalation and SSH remote access.

1. Log in to the Tower web interface. From the pane on the left, select **Inventories** and click the **+** sign to add a new inventory. Select the **Inventory** option.

2. Enter **webservers** as the name for this inventory project. Click **Save** in the lower-right corner to save the new project (see Figure B-2).

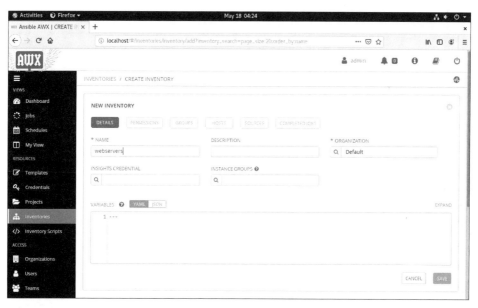

FIGURE B-2   Adding a New Inventory

3. After saving the new inventory, click **Hosts**. From the interface that shows up, click the **+** sign to add a new host. From there, add the name of the host you want to add and an optional description; then click **Save** to save the new host (see Figure B-3). Repeat this procedure for any other host you want to add.

FIGURE B-3   Adding Hosts to the Inventory

4. From the Hosts interface, scroll down to verify that the hosts were added successfully (see Figure B-4).

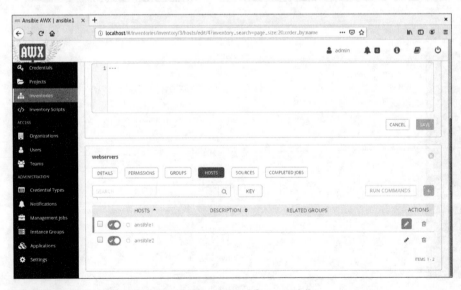

FIGURE B-4   Verifying That Hosts Were Added Successfully

5. After adding the hosts, you must add credentials. The credentials contain your user account and everything else that is needed to successfully connect to the

managed hosts. To add credentials, select **Credentials** from the Resources section in the pane on the left (see Figure B-5).

FIGURE B-5   Credentials Overview

6. From the Credentials interface, click **+** to add new credentials. Different items need to be provided. To start with, specify a name for the credential. Next, ensure that Machine is selected as the Credential Type (see Figure B-6).

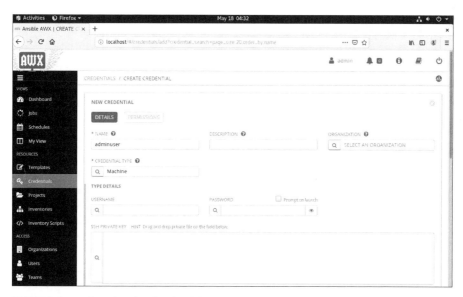

FIGURE B-6   Creating the Credentials

7. After entering the credentials' name and type, you must specify the username. This is the name of the remote user you set up on the managed hosts. Next, you must specify how to connect as this user. Different connection options are available. To authenticate with an SSH public/private key pair, you need to ensure the SSH private key is in the SSH PRIVATE KEY field. The easiest way to do so is to use the Files tool from the GNOME graphical interface and drag the id_rsa file to this field. (Set the **View Hidden Files** option in the Files tool.) See Figure B-7.

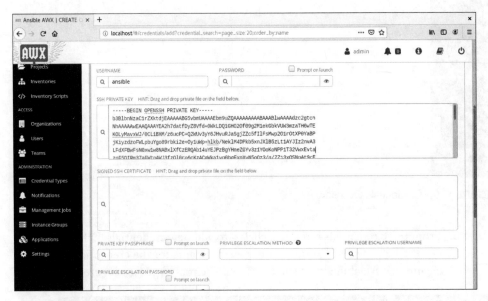

FIGURE B-7   Specifying How to Connect

8. After specifying the name of the remote user and the SSH key, you need to configure privilege escalation. Set this to **sudo** and enter the username **root** as the privilege escalation user. Assuming that no password is required to run sudo commands on the managed hosts, you do not need to enter anything else. So at this point you can click **Save** to save the credentials to your system (see Figure B-8).

FIGURE B-8   Configuring Privilege Escalation

9. Now that the credentials have been created, you can create a project. In the Ansible Tower project, you connect to the YAML files you want to use in your Ansible project. The standard is to provide these source files through some version control system, such as GitHub. To configure the project, from the Resources section in the pane on the left, click **Projects** to open the screen you see in Figure B-9.

FIGURE B-9   Projects Main Screen

10. From the Projects interface shown in Figure B-9, click **+** to add a new project. Enter the name **webservers** and ensure that the Organization name is set to Default. Next, from the SCM TYPE field, select **Git**. This adds a few new items to connect to the Git repository you want to use. If you have your own Git repository, feel free to use it; otherwise, use https://github.com/ sandervanvugt/ansible-demoproject as the sample project to connect to. Notice that your SCM might require additional credentials to connect; these are not included in Figure B-10. In Figure B-10 you see an overview of all settings entered so far. Click **Save** to save the project to Tower.

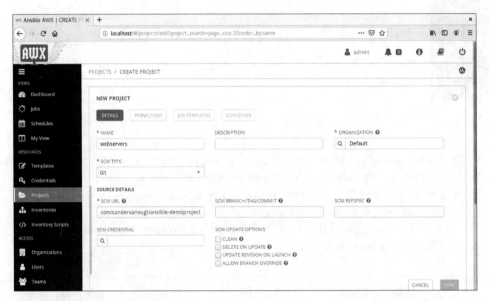

FIGURE B-10   Creating a Project

11. Now you are going to create a template. The template is the place where everything is connected and the actual job is going to be configured. From the Resources section in the pane on the left, click **Templates**, and from there click **+** to add a template. Select **Job Template** to open the interface that you see in Figure B-11.

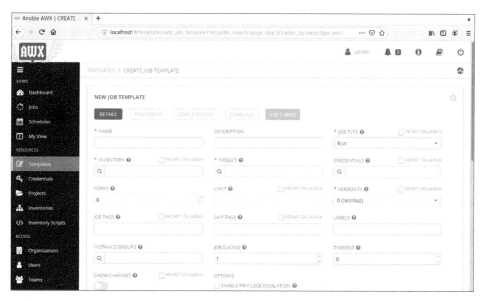

FIGURE B-11   New Job Template Start Screen

12. To define the template, you start with its name. Next, set the Job type to **Run**. Notice that you can also select **Check**, which will perform a dry run and syntax check based on the selected project. Next, use the drop-down list for the Inventory option to select the inventory you created earlier. Then use the drop-down list for the Project option to select the project that you previously created. After selecting the project, you get access to the playbooks it provides. Next, select the credentials you created earlier, and then select the option **Enable Privilege Escalation** to complete required settings for this template. See Figure B-12 for an overview of selected options. Scroll down to select the **Save** button to write the job settings to your system.

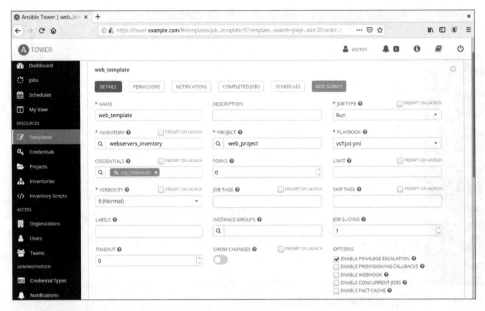

FIGURE B-12   Defining a Job Template

13. After you specify all template options, they are stored to the system. Scroll the template all the way to the bottom of the current screen (see Figure B-13). From there, click the rocket icon to launch a job based on this template.

FIGURE B-13   Accessing Saved Templates

14. After you launch a job, the Job status screen opens. From this screen you can see whether the job was able to run successfully. Notice the output in the right pane, which really is similar to the output you'll see when running Ansible commands directly from the command line. In case the process does go wrong (which is the case in the Figure B-14 output), read the command output; then try to understand and fix it.

FIGURE B-14   Analyzing Job Output

15. After you fix the problems, launch the rocket again to restart your job template. If all goes well, at this point it should show a Successful status. (In case you missed it, the problem shown in Figure B-14 is that host name resolution for the short hostname ansible1 is not set up in the /etc/hosts file on the Ansible Tower server.)

Summary

In this appendix you learned how to work with Ansible Tower. You read why using Tower may be convenient and how to set up an environment that is managed with Ansible Tower. You also learned how to run a project in Ansible Tower. Ansible Tower has many more features to offer, but the introduction in this appendix should be helpful to get you started.

Red Hat RHCE 8 (EX294) Cert Guide Exam Updates

Over time, reader feedback allows Pearson to gauge which topics give our readers the most problems when taking the exams. To assist readers with those topics, the authors create new materials clarifying and expanding on those troublesome exam topics. As mentioned in the Introduction, the additional content about the exam is contained in a PDF on this book's companion website, at http://www.pearsonitcertification.com/title/9780136872436.

This appendix is intended to provide you with updated information if Red Hat makes minor modifications to the exam upon which this book is based. When Red Hat releases an entirely new exam, the changes are usually too extensive to provide in a simple update appendix. In those cases, you might need to consult the new edition of the book for the updated content. This appendix attempts to fill the void that occurs with any print book. In particular, this appendix does the following:

- Mentions technical items that might not have been mentioned elsewhere in the book

- Covers new topics if Red Hat adds new content to the exam over time

- Provides a way to get up-to-the-minute current information about content for the exam

Always Get the Latest at the Book's Product Page

You are reading the version of this appendix that was available when your book was printed. However, given that the main purpose of this appendix is to be a living, changing document, it is important that you look for the latest version online at the book's companion website. To do so, follow these steps:

Step 1.   Browse to www.pearsonitcertification.com/title/9780136872436.

Step 2.   Click the **Updates** tab.

Step 3.   If there is a new Appendix B document on the page, download the latest Appendix B document.

> **NOTE** The downloaded document has a version number. Comparing the version of the print Appendix B (Version 1.0) with the latest online version of this appendix, you should do the following:
>
> - **Same version:** Ignore the PDF that you downloaded from the companion website.
>
> - **Website has a later version:** Ignore this Appendix B in your book and read only the latest version that you downloaded from the companion website.

Technical Content

The current Version 1.0 of this appendix does not contain additional technical coverage.

Glossary

A

ad hoc command   An Ansible command that uses a module to apply the desired state without making any change to the managed system.

anacron   A helper system to Linux cron, which makes sure that a job is started periodically every hour, day, week, or month, without specifically defining when exactly it should run.

Ansible Tower   A web-based platform that allows for management of Ansible environments from a browser.

ansible.cfg   The configuration file that Ansible uses to get information about required settings. Most parameters from ansible.cfg may be overwritten in playbooks.

AppStream   The package collection in RHEL 8 that offers access to nonessential packages. Packages in AppStream are provided as yum modules, which allows for different versions of the packages to be offered.

array   *See* list.

authorized_keys   The name of the file that is created for each user in the .ssh directory in the user home directory and contains public keys that enable password-less login for remote users who have copied over their public key to this file after generating a public/private key pair using ssh-keygen.

automation language   The format that is used to define the machine-readable code used to implement infrastructure as code.

AWX   The open-source upstream project for Ansible Tower.

B

block   A group of tasks that can be treated as one entity while working with conditionals.

C

check mode   A mode in which Ansible shows what happens if a playbook is executed but doesn't change anything. Running a playbook in check mode doesn't always show everything that would be changed because the result of executing one task may depend on the result of another task.

CI/CD   Continuous integration/continuous delivery; a way of easily developing software and updating software source code and making these new developments available as new versions to the end users using a CI/CD pipeline.

controller node   The node in the Ansible configuration where all the Ansible management commands are issued.

current state   The current configuration of a managed system.

CVS   Concurrent version system, a system that makes it possible to manage different versions of code while it is developed. CVS is a way to implement version control systems.

D

declarative approach   A way of working that uses configuration files (playbooks in the case of Ansible) instead of commands that declare the desired state and that are easy to roll out against the managed targets in an idempotent way.

desired state   The state that is defined in Ansible playbooks and that needs to be implemented on Ansible-managed systems.

DevOps   A contraction of the words *developers* and *operators*. It's a new way of working in which developers integrate operator tasks in their work and operators integrate developer tasks in their work.

dictionary   In Python, an unordered collection of items; also referred to as hashes. It is a collection of key-value pairs. In Python, a dictionary is defined as my_dict = { key1: 'car', key2:'bike' }. Because it is based on Python, Ansible enables users to use dictionaries as an alternative notation to arrays. Items in values in a dictionary do not start with a dash. Using dictionaries is one way; the alternative is to use a list. *See also* list, to compare differences.

E

EPEL repository   The Extra Packages for Enterprise Linux, a repository that contains packages from the Fedora project for use on Red Hat Enterprise Linux or CentOS but that have not officially been approved for these platforms.

F

fact   A system property that is detected while starting a playbook.

failure condition   The definition of what exactly is to be considered a failure when running Ansible playbooks.

filter   A tool that can be used to perform an action on the result of a variable. For instance, filters can be used to change the variable type from string to integer.

fork   A task that can be executed in parallel task execution.

G

Galaxy   The Ansible community website, accessible at https://galaxy.ansible.com, where Ansible roles and collections are provided.

Git repository   An online repository that developers can use to coordinate changes into software projects, including version control such that it is easy to roll back to the previous state of the software.

GPG   GNU Privacy Guard; an open-source implementation of PGP, in which public/private keys can be used to enhance security. In repositories, the repository GPG private key is used to sign packages. Next, the repository client needs to import the GPG public key of that repository to verify the package signature before packages are installed.

H

handler   A special type of task that runs only if triggered by another task.

hash   (In encryption) An encoded representation of a string that was created with the purpose of securing the original string.

hash   (In key-value pairs) *See* dictionary.

hashing algorithm   A mathematical formula used to generate a hash.

I

idempotent   A way of working in which Ansible ensures that running the same playbook multiple times will always result in the same code.

import   An option that enables items to be statically imported before any task will run. Task files and plays can be imported.

include   An option that enables items to be dynamically included depending on a conditional statement. Task files can be included.

infrastructure as code   A way of working in which the entire infrastructure of an IT environment is defined as code (like Ansible playbooks) that can easily be deployed to implement a new desired state.

init system   The system that is used on Linux to start essential system components after booting the system. Common init systems are BSD init (used on RHEL 5), Upstart (used on RHEL 6), and systemd (the default since RHEL 7).

inventory   A list of managed hosts. It may be provided as a static file or as a script that dynamically discovers manageable hosts (dynamic inventory).

item   An element in a list of variables.

J

Jinja2   A generic templating language for Python developers.

K

key-value   In a YAML dictionary, the key is the specific item that is to be defined. An example of a key is "name." The value is the specific value that is set to that name.

L

list   In variable definition, a key that can have multiple items as its value; also referred to as an array. Each item in a list starts with a dash (-). Individual items in a list can be addressed, using the index number (starting at zero), as in {{ network_interfaces[1] }}. Compare to how key-value pairs can be specified in a dictionary.

local fact   A fact that is defined as a local variable and is stored on the managed host.

lookup plug-in   A plug-in that allows access to external data sources.

M–O

magic variable   A reserved system variable that is stored as a default value and cannot be overwritten.

managed node   The node that is managed by Ansible.

module   The commands that are executed by using Ansible commands. Ansible modules provide the intelligence to Ansible.

P–Q

PAM   In Linux, Pluggable Authentication Modules. An advanced framework that allows for enhancement of standard Linux security, by offering libraries that can be used by developers of third-party security solutions.

parallel task execution   A process that determines the number of hosts on which tasks are executed at the same time.

pip   The Python software installer. A Python-based way to install software packages using Python (and not yum) repositories.

pipelines   *See* CI/CD.

play   A collection of tasks that is executed on a specific host or group of hosts in an Ansible playbook. Each play has a play header, providing details on what exactly to do and on which hosts it should be done.

playbook   A collection of one or more plays that is gathered in a playbook and contain tasks to be executed on specific hosts.

plug-in   Pieces of code that augment Ansible core functionality.

pool   A collection of software repositories in Red Hat Subscription Manager that a subscription offers an entitlement for.

project   A collection of playbooks and other configurations used to manage a specific managed environment.

provisioning   Deploying and installing systems.

public key fingerprint   A short representation of a public key, which can be used to verify a public key.

Python   A common scripting language. Ansible is written in Python.

R

random salt   Random data that is added to a hash function as defined by the encryption algorithm to generate hashed data.

register   A keyword that enables the result of a command to be stored in a variable.

requirements file   A file that can be used to define multiple roles that should be installed.

RHEL system role   An Ansible role created by Red Hat to standardize configuration tasks across different versions of Red Hat Enterprise Linux.

role   A collection of variables, templates, modules, and tasks developed to perform a specific task and can be embedded in a playbook easily.

S

serial task execution   A process that determines the number of hosts on which all tasks are executed before tasks will be executed on other hosts.

shell script   An executable file, written in ASCII text, that contains commands that will be executed by the Linux Bash shell.

subscription   An entitlement to use Red Hat software. Red Hat Enterprise Linux needs to be used with a subscription. Subscriptions are used to give users of RHEL access to software updates and optionally also support.

T–U

tag   A label that can be set on tasks, blocks, plays, and roles, which allows users to run only specific parts of the playbook.

task   A specification of a module and specific arguments needed to configure a desired state.

template   A configuration file that contains variables and, based on the variables, is generated on the managed hosts according to host-specific requirements.

V

vault   A secured environment that can be used to store variables in an encrypted way.

version control system   A structure that enables developers to easily work on software code and manage different versions and patches of the code.

W–X

when   A conditional statement that enables Ansible to run a specific task only if a specific condition is true.

WinRM   Windows Remote Management; the Windows software that may be used to manage Windows with Ansible.

Y–Z

YAML   The language that is used to write Ansible playbooks.

Index